T0332463

Multi–Disciplinary Advancement in Open Source Software and Processes

Stefan Koch
Bogazici University, Turkey

INFORMATION SCIENCE REFERENCE
Hershey · New York

Senior Editorial Director:	Kristin Klinger
Director of Book Publications:	Julia Mosemann
Editorial Director:	Lindsay Johnston
Acquisitions Editor:	Erika Carter
Development Editor:	Mike Killian
Production Coordinator:	Jamie Snavely
Typesetters:	Keith Glazewski & Natalie Pronio
Cover Design:	Nick Newcomer

Published in the United States of America by
Information Science Reference (an imprint of IGI Global)
701 E. Chocolate Avenue
Hershey PA 17033
Tel: 717-533-8845
Fax: 717-533-8661
E-mail: cust@igi-global.com
Web site: http://www.igi-global.com

Library of Congress Cataloging-in-Publication Data

Multi-disciplinary advancement in open source software and processes / Stefan Koch, editor.
       p. cm.
  Includes bibliographical references and index.
  Summary: "This book reviews the development, design, and use of free and open source software, providing relevant topics of discussion for programmers, as well as researchers in human-computer studies, online and virtual collaboration, and e-learning"--Provided by publisher.
  ISBN 978-1-60960-513-1 (hardcover) -- ISBN 978-1-60960-514-8 (ebook) 1. Open source software. 2. Computer software--Development. I. Koch, Stefan, 1974-
  QA76.76.S46M97 2011
  005.3--dc22
                                     2011000067

British Cataloguing in Publication Data
A Cataloguing in Publication record for this book is available from the British Library.

All work contributed to this book is new, previously-unpublished material. The views expressed in this book are those of the authors, but not necessarily of the publisher.

Table of Contents

Section 2

Section 3

Detailed Table of Contents

Section 1

Brian Fitzgerald, Lero – Irish Software Engineering Research Centre and University of Limerick, Ireland

Current estimates suggest widespread adoption of open source software (OSS) in organizations worldwide. However, the problematic nature of OSS adoption is readily evidenced in the fairly frequent reports of problems, unforeseen hold-ups, and outright abandonment of OSS implementation over time. Hibernia Hospital, an Irish public sector organization, have embarked on the adoption of a range of OSS applications over several years, some of which have been successfully deployed and remain in live use within the organization, whereas others, despite achieving high levels of assimilation over a number of years, have not been ultimately retained in live use in the organization. Using a longitudinal case study, we discuss in depth the deployment process for two OSS applications – the desktop application suite whose deployment was unsuccessful ultimately, and the email application which was successfully deployed. To our knowledge, this is the first such in-depth study into successful and unsuccessful OSS implementation.

Gregorio Robles ,Universidad Rey Juan Carlos, Spain
Jesús González-Barahona, Universidad Rey Juan Carlos, Spain
Daniel Izquierdo-Cortazar, Universidad Rey Juan Carlos, Spain
Israel Herraiz, Universidad Alfonso X el Sabi, Spain

Thanks to the open nature of libre (free, open source) software projects, researchers have gained access to a rich set of data related to various aspects of software development. Although it is usually publicly available on the Internet, obtaining and analyzing the data in a convenient way is not an easy task, and many considerations have to be taken into account. In this chapter we introduce the most relevant data sources that can be found in libre software projects and that are commonly studied by scholars: source code releases, source code management systems, mailing lists and issue (bug) tracking systems. The chapter also provides some advice on the problems that can be found when retrieving and preparing the data sources for a later analysis, as well as information about the tools and datasets that support these tasks.

Much of the data about free, libre, and open source (FLOSS) software development comes from studies of code forges or code repositories used for managing projects. This paper presents a method for integrating data about open source projects by way of matching projects (entities) across multiple code forges. After a review of the relevant literature, a few of the methods are chosen and applied to the FLOSS domain, including a comparison of some simple scoring systems for pairwise project matches. Finally, the paper describes limitations of this approach and recommendations for future work.

Agile sprints are short events where a small team collocates in order to work on particular aspects of the overall project for a short period of time. Sprinting is a process that has been observed also in Free Software projects: these two paradigms, sharing common principles and values have shown several commonalities of practice. This article evaluates the impact of sprinting on a Free Software project through the analysis of code repository logs: sprints from two Free Software projects (Plone and KDE PIM) are assessed and two hypotheses are formulated: do sprints increase productivity? Are Free Software projects more productive after sprints compared with before? The primary contribution of this article is to show how sprinting creates a large increase in productivity both during the event, and immediately after the event itself: this argues for more in-depth studies focussing on the nature of sprinting.

One of the major problems in software engineering education is the involvement of students in real world software projects. Industry projects are a solution, but in many cases they are hard to find and student participation can be problematic due to cultural, familiarization and other practical reasons. The abundance of Free / Libre Open Source Software (FLOSS) projects is a neat solution, offering multi-lingual, multicultural environments in virtually every application domain, at different levels of project size, maturity, organization etc. The paper analyzes how acquisition of practical experience on several basic and advanced software engineering topics can be achieved by working in a FLOSS project. The kind of skills that can be acquired are those requested by the Overview Report for Computing

Curricula by ACM and topics examined are those of the Software Engineering Body of Knowledge, by IEEE. Also software engineering areas that require special care or that may not prove suitable for such treatment are identified. Various isolated teaching cases pertaining to this approach are presented and discussed.

Section 2

The last few years have seen a rapid increase in the number of Free/Libre Open Source Software (FLOSS) projects. Some of these projects, such as Linux and the Apache web server, have become phenomenally successful. However, for every successful FLOSS project there are dozens of FLOSS projects which never succeed. These projects fail to attract developers and/or consumers and, as a result, never get off the ground. The aim of this research is to better understand why some FLOSS projects flourish while others wither and die. This article presents a simple agent-based model that is calibrated on key patterns of data from SourceForge, the largest online site hosting open source projects. The calibrated model provides insight into the conditions necessary for FLOSS success and might be used for scenario analysis of future developments of FLOSS.

The development of open source software is currently arousing increasing interest in the IT world. This research inquires some specific paths enlarging the traditional view over open source software in inquiring the US Department of Defense (DoD) and the dynamics associated its front- and back-office activities. We explain how distinguishing basic administration from operational constraints and weapon R&D dynamics introduces specific governance concerns among public and private stakeholders. By no longer defining open source solutions as mere goods, but as services characterized by a flow of knowledge, we particularly highlight new emerging strategies of technological acquisition. Our analysis leads to revise the traditional role focusing mainly on cost issues and introduces open source software with distinctive properties serving the management of innovation and technological agility at the level of complex systems, exemplified here with the constraints associated to weapon systems and the Network centric warfare doctrine.

An extensive empirical literature indicates that, even without formal intellectual property rights, innovators enjoy a variety of first-mover advantages and that 'imitation' is itself a costly activity. There is also accumulating evidence that an 'open' approach to knowledge production can deliver substantial efficiency advantages. This article introduces a formal framework incorporating all of these factors. We examine the relative performance of an 'open' versus a 'closed' (proprietary) regime, and explicitly characterize the circumstances in which an open approach, despite its effect on facilitating imitation, results in a higher level of innovation.

I consider a Vickrey-Salop model of spatial product differentiation with quasi-linear utility functions and contrast two modes of production, the proprietary model where entrepreneurs sell software to the users, and the open source model where users participate in software development. I show that the OS model of production may be more efficient from the point of view of welfare than the proprietary model, but that an OS industry is vulnerable to entry by entrepreneurs while a proprietary industry can resist entry by OS projects. A mixed industry where OS and proprietary development methods coexist may exhibit large OS projects cohabiting with more specialized proprietary projects, and is more efficient than the proprietary model of production from the point of view of welfare.

In this article, we consider the dynamics and competition between two software platforms (Open Source and proprietary software). Potential user-developers can adopt one of the two platforms in order to develop and sell new applications based on the platform. We consider the static issue first and then use a simple dynamic system where the dynamics comes from the development efforts (spillovers) made on each platforms. In this context, we first identify the conditions for the two platforms to coexist in the long run. From this baseline, we then consider different strategies for the editor. A first strategy is for the editor to "show the code" of its software, so as to develop more compatible products. A second strategy is to strategically monitor the compatibility degree between the proprietary and OS platform. In both cases, we analyze whether a mixed industry may be sustainable in the long run.

Chapter 11
Simulation-based Study of Community Governance and Conflict Management in
Emerging Global Participatory Science Communities 167

Despite significant research in open innovation, much less is known about why and how collective creativity emerges in open source scientific communities, as relatively little is known about organizing processes in such cyber-enabled Global Participatory Science (GPS) communities. One of the significant problems in understanding emergence of innovation involves how GPS communities govern and coordinate to maximize innovation output. We conduct an agent simulation study to examine the impact of culture and conflict management styles on collective creativity. Findings suggest that decentralized coordination schemes such as emergent selection such as found in utility communities and moderate degrees of assertiveness and cooperation for conflict management result in higher incidence of innovation

Chapter 12
Communication Network Characteristics of Open Source Communities 195

Empirical research has shown that social network structure is a critical success factor for various kinds of work groups. The authors extended this research to a new type of work group—the open source software project community—with the objective of exploring the role of communication networks within these intriguing projects. Using archival data from 143 open source project groups, the authors compiled six measures of social network structure and analyzed these in relation to four measures of group success. This study found that the social network structures of these project communities did not appear to be critical success factors at all, but rather they had no significant impact on success or their effect was opposite of that seen in prior studies of work groups. Various conjectures were suggested that might explain these results, offering opportunities for further research.

Chapter 13
Strategies for Improving Open Source Software Usability: An Exploratory Learning
Framework and a Web-Based Inspection Tool 218

The Open Source Software (OSS) movement has had enormous impact on how software is created and continues to attract interest from researchers, software developers and users. A factor that may be inhibiting OSS from achieving greater success is usability, a fundamental characteristic to user acceptance of software. Motivated by the uniquely user-driven nature of the open source model and the extensive user base that participates in OSS projects, the authors propose an exploratory learning method and an associated web-based inspection environment that enables non-experts to contribute to open source usability inspection. This tool uses patternbased usability guidelines to help identify usability knowledge during inspection. The method emphasizes outlining and exploration features which the authors have formally evaluated and the results of which are described. Data collected from a qualitative study indicates positive impact of the proposed method in helping end-users inspect software and achieve better results in discovering usability problems.

The motivational drivers of open source software developers have been researched by various investigators since about 2000. This work shows that developers are motivated by different extrinsic and intrinsic drivers, among them community aspirations, reciprocity and fairness, creative impulses, and monetary and career ambitions. There has been some work done in studying whether the profile of developer motivations is constant across open source projects or is sensitive to project organizational design. Among the many factors that could influence the mix of motives of OS developers is the license under which the work is performed. Licenses range in openness between those such as the GNU GPL that severely restrict the freedom of developers to mingle their OS code with proprietary code to those such as BSD licenses which allow programmers much greater latitude in integrating open source code with proprietary code. In addition to formal rules, meritocracies emerge to reward effort and performance, and also to direct, coordinate, and control other participants. The authors discuss these variables and how they may be related to motivations.

Preface

OPEN SOURCE SOFTWARE DEVELOPMENT PROJECTS: REVIEW ON EFFORT AND EFFICIENCY

In this section we will review literature on open source software development projects, focusing on their expended effort as well as achieved efficiency. The paper is based mostly on empirical analyses of open source communities. The main method employed is mining the associated software repositories which are publicly available and contain records of past interactions between participants, or between participants and the repository itself. We will present a short overview concerning this methodology, and reference some papers which deal with the technicalities in more detail. From that we will distill some characteristics found in open source software development projects, which includes foremost the high concentration on a few heads. We will then focus on the estimated effort expended for open source development projects, which in comparison to commercial organizational settings seems to be quite small, and relate these points to the efficiency that this form of software development achieves.

Introduction

In the last years, free and open source software, i.e. software under a license that grants several rights like free redistribution to the user, has become more and more important, with this importance now stretching beyond the mere use of well-known projects in both private and commercial settings (Fitzgerald, 2006; von Krogh and Spaeth, 2007). Examples for this type of adoption naturally include the operating system Linux with the utilities of the GNU project and various desktops as well as office packages, the Apache web server, data bases such as MySQL and many others.

It should be noted that several terms are in use within this field, most notably open source software and free software, which need to be discussed briefly. The term open source as used by the Open Source Initiative (OSI) is defined using the Open Source Definition (Perens, 1999), which lists a number of rights a license has to grant in order to constitute an open source license. These include most notably free redistribution, inclusion of source code, to allow for derived works which can be redistributed under the same license, integrity of author's source code, absence of discrimination against persons, groups or fields of endeavor, and some clauses for the license itself, its distribution, and that it must neither be specific to a product nor contaminate other software. The Free Software Foundation (FSF) advocates the term free software, explicitly alluding to "free" as in "free speech", not as in "free beer" (Stallman, 2002), which defines a software as free if the user has the freedom to run the program, for any purpose, to study how the program works, and adapt it to his needs, to redistribute copies and to improve the program, and release these improvements to the public. According to this definition, open source and free software are largely interchangeable. The GNU project itself prefers copylefted software, which is free software whose distribution terms do not let re-distributors add any additional restrictions when they redistribute or modify the software. This means that every copy of the software, even if it has been modified, must be free software. This is a more stringent proposition than found in the Open Source Definition, which just allows this. The most well-known and important free and open source license, the GNU General Public License (GPL) is an example for such a copyleft license, with the associated viral characteristics, as any program using or built upon GPLed software must itself be under GPL. There are a number of other licenses, some of which can be considered copyleft, like the X11 license or clarified versions of the original, vague Artistic License, and others which can be considered free or open source, like BSD, Apache or the Mozilla Public License and Sun Public License. In this paper, the term open source is used to refer to free software as well, if a particular license is of importance, this is noted.

More importantly, open source software is not only unique in its licenses and legal implications, but also in its development process and organization of work. The seminal work on this topic was written by Eric S. Raymond, 'The Cathedral and the Bazaar', in which he contrasts the traditional type of software development of a few people planning a cathedral in splendid isolation with the new collaborative bazaar form of open source software development (Raymond, 1999). In this, a large number of developer-turned users come together without monetary compensation to cooperate under a model of rigorous peer-review and take advantage of parallel debugging that leads to innovation and rapid advancement in developing and evolving software products. In order to allow for this to happen and to minimize duplicated work, the source code of the software needs to be accessible which necessitates suitable licenses, and new versions need to be released in short cycles.

This theoretical work is going to be our starting point in examining open source software development projects, and the implications for effort and efficiency as well as quality. It is necessary to base this discussion on empirical assessments of real-world projects. Empirical research on open source processes often employs the analysis of data available through mining the communication and coordination tools and their repositories. For this paper, we will mostly focus on this approach and results from several studies using it. Other approaches taken include ethnographic studies of development communities (Coleman and Hill, 2004; Elliott and Scacchi, 2004), sometimes coupled with repository mining (Basset, 2004).

The structure of this paper is as follows: We will start with a short introduction to mining software repositories, and then provide a discussion and empirical data concerning characteristics of open source software development projects based on this methodology. Then we are going to focus on the implications that these aspects have on effort, as well as efficiency and quality.

Software Repository Mining

Software development repositories contain a plethora of information on software and underlying, associated development processes (Cook et al., 1998; Atkins et al., 1999). Studying software systems and development processes using these sources of data offers several advantages (Cook et al., 1998): It is very cost-effective, as no additional instrumentation is necessary, and does not influence the process under consideration. In addition, longitudinal data are available, allowing for analyses that consider the whole project history. Depending on the tools used in a project, possible repositories available for analysis include source code versioning systems (Atkins et al., 1999; Kemerer and Slaughter, 1999), bug reporting systems, and mailing lists. In open source projects, repositories in several forms are also in use, and in fact form the most important communication and coordination channels as participants are not collocated. Therefore, there is only a small amount of information that cannot be captured because it is transmitted inter-personally. Repositories in use must also be available openly, in order to enable persons to access them and participate in the project.

Prior studies have included both in-depth analyses of small numbers of successful projects (Gallivan, 2001) like Apache and Mozilla (Mockus et al., 2002), GNOME (Koch and Schneider, 2002) or FreeBSD (Dinh-Tong and Bieman, 2005), and also large data samples, such of those derived from Sourceforge. net (Koch, 2004; Long and Siau, 2007). Primarily, information provided by version control systems has been used, but also aggregated data provided by software repositories (Crowston and Scozzi, 2002; Hunt and Johnson, 2002; Krishnamurthy, 2002), meta-information included in Linux Software Map entries (Dempsey et al., 2002), or data retrieved directly from the source code itself (Ghosh and Prakash, 2000).

Although this data is available, the task is made more complicated by the large size and scope of the project repositories or code forges, and the heterogeneity of the projects being studied (Howison and Crowston, 2004; Robles et al., 2009). Therefore, in the last years RoRs ("repository of repositories") have been developed, which collect, aggregate, and clean the targeted repository data (Sowe et al., 2007). Two examples are FLOSSMetrics and FLOSSmole. These RoRs usually hold data collected from project repositories, and some of them also store some analysis and metrics calculated on the retrieved data. The results (raw data, summary data, and / or analyses) will be stored in a database and accessible to the rest of the research community. The researcher therefore does not need to collect data independently.

Open Source Software Development Projects

Open source software development in many ways constitutes a new production mode, in which people are no longer collocated, and self-organization is prevalent. While there is one seminal description of the bazaar style of development by Raymond (1999), it should be noted that open source projects do differ significantly in the processes they employ (Scacchi et al., 2006), and that reality has been found to differ from this very theoretical description.

For example, there are strict release processes in place in several open source projects (Jorgensen, 2001; Holck and Jorgensen, 2004), and a considerable level of commercial involvement. Several ways have been discussed to describe different open source development processes, e.g. Crowston et al. (2006) operationalize a process characteristic based on the speed of bug fixing, Michlmayr (2005) used a construct of process maturity, while also concentration indices have been used to characterize development forms (Koch and Neumann, 2008). We find that there is considerable variance in the practices actually employed, as well as the technical infrastructure. The research on similarities and dissimilarities between open source development in general and other development models is still proceeding (Mockus et al., 2002; Koch, 2004; Scacchi et al., 2006), and remains a hotly debated issue (Bollinger et al., 1999; McConnell, 1999; Vixie, 1999).

Numerous quantitative studies of development projects and communities (Dempsey et al., 2002; Dinh-Trong and Bieman, 2005; Ghosh and Prakash, 2000; Koch and Schneider, 2002; Koch, 2004; Krishnamurthy, 2002; Mockus et al., 2002) have proposed process metrics like the commit, which refers to a single change of a file by a single programmer, or the number of distinct programmers involved in writing and maintaining a file or project to study open source work practices. One of the most consistent results coming out of this research is a heavily skewed distribution of effort between participants (Koch, 2004; Mockus et al., 2002; Ghosh and Prakash, 2000; Dinh-Tong and Bieman, 2005). Several studies have adopted the normalized Gini coefficient (Robles et al., 2004), a measure of concentration, for this.

The Gini coefficient is a number between 0 and 1, where 0 is an indicator for perfect equality and 1 for total inequality or concentration, and can be based both on commits or lines-of-code contributed, with studies showing no major difference. For example, Mockus et al. (2002) have shown that the top 15 of nearly 400 programmers in the Apache project added 88 per cent of the total lines-of-code. In the GNOME project, the top 15 out of 301 programmers were only responsible for 48 percent, while the top 52 persons were necessary to reach 80 per cent (Koch and Schneider 2002), with clustering hinting at the existence of a still smaller group of 11 programmers within this larger group. A similar distribution for the lines-of-code contributed to the project was found in a community of Linux kernel developers by Hertel et al. (2003). Also the results of the Orbiten Free Software survey (Ghosh and Prakash 2000) are similar, the first decile of programmers was responsible for 72 per cent, the second for 9 per cent of the total code.

A second major result regarding organization of work is a low number of people working together on file level. For example, Koch and Neumann (2008) have found that only 12.2% of the files have more than three distinct authors. Most of the files have one (24.0%) or two (56.1%) programmers and only 3% have more than five distinct authors, in accordance with other studies on file or project level (Koch, 2004; Krishnamurthy, 2002; Mockus *et al.*, 2002; Ghosh and Prakash, 2000).

Similar distribution can also be found on project level in large scale studies: For example, Koch (2004) in his study of several thousand projects found a vast majority of projects having only a very small number of programmers (67.5 per cent have only 1 programmer). Only 1.3 per cent had more than 10 programmers. Analyzing the 100 most active mature projects on Sourceforge.net, Krishnamurthy (2002) also showed that most of the projects had only a small number of participants (median of 4). Only 19 per cent had more than 10, 22 per cent only 1 developer. While this percentage is much smaller than found by Koch (2004), this is not surprising as Krishnamurthy only used the 100 most active projects, not the full population.

Effort of Open Source Software Development Projects

Effort Estimation

Any discussion on open source projects, their success, efficiency or quality is incomplete without addressing the topic of effort, and relating other constructs to it. Unfortunately, this effort is basically unknown, even to the leaders of these projects, and therefore needs to be estimated. In addition such an estimation offers important insights to stakeholders, e.g. in the context of decisions about how an ongoing project might be managed, whether to join or to remain in a project, as well as adoption decisions by current or prospective users, including companies deciding whether to pursue a related business model.

Software engineering research for many years has focused on the topic of effort estimation, and has produced numerous models and methods. The best known of these is probably COCOMO (Boehm, 1981), which offers an algorithmic formula for estimating effort based on a quantification of the lines of code; this was modified and updated with the publication of COCOMO II (Boehm et al., 2000). Other options for effort estimation include software equation (Putnam, 1978) approaches based on the function point metric (Albrecht and Gaffney, 1983), diverse machine-learning approaches and proprietary models such as ESTIMACS and SLIM. Many of these approaches are based on the general development project formulation introduced by Norden (1960), which develops a manpower function based on the number of people participating in a project at a given time. Differences in work organization in open source projects raise the question of whether participation in OS projects can be modeled and predicted using approaches created in the context of traditional software development, or whether new models need to be developed.

In general, we can employ two different approaches to estimating effort, one based on output, i.e. software and some measure of its size, the other based on evidence of participation. Especially the comparison of both approaches can yield important insights related to comparing open source to commercial software development, as the estimation based on size basically assumes an organization equivalent to commercial settings. In this paper, we will mostly focus on the results of this process, while for a more in-depth coverage, the reader is referred to Koch (2008), where the analysis is based on a set of more than 8000 projects. Other related work is limited (Koch and Schneider, 2002; Koch, 2004; Gonzalez-Barahona et al., 2004; Wheeler, 2005; Amor et al., 2006), and for the most part applies only basic models without further discussion, or indirect effort measures (Yu, 2006).

For participation-based estimation, the basis is formed by the work of Norden (1960), which models any development project as a series of problem-solving efforts by the manpower involved. The manpower involved at each moment in an open source project can be inferred from an analysis of the source code management system logs. The number of people usefully employed at any given time is assumed to be approximately proportional to the number of problems ready for solution at that time. The manpower function then represents a Rayleigh-type curve. While Norden postulates a finite and fixed number of problems, additional requests would lead to the generation of new problems to be worked on. While this effect might be small to negligible until the time of operation, it might be a driving factor later on. Therefore, while there are similarities in the early stages of a project, in the later stages, distinct differences in processes and organization of work show up, linked to differences in goal setting and eliciting. We will therefore explore this possible effect of work organization in the next section.

The first model in the output-based estimation category is the original COCOMO (Boehm, 1981), and while severe problems related to use of this model due to violated assumptions exist, it is still employed for comparison with other models and with existing studies (Gonzalez-Barahona et al., 2004; Wheeler, 2005). The necessary data can easily be gathered from the source code management system of any open source project, or by downloading the source code itself and submitting it to a counting program. The updated version COCOMO 2 (Boehm et al., 2000) eliminates some of these concerns, so forms another option. An approach that is similar to COCOMO in that it is also based on an output metric, is the function point method (Albrecht and Gaffney, 1983). This method in general offers several advantages, most importantly the possibility to quantify the function points relatively early, based on analysis and design. In estimating the effort it is difficult, especially for an outsider, to correctly quantify the function points, even after delivery. Another way of arriving at a number is to use the converse method of converting the function point count to lines-of-code (Albrecht and Gaffney, 1983; Boehm et al., 2000). The literature proposes a mean number of lines-of-code required to implement a single function point in a given programming language. Once the amount of function points for a given system is known, literature provides several equations, basically production functions, to relate this amount to effort, naturally all based on data collected in a commercial software development environment. Examples include Albrecht and Gaffney (1983), Kemerer (1987) or Matson et al. (1994), who propose both a linear and logarithmic model.

Organization and Effort

We first explore the differences that the organization of work in open source projects mean for manpower modeling based on the work of Norden (1960). As discussed, while Norden postulates a finite and fixed number of problems, additional requests from the user and developer community could lead to the generation of new problems to be worked on. Based on extensive modeling and comparisons using several alternative manpower functions for a set of more than 8000 projects (Koch, 2008), modified Norden-Rayleigh-functions incorporating this effect significantly outperform the classical variant over complete project lifespans. We can see this as proof that in the open source form of organization, additional requirements and functionalities are introduced to a higher degree than in commercial settings. Also several possible forms for adding this effect to the Norden-Rayleigh model have been explored (Koch, 2008): The features added seem to depend on the starting problem, more than on the cumulative effort expended up to that time. This highlights the importance of the first requirements, often the vision of the project founder, in determining future enhancements. Also, a different proportionality factor, i.e. learning rate, has to be assumed as compared to the main respectively initial project, with a quadratic function better suited to modeling the addition of new problems. These results underline how much open source software development is actually driven by the participants and users, who truly shape the direction of such a project according to their needs or ideas.

We next turn to an analysis of the differences between participation-based estimation and output-based estimation. As the approaches in the latter group are all based on data from commercial settings, these differences can give an idea about the relation between participation-based effort, and the effort that would be necessary to develop the same system in a different environment. The empirical analysis (Koch, 2008) shows distinctive differences: Estimates derived from Norden-Rayleigh modeling were tested against each output-based method, and were significantly lower. An analytical comparison is also possible between COCOMO in both versions (Boehm, 1981; Boehm et al., 2000), and the Norden-Rayleigh model because COCOMO is based on this. Londeix (1987) detailed how the Rayleigh-curve corresponding to a given COCOMO estimation can be determined. In this case the other direction is employed to find a parameter set in COCOMO corresponding to the Rayleigh-curve, derived from programmer participation. As COCOMO offers both development mode and a number of cost drivers as parameters, there is no single solution. Nevertheless, actually no solution is possible given the parameter space, so open source development cannot be modeled using the original COCOMO, which leads to the conclusion that development has been more efficient than theoretically possible. When the possible parameters of COCOMO II are explored, the result is once again that this project is very efficient as both cost drivers and scale factors replacing the modes of development in COCOMO II have to be rated rather favorably, but this time the resulting combinations are within the range.

These differences showing up between the effort estimates based on participation and output might be due to several reasons. First, open source development organization might constitute a more efficient way of producing software (Bollinger et al., 1999; McConnell, 1999), due mostly to self-selection outperforming management intervention. Participants might be able to determine more accurately whether and where they are able to work productively on the project overall, or on particular tasks. In addition, overhead costs are very much reduced. The second explanation might be that the difference is caused by non-programmer participation, i.e. people participating by discussing on mailing lists, reporting bugs, maintaining web sites and the like. These are not included in the participation-based manpower modeling due to the fact that data is based on the source code management systems. If the Norden-Rayleigh and COCOMO estimates are compared, COCOMO results for effort are eight times higher. If it were assumed that this difference could only come from the invisible effort expended by these participants, this effort must be enormous. It would account for about 88 percent of the effort, translating to about 7 persons assisting each programmer. As has been shown, in open source projects, the number of participants other than programmers is about one order of magnitude larger than the number of programmers (Dinh-Trong and Bieman, 2005; Mockus et al., 2002; Koch and Schneider, 2002), but their expended effort is implicitly assumed to be much smaller. We are therefore going to relate this to the the 'chief programmer team organization', proposed more than 30 years ago (Mills, 1971; Baker, 1972). This has also been termed the 'surgical team' by Brooks (1995), and is a form of organization where which system development is divided into tasks each handled by a chief programmer who has responsibility for the most part of the actual design and coding, supported by a larger number of other specialists such as documentation writers or testers.

Efficiency of Open Source Software Development Projects

Efficiency and Success

Before the issue of effects on the efficiency of open source projects from the organization of work is explored, a short discussion on conceptualization of efficiency as well as success of open source projects is necessary. These topics, especially success, are more difficult to define and grasp than in commercial software development. Consequently, there is increased discussion on how the success of open source projects can be defined (Stewart, 2004; Stewart et al., 2006; Stewart and Gosain, 2006; Crowston et al., 2003; Crowston et al., 2004; Crowston et al., 2006), using, for example, search engine results as proxies (Weiss, 2005), or measures like number of downloads achieved. Over time, research has indicated in this way several possible success measures, but aggregating those to have an overall picture has been a major problem. For example, Crowston et al. (2006) present more than 15 success measures, Stewart and Gosain (2006) also included subjective success measures from a survey. This leads to most studies choosing a different set of success measures, and for the most part not aggregating the chosen set of different measures.

Efficiency and productivity in software development is most often denoted by the relation of an effort measure to an output measure, using either lines-of-code or, preferably due to independence from programming language, function points (Albrecht and Gaffney, 1983). This approach can be problematic even in an environment of commercial software development due to missing components especially of the output, for example also Kitchenham and Mendes (2004) agree that productivity measures need to be based on multiple size measures.

As discussed, the effort invested is normally unknown and consequently needs to be estimated, and the participants are also more diverse than in commercial projects as they include core team member, committers, bug reporters and several other groups with varying intensity of participation. Besides, also the outputs can be more diverse. In the general case, the inputs of an open source project can encompass a set of metrics, especially concerned with the participants. In the most simple cases the number of programmers and other participants can be used. The output of a project can be measured using several software metrics, most easily the lines-of-code, files, or others. This range of metrics both for inputs and outputs, and their different scales necessitates the application of a more sophisticated and appropriate method. Many of the results presented in the next two chapters are therefore based on applying Data Envelopment Analysis (DEA) to this problem. DEA (Farell, 1957; Charnes et al., 1978; Banker et al., 1984) is a non-parametric optimization method for efficiency comparisons without any need to define any relations between different factors or a production function. In addition, DEA can account for economies or dis-economies of scale, and is able to deal with multi-input, multi-output systems in which the factors have different scales.

The main result of applying DEA for a set of projects is an efficiency score for each project. This score can serve different purposes: First, single projects can be compared accordingly, but also groups of projects, for example those following similar process models, located in different application domains or simply of different scale can be compared to determine whether any of these characteristics lead to higher efficiency.

Organization and Efficiency

In this section, we will give an overview of the interrelationship between different attributes of open source projects characterizing their organization of work, as well as infrastructure, and their efficiency. The first element to be explored naturally is the generally large number of participants. Following the reasoning of Brooks, an increased number of people working together will decrease productivity due to exponentially increasing communication costs (Brooks, 1995). Interestingly, this effect has not turned up in prior studies (Koch, 2004; Koch, 2007). This leads to the interesting conclusion that Brooks's Law seemingly does not apply to open source software development. There are several possible explanations for this, which include the very strict modularization, which increases possible division of labor while reducing the need for communication. Also the low number of programmers working together on single files can be taken as a hint for this. We will also explore the notion of superior tool and infrastructure use as a possible factor later.

As empirical results have shown that the effort within open source projects is distributed very inequally, which seems to be a major characteristic of this type of organization, any effects this could have on efficiency should also be explored. Using a data set of projects from SourceForge and DEA, Koch (2008a) showed that there is indeed no connection: There was no significant difference in efficiency between projects with different levels of inequality, so this form of organization does not seem to incur a penalty. In some works, also license is hypothesized as having an impact on success or efficiency. Subramanian et al. (2009) found such an effect, as did Stewart et al. (2006), while Koch (2008a) did not.

Finally, the infrastructure employed for communication and coordination naturally shapes the work done in a project. It has been hypothesized that the advent of the Internet and especially the coordination and communications tools are at least a precondition for open source development (Raymond, 1999; Rusovan et al., 2005; Robbins, 2005). For example, Michlmayr (2005) has used a sample of projects to uncover whether the process maturity, based on version control, mailing lists and testing strategies, has had any influence on the success of open source projects, and could confirm this. Koch (2009) has analyzed the impact of adoption of different tools offered by SourceForge as well as tool diversity on project efficiency using DEA, and found surprising results: In a data set of successful projects, actually negative influences of tool adoption were found, while the results were more positive in a random data set. Two explanations were proposed for this, with one being that projects, especially larger ones, might be using other tools. The second explanation is that tools for communicating with users and potential co-developers can become more of a hindrance in successful projects, as they could increase the load to a degree that it detracts attention and time from the developers, which might be better spent on actual development work. In general, the successful projects also show a more progressed status, so actually these results seem to correspond to the results of Stewart and Gosain (2006), who stress the importance of development stage as moderator in project performance. In addition, these projects in general have a higher number of developers, which, counter-intuitively, seems to be linked to negative effects of communication and coordination tool adoption. One explanation might be that projects with problems in communication and coordination due to team size adopt tools to a higher degree, which can not completely solve the problem after it has passed some threshold. Therefore projects adopting these tools have a lower efficiency, but that might be even lower without tool adoption. The same reasoning could apply for communication channels with users: Tool adoption alone might be unable to prevent total communication overload.

Organization and Quality

In addition to effects of organization on efficiency, quality is a major concern in software development, and a hugely debated topic in open source (Dinh-Trong and Bieman, 2005; Stamelos et al., 2002; Zhao and Elbaum, 2000). We will therefore highlight a few results which link elements of organization to the quality achieved, although related studies are quite rare. For capturing this, attributes of the development process as used before need to be related to characteristics of quality for which diverse metrics from software engineering like McCabe's cyclomatic complexity (McCabe, 1976) or Chidamber and Kemerer's object-oriented metrics suite (Chidamber and Kemerer, 1994) can be employed. Koch and Neumann (2008) have attempted such an analysis using Java frameworks, and found that a high number of programmers and commits, as well as a high concentration is associated with problems in quality on class level, mostly to violations of size and design guidelines. This underlines the results of Koru and Tian (2005), who have found that modules with many changes rate quite high on structural measures like size or inheritance. If the architecture is not modular enough, a high concentration might show up as a result of this, as it can preclude more diverse participation. The other explanation is that classes that are programmed and/or maintained by a small core team are more complex due to the fact that these programmers 'know' their own code and don't see the need for splitting large and complex methods. One possibility in this case is a refactoring (Fowler, 1999) for a more modular architecture with smaller classes and more pronounced use of inheritance. This would increase the possible participation, thus maybe in turn leading to lower concentration, and maintainability together with other quality aspects. Underlining these results, MacCormack et al. (2006) have in a similar study used design structure matrices to study the difference between open source and proprietary developed software, without further discrimination in development practices. They find significant differences between Linux, which is more modular, and the first version of Mozilla. The evolution of Mozilla then shows purposeful redesign aiming for a more modular architecture, which resulted in modularity even higher than Linux. They conclude that a product's design mirrors the organization developing it, in that a product developed by a distributed team such as Linux was more modular compared to Mozilla developed by a collocated team. Alternatively, the design also reflects purposeful choices made by the developers based on contextual challenges, in that Mozilla was successfully redesigned for higher modularity at a later stage. On project level, there is a distinct difference: Those projects with high overall quality ranking have more authors and commits, but a smaller concentration than those ranking poorly. Thus, on class level a negative impact of more programmers was found, while on project level a positive effect. This underlines a central statement of open source software development on a general level, that as many people as possible should be attracted to a project. On the other hand, these resources should, from the viewpoint of product quality, be organized in small teams. Ideally, on both levels, the effort is not concentrated on too few of the relevant participants. Again, this seems to point to the organizational form of 'chief programmer team organization' (Mills, 1971; Baker, 1972; Brooks, 1995).

Conclusions

In this paper, we have surveyed the available literature related to characteristics of open source software development projects, and implications for effort and quality. Most of the empirical works have been based on mining the associated software repositories, and the results show that this is a promising way of achieving insights into projects and their characteristics.

One of the main principles and results found is the high concentration of programming work on a small number of individuals, which seems to hold true for most projects, similar to a very skewed distribution between projects. In addition, the number of people working on files cooperatively is quite small, with commercial involvement even increasing this trend. Under some circumstances, this high concentration can be linked to problems in quality and maintainability. The number of programmers attracted to a project forms a main focus point, and generally has positive implications: Having more programmers, quite interestingly and contrary to software engineering theory, does not reduce productivity, and does not negatively affect quality, if the concentration is kept in check. When considering the effort, estimations based on programmer involvement are significantly below estimations based on project output. Besides high efficiency due to self-organization and absence of management overhead, this points to an enormous effort expended by non-programming participants. Many of these results point to one especially important characteristic that determines success of an open source projects, which is modularity. A modular architecture allows for high participation while avoiding the problems of high concentration on a lower level like file or class.

There are many avenues for future research which are open in the context of open source software development, and a few have been touched upon here. The topic of effort and effort estimation is far from closed yet, and especially participants other than programmers are not adequately reflected here. Also the relations between projects, for example inclusion of results or reuse, and linking this to efficiency, effort and organization, similar to a market versus hierarchy discussion would be highly interesting. There are numerous works that have used social network analysis, e.g. by Grewal et al. (2006) or Oh and Jeon (2007), both between as well as within projects, and this could be an interesting lens through which to inspect the chief programmer team aspect discussed here. Also Dalle and David (2005) have started to analyze the allocation of resources in projects. Finally, the definition of success for open source projects is still difficult, and this uncertainty undermines some of the results from other studies or aspects.

Stefan Koch
Bogazici University, Turkey

REFERENCES

Albrecht, A. J., & Gaffney, J. E. (1983). Software Function, Source Lines of Code, and Development Effort Prediction: A Software Science Validation. *IEEE Transactions on Software Engineering, 9*(6), pp. 639-648.

Amor, J. J., Robles, G., & Gonzalez-Barahona, J. M. (2006). Effort estimation by characterizing **developer** activity. In *Proc. of the 2006 International Workshop on Economics Driven Software Engineering Research*. International Conference on Software Engineering, Shanghai, China, pp. 3-6.

Atkins, D., Ball, T., Graves, T., & Mockus, A. (1999). Using Version Control Data to Evaluate the Impact of Software Tools. In *Proc. 21st International Conference on Software Engineering*. Los Angeles, CA, pp. 324-333.

Baker, F. T. (1972) Chief Programmer Team Management of Production Programming. *IBM Systems Journal, 11*(1), pp. 56-73.

Banker, R.D., Charnes, A., & Cooper, W. (1984). Some Models for Estimating Technical and Scale Inefficiencies in Data Envelopment Analysis. *Management Science, 30*, 1078-1092.

Basset, T. (2004). Coordination and social structures in an open source project: Videolan. In Koch, S.,r(eds.), *Open Source Software Development*, pages 125-151. Hershey, PA: Idea Group Publishin..

Boehm, B.W. (1981). *Software Engineering Economics*. Englewood Cliffs, NJ: Prentice Hall.

Boehm, B. W., Abts, C., Brown, A. W., Chulani, S., Clark, B. K., Horowitz, E., Madachy, R., Reifer, D. J., & Steece, B. (2000). *Software Cost Estimation with COCOMO II*. Upper Saddle River, NJ: Prentice Hall.

Bollinger, T., Nelson, R., Self, K. M., & Turnbull, S. J. (1999). Open-source methods: Peering through the clutter. *IEEE Software, 16*(4), 8-11.

Brooks Jr., F. P. (1995). *The Mythical Man-Month: Essays on Software Engineering*. Anniversary ed., Reading, MA: Addison-WesleA.

Charnes, A., Cooper, d., & Rhodes, E. (1978). Measuring the Efficiency of Decision Making Units. *European Journal of Operational Research, 2*, 429-444.

Chidamber, S. and Kemerer, C. F. (1994). A metrics suite for object oriented design. *IEEE Transactions on Software Engineering, 20*(6), 476-493.

Coleman, E. G., & Hill, B. (2004). The social production of ethics in debian and free software communities: Anthropological lessons for vocational ethics. In Koch, S., (ed.), *Open Source Software Development*, pages 273-295. Hershey, PA: Idea Group Publishin..

Cook, J. E., Votta, L. G., & Wolf, A. L. (1998). Cost-effective analysis of in-place software processes. *IEEE Transactions on Software Engineering, 24*(8), pp. 650-663.

Crowston, K., & Scozzi, B. (2002). Open source software projects as virtual organizations: Competency rallying for software development. *IEE Proceedings - Software Engineering, 149*(1), 3-17.

Crowston, K., Annabi, d., & Howison, J. (2003). Defining Open Source Software Project Success. In *Proceedings of ICIS 2003*, Seattle, WA.

Crowston, K., Annabi, H., Howison, d., & Masango, C. (2004). Towards A Portfolio of FLOSS Project Success Measures. In *Collaboration, Conflict and Control: The 4th Workshop on Open Source Software Engineering (ICSE 2004)*, Edinburgh, Scotland.

Crowston, K., Howison, d., & Annabi, H. (2006). Information systems success in free and open source software development: theory and measures. *Software Process: Improvement and Practice, 11*(2*), 123-148.*

Crowston, K., Li, Q., Wei, K., Eseryel, Y., & Howison, J. (2007). Self-organization of teams for free/libre open source software development. *Information and Software Technology, 49,* 564-575.

Dalle, J.-M., & David, P.A. (2005). The Allocation of Software Development ressources in Open Source Production Mode. In Feller, J., Fitzgerald, B., Hissam, S. d., & Lakhani, K. R., editors, *Perspectives on Free and Open Source Software,* pages 297-328. Cambridge, MA: MIT PresA.Dempsey, B. J., Weiss, D., Jones, P., & Greenberg, J.(2002). Who is an open source software developer? *CACM, 45*(2), 67-72.

Dinh-Trong, T.T., & Bieman, J. M. (2005). The FreeBSD Project: A Replication Case Study of Open Source Development. *IEEE Transactions on Software Engineering, 31*(6), 481-494.

Elliott, M. S., & Scacchi, W. (2004). Free software development: Cooperation and conflict in a virtual organizational culture. In Koch, S. (ed.), *Open Source Software Development,* pages 152-172. Hershey, PA: Idea Group Publishing.

Farell, M.J. (1957). The Measurement of Productive Efficiency. *Journal of the Royal Statistical Society,* Series A 120(3), pp. 250-290.

Fitzgerald, Brian (2006). The Transformation of Open Source Software. *MIS Quarterly, 30*(3), 587-598.

Gallivan, M. J. (2002). Striking a balance between trust and control in a virtual organization: A content analysis of open source software case studies. *Information Systems Journal, 11*(4), 277-304.

Ghosh, R., & Prakash, V. V. (2000). The Orbiten Free Software Survey. *First Monday, 5*(7).

Gonzalez-Barahona, J.M., Robles, G., Ortuno Perez, M., Rodero-Merino, L., Centeno-Gonzalez, J., Matellan-Olivera, V., Castro-Barbero, E., & de-las Heras-Quiros, P (2004). Analyzing the anatomy of GNU/Linux distributions: methodology and case studies (Red Hat and Debian). In Koch, S. (Ed.), *Free/Open Source Software Development.* Hershey, PA: Idea Group Publishing.

Grewal, R., Lilien, G. L., & Mallapragada, G. (2006). Location, Location, Location: How Network Embeddedness Affects Project Success in Open Source Systems. *Management Science, 52*(7), 1043-1056.

Hertel, G., Niedner, S., & Hermann, S. (2003). Motivation of software developers in open source projects: An internet-based survey of contributors to the Linux kernel. *Research Policy, 32*(7), 1159-1177.

Holck, J., & Jorgensen, N. (2004). Do not check in on red: Control meets anarchy in two open source projects. In Koch, S., editor, *Free/Open Source Software Development,* pages 1–26. Hershey, PA: Idea Group Publishing.

Howison, J., & Crowston, K. (2004). The perils and pitfalls of mining SourceForge. In *Proc. of the International Workshop on Mining Software Repositories.* Edinburgh, Scotland, pp. 7-11.

Hunt, F., & Johnson, P. (2002). On the pareto distribution of sourceforge projects. In: *Proc. Open Source Software Development Workshop.* Newcastle, UK, (pp. 122-129).

Jorgensen, N. (2001). Putting it all in the trunk: Incremental software engineering in the FreeBSD Open Source project. *Information Systems Journal, 11*(4), 321–336.

Kemerer, C. F., (1987). An Empirical Validation of Software Cost Estimation Models. *CACM, 30*(5), pp. 416-429.

Kemerer, C. F., & Slaughter, S. (1999). An Empirical Approach to Studying Software Evolution. *IEEE Transactions on Software Engineering, 25*(4), 493-509.

Kitchenham, B., & Mendes, E. (2004). Software Productivity Measurement Using Multiple Size Measures. *IEEE Transactions on Software Engineering, 30*(12), 1023-1035.

Koch, S. (2004). Profiling an open source project ecology and its programmers. *Electronic Markets, 14*(2), 77-88.

Koch, S. (2007). Software Evolution in Open Source Projects - A Large-Scale Investigation. *Journal of Software Maintenance and Evolution, 19*(6), 361-382.

Koch, S. (2008). Effort Modeling and Programmer Participation in Open Source Software Projects. *Information Economics and Policy, 20*(4), 345-355.

Koch, S. (2008a). Measuring the Efficiency of Free and Open Source Software Projects Using Data Envelopment Analysis. In Sowe, S.K., Stamelos, I., & Samoladas, I. (eds.): *Emerging Free and Open Source Software Practices*, pp. 25-44, Hershey, PA: IGI Publishing.

Koch, S. (2009). Exploring the Effects of SourceForge.net Coordination and Communication Tools on the Efficiency of Open Source Projects using Data Envelopment Analysis. *Empirical Software Engineering, 14*(4), 397-417.

Koch, S., & Neumann, C. (2008). Exploring the Effects of Process Characteristics on Product Quality in Open Source Software Development. *Journal of Database Management, 19*(2), 31-57.

Koch, S., & Schneider, G. (2002). Effort, Cooperation and Coordination in an Open Source Software Project: Gnome. *Information Systems Journal, 12*(1), 27-42.

Krishnamurthy, S. (2002). Cave or community? an empirical investigation of 100 mature open source projects. *First Monday, 7*(6).

Londeix, B. (1987). *Cost Estimation for Software Development.* Addison-Wesley, Wokingham, UK.

Long, Y., & Siau, K. (2007). Social Network Structures in Open Source Software Development Teams. *Journal of Database Management, 18*(2), 25-40.

MacCormack, A., Rusnak, J., & Baldwin, C.Y. (2006). Exploring the Structure of Complex Software Designs: An Empirical Study of Open Source and Proprietary Code. *Management Science, 52*(7), 1015-1030.

Matson, J. E., Barrett, B. E., & Mellichamp, J. M. (1994). Software Development Cost Estimation Using Function Points. *IEEE Transactions on Software Engineering, 20*(4), 275-287.

McCabe, T. (1976). A complexity measure. *IEEE Transactions on Software Engineering, 2*(4), 308-320.

McConnell, S. (1999). Open-source methodology: Ready for prime time? *IEEE Software, 16*(4), 6-8.

Michlmayr, M. (2005). Software Process Maturity and the Success of Free Software Projects. In Zielinski, K. and Szmuc, T. (eds.): *Software Engineering: Evolution and Emerging Technologies*, pp. 3-14, Amsterdam, The Netherlands: IOS Press.

Mills, H. D. (1971). *Chief Programmer Teams: Principles and Procedures*. Report FSC 71-5108. IBM Federal Systems Division.

Mockus, A., Fielding, R., & Herbsleb, J. (2002). Two case studies of open source software development: Apache and Mozilla. *ACM Transactions on Software Engineering and Methodology, 11*(3), 309-346.

Norden, P. V. (1960). On the anatomy of development projects. *IRE Transactions on Engineering Management, 7*(1), 34-42.

Oh, W., & Jean, S. (2007). Membership Herding and Network Stability in the Open Source Community: The Ising Perspective. *Management Science, 53*(7), 1086-1101.

Perens, B. (1999) 'The Open Source Definition', in DiBona, C. et al. (eds.), *Open Sources: Voices from the Open Source Revolution,* CambridgetsMA: O'Reilly & Associates.

Putnam, L. H. (1978. 'A general empirical solution to the macro software sizing and estimating probem', *IEEE Transactions on Software Engineering, 4*(4p. 345-361.

Raymond, E.S. (1999). *The Cathedral and the Bazaar.* CambridettsMA: O'Reilly & Associates.

Robbins, J. (2005). Adopting Open Source Software Engineering (OSSE) Practices by Adopting OSSE Tools. In Feller, J., Fitzgerald, B., Hissam, and., & Lakhani, K.R. (eds), *Perspectives on Free and Open Source Software*, Cambridge, MA: MIT Press.

Robles, G., Koc and., & Gonzalez-Barahona, J. M. (2004). Remote analysis and measurement of libre software systems by means of the CVSanalY tool. In *ICSE 2004 - Proceedings of the Second International Workshop on Remote Analysis and Measurement of Software Systems (RAMSS '04)*, pages 51–55, Edinburgh, Scotland.

Robles, G., Gonzalez-Barahona, J.M., & Merelo, J.J. (2006). Beyond source code: The importance of other artifacts in software development (a case study). *Journal of Systems and Software, 79*(9), 1233-1248.

Robles, G., González-Barahona, J. M., Izquierdo-Cortazar, D., & Herraiz, I. (2009). Tools for the study of the usual data sources found in libre software projects. *International Journal of Open Source Software & Processes, 1*(pp. 24-45.

Rusovan, S., Lawfor and., & Parnas, D.L. (2005). Open Source Software Development: Future or Fad? In Feller, J., Fitzgerald, B., Hissam, and., & Lakhani, K.R. (eds), *Perspectives on Free and Open Source Software*, Cambridge, MA: MIT Press.

Scacchi, W., Feller, J., Fitzgerald, B., Hissa and., & Lakhani, K. (2006). Understanding Free/Open Source Software Development Processes. *Software Process: Improvement and Practice, 11*(pp. 95–105.

Sowe, S. K., Angelis, L., Stamelos, I., & Manolopoulos, Y. (2007) Using Repository of Repositories (RoRs) to Study the Growth of F/OSS Projects: A Meta-Analysis Research Approach. *OSS 2007,* pp. 147-160.

Stallman, Richard M. (2002). *Free Software, Free Society: Selected Essays of Richard M. Stallman.* Boston, Massachusetts: GNU Press.

Stamelos, I., Angelis, L., Oikonomo and., & Bleris, G.L. (2002). Code quality analysis in open source software development. *Information Systems Journal*, pp. 43-60.

Stewart, K.J. (2004). OSS Project Success: From Internal Dynamics to External Impact. In *Collaboration, Conflict and Control: The 4th Workshop on Open Source Software Engineering (ICSE 2004)*, Edinburgh, Scotland.

Stewart, K.J., Ammeter, and., & Maruping, L.M. (2006). Impacts of Licence Choice and Organisational Sponsorship on User Interest and Development Activity in Open Source Software Projects. *Information Systems Research, 17*(pp. 126-144.

Stewart, K. J.and Gosain, S. (2006). The Moderating Role of Development Stage in Affecting Free/Open Source Software Project Performance. *Software Process: Improvement and Practice, 11*(pp. 177-191.

Subraminian, C., Sen, R. and Nelson, M.L. (2009). Determinants of open source software project success: A longitudinal study. *Decision Support Systems*, 46, pp. 576-585.

Vixie, P., 1999. Software Engineering.n : DiBona, C., Ockman, S., Stone, M. (Eds.), *Open Sources: Voices from the Open Source Revolution.* Cambridge, MA: O'Reilly & Associ100..

von Krogh,eorand Spaeian S. (200 , "The open source software phenomenon: Characteristics that promote reseah.", *Journal of Strategic Information Systems, 16*(pp. 236–253.

Weiss, D. (2005). Measuring Success of Open Source Projects Using Web Search Engines. In *Proceedings of the 1st International Conference on Open Source Systems*, pp. 93-99, Genoa, Italy.

Wheeler, D. (, 2005). More Than a Gigabuck: Estimating GNU/Linux's Size - Version 1.07 (updated 2002). Retrieved May 21, 2010, from http://www.dwheeler.com/sloc/redhat71-v1/redhat71sloc.html

Yu, L. (2006). Indirectly predicting the maintenance effort of open-source software. *Journal of Software Maintenance and Evolution, 18*(pp. 311-332.

Zhao, L., Elbaum, S. (2000). A survey on quality related activities in open source. *Software Engineering Notes, 25*(pp. 54-57.

Section 1

Chapter 1

Open Source Software Adoption:
Anatomy of Success and Failure

Brian Fitzgerald
Lero – Irish Software Engineering Research Centre and University of Limerick, Ireland

ABSTRACT

Current estimates suggest widespread adoption of open source software (OSS) in organizations worldwide. However, the problematic nature of OSS adoption is readily evidenced in the fairly frequent reports of problems, unforeseen hold-ups, and outright abandonment of OSS implementation over time. Hibernia Hospital, an Irish public sector organization, have embarked on the adoption of a range of OSS applications over several years, some of which have been successfully deployed and remain in live use within the organisation, whereas others, despite achieving high levels of assimilation over a number of years, have not been ultimately retained in live use in the organization. Using a longitudinal case study, we discuss in depth the deployment process for two OSS applications – the desktop application suite whose deployment was unsuccessful ultimately, and the email application which was successfully deployed. To our knowledge, this is the first such in-depth study into successful and unsuccessful OSS implementation.

INTRODUCTION

Open source software (OSS) has elicited a great deal of research interest across a range of disciplines since the term was introduced in 1998. Much

DOI: 10.4018/978-1-60960-513-1.ch001

of this research, however, has focused *inward* on the phenomenon itself, studying the motivations of individual developers to contribute to OSS projects, or investigating the characteristics of specific OSS products and projects, for example. Far less has been done in looking *outward* at the process of OSS adoption and implementation in organizations. The need for rigorous research into this process is important for several reasons: Firstly, recent estimates suggest widespread adoption of OSS: A survey of public administrations in 13 European countries reported that 78% were using open source (Ghosh and Glott, 2005). Similarly, a large-scale survey in the US estimated that 87% of organizations were using open source software (Walli et al., 2005). However, these surveys did not distinguish between primary adoption (the initial decision to adopt at the organizational level) and secondary OSS adoption (the actual implementation process which involves adoption by individuals throughout the organization). Primary and secondary adoption have been identified as quite different scenarios (Gallivan, 2001; Zaltman et al., 1973). This distinction and the problematic nature of OSS adoption is readily evidenced in the fairly frequent (and somewhat controversial) reports of problems, unforeseen hold-ups, and outright abandonment of OSS implementation over time (e.g. Birmingham City Council (Thurston, 2006); Crest Electronics (Turner, 2005); Scottish Police (Niccolai, 2005), Newham Council (McCue, 2004).

Here we present the case of Hibernia Hospital, an Irish public sector organization, who embarked on the adoption of a range of OSS applications. Some of these applications have been successfully deployed and remain in live use within the organisation, whereas others, despite achieving high levels of assimilation over a number of years, have not been ultimately retained in live use in the organization. Using a longitudinal case study, we discuss in depth the deployment process for two OSS applications—a desktop application suite whose deployment was ultimately unsuccessful and abandoned, and an email application which was successfully deployed. To our knowledge, this is the first such study into successful and unsuccessful OSS implementation, although there have been several studies of OSS adoption (e.g. Lundell et al., 2006; Rossi et al., 2006; Ven et al., 2006; Zuliani and Succi, 2004).

As a starting point, we drew on Gallivan's (2001) process framework for studying secondary adoption of technology. This framework extends the classical diffusion of innovation theory of Rogers (1962-2003) by drawing on critiques of this theory (e.g. Fichman, 1992; Fichman and Kemerer, 1999; Moore and Benbasat, 1991). Our goal in this study was not to test a factor model of OSS deployment but rather to provide a rich description of the process of successful and unsuccessful OSS adoption in a single organizational context, with a focus more on theory development rather than theory testing.

Furthermore, researchers have identified a tendency in traditional innovation adoption research towards a pro-innovation bias (Fichman, 2004; Rogers, 2003). As a result, innovation is invariably seen as beneficial and positive for all participants, and, indeed, more has been written about successful adoption than rejection. Thus, our study here of the successful and failed adoption of OSS products can provide useful insights and contrasts which can contribute to theory development in this area.

The remainder of the paper is structured as follows. In section 2, we discuss the process model approach adopted here and present the conceptual framework we use in the study. Following this, section 3 discusses the research approach adopted. Section 4 presents the adoption process trajectories for both OSS applications in Hibernia. Following this, in section 5 we discuss this deployment using the framework derived in Section 2. Finally, the conclusions and the implications of the study for a theory of OSS deployment are discussed.

CONCEPTUAL GROUNDING

Process vs. Factor Research Models

Process and factor approaches have been identified as alternative but complementary approaches to research (e.g. Markus and Robey, 1988; Mohr,

1982). Briefly summarising, factor research is concerned with identifying predictor and outcome variables. These are cast as independent and dependent variables and the research focus tends towards rigorous measurement of the variables and statistical analysis of the relationship between them. The variables are assumed to be causally related with the predictor/independent variable accounting for variation in the outcome/dependent variable. However, such research cannot provide any in-depth explanation as to how and why the variables may be related (Newman and Robey, 1992). Process model research, on the other hand, seeks to elaborate the story of the underlying dynamics which reveals how and why outcomes are reached over time. In this study, given the lack of research on organizational adoption of OSS, successful or otherwise, a process model which could afford increased understanding of significant OSS adoption events was important.

While process and factor models are acknowledged as complementary, researchers have warned against combining into a single model (Markus and Robey, 1988; Newman and Robey, 1992; Mohr, 1982). This argumentation is based on the fact that the models differ in form and operate a different model of causality. That is rather than a 'push type' causality of factor models where the levels of the independent variables cause the levels of the dependent variables, in the process model

approach, outcomes are implied by preceding events—a 'pull-type' causality.

Notwithstanding this argument, several researchers have combined process and factor models to good effect (Gallivan, 2001; Sambamurthy and Poole, 1992; Shaw and Jarvenpaa, 1997). Indeed, combining factor and process models has been advocated when the focus is on understanding the adoption events and the factors that promote or constrain adoption outcomes (Gallivan, 2001; Shaw and Jarvenpaa, 1997). Therefore a somewhat hybrid model was followed here in that an overall conceptual framework of innovation adoption was identified, primarily as a conceptual lens to theoretically ground the study (Klein and Myers, 1999) and also as a means of bounding the study focus (Newman and Robey, 1992).

Innovation Adoption Research

In a review of technology diffusion research, Fichman (1992) proposes a 2x2 matrix of innovation adoption contexts where the axes are locus of innovation adoption (individual or organization) and class of technology to be adopted (low user interdependencies and knowledge burden versus high user interdependencies and knowledge burden). The model is presented in Figure 1.

Fichman argues that the assumptions underpinning traditional innovation adoption models hold

Figure 1. IT diffusion classification matrix (from Fichman, 1992; Gallivan, 2001)

best for the lower-left quadrant in Figure 1. In our study, we focus on organizational adoption of open source which is best characterised by organizational mandate to use the technology and also extensive knowledge required to overcome barriers to implementation and use. This is represented by the upper-right quadrant in Figure 1.

Such a characterisation of OSS as a technology subject to organizational mandate, high user interdependencies and high knowledge burden is justifiable for a number of reasons. Firstly, the OSS products that we focus on in this study include desktop and email application platforms. Both of these represent horizontal infrastructure systems in widespread use within organizations. As such they would be subject to the IT governance policy within an organization, and use of these systems would typically be organization-wide.

Furthermore in terms of knowledge burden, Fichman and Kemerer (1999) argue that IT assimilation may be hindered by knowledge barriers due to the learning required to obtain the necessary deep knowledge and skills to successfully deploy complex technologies. These knowledge barriers cause deployment to be a risky venture for an organization, but it may still undertake deployment so as to be in a position to avail of benefits at the appropriate time.

These issues are especially pertinent in the case of OSS. Given the fact that OSS is quite a new phenomenon, there is no well-established and codified base of knowledge that can guarantee successful deployment. OSS adoption represents a significant risk and a fundamental change in how software is acquired and maintained (Agerfalk and Fitzgerald, 2008). For example, there is usually no vendor to market an OSS product and verify that the product meets required functionality. Nor is there the automatic provision of the guaranteed maintenance contract that comes with the acquisition of proprietary software. These issues represent a considerable knowledge burden for organizations that embark on the process of OSS adoption.

A Conceptual Framework for the Innovation Adoption Process

Gallivan (2001) draws on a wide range of innovation adoption research, including Rogers diffusion of innovation, Davis' (1989) TAM model and, particularly the Theory of Planned Behavior (Ajzen, 1985) to propose a process framework specifically addressing secondary adoption and organizational assimilation of technology (see Figure 2).

This framework operates at quite a high-level in identifying issues relevant to the IT adoption process. Here we briefly discuss the components of the framework and how they are relevant in an

Figure 2. Secondary adoption process (adapted from Gallivan, 2001)

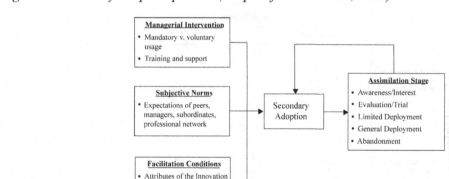

open source context. Later, we use this framework to structure our discussion of the deployment process for the various OSS applications in Hibernia.

Managerial Intervention

Managerial intervention refers to the actions taken and resources made available by management to expedite secondary adoption. Gallivan identifies issues such as voluntariness of adoption, training and support here. Voluntariness has also been proposed as a significant factor in other innovation research (Moore and Benbasat, 1991), and the issue of organizational mandate in relation to OSS adoption was discussed above.

Management support is undoubtedly critical for radical, high-risk initiatives such as OSS deployment since it contravenes the traditional model where ongoing support is legally guaranteed by a vendor. Indeed, management support is likely to become even more important in the future as OSS adoption moves out of the domain of invisible infrastructure systems to more visible, high-profile applications.

Subjective Norms

Subjective norms have to do with individual beliefs about how relevant peers and co-workers expect them to behave in relation to the technology. This can lead to greater effort to learn about and adopt an innovation or even cause abandonment of a technology. This issue has resonances with attributes of the innovation, such as compatibility and image, discussed below.

From a values and norms perspective, the ideology represented by OSS may have significant implications. The importance of ideological values has been illustrated in several studies of OSS. For example, Stewart and Gosain (2006) identify how adherence to an overarching OSS community ideology facilitates team effectiveness. Similarly, the protracted and heated dispute over several years among the Linux kernel development community concerning the use of a proprietary version control system (BitKeeper) represented an ideological crisis for many in that community, and certainly influenced the choice of adoption and non-adoption of the technology (Shaikh, 2006).

Facilitating Conditions: Attributes of the Innovation and Organization

Much prior research on innovation adoption has focused on attributes of the technology and the organization. Rather than discuss exhaustively the range of attributes that have been identified, a number of attributes are briefly presented here and we discuss how they are relevant to an OSS context.

Attributes of the Innovation

Rogers (2003) identifies five key perceived attributes of an innovation that influence the outcome of the adoption process:

- **Relative advantage:** the extent to which an innovation is perceived as being better than its precursor.
- **Compatibility:** the degree to which an innovation is perceived as being consistent with the existing values, norms, needs and past experiences of potential adopters.
- **Complexity:** the degree to which an innovation is perceived as difficult to understand and use.
- **Trialability:** the degree to which an innovation can be experimented with.
- **Observability:** the degree to which the results of an innovation are visible to others.

In short, Rogers suggests that innovations will diffuse more quickly and successfully when they are readily trialable, of high relative advantage, compatible with the status quo, not too complex to use, and where use is readily observable to others. These attributes have been confirmed in many studies. Additional attributes, such as image and voluntariness, have been identified (Moore and Benbasat, 1991), and indeed some attributes have been found to overlap—relative advantage and compatibility, for example (Moore and Benbasat, 1991; Carter & Belanger, 2006). While Rogers' work is applicable to innovation in general, in the specific category of IT adoption, the technology assessment model (TAM) has been proposed by Davis (1989) with two central attributes—perceived usefulness and perceived ease of use. These are subsumed by the Rogers attributes of relative advantage and complexity respectively.

These attributes are readily apparent in the context of OSS. In terms of relative advantage, compatibility and complexity, for example, many OSS products have been purposefully designed to replicate proprietary counterparts. There should therefore be a sense of familiarity thus mitigating adoption problems in relation to these attributes. On the other hand, the observability of OSS use is less obvious due to the strategy of replicating proprietary software. For example, it is very difficult to tell the difference between MS Word, Excel and Powerpoint and the respective OpenOffice counterparts, Writer, Calc and Impress, merely by looking at users working online on these applications.

Given that acquisition of OSS products is usually extremely straightforward, often as simple as a zero-cost download from a web site, trialability is greatly facilitated in the specific case of OSS. Indeed, many OSS implementations up to now have been deployed by technologically-literate IT personnel who have not sought organizational approval to acquire the products.

In Rogers's work, image is considered to be subsumed in relative advantage, but Moore and Benbasat concur with previous studies which have shown image to be a separate factor (Tornatzky and Klein, 1982). Image is defined as the degree to which an innovation can enhance one's image or social status. This has emerged as a complex issue in relation to open source. Studies of the motivation of OSS developers reveal that the intrinsic satisfaction of belonging to a meritocratic community where talented developers can progress to become core developers is a powerful force (e.g. Kuk, 2006; Lakhani and Wolf, 2006). Similarly, from a user perspective, public administrations, particularly in Europe, have been enthusiastically seeking to deploy open source, seeing it as a positive initiative which frees them from the constraints of a proprietary software industry. However, other reports have found that developers do not necessarily embrace open source (Zachary, 2003), and equally, from a user perspective, there may be resistance to the use of open source products (van Reijswoud, 2005).

Organizational Attributes: Absorptive Capacity

Fichman (1992) recommends that theoretical frameworks of traditional innovation research be complemented by additional perspectives, including absorptive capacity (Cohen and Levinthal, 1990). Absorptive capacity refers to an organization's ability to recognise the value of new information, absorb it and subsequently leverage it productively. An absorptive capacity perspective has been used by Daniel et al. (2006) to study OSS development group performance in relation to knowledge acquisition and transfer. However, absorptive capacity certainly seems relevant for OSS adoption more generally. The ever increasing number of OSS applications appearing in the marketplace represents a significant knowledge challenge to be overcome—for example, the knowledge of what applications exist, which ones are most viable, how well they are supported, what functionality they offer, how they may be integrated with other OSS or proprietary applications. Indeed, developers in the past have referred to the "exhilarating succession of problem-solving challenges" when installing OSS products (Sanders, 1998). Furthermore, given that there is no tried and tested roadmap indicating a clear series of steps to guarantee successful deployment, organizations cannot expect to have the type of lengthy experience with OSS deployment that could guarantee success. Thus, the process of OSS implementation is clearly one where absorptive capacity may play a crucial role.

Secondary (Individual) Adoption Process

Gallivan suggests this component to address the details of the organizational implementation process whereby individuals throughout the organization adopt the innovation. This is taken to include when and how the innovation is adopted, what obstacles are encountered and how these influence the outcome and the degree of organizational assimilation.

Level of OSS Assimilation

Given that technology acquisition and deployment represent different assimilation events, the level or degree of assimilation can be viewed as a staged process from awareness/interest through to general deployment. The following, adapted from Fichman & Kemerer (1997), indicate the range of OSS assimilation levels experienced over time in Hibernia.

- **Awareness/Interest:** Key decision makers in organization aware of OSS and actively committed to learning more
- **Evaluation/Trial:** Organization has acquired specific OSS products and has initiated evaluation or trial
- **Limited Deployment:** Organization has established a program of regular but limited use of OSS products

- **General Deployment:** Organization is using OSS products for at least one large and mission critical system
- **Abandonment:** Organization has discontinued live use of OSS products

RESEARCH APPROACH

At a high level, research epistemologies may be classified as positivist, interpretivist or critical (Chua, 1986), although Klein and Myers (1999) recognise that classifying individual research studies is not always straightforward. To the extent that positivist research involves quantifiable measures, formal hypothesis testing and the pursuit of statistical generalization, this research study is not primarily a positivist one. Likewise given that critical research seeks to elucidate the negative and discriminatory conditions inherent in the status quo, this study does not follow a critical approach. Interpretivist research assumes the social construction of reality through language and shared meanings, and explicitly recognises the importance of a deep understanding of the context in all its inherent complexity. This research is largely compatible with these assumptions and our epistemology is thus closest to the interpretivist one. However, this classification should be tempered with our use of a high-level conceptual framework to ground the research, and to which we also link our findings. Nevertheless, Klein and Myers (1999) recommend the use of a conceptual framework in interpretivist research for such a purpose.

We sought to develop a rich understanding and insight based on a deep analysis of a single case context—what has been termed a "revelatory case" (Yin, 1994). This is also relevant given that there are undoubtedly political and social factors at play in IT assimilation (Fichman & Kemerer, 1999), which are difficult to elucidate in survey research, for example. Also, by definition postal surveys usually only elicit information from a

Table 1. Data sources

Activity	Criteria
22 interviews in Hibernia and with relevant external experts	Interviews with 17 IT staff, OSS users and management in Hibernia over the period Feb 2003 to Nov 2006 Interviews with three consultants from three local organisations providing support to Hibernia (Feb 2004, Jun 2004) Interviews with two Government and Health Board personnel about general OSS implementation policy issues in the health sector in Ireland (Nov 2004 and Jun 2005)
Fortnightly half-day workshops	In context of a joint research project, half-day OSS implementation workshops held fortnightly in the period Mar - Dec 2004
Informal meetings/interviews	Frequent informal interviews/meetings with relevant staff refine/clarify issues in the period Feb 2003 to Nov 2006
Project Documentation	Various reports and presentations relevant to the OSS implementation process
Feedback presentations	Findings were presented at three workshops attended by relevant staff

single key informant (or perhaps two) in an organisation. Thus, there is merit in investigating the view of multiple stakeholders in a particular case context, particularly for the complex secondary adoption process (Fichman, 1992; Gallivan, 2001; Rogers, 2003). Also, just as quantitative research highlights findings that are of greatest statistical significance, in qualitative research, the aptness of a respondent's quote can memorably highlight the essence of the research.

Given that the OSS implementation process in Hibernia was not uniformly successful, we chose to focus on two example implementations—the desktop application suite which was unsuccessfully deployed and the email suite which was successful, thus representing 'extreme cases' (Miles and Huberman, 1994). Both applications are broadly similar—they are applicable to users throughout the organization, and there are strong proprietary alternatives in each case. Furthermore, by limiting our study to a single case context, certain factors are controlled to some extent—organizational attributes, for example. This makes it easier to isolate the salient elements influencing the success or failure of the process.

Data Collection and Analysis

In terms of data collection, a number of sources were drawn on (see Table 1). Over a three-year period, a series of formal face-to-face interviews, and more informal telephone interviews and meetings, were conducted with IT staff, key users and relevant management. In addition, interviews were conducted with external consultants from local firms who provided technical support for Hibernia's OSS implementation, and also with external experts who were familiar with overarching IT policy issues in the hospital sector. Formal interviews were generally of one to two-hour duration. These interviews were complemented by comprehensive reviews of documents and presentations, and fortnightly project workshops of half-day duration over a 12-month period. Furthermore, in the context of a collaborative funded research project between the author's university and Hibernia, there was prolonged and extensive access and interaction with the relevant personnel. Thus, clarification and refinement of emergent issues happened frequently through informal interviews and meetings with key personnel.

While the initial primary adoption of OSS in Hibernia was a straight-forward organizational decision, it soon became obvious that the secondary adoption of specific OSS applications by individuals throughout the organization would not be straightforward. Given this, we drew on the conceptual framework (Figure 2) which had been specifically designed to investigate secondary adoption (Gallivan, 2001). Data analysis occurred over two phases. Firstly, all the data gathered over the entire duration of the study was analysed from the high level perspective of the conceptual framework. Examples of issues which related to managerial intervention, subjective norms, organizational attributes, and attributes of the innovation were identified. Following this, in a second coding phase, the specific details which underpinned the high-level constructs were identified thereby elaborating the high-level constructs of the framework. The method of constant comparison (Glaser and Strauss, 1967; Miles and Huberman, 1994) was used here as both cases of successful and unsuccessful OSS deployment were also drawn on to help isolate the most salient issues.

While generally guided by an interview protocol which specified the specific topics of research interest, interviews were conducted in a reflexive manner, in that it was accepted that responses to certain questions could stimulate new awareness and interest in particular issues which could then require additional probing. This strategy is also recommended by Eisenhardt (1989) who labels it "controlled opportunism". This probing was also a feature of the informal interviews and meetings which followed the formal interviews.

Reliability and Validity Issues

Research reliability is concerned with the consistency with which research results can be replicated. A frequent criticism of interpretivist research is that due to its subjective nature, replication is problematic. While acknowledging that interpretivist analysis would not expect all researchers to interpret the findings in exactly the same way, it is important that the research process be transparent and accessible to others. To help address research reliability, Yin (1994) recommends the use of a case study database and protocol. This strategy has been operationalised in other interpretivist case studies (e.g. Kirsch, 2004) and we followed a similar approach here. A case study database

was established which contained the raw field notes, transcribed interviews, and coding of this data according to our conceptual framework. The case study protocol specifies the criteria for selecting the case applications, the choice of whom to interview, and the interview protocol in terms of broad interview questions.

Research validity is concerned with whether the actual research in practice matches what it purports to be about. In interpretive research this is primarily concerned with the "truth value" of the research (Miles and Huberman, 1994).

Construct validity deals with the extent to which the constructs as operationalized relate to the research phenomenon being studied. In this study, given the lack of research on OSS adoption, and our goal of theory development, construct validity was important. Yin (1994) describes three tactics to deal with construct validity: the use of multiple sources of evidence, the establishment of a chain of evidence, and key informants reviewing draft findings. In this case, the collection of data on the same phenomenon from multiple interviewees both within and external to Hibernia, together with information gleaned from project documents and presentations, helped address the multiple sources of evidence criterion. In relation to the chain of evidence criterion, this was addressed through the establishment of a case study database, the rigorous analysis and coding of data according to the conceptual framework, illustration of the theoretical constructs with quotes from interviewees who fulfilled a variety of roles in the implementation, and the process description of the deployment trajectory over time. Finally, key informant review and feedback was addressed in several workshops in the context of a joint research project on OSS implementation in Hibernia, and also several draft reports and presentations on the topic were reviewed by Hibernia staff.

External validity is concerned with the extent to which a study's findings can be generalised. One of the limitations of this study might appear to be the fact that it is based on a single case and thus there is limited scope for generalization. However, Lee and Baskerville (2003) identify a fundamental and long-standing misapplication of generalization whereby researchers have solely focused on statistical sampling-based generalizability from a sample to a population, and have sought to overcome the perceived problem of attempting to generalize to other settings beyond the current one. Following this conventional model, researchers have suggested increasing sample size or number of case study organizations, but Lee and Baskerville argue cogently for the ultimate futility of this flawed strategy. They propose an overarching framework that proposes four distinct categories of generalizing, only one of which corresponds to statistical sampling-based generalization. One of the other categories in their framework, that of generalizing from empirical description to theoretical statements, is more applicable to our research study. This view of generalizing from thick description to theoretical concepts, specific implications and rich insight is also recommended as a strategy by Walsham (1993) and Klein and Myers (1999, p.75) who argue for such a theoretical link as being key to distinguish "interpretive research…from just anecdotes". In this study, the findings were analysed and integrated using the theoretical framework derived from Gallivan (2001).

OSS ADOPTION IN HIBERNIA HOSPITAL

Hibernia Hospital, which began as a merger of two of the oldest hospitals in Ireland, operates in a public sector environment, employing around 3,000 staff directly, which would make it quite a large organization by Irish standards. Similar to many other organizations worldwide, Hibernia's IT budget had undergone a significant contraction since 2000 in the wake of the increased budget in the lead up to the Y2K. For example, in 2003, Hibernia faced an overall budgetary shortfall of

€17 million. Further compounding this issue, was the fact that Hibernia would face an annual expenditure in the region of €1 million just to achieve compliance with the licensing conditions in the proprietary software products in use. It was clear that this level of funding would not be available. Thus, Hibernia was faced with the choice of either reducing the overall level of service to cope with cost restrictions, or embarking on some radical innovation in implementing less costly alternatives. Consequently, it began to investigate what could be found in the open source market-place. The IT staff in Hibernia undertook an extensive phase of desk research into various OSS products over a six-month period. The quality of the exchanges on SourceForge and Slashdot were sufficient to convince the IT Manager that OSS was worth investigating further. Some direct experimentation with downloaded OSS programs was then sufficient to convince him that the risk involved was acceptable.

StarOffice Desktop Suite

StarOffice is available from Sun Microsystems who were also the driving force behind OpenOffice. Some proprietary software is bundled with StarOffice, which prevents it being offered on the same terms as the pure open source, OpenOffice, with which it shares a common code base. Hibernia decided to implement StarOffice, as Hibernia could then purchase support from Sun. This was considered important to mitigate the risk in embarking on a radical new initiative such as OSS deployment.

In February 2002, Hibernia began the roll-out of Sun's StarOffice 5.2 desktop suite. This deployment was very problematic for users and the technical staff. However, this was felt to be largely due to problems in that version of StarOffice. In September 2002, StarOffice 6.0 was deployed with some support from Sun. However this was also troublesome. The IT Manager wanted to pursue a thin client strategy based around the concept that all applications should be downloaded from the network where practical. The StarOffice package was initially loaded onto a single Linux server, but this became overwhelmed, and it was then clustered to sustain a dual server strategy. Despite this, users continued to lose network connections in an unpredictable fashion. This inevitably increased frustration and tension amongst the entire workforce who were dependent on these tools. The IT Manager conceded that:

"we stuck with the network solution too long. It was only after a series of ferocious encounters with users—and with my own staff—that I recognised that we had to shift".

StarOffice was reinstalled on the desktop instead for those who wanted it, which did improve the situation somewhat according to technical staff, In November 2003, Hibernia installed StarOffice 7.0. This solved many of the existing problems, to the extent that the IT Manager could report that there were no open bug reports in Hibernia for StarOffice 7.0. Nevertheless, the users' perception of the StarOffice system appears to have been damaged irreparably.

Further compounding the problems was the fact that when Hibernia started StarOffice implementation in 2002, there was very little by way of training material. Thus, a lot of material had to be prepared internally which increased the workload for IT staff and trainers.

Even though the move to StarOffice was mandated, not everyone was obliged to migrate. The CEO, although a committed supporter who mandated the move to OSS, did not become a StarOffice user. In addition to this, Hibernia comprises many largely autonomous units which behave independently and raise research funds to support their activities. Across these units about 120 users chose to ignore the overall move to StarOffice. Typically, these users had sufficient funds to remain independent of central IT support. However the IT Manager informed them that this would have consequences in that they would have to assume responsibility themselves for ensuring that the hardware which they use is upgraded, and provide resources for future maintenance upgrades, etc.

Email Platform

Prior to the move to OSS, Hibernia's email system was a proprietary one with a 500-user license limit. This limit had been reached and the IT Manager had to refuse recurring requests for new email accounts. Hibernia initially adopted the SuSE eMail application which was an open source email platform supported by Novell following acquisition of SuSE Linux. Given that there was no upper limit on the number of user email accounts with the SuSE eMail application, Hibernia sought to satisfy increased user demand for extra email accounts. However, when it reached about 700 user email accounts, the SuSE eMail system became prone to frequent problems of hanging and crashing. Hibernia had paid a consultant a once-off fee to implement the SuSE application initially. As with StarOffice, Hibernia sought to establish a support contract for SuSE eMail with Novell. However, the IT Manager reported that Novell at the time did not appear to be interested in offering an ongoing support contract for SuSE eMail. In the absence of a solution to the problems with SuSE eMail, Hibernia began to look for an alternative open source email platform. A multi-product open source email platform was established, comprising the Postfix mail transport agent, OpenLDAP directory access protocol service, SpamAssassin mail filter, and the SquirrelMail email client. After some initial teething problems with integration, this mixed architecture emerged as an extremely stable and scaleable email solution. Given that there were no license-imposed constraints on the number of users, Hibernia initiated a policy whereby all staff were entitled to an email account. Hibernia's IT staff were also able to add functionality to re-route emails to mobile phones and user PDAs. This, together with the impressive filtering capability of SpamAssassin, caused the email platform to be received very favourably by the general user base. At present, Hibernia supports more than 3,000 email accounts. Also, the system scope has been expanded to incorporate certificate-based external email access for about 350 authorised users. Overall, the IT Manager believes that "it would be unthinkable and completely unacceptable" to revert to a 500-user license again.

DISCUSSION OF OSS ADOPTION IN HIBERNIA HOSPITAL

Here we discuss the different implementation trajectories for both open source applications within Hibernia using the conceptual process framework derived above.

Managerial Intervention

Mandatory vs. Voluntary Usage

As already mentioned, the decision to move to OSS was given full support by the CEO, largely on the basis that there was no other choice given the cuts in the IT capital budget. Thus, the use of StarOffice was seen as mandatory. This had significant negative implications. Firstly, as the Secretary Manager put it:

We did not think that StarOffice had been given to us as a bonus. Rather we felt that Microsoft Office had been taken away.

However, even in the case of StarOffice, as already mentioned, a number of users who had sufficient resources were able to opt out of the migration. Also, one department who dealt primarily with fund-raising from external stakeholders argued for the need to remain with the proprietary system due to having to liaise with these external agencies who solely used proprietary software.

On the other hand, this issue of mandatory usage did not arise in the case of the email platform suite. Hibernia was offering an additional service in terms of email access to those who sought it and who had not been able to get email access in the past. Thus, the email platform was implemented in the context of voluntary user demand rather than there being any perception of mandatory usage by management.

Training and Support

The Secretary Manager was critical of the process by which StarOffice was initially implemented. There was no effective buy-in process in her opinion. A small pilot group which included just one secretary comprised the initial trial. This was inadequate given that the most active users of StarOffice would be the cohort of secretaries in Hibernia. The Secretary Manager suggested that

StarOffice was sold as the same thing as Microsoft Office. A two-page brochure was provided and it was suggested that no training would be needed really.

However, even though StarOffice and MS Office are largely functionally equivalent, menus are constructed differently and terminology is slightly different. Thus, commonly-used options such as Print Preview or Track Changes are labelled differently or are in different sub-menus, with different key-stroke short-cuts. This contributed to a greater feeling of unfamiliarity and incompatibility than is probably warranted given the similarities between the applications.

Given these problems with the deployment of earlier versions of StarOffice, a widespread training and awareness program was created to ensure that the user community could be briefed on the new features in StarOffice version 7.0. While this could certainly address user perceptions in relation to issues of complexity, relative advantage and compatibility, it was not enough to overcome the very negative perceptions associated with StarOffice in Hibernia—this despite the fact that Hibernia have no unresolved problem reports for StarOffice 7.0.

While there was no specific training or extra support in the case of email, any differences between the original proprietary application and the subsequent OSS application have not been perceived as problematic. However, since the user base from email climbed from 500 to over 3,000, the vast majority of the users did not have an existing email application in their work context which they had learned and now needed to unlearn. Also, the fact that there are no alternative email applications elsewhere in Hibernia with which unfavourable comparisons could be drawn helps to minimise this as a problem.

Subjective Norms

In the case of StarOffice, the user base perceived usage as mandatory for those who did not have the resources to maintain an alternative. This led to feelings of resentment which were quick to emerge when problems became apparent. Interestingly, rather than being seen as renegades who failed to comply, the departments and users who were able to remain on the proprietary platform were envied by their colleagues. The Secretary Manager described it:

You meet people and hear that they are using Microsoft, and immediately you ask them how they managed to do that.

One of the key complaints from the administrative staff in Hibernia who moved to the StarOffice platform was that they feared being de-skilled in relation to their employment prospects if they didn't have skills in popular proprietary applications. In fact, users readily admitted that they would have preferred not to have switched from the proprietary desktop systems to OSS. Additionally, there was further resentment in

some quarters to the move to OSS systems, in that some staff appear to feel somewhat 'short-changed' and believe their work is under-valued if they are asked to use OSS systems which cost less that those being used by their counterparts in hospitals elsewhere using proprietary systems.

Attributes of the Innovation

The discussion above identified several innovation attributes that have been found in previous research to influence innovation adoption. Here we discuss the ones most salient to the OSS adoption in this study—image, relative advantage, trialability and observability.

Image

Perhaps the most significant issue for StarOffice was the fact that it quickly gained a negative image, and despite improvements in newer versions of the software, this negative image persisted. One user admitted that when StarOffice was proposed, there was a widespread perception that this was a cheap and antiquated package from "Jurassic Park" which would have limited functionality. This user was genuinely surprised to hear that StarOffice was a modern application which was actively being developed. This negative view was confirmed by an Informatics Nurse who suggested that StarOffice ran into "bad publicity from the outset".

There was a fairly widespread perception within Hibernia that it is prone to disadvantage due to its being on the North side of Dublin, an area traditionally perceived as being disadvantaged (at least by those who are from there), and that StarOffice was just another example of this disadvantage working against them. Indeed, in typical Northside Dublin fashion, users have coined the succinct and disparaging term, "Star Bleedin' Office", to refer to the system.

Significant in this perception was the fact that no other hospital in Ireland had chosen to implement an open source desktop. The Secretary Manager suggested that the budget-cutting rationale behind the implementation of StarOffice caused it to be perceived as a "poor man's Microsoft", and as a result there was a pre-conceived expectation that it would be problematic.

The negative effect of StarOffice was even suggested to underpin an increased level of absenteeism and stress-related sick leave, according to the Occupation Health department. While, there was no rigorous analysis of employee absences to support this, there was a belief that the stress of moving to StarOffice had been a factor in many stress-related and work leave/absences. It will be interesting to see if the level of stress-related absences also increases when Hibernia revert to a proprietary platform.

The StarOffice image has become quite notorious within Hibernia, to the extent that at meetings to discuss new IT projects, managers have been heard to express the hope that it would not be "another StarOffice". Also, the negative image of StarOffice extended beyond Hibernia. One user described emailing an attachment, which had been saved in StarOffice's proprietary format by default, to a colleague externally. This colleague couldn't open the attachment, and emailed a response saying that the attachment was in that "StarOffice gobbledy-gook".

In sharp contrast, the email platform has no such similar baggage of negative image. While there were problems during the implementation of SuSE eMail, these were quickly overcome when an alternative email system was implemented. Also, these problems only manifested themselves when more than 200 additional users had been given email access. Thus, there was no sense in which the user service had been disimproved in any way. This has resonances with the relative advantage issue discussed next.

Relative Advantage

Clearly, the initial problems with StarOffice caused users to perceive their original proprietary system as better. There were several problems, particularly with Impress, the StarOffice equivalent of MS PowerPoint. An Informatics Nurse described it:

"I have seen people crying because of Impress. One day I was working on a presentation which I was due to give at 8:30 the following morning. At 5:30pm I checked it and it had become just one blank sheet. I had to go home and recreate it from memory in PowerPoint".

Interestingly, the Informatics Nurse also recalled losing several chapters of her thesis when using MS Word in the past, but there was a sense in which she felt less vulnerable about that. The IT Manager also recalled giving a seminar on OSS at an IT conference attended by several hundred delegates, and his Impress presentation stalled. It was not a happy experience, and certainly, the software which supports people publicly presenting, is not one where problems will be tolerated to say the least. This issue is interesting since only a very small number of actual users would need to deliver presentations, and thus the problems experienced due to the use of Impress were not all that widespread overall. Nevertheless, users seemed to very readily empathise with the negative scenario of problems with a public presentation.

While StarOffice and MS Office are more or less equivalent functionally, there are some differences, and these were were cited in some cases as a reason for not migrating to StarOffice. For example, the Finance Department cited the row number limit in StarOffice Calc which is less than that of MS Excel, as a reason for not migrating.

However, when things settled, particularly following the installation of StarOffice 7.0, a number of benefits became evident in the OSS solution. For example, one of the benefits has been the capacity of StarOffice to exploit its in-built

XML capabilities. This is a very powerful feature of the application which enables documents to be structured in such a way that processing logic is built into different sections of the document, i.e. an on-line HR form request, for example, which is then automatically routed to the HR department for processing. This is a significant new feature and provides additional functionality over what was previously offered in Hibernia's proprietary desktop applications.

Also, the StarOffice suite contained an option to create PDF output, which was not available in the MS Office implementation in Hibernia. This was mentioned as a positive benefit by several interviewees. While the Impress application was clearly the most notable problem point, there was support for the other StarOffice applications. Indeed, an interviewee expressed a distinct preference for StarOffice's Calc over MS Office Excel spreadsheet software. However, such perceptions did not scale into an overarching perception of the relative advantage of StarOffice over the proprietary system it replaced.

In the case of email, Hibernia was able to satisfy additional requests for email accounts, thus offering an improved service. While there were significant problems around the use of SuSE eMail, these were very short-lived as Hibernia was able to overcome them quite quickly by implementing an alternative OSS email suite. Again, these problems only occurred after more than 200 additional email accounts had been added, so there was no real perception that the OSS system was operating at a disadvantage. This option of replacing StarOffice was not possible, and even though the problems were ironed out in subsequent installations of StarOffice, it was still perceived as StarOffice and viewed with suspicion.

Also, there were differences with the StarOffice scenario in that users were not aware of alternative email applications in simultaneous use in other departments. Furthermore, users did not typically have an alternative email application at home, which was frequently the case where MS Office was installed on home computers.

Trialability

Trialabilty was a very salient issue in Hibernia's OSS deployment. At the initial stage, Hibernia's IT staff were able to download and experiment with several OSS applications of potential interest. Given the budget situation, the fact that this was a zero-cost exercise was important. Also when Hibernia experienced problems with the SuSE eMail implementation, IT staff were again able to experiment with a range of alternative OSS email applications and quickly implement a very successful and scaleable email solution.

This mode of OSS implementation has continued. When selecting an online e-learning system, Hibernia trialed a number of OSS e-learning systems before selecting the one which appeared to meet their needs best.

Interestingly, this easy trialability appears to have implications for the training and support process in that there was less attention paid to it. If it had been a high cost initiative it would certainly have had a higher profile within the organization and, as a consequence, more attention would have been paid to implementation issues such as pilot testing, training and support. The IT Manager summarised the dilemma:

"If you have a product which costs €1 million—it may seem appropriate to spend €500K on consulting. However if the product costs nothing—then spending €500K somehow seems to be a more difficult decision to take—yet the saving is still €1 million".

Hibernia have learned this lesson and, for example, created a more comprehensive user awareness and training package to support the implementation of StarOffice 7.0.

Observability

Rogers suggests that the extent to which results of an innovation are observable to others will affect its rate of diffusion. However, given that Hibernia wanted to achieve as smooth a transition as possible, the goal was to minimise and downplay the observability of the differences between StarOffice and MS Office to try ensure they would be perceived identically. This is often not difficult in an OSS context since applications have typically been designed to replicate the functionality of proprietary systems. Thus, rather than trying to publicly triumph the use of StarOffice as progressive and something to be enthusiastically yearned for, the emphasis was on downplaying the issue of observability. Given the negative image that has come to be associated with OSS in Hibernia, there is a conscious move to not identify IT applications as open source. Thus, the issue was not highlighted in the case of the email application. Similarly, when Hibernia implemented an OSS e-learning system subsequently, the fact that the systems being trialed were open source was deliberately downplayed as much as possible.

Organizational Attributes: Absorptive Capacity

Hibernia's absorptive capacity in relation to open source adoption was extremely important. The IT Manager accepted that the initial roll-out of StarOffice had been poorly conceived, and Hibernia had learned from that for subsequent implementations of OSS. Clearly, there was an element of risk in proceeding on the OSS path, since ongoing product support would not be provided in the usual way. Thus, there was a need for a complete rethink of the support strategy. In the past Hibernia had always purchased support from a competent third-party provider. While with OSS this option still existed to some extent, there was a significant difference in expectation associated with OSS, as support was essentially derived from a series of bulletin boards, complemented with external consultancy initially until Hibernia became competent.

Also, it helped that a number of key staff—particularly in the computer operations department—rapidly adapted to the new OSS environment, and the IT Manager described the operations team as the "leaders in the overall adoption of OSS". The bulk of the overall OSS search selection and implementation was actually carried out by the hospital staff. This necessarily involved a process of learning/experimentation. As the staff confidence and familiarity with OSS products grows, the learning cycles were correspondingly shortened. It also helped that Hibernia already had a strong experience of UNIX applications to draw on. So the transition was not as radical as it would have been if staff experience was simply based on GUI-enabled systems administration. In the words of the Linux Systems Administrator, "We are not afraid of the command line interface".

Evidence of increased absorptive capacity in relation to open source is readily evident in the email application deployments. When Hibernia encountered insurmountable problems in relation to the open source SuSE eMail application, IT staff quickly sourced an alternative suite of email applications. This integration of an entire suite of disparate open source email applications into a single integrated email platform represented a significant technological challenge, from identifying suitable applications in the first place, to integrating them into an overall working application.

CONCLUSION

Table 2 summarises the differences in the deployment process for both the OSS desktop and email applications within Hibernia. Rather than elaborating the individual issues here, we will focus more holistically on interaction among the framework elements, as this had a significant influence on OSS implementation. Following this we discuss

Table 2. OSS deployment within Hibernia

	StarOffice Desktop	Email Platform
Managerial Intervention		
- Mandatory v voluntary usage	Usage seen as mandatory for those who could not afford to maintain proprietary alternative.	Access to email application provided upon request, thus usage not perceived as mandatory.
- Training and support	Differences between OSS and proprietary systems downplayed. Low level of training initially using in-house developed material.	No specialised training necessary. No incumbent proprietary system to unlearn.
Subjective Norms		
	Mandatory usage for users who could not afford to maintain proprietary led to StarOffice being perceived as inferior. Staff fear of being deskilled if using OSS, and also that work undervalued if using 'cheap' OSS.	More than 2500 additional users requests for email accounts were satisfied. Thus, uniformly perceived as beneficial.
	Those who opted out of the move to StarOffice envied rather than resented.	Also no alternative email system with against which unfavourable comparisons could be drawn.
Innovation Attributes		
- Image	StarOffice seen as cheap and antiquated "Jurassic Park" option for the disadvantaged. Widespread negative image of StarOffice both within and external to Hibernia.	Email access seen by many as a new privilege which hadn't been available in the past.
- Relative Advantage	Problems and instability led to StarOffice being perceived as inferior. Impress problems particularly cited. Benefits of StarOffice not widely appreciated.	Email a new application for the majority, thus no relative comparison. Also, problems with intermediate SuSE email quickly resolved, and new functionality (routing of email to PDAs) appreciated.
- Trialability	Trialability important, but limited due to lack of alternative OSS desktop suites.	Trialablity critical as Hibernia experimented with a number of OSS email applications.
- Observability	StarOffice and MS Office appear identical on casual observation. Thus, OSS usage is not readily apparent and observable.	Downplayed due to negative image associated with OSS. Not a major issue as no alternative email application in use to compare against.
Organization Attributes		
- Absorptive Capacity	Important as OSS represents new model of software acquisition, implementation and support. Prior learning evident in implementation of StarOffice 7.0.	Very relevant in this case as the first OSS email application had to be replaced by a suite of individual OSS email applications in a novel mixed architecture. High knowledge burden in selecting right applications to include in this architecture and configuring to work successfully together.

the implications of the study for research and practice, and discuss the limitations of the study.

Firstly, we focus on trialability and absorptive capacity as these served primarily to facilitate OSS adoption in this study. Trialability of OSS ensured that Hibernia could experiment with OSS applications in the first place and be reasonably confident that the OSS applications available could meet their needs. Also, when problems occurred as in the case of the initial OSS email implementation, an alternative could be found which solved the problem. However, while trialability certainly facilitates the primary adoption of OSS, it is absorptive capacity which ensures that the best OSS candidates are selected and successfully integrated and implemented, thereby facilitating successful secondary adoption.

However, other interlinked elements, such as voluntary versus mandatory adoption and image of the innovation, manifest themselves in such a way as to impede the assimilation of OSS within Hibernia.

Firstly, by being perceived as mandatory due to the necessity of cost-cutting, the adoption of StarOffice was inevitably perceived as reactive. Then when it emerged that some 'more privileged' users could opt out of the move, this two-tier scenario significantly contributed to the negative image bestowed upon StarOffice. When problems occurred, these served to fuel a disproportionately negative perception of StarOffice, despite the fact that it offered certain extra functionality, and that a steady state with no open bug reports was eventually reached following the implementation of StarOffice 7.0. Interestingly, the email application shared a similar deployment trajectory in that it too faced problems initially, which likewise were subsequently overcome, and also there were advantages in the OSS email system over the original proprietary system. However, the critical difference appears to be that the move to email was not seen as a top-down mandate, rather users could request an email account. Furthermore, there was no cohort using an alternative system who might be perceived as privileged.

The issue of observability was interesting in the Hibernia OSS adoption process. It would not be obvious at a casual glance wthether a user was using StarOffice or MS Office. In the case of email, the fact that the vast majority of users got access to email for the first time within Hibernia would have highlighted the observability issue, in that users were emailing who had not done so before. Thus, this was quickly evident and led to more requests for email accounts. However, due to the negative image of open source that arose from the StarOffice experience, Hibernia sought

to downplay the fact that proposed applications, such as e-learning, were open source.

Implications for Research

The study identifies several issues and streams of research which could be further elaborated. To our knowledge, it is the first rigorous analysis of successful and unsuccessful OSS adoption. Our focus on a single case context is also noteworthy as certain important factors inevitably differ across organizations in a multiple case study context, thus making it more difficult to interpret the actual influence and role of individual elements. The study illustrates how a hybrid process variance model can shed light on the innovation adoption process, and in particular, illustrating the complex interaction between the various elements.

The link between trialability and actual deployment of OSS was significant in this study, particularly in the case of email. This also seems to be borne out in OSS adoption more generally. Onetti and Capobianco (2005) report a case study of a software company who offered both traditional proprietary and OSS products. The company found that the ratio of prospects who eventually become actual customers was markedly higher in the case of OSS. Funambol found that in contrast to its traditional sales process for proprietary software, when contacted about OSS products, the prospective customers had already downloaded and actually trialed the OSS product, and were far more likely to become customers paying for support. This altered the business flow from "sales push" to "user pull" (Onetti and Capobianco, 2005).

The Hibernia study also supports the contention by Fichman (1992) and Gallivan (2001) that innovations which involve organizational mandate and high knowledge require the integration of new metaphors and constructs into the research model. The high knowledge burden in successfully deploying OSS supports the view that absorptive capacity is an important issue, and this facet could be further elaborated to potential good effect. Another potentially promising perspective identified by Fichman (1992) is that of critical mass theory (Markus, 1987). This was clearly an issue in this study as the cohort of users who opted out of the move to StarOffice served to weaken the critical mass, whereas the increased number of users who received email accounts worked in the opposite direction.

The critical mass issue is linked to the issue of network externality effects. Some technologies become more valuable through the increasing returns to adoption that arise from the incremental contribution of other adopters. The basic argument is that for some technologies, the potential benefits are greatest when the entire ecosystem of users, suppliers and mediating institutions are in place to fully leverage the deployment of the technology. These increasing returns can arise through positive network externality effects (Katz & Shapiro, 1986), which are readily apparent in OSS, as the phenomenon is fundamentally predicated upon drawing sufficient voluntary interest from a worldwide network of talented hackers with complementary skills to produce industry-quality software products (Feller et al., 2008). Furthermore, the commercial business model of open source is frequently based on creating a lucrative service and support market by leveraging the zero purchase cost to create a large base of potential customers.

It is also abundantly clear that in the case of OSS a focus on secondary adoption is important. As already mentioned, estimates of OSS adoption by organizations vary greatly. However, it is certainly the case that there could be a marked gap between the initial acquisition of OSS and its eventual large-scale secondary adoption by a critical mass of individual users. Indeed, the essential characteristics of OSS render it very prone to such an assimilation gap: The widespread media coverage leads to high awareness of the concept, while its zero cost results in a very low barrier to initial acquisition. However, the newness of the phenomenon, the manner in which it transgresses traditional software support options, and the lack of any tried and tested approach which could guarantee successful implementation—these all serve to exacerbate the potential assimilation gap between initial acquisition and widespread adoption.

Again, related to this are two elements which were found to be extremely influential in this study—voluntariness of adoption and image of the innovation. While these factors have been identified in some prior research (e.g. Moore and Benbasat, 1991), the issues, and in particular the inter-relationship between them, have not been studied in detail. Voluntariness of adoption is linked to critical mass as organizational mandate can decree that a technology be universally adopted. However, this has implications for how the innovation will be perceived especially by those who feel compelled to use it, thereby affecting the image of the innovation. Furthermore, in previous research, image is assumed to have a positive effect—the use of the innovation is expected to be image-enhancing. In this study, it was certainly the case that innovations are not always seen as conveying a positive image and universally welcomed by those who are expected to use them—the fear of deskilling and the perception of work being undervalued, for example, This has resonances with Fichman's (2004) critique of the dominant paradigm which typically assumes that technology innovation is universally welcomed and perceived as beneficial by all stakeholders. This was certainly not the universal perception from the outset in Hibernia.

Implications for Practice

The study also has a number of implications for organizations who are embarking on OSS adoption. At a higher-level, an open question in prior research has been whether IT implementation should follow a 'big bang' or phased approach, as successful implementations have been reported with both approaches (Fichman, 2004). This is also an open question for OSS migration with researchers recommending both 'big bang' approaches (Ven et al., 2006) and phased pilot approaches (Zuliani and Succi, 2004). The findings of this study would support the 'big bang' approach for each <u>individual</u> OSS application, primarily to avoid the situation where opting out of migration is seen as the preserve of those more privileged, thereby creating image and relative advantage problems subsequently.

This is also related to the issue of whether an organization treats OSS adoption as a mandatory or voluntary initiative. If mandatory, then it is important that OSS is not perceived as a low-cost 'second-rate' alternative, thereby relegating it to an inferior status which individual adopters seek to avoid.

Trialability is more or less a given in OSS, thus ensuring that the initial experimentation with OSS is facilitated. However, the zero cost trialability of OSS should not cause organizations to downplay the importance of implementation issues such as pilot tests, training and support. Also, in the absence of any comprehensive vendor support and marketing, absorptive capacity becomes critical. Identifying potential OSS solutions in the first place is not a trivial issue. Generally, there are no vendors who can answer questions on the suitability and functionality of the software or provide details on reference implementation sites. Similarly, porting OSS to new platforms and integrating OSS systems with other proprietary and OSS systems is far from trivial, as is ongoing support. In this study, some expert consultancy was sourced locally to help with initial implementation issues, but these abilities were acquired in-house over time.

Limitations of Study

One of the possible limitations of this research is that it is a single case study, although we would argue that this should be tempered by the fact

that this also afforded an in-depth insight into the process, and also allowed for the keeping constant of potentially confounding factors. Of more importance perhaps is the fact that the organization is a public sector one, and there could be important differences in the OSS adoption process for organizations in other industry sectors.

Also, this study focused on desktop and email applications, both of which are highly visible mass-market applications with strong market-leading proprietary alternatives. By contrast, less visible back-office infrastructure applications such as servers running Linux, Apache, Samba, and the like, may operate differently. Our experience would suggest that the OSS is already dominant in that sector. Similarly, the Hibernia experience would suggest that OSS can be a perfectly acceptable solution for niche applications such as e-learning, particularly when these systems are introduced without having any incumbent system to replace.

Overall, one can conclude that OSS is a very viable alternative for organizations. The main problems arise in the implementation process, rather than arising due to problems of a technical nature, as the latter are usually ironed out very quickly. Indeed, the acid test is perhaps the fact that despite any problems with StarOffice, Hibernia operated effectively as a hospital throughout this period.

ACKNOWLEDGMENT

I would like to acknowledge in particular the helpful feedback from Geoff Walsham, and also the suggestions of the Editor and two anonymous reviewers. This work has been financially supported by the Science Foundation Ireland (SFI) award to Lero—the Irish Software Engineering Research Centre, and the EU FP6 project OPAALS and EU FP 7 project NEXOF-RA.

REFERENCES

Agerfalk, P., & Fitzgerald, B. (2008). Outsourcing to an Unknown Workforce: Exploring Opensourcing as a Global Sourcing Strategy. *Management Information Systems Quarterly, 32*(3), 385–410.

Ajzen, I. (1985). From Intentions to Actions: A Theory of Planned Behavior. In Kuhl, J., & Beckmann, J. (Eds.), *Action Control: From Cognition to Behavior* (pp. 11–39). New York, NY: Springer.

Carter, L., & Belanger, F. (2006). The Influence of Perceived Characteristics of Innovating on e-Government Adoption, *Electronic. Journal of E-Government, 1*(2).

Chua, W. (1986). Radical Developments in Accounting Thought. *Accounting Review, 61*, 601.

Cohen, W. M., & Levinthal, D. A. (1990). Absorptive Capacity: A New Perspective on Learning and Innovation. *ASQ, 35*, 128–152. doi:10.2307/2393553

Daniel, S., Agarwal, R., & Stewart, K. (2006) An absorptive capacity perspective on OSS development group performance, *27th International Conference on Information Systems,* Milwaukee Dec 2006.

Davis, F. (1989). Perceived Usefulness, Perceived Ease of Use, and User Acceptance of Information Technology. *Management Information Systems Quarterly, 13*, 319–340. doi:10.2307/249008

Eisenhardt, K. (1989). Building theory from case study research. *Academy of Management Review, 14*(4), 532–550. doi:10.2307/258557

Feller, J., Finnegan, P., Fitzgerald, B., & Hayes, J. (2008). From peer production to productization: a study of socially-enabled business exchanges in open source service networks. *Information Systems Research, 19*(4). doi:10.1287/isre.1080.0207

Fichman, R. G. (1992). Information Technology Diffusion: A Review of Empirical Research," in J.l. DeGross, J.D. Becker, and J.J. Elam (Eds.), *13th International Conference on Information Systems*, Dallas, TX, pp. 195-206.

Fichman, R. G. (2004). Going Beyond the Dominant Paradigm for IT Innovation Research: Emerging Concepts and Methods. *Journal of the Association for Information Systems, 5*(8).

Fichman, R. G., and Kemerer, C. F. The Assimilation of Software Process Innovations: An Organizational Learning Perspective, *Management Science* (43:10), 1997, pp. 1345-1363.

Fichman, R. G., & Kemerer, C. F. (1999). The Illusory Diffusion of Innovation: An Examination of Assimilation Gaps. *Information Systems Research, 10*(3), 255–275. doi:10.1287/isre.10.3.255

Gallivan, M. (2001). Organizational adoption and assimilation of complex technological innovations: development and application of a new framework. *Database, 32*(3), 51–85.

Ghosh, R and Glott, R (2005) Results and policy paper from survey of Government authorities, Technical report, MERIT, University of Maastricht, Free/Libre and Open Source Software: Policy Support.

Glaser, B., & Strauss, A. (1967). *The Discovery of Grounded Theory*. Chicago: Aldine.

Kaplan, B., & Duchon, D. (1988). Combining qualitative and quantitative methods in IS research: a case study. *Management Information Systems Quarterly, 12*(4), 571–587. doi:10.2307/249133

Katz, M.L., and Shapiro, C. "Technology Adoption in the Presence of Network Externalities," *Journal of Political Economy* (94:4) 1986, pp 822-841.

Kirsch, L. (2004). Deploying common systems globally: the dynamics of control. *Information Systems Research, 15*(4), 374–395. doi:10.1287/isre.1040.0036

Klein, H. K., & Myers, M. D. (1999). A Set of Principles for Conducting and Evaluating Interpretive Field Studies in Information Systems. *Management Information Systems Quarterly*, *23*(1), 67–93. doi:10.2307/249410

Kuk, G. (2006) Strategic Interaction and Knowledge Sharing in the KDE Developer Mailing List," *Management Science*, (52:7), pp 1031-1042

Lakhani, K., & Wolf, B. (2005) Motivation and Effort in Free/Open Source Software Projects: The Interplay of Intrinsic and Extrinsic Motivations, in Feller, J, Fitzgerald, B, Hissam, S, and Lakhani, K. (2005) (Eds) *Perspectives on Free and Open Source Software*, MIT Press, Cambridge.

Lee, A. S., & Baskerville, R. L. (2003). Generalizing Generalizability in Information Systems Research. *Information Systems Research*, *14*(3), 221–243. doi:10.1287/isre.14.3.221.16560

Lundell, B., Lings, B., & Lindqvist, E. (2006). Perceptions and uptake of open source in Swedish organizations. In *Damiani, E, Fitzgerald, B, Scacchi, W and Succi, G (2006) Open Source Systems* (pp. 155–164). New York: Springer-Verlag.

Markus, M. L. (1987). Toward a 'Critical Mass' Theory of Interactive Media: Universal Access, Interdependence and Diffusion. *Communication Research*, *14*, 491–511. doi:10.1177/009365087014005003

Markus, M. L., & Robey, D. (1988). Information Technology and Organizational Change: Causal Structure in Theory and Research. *Management Science*, *34*(5), 583–598. doi:10.1287/mnsc.34.5.583

McCue. (2004) London council ditches Linux plans, http://news.zdnet.co.uk/software/0,1000000121,39118909,00.htm, last accessed on 8 Jan 2007.

Miles, M., & Huberman, A. (1994). *Qualitative Data Analysis: A Sourcebook of New Methods*. Sage, Beverley Hills.

Mohr, L. B. (1982). *Explaining Organizational Behavior*. San Francisco, CA: Jossey-Bass.

Moore, G. C., & Benbasat, I. (1991). Development of an Instrument to Measure Perceptions of Adapting an Information Technology Innovation. *Information Systems Research*, *2*(3), 192–222. doi:10.1287/isre.2.3.192

Newman, M., & Robey, D. (1992). A Social-Process Model of User-Analyst Relationships. *Management Information Systems Quarterly*, *16*(2), 249–265. doi:10.2307/249578

Niccolai, J. (2005) Scottish police pick Windows in software line-up, *InfoWorld*, http://www.infoworld.com/article/05/08/11/HNscottishpolice_1.html, last accessed 20 Dec 2006

Onetti, A., & Capobianco, F. (2005) Open source and business model innovation. the Funambol case, in Scotto, M and Succi, G (Eds) *Proceedings of First International Conference on Open Source (OSS2005)*, Genoa, 11-15 July 205, pp. 224-227.

Rogers, E. (1962). *Diffusion of Innovations*. NY: The Free Press.

Rogers, E. (2003). *Diffusion of Innovations* (5th ed.). NY: The Free Press.

Rossi, B., Russo, B., & Succi, G. (2006). A study of the introduction of OSS in public administration. In *Damiani, E, Fitzgerald, B, Scacchi, W and Succi, G (2006) Open Source Systems* (pp. 165–172). New York: Springer-Verlag.

Sambamurthy, V., & Poole, M. S. (1992). The Effects of Variations in Capabilities of GDSS Designs on Management of Cognitive Conflict in Groups. *Information Systems Research*, *3*(3), 225–251. doi:10.1287/isre.3.3.224

Sanders, J. (1998). Linux, open source, and software's future. *IEEE Software, 15*(5), 88–91. doi:10.1109/52.714831

Shaikh, M. (2006) Version Control Software in the Open Source Process: A Performative View of learning and Organizing in the Linux Collectif, Unpublished Thesis, London School of Economics.

Shaw, T., & Jarvenpaa, S. L. (1997). Process Models in Information Systems, *IFIP WG8.2 Working Conference on Information Systems and Qualitative Research*, May 31-June 3, Philadelphia, PA.

Stewart, K., & Gosain, S. (2006). The impact of ideology on effectiveness in open source software development teams. *Management Information Systems Quarterly, 30*(2), 291–314.

Thurston, R. (2006), Criticism mounts over Birmingham's Linux project, last accessed on 15 Jan 2007 at: http://www.zdnet.com.au/news/software/soa/Criticism_mounts_over_Birmingham_s_Linux_project/0,130061733,339272293,00.htm

Tornatzky, L., & Klein, K. (1982). Innovation Characteristics & Innovation Adoption Implementation: A Meta-Analysis of Findings. *IEEE Transactions on Engineering Management, EM-29*, 28–45.

Turner, A. (2005), Linux misses Windows of opportunity, last accessed on 15 Jan 2007 at http://www.theage.com.au/articles/2005/09/26/1127586780339.html?from=top5

Van Reijswoud, V. (2005) OSS for development: myth or reality? last accessed 17 Jan 2007 at http://www.calibre.ie/events/limerick/docs/calibre_Reijswoud_presentation.pdf

Ven, K., Van Nuffel, D., & Verelst, J. (2006). The introduction of OpenOffice.org on the Brussels Public Administration. In *Damiani, E, Fitzgerald, B, Scacchi, W and Succi, G (2006) Open Source Systems* (pp. 123–134). New York: Springer-Verlag.

Walli, S., Gynn, D., & von Rotz, B. (2005) The Growth of Open Source Software in Organizations, available at http://www.optaros.com/en/publications/white_papers_reports (last accessed 31 Jul 2006)

Walsham, G. (1993). *Interpreting Information Systems in Organizations*. UK: Wiley.

Yin, R. (1994). *Case Study Research: Design and Methods* (2nd ed.). California: Sage Publications.

Zachary, G. (2003) Ghana, Information Technology and Development in Africa, http://www.cspo.org/products/articles/BlackStar.PDF (Current 11 Aug 2006)

Zaltman, G., Duncan, R., & Holbeck, J. (1973). *Innovations & Organizations*. New York: Wiley & Sons.

Zuliani, P., & Succi, G. (2004) Migrating public administrations to open source software, *Proceedings of e-Society IADIS International Conference*, Avila, Spain, 2004.

Chapter 2
Tools and Datasets for Mining Libre Software Repositories

Gregorio Robles
Universidad Rey Juan Carlos, Spain

Jesús González-Barahona
Universidad Rey Juan Carlos, Spain

Daniel Izquierdo-Cortazar
Universidad Rey Juan Carlos, Spain

Israel Herraiz
Universidad Alfonso X el Sabi, Spain

ABSTRACT

Thanks to the open nature of libre (free, open source) software projects, researchers have gained access to a rich set of data related to various aspects of software development. Although it is usually publicly available on the Internet, obtaining and analyzing the data in a convenient way is not an easy task, and many considerations have to be taken into account. In this chapter we introduce the most relevant data sources that can be found in libre software projects and that are commonly studied by scholars: source code releases, source code management systems, mailing lists and issue (bug) tracking systems. The chapter also provides some advice on the problems that can be found when retrieving and preparing the data sources for a later analysis, as well as information about the tools and datasets that support these tasks.

1. INTRODUCTION

In libre software[1] projects communication and organization are heavily dependent on the use of telematic means. Face-to-face communication is rare, and Internet-based tools are the most common means for a developer to interact with the code and with other developers.

Fortunately for researchers, the data produced by those interactions is usually stored and offered publicly over the Internet. The repositories for these data contain information valuable to understand the development process, and can be analyzed in combination with the most classical

DOI: 10.4018/978-1-60960-513-1.ch002

data source: source code. In addition, the ability of having detailed information from the past (since it is usually archived for long periods of time) offers the possibility of performing also longitudinal and evolutionary analysis.

Research groups worldwide have already taken benefit from the availability of such a rich amount of data sources in the last years. Nonetheless, the access, retrieval and fact extraction is by no means a simple task and many considerations and details have to be taken into account to successfully retrieve and mine the data sources.

This chapter offers a detailed description of the most common data sources that can generally be found for libre software projects on the Internet, and of the data that can be found in them: **source code releases**, **source code management systems** (in the following, SCM), **mailing lists archives**, and **issue or bug tracking system** (in the following, BTS). In addition, we present some tools and datasets that might help researchers in their data retrieval and analysis tasks.

Mining and analyzing these data sources offer an ample amount of possibilities that surpass or complement other data-acquiring methodologies such as surveys, interviews or experiments. The amount of data that can be obtained, in a detailed way and in many cases for the whole lifetime of a software project, gives a precise description of the history of a project (Bauer and Pizka, 2003). In this sense, we have access to the activities (the what), the points in time (the when), the actors (the who) and sometimes even the reason (the why) (Hahsler and Koch, 2005). Compared to surveys, mining these data sources allow to access data for thousands of developers and a wide range of software projects. Most of these efforts can be considered as non-intrusive, as researchers can analyze the projects without interacting with developers, which is friendly to them. But even in a small environment, e.g., when evaluating the impact of software tools in a small team (Atkins et al., 2002), the use of data from one or more of these sources provides additional insight. Fur-

thermore, mining software repositories has many advantages compared to conducting experiments as real-world software projects are taken into consideration (Mockus and Votta, 2000, Graves and Mockus, 1998).

2. FIRST STEPS BEFORE THE ANALYSIS

There are some steps to be walked before the analysis of data from libre software projects can be started. First of all, the relevant data sources have to be identified. After that, the data has to be retrieved from the corresponding data repositories. Only then, the researcher can really start to analyze the data.

It is important to notice that there may be several ways of accessing the same kind of data, depending on the project and how it handles it. There are several different tools and systems that projects use, and they also have different usage conventions. For instance, the use of tags, comments, among others, may differ from one project to another, and can be of paramount importance to tell bugs appart from new feature requests in a BTS. The complexity and feasibility of both identification and retrieval depend, therefore, of the project. Figure 1 shows a diagram with all the steps that have to be accomplished for any source considered in the studies.

In general terms, the identification of the data source depends mostly on its significance for the software development of a project. Hence, identifying the source code releases, the SCM system, the mailing lists or the BTS is usually not problematic, since it lies in the interest of the projects to publish them clearly and openly. In these cases, the largest drawback may be is the lack of historical data. Sometimes a project only maintains a partial set of the data (eg, the most recent), and can even not maintain any set at all (eg, because a given tool is available but not used by developers). This situation is common for software re-

Figure 1. Whole process: from identification of the data sources to analysis of the data

leases, where finding past releases of the software is sometimes not possible. Other situations where this might happen is when a development tool has not been used in the early stages of development. This is the case of many projects that started using a SCM system only once the project had gained some momentum. Having only partial data can also be the result of a migration from one tool to another, losing in the way some information, if not all (common in the migration to a different SCM). Or having part of the information in a first stage SCM usage and part of the history in a new SCM. When identifying data sources, these considerations have to be taken into account.

There exist also some other data sources for libre software projects that are not so obvious and hence their identification is not straightforward. For instance, organizational information that is embedded into some format and that is beyond the use of standard tools as SCM systems, mailing lists and BTS, or information maintained by third parties (such as software distributors). In general, such type of information is project-dependent and can be only obtained for one project or a small number of them. This is the case for packaging systems such as the .deb format used in Debian and Debian-based distributions or the .rpm Red Hat package system in use in Red Hat and other distributions.

Beyond this, we can find project-related information in other places such as the Debian Popularity Contest (Robles et al., 2006b) or the Debian Developer database (Robles et al., 2005), and above all, the Ultimate Debian Database (Nussbaum and Zacchiroli, 2010), which contains information about all the packages in Debian and Ubuntu, including defects. Other data sources may

also be considered; for instance, in KDE there is a file that is used to list all the ones who have write access to their SCM repository. Another example is given in a study by Tuomi (Tuomi, 2004) in which the credits file, a text file listing all important contributors to the project, of the Linux kernel are studied in detail. Identification of the data sources requires in such cases specific knowledge on the project and is difficult if not impossible to be generalized.

Once a data source has been identified, the relevant data has to be retrieved to a local machine in order to be analyzed (see Figure 1). Although this process may not seem to be very difficult at first, previous experiences have shown that some considerations and good practices should be followed in this step as reported by Howison et al. in the retrieval of information from the web pages hosted at SourceForge (Howison and Crowston, 2004). For instance, the analysis of the credits file, which can be found together with the sources in many projects, has to deal with the complexity that there is no standardized way of naming the authors, so projects follow their own conventions.

Fortunately, there are several datasets available that have been composed by retrieving information about libre software projects from their repositories on a regular basis, and which are available for researchers in a more friendly way. As well as making it easier to retrieve data, these datasets ensure the repeatability and verifiability of the empirical studies using them, because the datasets are public and shared among all the research community. From a research point of view, these datasets are preferable to the mining tools, because they have been validated against the original sources. From the libre software projects point of view, using these datasets releaves them from the stress that their servers must undergo when mined for research purposes, because the mining process is only done once. In the follwing, the FLOSSMetrics dataset (Herraiz et al., 2009) will be used as a case example, although there are some other options as well, like the FLOSS-Mole dataset (Howison et al., 2006). Hindle *et al.* (Hindle et al., 2010) describe some other datasets that might be of interest.

In the next sections we will enter into detail in the process of data extraction and data storage once the data has been properly retrieved from the information source to a local machine.

3. SCM SYSTEM META-DATA

Generally speaking, most libre software projects use a SCM system to manage file versions during the development process. They are used to track changes and past states of a software project. Thus, they allow for the obtention of the current and any past state of the code, as well as the information of how each change was made. This permits the researcher to observe the evolution of a software product.

SCM systems also store a set of meta-data of the changes. These meta-data can be tracked and analyzed. This information is usually related to the interactions that occur among developers and the SCM systems. In general the information is only related to actions that comprehend write access while reading (downloading the sources) or obtaining other information (diffs, among others) cannot be tracked in that way. For instance, along with a change, valuable information is recorded, like the date of change, the full path where the change occurred, user who committed or the comment written by the committer[2].

CVSAnalY[3] (Robles et al., 2004) is one of the tools that analyzes the interactions that occur between developers and the most used SCM systems in libre software projects at the current

time, based on the analysis of the log of the SCM. At the moment of writing, CVSAnalY supports CVS, Subversion and Git repositories.

Most of the SCM systems keep common information about all interactions (commits) with developers. Depending on the SCM, there are two types of repositories: centralized and distributed. In centralized repositories, developers interact directly with a central server (this is the case of CVS or Subversion) that keeps the whole history of the project. In distributed systems, every developer stores a complete copy of the repository, with all the history, and interact with it locally. Later on, a *merge* takes place with other branches of the repository, so her work can be shared with other developers. The main differences between these two types of repositories are that in distributed systems developers do not need an Internet connection to interact with the repository, and that the whole history of the project is not kept in only one centralized repository. This last difference has deep implications for research, because having the whole history of the project locally removes any kind of dependency with the libre software project management for research purposes.

SCM systems keep certain information when a change is committed: committer name, date, file, revision and an explanatory comment introduced by the committer. Each SCM has its own peculiarities and extra information. In the CVS case the number of lines added and removed is provided by default. And in the case of the distributed SCM systems, the real author of the commit and the actual date can also be stored. As it can be seen, distributed systems make a difference between committer and author. This is remarkable due to the fact that centralized SCM systems store information about who committed a change and when this was ordered (keeping track of the server time). On the other hand, distributed SCM systems also keep information from the real author (for instance, people who do not have commit rights in the main repository) and when this change

Figure 2. Process of the CVSAnalY tool

took place (the real date and not the date found in the server).

There is some file-specific information that can also be extracted, as for instance if the file has been removed[4]. On the other hand, the human-inserted comment can also be parsed in order to see if the commit corresponds to an external contribution or even to an automated script (although this problem is fixed by distributed SCM systems).

Basically CVSAnalY consists of three main steps: preprocessing, insertion into database and post-processing. But they can be subdivided into several more as it has been done in Figure 2. In the following subsections the inner functioning of CVSAnalY will be presented, focusing on details of its use with CVS. Its use with other SCM systems is similar.

3.1. Preprocessing: Retrieval and Parsing

Preprocessing includes downloading the sources from the repository of the project in study. Once this is done, the logs are retrieved and parsed to transform the information contained in log format into a more structured format (SQL for databases or XML for data exchange). For Subversion and Git repositories, CVSAnalY also supports retrieving directly the log using the URL repository, although checking out a copy of the repository is the recommended way of operation.

The following is a CVS log excerpt for the AUTHORS file of the KDevelop project[5]. It gives the last three revisions (from revision 1.47 to 1.49) done during the last months of the year 2003 until mid-2004. Log messages from other

SCM systems, such as Subversion, *git* or *Bazaar* look similar.

While being parsed, each file is also matched for its type. Usually this is done by looking at its extension, although other common filenames (for instance README or TODO) are also looked for. The goal of this separation is to identify different contributor groups that work on the software, so besides source code files the following file types are also considered: documentation (including web pages), images, translation (generally internationalization and localization), user interface and sound files. Files that don't match any extension or particular filename are accounted as unknown. This discrimination follows the criteria that have been presented in section 6.2, although it lacks the possibility of looking at the content of the files as we only consider filenames (because this is the only information that appears in the CVS logs).

CVS also has some peculiarities when introducing contents for the first time (this action is called initial check-in). The initial version (with version number 1.1.1.1) is not considered in our computation as it is the same as the second one (which has version number 1.1).

Comments attached to commits are usually forwarded to a mailing list so that developers keep track of the latest changes in CVS. Some projects have established some conventions so that certain commits do not produce a message to the mailing list. This happens when those commits are supposed to not require any notification to the rest of the development team. A good example of the pertinent use of *silent* commits comes from the existence of bots that do several tasks automatically.

In any case, such conventions are not limited to non-human bots, as human committers usually may also use them. In a large community we can argue that *silent* commits can be considered as not contributory (i.e., changes to the head of the files, for instance a change in the license or the year in the copyright notice, or moving many files from one location to another). Therefore, we have set a flag for such commits in order to compute them separately or leave them out completely in our analysis.

For instance, the developers of the KDE project mark such commits with the comment *CVS_SILENT* as it can be seen from following log excerpt extracted from the kdevelop_scripting.desktop file of the KDevelop CVS module. In this case it is due to a change to a *desktop* file, a file type that is related to the user interface. Being this change not considered interesting for other developers to know about, the author of this commit decided to make this commit *silently*.

Write access to the SCM system is not given to anyone. Usually this privilege is granted only to those contributors who have reached a compromise with the project and the project's goals. But external contributions -commonly called patches, that may contain bug fixes as well as implementation of new functionality- from people outside the ones who have write access (committers) are always welcome. In distributed SCM systems, external contributions can be explicitly marked in the log of a commit. There exist a main repository where people could commit, but there are some external developers that could not have access to submit changes. In this case, those developers create a patch that later will be applied in the main branch (or merged), but the main difference is that the initial information (when this was committed and by who) will be kept in the main repository, while in centralized ones, this does not work that way.

In centralized repositories, it is a widely accepted practice to mark an external contribution with an authorship attribution when committing it. Thus, we have constructed certain heuristics

to find and mark commits due to such contributions. The heuristics we have set up are based on the appearance of two circumstances: patch (or patches in its plural form) together with a preposition (from, by, of, and other) or an e-mail address or an indication that the code had been attached to a bug fix in the BTS. The regular expressions that have been used are following:

As an example, the following slightly modified excerpt taken from the kdevelop.m4.in file from the KDevelop module in the KDE CVS repository shows a patch applied by a committer with username "dymo" that was submitted originally by Willem Boschman:

All these efforts have in common that they perform text-based analysis of the comments attached by committers to the changes they perform. The range of possibilities in this sense is very ample. For instance, Mockus *et al.*, and later on in an enhanced manner Amor *et al.*, have tried to identify the reasons for changes (classifying changes as adaptive, perfective or corrective) in the software using text-analysis techniques (Mockus and Votta, 2000, Amor et al., 2006).

3.2. Data Processing and Storage

Once the logs have been parsed and transformed into a more structured format, some summarizing and database optimization information is computed and data is stored into a database.

Usually the output of the previous parsing consists of a single database table with an entry per commit. This means that information is stored in a raw form, the table containing possibly millions of entries depending on the size and age of a project. Information is hence in a raw format and in an inconvenient way if we consider getting statistical information for developers and projects from it.

A first step in this direction is to make use of normalization techniques for the data. In this sense, committers are assigned a unique numerical identification and if further granularity is needed, procedures have been implemented to do the same at the directory and file level. For the sake of optimization this has been introduced during the parsing phase so additional queries do not have to be performed. The next step is to gather statistical information on both committers and modules. These additional tables will give detail on the interactions by contributors or to modules, which is one of the most frequent information that is asked.

Additional information that makes evolutionary analyses possible is the number of contributions by developers and to modules. Hence, the same statistical queries that have been obtained for committers and modules for the summarizing tables can be obtained in a monthly or weekly basis since the date the repository was set up.

In general terms, when a change is submitted, this information implies changes in several files and these set of files are committed in the same commit. Unfortunately CVS does not keep track of which files have been committed at the same time. The absence of this concept in CVS may bring some distortion into the analysis. We have therefore implemented the sliding window algorithm proposed by German (Germán, 2004) and Zimmermann et al. (Zimmermann et al., 2005) that identifies atomic commits (also known as *modification requests* or transactions) by grouping commits from the CVS logs that have been done (almost) simultaneously. This algorithm considers that commits performed by the same committer in a given time interval (usually in the range of seconds to minutes) can be considered as an atomic commit. If the time window is fixed, the amount of time that is considered from the first commit to the last one is a constant value. For a sliding time window, the time interval is not constant; the time window is restarted for every new commit that belongs to the same transaction until no new commit occurs in the (new) time slot (Zimmermann et al., 2005).

The post-process is composed of several scripts that interact with the database, statistically analyze

its information, compute several inequality and concentration indexes and generate graphs for the evolution over time for a couple of interesting parameters (commits, committers, LOCs...). Results could be shown in several formats, which are explained in more detail in (González-Barahona et al., 2010)) for the case of FLOSSMetrics.

4. MAILING LISTS ARCHIVES (AND FORUMS)

Mailing lists and forums are the key elements for information dissemination and project organization in libre software projects. Without almost any exception, libre software projects provide one or more mailing lists. Depending on the project, many mailing lists may exist for several target audiences. So, for instance, SourceForge recommends to open three mailing lists: a technical one for developers, another one to give support to users and and a third one that is used for announcing new releases.

Mailing lists are programs that forward e-mail messages they receive to a list of subscribed e-mail addresses. More sophisticated mailing list managers have plenty of functionality which allows for easy subscription, unsubscription, storage of the messages that have been sent (known as the archives), and avoidance of spam, among others.

Forums are web-based programs that allow visitors to interact in a similar manner as in an e-mail thread with the difference that in this case all the process goes through HTML forms and that results are visible on the web.

Both mailing lists and forums are based on similar concepts and their differences lie in their implementation and the need for different clients to participate in them. Mailing lists require the use of an e-mail client, while forums can be accessed through web browsers. As their concept is the same, there exist some software programs that transform mailing lists messages to a forum-like interface and vice-versa. Because of that, in this chapter we focus on mailing lists, specifically on one of the most used mailing lists managers called GNU Mailman[6] and the RFC 2822 (Internet Message Format) and RFC 4155 (also known as MBOX) formats in which it generally stores and publishes the archives.

4.1. Format of Archives

As mentioned above, generally all mailing list managers offer the possibility of storing all posts (the archives) and making them publicly available through a web interface. This offers the possibility for newcomers to go through the history and to gain knowledge on technical as well as organizational details of a project.

The archives are also offered in text files following the MBOX format. MBOX is a format used traditionally in UNIX environments for the local storage of e-mail messages. It is a plain text file that contains an arbitrary number of messages. Each message is composed of a special line followed by an e-mail message in the RFC-2822 standard format. The special line that allows to differentiate messages consists of the keyword "From" followed by a blank space, the poster's e-mail address, another blank space and finally the date the message was sent. The RFC-2822 format can be divided into two parts: (a) headers, that contain information for the delivery of the message and (b) the content, which is the information to be delivered to the receiver; the standard only allows lines of text, so filtering has to be implemented if an image or other information is attached.

Mailing lists in MBOX format can be analyzed by means of the MailingListStats, or *mlstats* for short, tool[7]. Given an URL of the archives of the mailing lists, *mlstats* outputs the information extracted from the headers and the content of the message in database format for further processing and analysis.

Below is an excerpt of a post sent to a mailing list that has been stored following the RFC-2822 standard. Is is an automatic message sent April

30 2005 to the GNOME CVS mailing list. This list keeps track of all the commits that are done to the CVS system of the GNOME project. This assures that subscribers are aware of the latest changes in the CVS. The content of the message, the description of the modification that had been performed, has been omitted in the excerpt.

From the message excerpt above, we can see some of the headers that are described in the standard. The most important ones are following: *From* (e-mail address, sometimes also real name, of the sender), *Sender* (address of the responsible entity for the last transmission), *Reply-To* (address the author wants to be replied), *To* (address(es) of the receiver(s)), *Cc* (e-mail address(es) of the receiver(s) that should receive a copy), *Bcc* (addressee(s) with *carbon* copy), *Subject* (usually contains a brief description of the topic), *Received* (contains address of the intermediate machine that has transferred the message), *Date* (when the message was sent given by the sender machine), *Message-ID* (unique identifier of this message), *In-reply-to* (Identifier of the parent message to which the current one is a response), and *References* (identifications (message-IDs) of all the other messages that are part of the conversation thread).

In addition to the data that can be found in the headers, some other information could be obtained from analyzing the content of the messages. In this regard, Weigerber *et al.* analyze the type of patches first sent to mailing lists and later on integrated into the source code tree of the project (Weißgerber et al., 2008).

5. BUG-TRACKING SYSTEMS

BTS are used in libre software projects to manage the incoming error and feature enhancement reports from users and co-developers. The use of BTS is relatively extended and the most known tool in this area is BugZilla[8], a BTS developed by the Mozilla project that has been adopted by other large projects as well. Hence Bugzilla is the system we study in this chapter, although conceptually all other systems should work similarly.

Bugzilla allows to manage all bug reports and feature requests by means of a publicly available web interface. Besides the reports, it also offers the possibility of adding comments so that developers may ask for further information about the error or other end-users may comment it. Beyond Bugzilla, other tools exist with similar features, as for instance GNATS (the one used in the FreeBSD project). SourceForge and other web platforms that support software development have implemented their own BTS for the projects they host.

5.1. Data Description

Bugzilla stores in its database specific information for each bug report. The fields that can be usually found are following[9]:

- Bugid: Unique identifier for any bug report.
- Description: Textual description of the error report.
- Opened: Date the report was sent.
- Status: Status of the report. It can take one of the following status: new, assigned (to a developer to fix it), reopened (when it has been wrongly labeled as resolved), needinfo (developers require more information), verified, closed, resolved and unconfirmed.
- Resolution: Action to be performed on the bug. It can take following status: obsolete (will not be fixed as it is a bug to a previous, already solved issue), invalid (not a valid bug), incomplete (the bug has not been completely fixed), notgnome (the bug is not of GNOME, but of a component of another project, as for instance X window system or the Linux kernel), notabug (the issue is not really a bug), wontfix (the developers consider not to correct this error for any reason) and fixed (the error has been corrected).

- Assigned: Name and/or e-mail address of the developer in charge of fixing this bug.
- Priority: Urgency of the error. It can take following values: immediate, urgent, high, normal and low. Usually this field is modified by the bugmaster as users do not have sufficient knowledge on the software to know the correct value.
- Severity: How this error affects the use and development of the software. Possible values are (from high severity to lower one): blocker, critical, major, normal, minor, trivial and enhancement.
- Reporter: Name and e-mail address of the bug reporter.
- Product: Software that contains the bug. Usually this is given at the tarball level.
- Version: Version number of the product. If no version was introduced, *unspecified* is given. Also, for enhancements the option *unversioned enhancement* may be chosen.
- Component: Minor component of the product.
- Platform: Operating system or architecture where the error appeared.

Usually all fields (besides the automatic ones like *bugid*, the opening date or its status) are filled out the first time by the reporter. Larger projects usually have some professional or volunteer staff that review the entries in order to adjust the information (Villa, 2003, Villa, 2005). This is especially important for fields like priority or severity as end-users hardly have no knowledge or experience on how to evaluate these fields.

5.2. Data Acquisition and Further Processing

For the analysis of the data stored in a BTS, we have created Bicho, a tool that is specifically devoted to extract data from Bugzilla [10] The architecture of Bucho is described in Figure 3. Although the retrieval of the data could theoretically

Figure 3. Architecture of the Bugzilla Analyzer

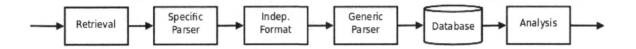

be simplified by obtaining the database of the Bugzilla system from the project administrators, we thought that retrieving the data directly from the web interface would be more in accordance with the non-intrusive policy that all other tools described in this chapter follow.

When designing and developing Bicho, we had to deal with several problems to retrieve the Bugzilla data. After crawling for all web pages (one per bug) and storing them locally, we had to transform the HTML data into an intermediate log-type format, as not all fields were given for all bugs due probably to a transition from a previous system. Probably also because of this, there may have been some information loss and some ids could not be tracked. Other problems that we found, were the existence of wrong date entries for some bugs and comments. As the bug report ids are sequential, we could fix these entries when we found out that the date was wrong. We applied the same solution to comments with erroneous dates, as comments are also posted sequentially and cannot be introduced before the bug report has been submitted.

In recent versions of Bugzilla, it is possible to obtain the data in XML format which simplifies in a great manner the data extraction[11]. At the time of writing this chapter, the use of the XML interface was not as common as the authors would wish, so retrieving the data from parsing web pages was the unique non-intrusive manner at that time. In any case, the Bugzilla analyzing tool has been designed in such a way that only by removing some parts (specifically the specific HTML-parser which parses into the independent format) and by modifying the generic parser we

could reuse the rest of the modules without major changes using the XML query format. This is also valid for other BTS, as GNATS.

One of the issues of BTS is that in general the most relevant information in a bug report is included in natural language (usually in English) in the *Description* field . Bettenburg *et al.* have proposed a tool that extracts structural information such as source code (i.e., patches), listings, etc. from it (Bettenburg et al., 2008).

Finally, it is worth to mention that Bicho works with the current version of the SourceForge tracker, the GNOME and KDE bugzilla and partially with the BTS used by the Apache Software Foundation community (which uses Jira and Bugzilla).

6. SOURCE CODE

We should begin with the concept of release. It is important due to the fact that it points out the main milestone happened during the life of a project. It usually has a common nomenclature, the release number, which is akin to "MM. mm.bb". Where "MM" means the number of the major release, "mm" means the number of minor releases and "bb" connotes some bug fixes and small improvements.

As software development projects, source code is the central point of all interactions, being a primary way of communication and playing a major signaling and coordination role. According to (Lanzara and Morner, 2003), source code "is transient knowledge: it reflects what has been programmed and developed up to that point, resuming

Figure 4. Process of source code analysis

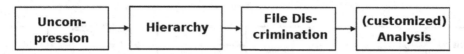

past development and knowledge and pointing to future experiments and future knowledge.".

The study of the source code, as the main product of the software development process, is a matter that has been done for over fourty years now. But not only *traditional* source code (i.e., programmed in a programming language) can be taken into account, but also all the other elements that make the software, such as documentation, translation, user interface and other files (Robles et al., 2006a).

The analysis usually starts with a source code base that is stored in a directory (or alternatively in a compressed directory, usually in tar.gz or tar. bz formats common in the libre software world). After decompressing the tarball, if needed, the hierarchical structure of the source code tree is identified and stored.

Then, files can be grouped into several categories depending on type (as will be described below) which allows for a more specific analysis. This means, for instance that source code files in a programming language can be analyzed differently than images or documentation files. On the other hand, the discrimination for files with source code can be finer, identifying the programming language and offering the possibility of using alternative metrics depending on it. As a consequence, object oriented metrics could be applied to files containing Java code, but would not be required for files that are written in assembler language.

The whole process can be observed in Figure 4: after (possibly) decompressing, the directory and file hierarchy is obtained, then files are discriminated by their type and finally analyzed, if possible taking into consideration the file type that has been identified in the previous step. In

the following subsections the different steps are described more in detail.

6.1. Hierarchical Structure

The structure of directories and files of a software program (and how it changes over time) has already been the focus of some research studies (Capiluppi, 2004, Capiluppi et al., 2004). The idea is that the technical architecture and probably therefore the organization of the development team is mapped by the tree hierarchy of directories. So, from a directory hierarchy, we could infer the organizational structure of a libre software development project.

6.2. File Discrimination

File discrimination is a technique that is used to specifically analyze files on behalf of their content (Robles et al., 2006a). The most common way of discriminating files is by using heuristics, which may vary in their accuracy as well as in the granularity of their results.

A first set of heuristics may determine the type of a file by considering its extension. File extensions are non-mandatory, but usually conventions exist so that the identification of the content of a file can be made easier and to enable the automation of administrative tasks.

Hence, a first step for file discrimination consists of having a list of extensions that links to the content of the file. In this context, the *.pl* extension is indicative for a file that contains programming instructions while a *.png* can be considered as an image file. Of course, this can be done at several granularity levels, meaning that a *.c* file is a file that with high probability contains programming

Table 1. (Incomplete) set of matches performed to identify the different file types

File type	Extension/file name matching
documentation	*.html *.txt *.ps *.tex *.sgml
images	*.png *.jpg *.jpeg *.bmp *.gif
i18n	*.po *.pot *.mo *.charset
ui	*.desktop *.ui *.xpm *.theme
multimedia	*.mp3 *.ogg *.wav. *.au *.mid
code	*.c *.h *.cc *.pl *.java *.s *.ada
build	configure.* makefile.* *.make
devel-doc	readme* changelog* todo* hacking*

Table 2. Examples of first line indicating that the file is written in Python, Shell or Perl respectively

#! /usr/bin/python
#! /usr/bin/sh
#! /usr/bin/perl

language, being that the programming language C code. Table 1 shows an excerpt of the list of file extensions that can be used.

The file types that can be considered are documentation, images, internationalization (i18n) and localization (l10n), user interface (ui), multimedia and code files. For the latter type, a more detailed analysis and discrimination between source code that is part of the software application (code) from the one that helps in the building process (generally Makefiles, configure.in, among others) and from documentation files that are tightly bound to the development and building process (such as README, TODO or HACKING) can be made.

A second step in the process of file discrimination includes inspection of the content of the files both to check if the identification made by means of matching file extensions is correct and to identify files that have no extension or whose extension is not included in the previous list.

In this case, heuristics are generally content-specific and may go more in depth depending on the detail of discrimination we are looking for. One of the most common ways to improve file discrimination by looking at the file content is to analyze the first line. There exists some convention in source code files that denotes that

the programming language that they contain. For instance, in the case of a file written in the Python, *Bourne again* shell or Perl programming languages (examples can be found in Table 2), the first line could contain respectively the following information[12].

In the case of programming languages, further information can be gained from the structure of the code, by the identification of specific keywords or other elements such as specific comments. For text files (especially the ones that are based on mark-up languages), tags and other specific elements may help in the identification process. Finally, other algorithms can be taken into account, as the information returned by the UNIX *file* command on the file type (which also identifies some of the binary formats, especially useful in the case of images).

Some of the previous discrimination techniques are already in use in some tools, most notably in SLOCCount (see (Wheeler, 2001, Robles et al., 2006b)). As SLOCCount counts the number of lines of code it is only concerned with identifying source code files and identifying the programming language in which they are written, not considering all other file types that we have taken into consideration in this work (documentation, translations, and other).

6.3. Software Complexity

Source code allows for measurement of different software properties, known as product metrics. Among the most widely analyzed properties, we find size and complexity. To measure size, we recommend the aforementioned tool SlocCount.

For complexity, there are different tools available, which are language-dependent. In this chapter we describe the CMetrics tool [13], which can measure complexity metrics for the C programming language. We describe here the metrics, and for more details about the tools, readers can refer to the provided URL.

CMetrics can measure two different groups of metrics: McCabe's cyclomatic complexity and Halstead's Software Science metrics.

6.3.1. McCabe's Cyclomatic Complexity

McCabe introduced his cyclomatic complexity metric in the seventies decade of the past century (McCabe, 1976). In spite of its age, it remains widely used in industry and research. This metric indicates the number of regions in a graph. For a graph G with n vertices, e edges, and p exit points (e.g., function returns in the case of C), the complexity v is defined as follows:

$$v(G)=e-n+2p \qquad (1)$$

Figure 5 contains a sample graph, that may represent the different execution paths of a program. Any graph has at least one region (the surrounding region). Therefore, the minimum value of the cyclomatic complexity of a program is 1. Any program can be easily represented as a graph, with simple rules such as representing IF statements by bifurcation points, or closed loops corresponding to regions, etc.

The rationale behind the metric is that all the edges that delimit a region form a *circuit* that must be tested. The more regions a program has, the more testing it will need, and the more complex the program is.

Because of that, for the case of the C programming language, this metric is defined at the function level. It can be aggregated for files using different approaches (calculating the maximum among all the functions, average, median, etc).

Figure 5. Sample graph that represents the flow of a program. The cyclomatic complexity is the number of regions in the graph. Any graph has at least one region (the surrounding region). So the minimum value of the cyclomatic complexity is 1. In the graph shown in this figure, the value of the cyclomatic complexity is 5

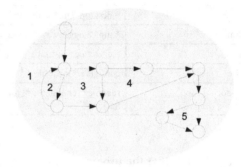

6.3.2. Halstead's Software Science Metrics

This is a set of metrics, known as Software Science metrics, that were introduced by Halstead in a book published in the seventies (Halstead, 1977), although a more recent publication with a good description of these metrics is the book by Kan (Kan, 2003). CMetrics can measure four metrics of this set: length, volume, level and mental discriminations. These metrics, that are defined at the file level, are based on the redundancy of *operands* and *operators* in a program.

For the case of C, operands are string constants and variable names, and operators are symbols (like +,-,++,-), the * indirection, the sizeof operator, preprocessor constants, statements (like if, while), storage class specifiers (like static, extern), type specifiers (like int, char) and structures specifiers (struct and union).

The metrics are obtained by counting the number of distinct operators n_1, number of distinct operands n_2, total number of operators N_1, and total number of operands N_2. The length L of a program is the total number of operators and operands:

$$L = N_1 + N_2 \qquad (2)$$

The volume V of a program is defined as

$$V = N \cdot \log_2(n_1 + n_2) \qquad (3)$$

The level lv of a program is defined as:

$$lv = \frac{2}{n_1} \frac{n_2}{N_2} \qquad (4)$$

The inverse of this metric is sometimes mentioned as *difficulty*.

The effort E that a programmer needs to invest to comprehend the program is defined as

$$E = \frac{V}{lv} \qquad (5)$$

This metric is sometimes denominated *number of mental discriminations* that a developer must do to understand a program.

6.4. Analysis of Other Files

Besides source code written in a programming language, we identify other artifacts that compose the sources of libre software projects. (Robles et al., 2006a) shows the many possibilities that arise from the study of those files, but other references to this issue may be found in related literature. Some authors have focused on the analysis of the change log files (Capiluppi et al., 2003) as they usually follow a common pattern in libre software projects, although sometimes this pattern is slightly different from the standardized way used in GNU projects[14].

Translation files may be used to keep track of the amount of translation work that has been accomplished to the moment and hence have a quantitative manner of knowing the support of that software in a given language.

Regarding licenses, in addition of a reference to the licensing terms that can be found at the top of the code files, usually projects have a text file which includes the full text of the license. The filename may give enough evidence for the type of license that a project uses, but other ways can also be considered. One that we have been trying with is the use of a locality-sensitive hash like nilsimsa (Chang and Mockus, 2008). This type of hashes return codes with small changes for inputs that differ only slightly. As intellectual property issues have become a recent area of interest among industry, some approaches (and tools, such as FOSSology) have been presented that target these problems (Gobeille, 2008).

Finally, the amount of documentation for a software system could be a good topic for empirical research. In this sense, the *doceval*[15] tool offers a way of assessing and partially evaluating the documentation that can be found in the sources of libre software projects (Robles et al., 2006c).

7. DATASETS FOR EMPIRICAL RESEARCH

When retrieving data from libre software communities, researchers find a lack of congruence in the available data because there are plenty of different repositories of information (SCM, Mailing lists or BTS) where each of them uses a specific technology (e.g. for SCM the most common are CVS, Subversion, Git, Mercurial or Baazar, but there are even more).

Also, in a recent investigation, Robles (Robles, 2010) found that only one of the papers published in the Mining Software Repositories conference fulfilled the requirements to be replicated. The rest of papers published in that conference since 2004 did not fulfill the requirements for validation and replication. This was partly due to the fact that researchers use their own tools and do not share the resulting datasets. In empirical research, validation, verification and replication are essential requirements. To foster these desired properties, several initiatives have aroused to offer datasets of libre software repositories. This means that researchers do not have to mine directly the repositories, and obtain the needed data in a research friendly manner. Libre software projects themselves also benefit of this approach, because it relieves their servers of the stress that mining supposes.

These datasets have been denominated *meta repositories* in (González-Barahona et al., 2010), that have identified some of the most common problems that researchers must face when mining software repositories: different representation of the same data, performance issues when performing large analysis, lost data, damage to the analyzed project infrastructure or lack of expertise. They review some of these datasets:

- FLOSSMole (Howison et al., 2006): This is a collection of datasets. This currently stores data from SourceForge, Freshmeat, Rubyforge, ObjectWeb, the FSF, Tigris, Google Code, Github and Savannah.
- FLOSSMetrics (Gonzalez-Barahona et al., 2010): This is a FP6 project funded by the European Comission. The data stores in FLOSSMetrics comes from FLOSS projects and it currently stores databases from more than 2,800 projects. This project deepens in the repositories offering a set of queries which directly answer different questions related to the community evolution and other facts.
- SRFA (Antwerp and Madey, 2008): The Sourceforge Research Data Archive stores several years of information directly donated by SourceForge.
- PROMISE (Sayyad Shirabad and Menzies, 2005): The PROMISE Software Engineering Repository contains several examples of the period 2004-2006. This information is used to train defect prediction or cost estimation .

We strongly recommend to try to reuse some of these datasets before trying to mine directly a software repository. Only in the case that either the project or the repository that we need is not included in those datasets, using mining tools against the project is justified. In that case, it is also strongly recommended to take the caution to make the study replicable, following the advice given by Robles (Robles, 2010). In any case, the *meta repositories* will usually accept external contributions of data, and even they will accept simply a suggestion to include some data in the dataset, providing the necessary pointers to the project or the repository.

8. SUMMARY AND CONCLUSIONS

Libre software projects offer a vast amount of information about their development process and the resulting product. Although this information is publicly available over the Internet, researchers should take into consideration the many *hidden* problems that may occur when obtaining and properly analyzing these data. In this chapter we have given some insight into the most data sources in research, its problems, how to circumvent them and, if possible, have provided and introduced tools and reusable datasets that may help when researchers mine them.

Despite the possibilities that the vast amount of publicly available information from libre software projects offer, there are a number of problems, threats and challenges that researchers have to consider when using these data for their activities.

There is a big challenge in merging information from various sources. For instance, correlating bugs in the BTS to commits in SCM and to code in the source code is a tricky task that requires complex methods. In addition, these methods may have to be changed from project to project as the dynamics may be different among them (i.e., in some projects, committers indicate the bug report number in the commit message, while in others patches are not handled via a BTS but through a mailing list)

Finally, as mining libre software projects has become popular among scientists, many projects have suffered from an overflow of data gathering petitions, both automatically by means of tools or directly from humans in the sense of invitations to participate in surveys. In the specific case of tools, sometimes retrieving data has caused the slow down, or denial of service, of servers where the infrastructure of the project is installed, resulting in the tool being banned. To avoid these problems, we strongly recommend some of the reusable datasets described in this chapter. This will also have the accompanying benefit of making it easier to validate, verify and replicate any study, which are essential properties of any empirical scientific discipline.

9. ACKNOWLEDGMENT

This work has been funded in part by the European Commission, under the FLOSSMETRICS (FP6-IST-5-033547), QUALOSS (FP6-IST-5-033547) and QUALIPSO (FP6-IST-034763) projects, and by the Spanish CICyT, project SobreSalto (TIN2007-66172) and by SEDEPECA. This chapter is based in part in a paper was published in IJOSSP (Robles et al., 2009).

REFERENCES

Amor, J. J., Robles, G., & González-Barahona, J. M. (2006). Discriminating development activities in versioning systems: A case study. In *Proceedings PROMISE 2006: 2nd. International Workshop on Predictor Models*.

Antwerp, M. V., & Madey, G. (2008). Advances in the sourceforge research data archive. In *WoPDaSD*.

Atkins, D. L., Ball, T., Graves, T. L., & Mockus, A. (2002). Using version control data to evaluate the impact of software tools: A case study of the version editor. *IEEE Transactions on Software Engineering*, *28*(7), 625–637. doi:10.1109/TSE.2002.1019478

Bauer, A., & Pizka, M. (2003). The contribution of free software to software evolution. In *Proceedings of the International Workshop on Principles of Software Evolution (IWPSE)*, Helsinki, Finland. IEEE Computer Society.

Bettenburg, N., Premraj, R., Zimmermann, T., & Kim, S. (2008). Extracting structural information from bug reports. In *MSR '08: Proceedings of the 2005 Working Conference on Mining software repositories*.

Capiluppi, A. (2004). Improving comprehension and cooperation through code structure. In *Proceedings of the 4th Workshop on Open Source Software Engineering, 26th International Conference on Software Engineering*, Edinburg, Scotland, UK.

Capiluppi, A., Lago, P., & Morisio, M. (2003). Evidences in the evolution of OS projects through changelog analyses. In *Proceedings of the 3rd International Workshop on Open Source Software Engineering*, Orlando, Florida, USA.

Capiluppi, A., Morisio, M., & Ramil, J. F. (2004). Structural evolution of an Open Source system: a case study. In *Proceedings of the 12th International Workshop on Program Comprehension*, pages 172–183, Bari, Italy.

Chang, H.-F., & Mockus, A. (2008). Evaluation of source code copy detection methods on FreeBSD. In *MSR '08: Proceedings of the 5th Working Conference on Mining software repositories*.

Germán, D. M. (2004). Mining CVS repositories, the softChange experience. In *Proceedings of the International Workshop on Mining Software Repositories*, Edinburgh, UK.

Gobeille, R. (2008). The fossology project. In *MSR '08: Proceedings of the 5th Working Conference on Mining software repositories*.

González-Barahona, J. M., Izquierdo-Cortazar, D., & Squire, M. (2010). Repositories with public data about software development. *International Journal of Open Source Software and Processes*, *2*(2), 1–13.

Gonzalez-Barahona, J. M., Robles, G., & Dueñas, S. (2010). Collecting data about floss development: the flossmetrics experience. In *FLOSS '10: Proceedings of the 3rd International Workshop on Emerging Trends in Free/Libre/Open Source Software Research and Development*, pages 29–34, New York, NY, USA. ACM.

Graves, T. L., & Mockus, A. (1998). Inferring change effort from configuration management databases. In *5th IEEE International Software Metrics Symposium*, pages 267–, Bethesda, Maryland, USA.

Hahsler, M., & Koch, S. (2005). Discussion of a large-scale open source data collection methodology. In *Proceedings of the Hawaii International Conference on System Sciences (HICSS-38)*, Big Island, Hawaii, USA.

Halstead, M. H. (1977). *Elements of Software Science*. New York, USA: Elsevier.

Herraiz, I., Izquierdo-Cortazar, D., Rivas-Hernandez, F., Gonzalez-Barahona, J. M., & Robles, G. nas Dominguez, S. D., Garcia-Campos, C., Gato, J. F., & Tovar, L. (2009). FLOSSMetrics: Free / libre / open source software metrics. In *Proceedings of the 13th European Conference on Software Maintenance and Reengineering (CSMR)*. IEEE Computer Society.

Hindle, A., Herraiz, I., Shihab, E., & Jiang, Z. M. (2010). Mining Challenge 2010: FreeBSD, GNOME Desktop and Debian/Ubuntu. In *Proceedings of the 7th IEEE International Working Conference on Mining Software Repositories*, pages 82–85. IEEE Computer Society.

Howison, J., Conklin, M., & Crowston, K. (2006). Flossmole: A collaborative repository for floss research data and analyses. *International Journal of Information Technology and Web Engineering*, *1*, 17–26.

Howison, J., & Crowston, K. (2004). The perils and pitfalls of mining SourceForge. In *Proceedings of the International Workshop on Mining Software Repositories*, pages 7–11, Edinburg, Scotland, UK.

Kan, S. H. (2003). *Metrics and Models in Software Quality Engineering* (2nd ed.). Addison-Wesley Professional.

Lanzara, G. F., & Morner, M. (2003). The knowledge ecology of open-source software projects. In *Proceedings of the 19th EGOS (European Group of Organizational Studies) Colloquim*.

McCabe, T. J. (1976). A complexity measure. *IEEE Transactions on Software Engineering*, *2*(4), 308–320. doi:10.1109/TSE.1976.233837

Mockus, A., & Votta, L. G. (2000). Identifying reasons for software changes using historic databases. In *Proc Intl Conf Softw Maintenance*, pages 120–130.

Nussbaum, L., & Zacchiroli, S. (2010). The Ultimate Debian Database: Consolidating Bazaar Metadata for Quality Assurance and Data Mining. In *7th IEEE Working Conference on Mining Software Repositories (MSR)*. IEEE Computer Society.

Robles, G. (2010). Replicating msr: A study of the potential replicability of papers published in the mining software repositories proceedings. pages 171–180.

Robles, G., González-Barahona, J. M., & Guervós, J. J. M. (2006a). Beyond source code: The importance of other artifacts in software development (a case study). *Journal of Systems and Software*, *79*(9), 1233–1248. doi:10.1016/j.jss.2006.02.048

Robles, G., González-Barahona, J. M., Izquierdo-Cortazar, D., & Herraiz, I. (2009). Tools for the study of the usual data sources found in libre software projects. *International Journal of Open Source Software and Processes*, *1*(1), 24–45.

Robles, G., González-Barahona, J. M., & Michlmayr, M. (2005). Evolution of volunteer participation in libre software projects: evidence from Debian. In *1st International Conference on Open Source Systems*, pages 100–107, Genoa, Italy.

Robles, G., Gonzalez-Barahona, J. M., Michlmayr, M., & Amor, J. J. (2006b). Mining large software compilations over time: Another perspective of software evolution. In *Third International Workshop on Mining Software Repositories*, pages 3–9, Shanghai, China.

Robles, G., Koch, S., & González-Barahona, J. M. (2004). Remote analysis and measurement of libre software systems by means of the CVSAnalY tool. In *Proc 2nd Workshop on Remote Analysis and Measurement of Software Systems*, pages 51–56, Edinburg, UK.

Robles, G., Prieto-Martínez, J. L., & González-Barahona, J. M. (2006c). Assessing and evaluating documentation in libre software projects. In *Proceedings of the Workshop on Evaluation Frameworks for Open Source Software (EFOSS 2006)*.

Sayyad Shirabad, J., & Menzies, T. (2005). *The PROMISE Repository of Software Engineering Databases*. Canada: School of Information Technology and Engineering, University of Ottawa.

Tuomi, I. (2004). Evolution of the Linux Credits file: Methodological challenges and reference data for Open Source research. *First Monday*, *9*(6). http://www.firstmonday.dk/issues/issue9_6/ghosh/.

Villa, L. (2003). How gnome learned to stop worrying and love the bug. In *Otawa Linux Symposium*, Otawa.

Villa, L. (2005). Why everyone needs a bugmaster. In linux.conf.au, Canberra.

Weißgerber, P., Neu, D., & Diehl, S. (2008). Small patches get in! In *MSR '08: Proceedings of the 2005 Working Conference on Mining software repositories*.

Wheeler, D. A. (2001). More than a gigabuck: Estimating GNU/Linux's size. http://www.dwheeler.com/sloc/redhat71-v1/redhat71sloc.html.

Zimmermann, T., Weißgerber, P., Diehl, S., & Zeller, A. (2005). Mining version histories to guide software changes. *IEEE Transactions on Software Engineering*, *31*(6), 429–445. doi:10.1109/TSE.2005.72

ENDNOTES

[1] In this chapter the term "libre software" will be used to refer to any software licensed under terms that are compliant with the definition of "free software" by the Free Software Foundation, and the definition of "open source software" by the Open Source Initiative, thus avoiding the controversy between those two terms.

[2] A committer is a person who has write access to the repository and does a commit -an interaction- with it at a given time.

[3] http://projects.libresoft.es/wiki/cvsanaly

[4] In a SCM system there is actually no file deletion, as the file can be recovered any time in the future

[5] KDevelop is an IDE (Integrated Development Environment) for KDE. More information can be obtained from http://kdevelop.org/.

[6] The MailMan's project web site can be found at following URL: http://www.gnu.org/software/mailman/.

[7] http://libresoft.es/tools/mlstats

[8] http://www.bugzilla.org/

[9] The ones shown next are the ones that can be found for the GNOME Bugzilla system. Bugzilla can be adapted and modified, so the fields may (and will) change from project to project.

[10] http://projects.libresoft.es/wiki/bicho

[11] For instance, bug #55,000 from the KDE BTS, which can be accessed through the web interface at http://bugs.kde.org/show_bug. cgi?id=55000 may also be obtained in XML at following URL: http://bugs.kde.org/xml. cgi?id=55000.

[12] The location of the binaries may depend from system to system, although the standard location for them is the /usr/bin directory.

[13] http://tools.libresoft.es/cmetrics

[14] In the GNU coding standards, some conventions for change log files are given, see http:// www.gnu.org/prep/standards/html_node/ Change-Logs.html

[15] *doceval* can be obtained from https://forja. rediris.es/projects/csl-doceval/.

Chapter 3
Integrating Projects from Multiple Open Source Code Forges

Megan Squire
Elon University, USA

ABSTRACT

Much of the data about free, libre, and open source (FLOSS) software development comes from studies of code forges or code repositories used for managing projects. This paper presents a method for integrating data about open source projects by way of matching projects (entities) across multiple code forges. After a review of the relevant literature, a few of the methods are chosen and applied to the FLOSS domain, including a comparison of some simple scoring systems for pairwise project matches. Finally, the paper describes limitations of this approach and recommendations for future work.

INTRODUCTION

Free, libre or open source software (FLOSS) development teams often use centralized code forges, or repositories, to help manage their project code, to provide a place for users to find the product, and to organize the development team. Although many FLOSS projects host their own code repository and tools, many projects use the tools hosted at a third-party web site (such as Sourceforge, ObjectWeb, or Rubyforge). These code forges provide basic project/team management tools, as well as hosted space for the source code downloads, a version control system, bug tracking software, and email mailing lists. There are also directories of FLOSS software (such as Freshmeat and the Free Software Foundation directory) that try to gather into one convenient place material about projects interesting to a particular community.

DOI: 10.4018/978-1-60960-513-1.ch003

Much open source software engineering research has been focused on gathering metrics from code repositories. Many aspects of the repository-based software development process have been studied in depth, and repository data collection is important for these studies (see Conklin, 2006 for background). The FLOSSmole project (Howison, Conklin, and Crowston, 2005) was created to consolidate metadata and analyses from some of these repositories and directories into a centralized collaboratory for use by researchers in industry and academia. As of this writing, FLOSSmole includes data and analyses from Sourceforge, Freshmeat, Rubyforge, ObjectWeb, Debian project, and the Free Software Foundation (FSF) directory of free software. One of the challenges mentioned in Conklin (2006) in creating this kind of collaboratory is in integrating the data from these various sources. It seems reasonable that a project might be listed on several directories *and* have a listing on a code forge. However, sometimes a project will be listed in multiple forges too, usually because the project has migrated from one forge to another over time, or because the project wishes to "grab" the unique namespace for its project on a certain forge so it will register at that forge without an intention to ever actually use that space.

In any case, when integrating project data from multiple sources, we must first identify which project pairs are matches. In other words, we want to find out which projects are listed on multiple forges. For example, is the *octopus* project on ObjectWeb the same as the *octopus* project on Sourceforge or the project also called *octopus* on Freshmeat? If we can devise a scoring system for determining whether a project pair is a match, then can we automate the matching process?

The focus of this article is entity matching (and duplicate identification) for this kind of data integration, as applied to the domain of FLOSS projects. Section 2 outlines some terminology from the study of data integration problems and gives a background of entity matching algorithms. Section 3 describes the FLOSS domain in terms of entities and duplicates. Section 4 gives an example of applying some of the algorithms for entity matching to this domain. Section 5 outlines limitations of this work and gives recommendations for future study.

ABOUT ENTITY MATCHING

The act of integrating multiple data sets and finding the resulting duplicate records ("matches") is nearly as old as database processing itself. In practice and in the literature, this set of processes is known by many names (Bitton and DeWitt, 1983; Hernandez and Stolfo, 1985; Winkler, 1999; Garcia-Molina, 2006): merge/purge, object identification, object matching, object consolidation, record linkage, entity matching, entity resolution, reference reconciliation, deduplication, duplicate identification, and name disambiguation. The term *entity matching* will be used in this article.

Within the larger activity of data integration, the act of matching entities is not to be confused with the act of schema reconciliation. Schema reconciliation refers to the act of matching up columns or views in different data sources, and using data or metadata to make the match. For a trivial example, suppose a field in Table A is called *url* but it is called *home_page* in Table B. To resolve these schemas, the analyst could create a global schema or view that encapsulates both underlying schemas. This task can be done manually, or can be automated through various machine learning techniques (such as Batini and DeWitt, 1986; Doan, Domingos and Halevy, 2001; Rahm and Bernstein, 2001). Schema reconciliation and entity matching are related, but not identical, tasks of data integration. Most often the schema reconciliation will happen first, followed by the "merge" task, and finally by the eventual "purge" of duplicate data. However, if data sources are kept separate throughout the matching process, then the act of schema reconciliation could include a "merge" between disparate entities.

Agree/Disagree and Frequency-Based Matching

The simplest form of entity matching is what we will call the agree/disagree method: take two data sets A and B and compare them pairwise for matches based on one or more attributes. The pairs will either agree or disagree on zero or more of the attributes, and thus a weight for the match can be determined.

In trying to improve agree/disagree entity matching, Doan, Lu, Lee, and Han (2003) use frequencies of values to determine the probability of a match (see Winkler, 1999 for another brief explanation of this work). Newcombe in Winkler (1999) asserts two premises: (a) that matches are easier and more accurate when particular values in the fields are considered (as opposed to only considering all pairwise matches between two data sets on a common field), and (b) that two rare values are more easily and accurately matched than two common values. The example given in the Winkler paper is to compare the process of matching the following: two records listing the name ZbigniewZabrinsky, two records listing the name James Smith, and any two records with first and last names. The two records for ZbigniewZabrinsky are likely to be more easily and accurately matched than James Smith due to the rarity of the field values. The author also writes that, on a practical note, first and last name values alone are usually not very good for performing matches of human beings. He suggests first that other attributes such as address, date of birth, etc. should be considered in order to reduce false positives, and also that more sophisticated techniques for string comparison should be implemented.

Disjoint Sets

In Doan, et al. (2001), the authors consider the problem of how to match 'person' records using disjoint attributes and a 'typical person' profile. For instance, the example given in the paper is that the two records {Mike Smith, age 9} and {Mike Smith, salary $200,000} are not likely to be the same person based on a profile indicating that a typical person with an annual salary of $200,000 is older than 9 years. The authors compare their system to a traditional agree/disagree system of matching, and show that disjoint attributes can be effective if paired with shared attributes.

ENTITY MATCHING METHODS FOR FLOSS DATA

This portion of the article describes the way each of these entity matching methods can be used to determine matches between projects in the FLOSSmolecollaboratory (Howison, et al, 2005). FLOSSmole is a research collaboratory for open source data. The project contains raw data and analyses from six of the available source code forges, and contains data from as far back as 2003. The FLOSSmole data is collected in two ways: through donations either given by people who run the forges or by researchers, and through automatic spidering of the code forge web sites. After the data is donated or collected, it is cleaned and aggregated. Finally the data is provided in various raw and summary formats for use by the general public under an open source license.

By way of introduction to the FLOSSmole data, Table 1 shows the relative sizes of the repositories or forges, and Table 2 shows a partial

Table 1. Forges and repository sizes (FLOSSmole data, April, 2008)

Forge	Total Number of Projects Listed
Sourceforge	149,171
Freshmeat	44,379
Rubyforge	5,534
Objectweb	120
Free Software Foundation	5,395
Debian Project	24,922

Table 2. Project metadata: relevant attributes to use when matching projects, (FLOSSmole data, April, 2008)

Attribute	Forge *Sourceforge, Freshmeat, Rubyforge, Objectweb, Free Software Fndn.*				
	SF	FM	RF	OW	FSF
Short Name (unixname)	X	X	X	X	X
Long Name	X	X	X	X	X
Description	X	X	X	X	X
URL	X	X	X	X	X
License Type(s)	X	X	X	X	X
Programming Language(s)	X	X	X	X	X
Operating System(s)	X	X	X	X	
Topic(s)	X	X	X	X	
Intended Audience(s)	X	X	X	X	
User Interface(s)	X	X			X
Environment(s)			X	X	
List of Developer(s)	X	X	X	X	X

list of the project attributes available for each of these repositories or forges in FLOSSmole at the time of this writing. These project attributes are the most likely candidates for the job of matching projects. (There are dozens of other attributes about each project in FLOSSmole, such as registration date or project status or number of downloads, but these are not likely to be helpful in matching projects across repositories.)

Most of these attributes shown in Table 2 are self-explanatory. However, some confusion can arise when differentiating between the short name and the long name for a project. The short name is usually an internal-to-the-repository name that is given to the project at the time of its creation. Some repositories use this as a sort of primary key for the project in its database. The long name of a project is the more descriptive name for a project. It can change over time, it can include spaces and special formatting characters, and it typically more descriptive than the short name. Values for all of the attributes shown in the list in Table 2 are chosen by the project administrators,

and except for short name and long name, they can all be NULL. License type, operating system, topic, audience, interface, environment and developers, can have multiple values.

The next three sections describe a few of the obvious choices for attributes from this list that can be used to establish matches between projects. One choice from Table 2 that may initially look promising is "List of Developers". Since this attribute is actually a list of developers who work on each project, what better way to differentiate or match two projects? (If the list of developers is the same for the two projects, then the two projects are likely to be a match.) The problem with this is that developers are entities themselves, and matching developers between repositories requires an entirely separate list of attributes (developer name, developer email, developer skills, role on project, etc). In addition, developer information is often intentionally obfuscated by the developer themselves, and in some cases by the forge maintainers. Finally, as Robles and Gonzalez-Barahona (2005) described,

Figure 1. Number of projects at each repository that list a home page at another repository (FLOSSmole data, April, 2008)

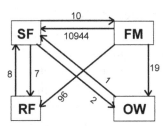

Figure 2. Number of projects at each repository that share an identical short project name

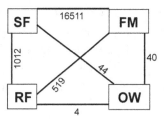

Matching by Project Names

Figure 2 shows the number of short project names shared in common between each pair of projects. For instance, *starfish* is a project listed on both Sourceforge and Rubyforge. On Rubyforge, it is described as a "tool to make programming ridiculously easy", but on Sourceforge the *starfish* project is described as a password management application. There are 1012 projects with shared names on Rubyforge and Sourceforge. A similar problem exists between the project names on Sourceforge and ObjectWeb. For example, the project called *octopus* exists on both these forges and appears to be a completely different application: on Sourceforge this is an Eclipse plug-in, but on ObjectWeb *octopus* is an ETL data warehousing tool. Of the 125 applications (total) listed on ObjectWeb, 44 have names that are shared with a Sourceforge project. The Sourceforge project may (as in the case of *lemonldap*) or may not (as in the case of *octopus*) be the same project. On Freshmeat, there also is a project called *octopus*, but this one is a financial trading application.

Most forges require projects to have a unique name (sometimes called the "unixname") within that forge. For example, once a project called *starfish* has been added to Sourceforge, another one cannot be added with the same short unixname. However, multiple projects can have the same "display name"; Sourceforge projects *starfish* and *xstarfish* both have the display name of "starfish". On Sourceforge, 60% of projects have unixnames

there could be significant privacy implications to using developer data without the express consent of the developers themselves. Section 5 discusses broadening project entity matching to include developers, but the remainder of this article will exclude developers as entities and will retain the focus on project matching only.

Matching by URLs

Matching projects by URL has two possible: projects listed on different forges might both display the same external URL, or projects on one forge might actually list the project site on a competing forge as the home page of record. The diagram shown in Figure 1 depicts each forge/directory in FLOSSmole and how many of its projects list another forge as the actual hosting home page. For example, in the diagram, the topmost arrow shows 10 projects on Sourceforge (SF) that actually have Freshmeat (FM) listed as the home page. The arrow notation is used to show a direction of the relationship (e.g. 10,944 Freshmeat projects show a home page on Sourceforge, but only 10 Sourceforge projects list a Freshmeat home page). Pairs of forges with no URLs in common do not show an arrow. (No Rubyforge projects list ObjectWeb URLs, and vice versa.) As is befitting its status as a directory, rather than a respository, Freshmeat has the highest numbers on its outbound arrows—it lists the most projects that actually have a homepage on another forge.

that are different from their display names (April 2008 FLOSSmole data). Note that the FSF directory has only a requirement for case-sensitive uniqueness in project names. Not shown on the graph, the FSF lists project pages for both *ANT* (telephony application) and *ant* (build tool). There are 54 such ambiguously named projects listed on FSF.

Matching by Other Attributes

It may be possible to determine the accuracy of each matched pair further by attempting to match the project owner or developer names, emails, or usernames as in Robles and Gonzalez-Barahona (2005). Or, it may be possible to find a matched pair through the textual description of the project, or through the project license type, the programming language(s), operating system(s), or other metadata about the project. Each of these possible match fields requires that the project administrator has accurately filled in the metadata for his/her project. If the administrator never bothered to fill in the programming language for the project on one or both of the sites where the project is listed, then it will not be possible to disambiguate by finding a match on this item.

Table 3 summarizes a few of the most common attribute statistics for 149,171 Sourceforge projects as measured in April 2008. It is also interesting to discover that of those 81% of proj-

Table 3. Numbers of Sourceforge projects with and without certain attribute data, (FLOSSmole, April, 2008 data)

Project Attribute	Projects listing at least one	Projects listing none
Programming Language	April-2008: 75,012 (50%)	April-2008:74,159 (50%)
License Type	April-2008: 121,010 (81%)	April-2008:28,161 (19%)
Operating System	April-2008:17,737 (12%)	April-2008: 131,434 (88%)

ects that list a license type, over half use the Gnu General Public License (GPL).

Advanced Methods

In our attempt to match FLOSSmole projects by common URLs, names, or any other combination of attributes, we are still performing basic agree/disagree entity matching. Our brief review of the database literature on entity matching indicates that these methods do work for some cases, but can be optimized and improved. This section discusses the improvements we added, and Section 4 will explain the results of our application.

Frequency-Based Matching and String Metrics

The first improvement made to the agree/disagree entity matching is to consider how to apply a form of frequency matching on the name field. Recall that Winkler (1999) explains that rare names (ZbigniewZabrinsky) are more easily matched than common names (James Smith). "Rare" and "common" are determined by an already-existing set of names and their general frequency rankings in the population. In the case of FLOSS projects, there is no such ranking for software project names, but a corollary might be that projects with dictionary words for names (e.g. the *octopus* and *starfish* examples) are more likely to be non-matches than projects with unusual, non-dictionary names (e.g. *sqlite-ruby* or *lemonldap*). Because there is also a difference between the unique unixname and the non-unique display name for each project, we ask: which of these fields should be used to consider the frequency match? In Section 4, we answer with "both", and we experiment with scoring these matches differently.

Another improvement we considered was to look at string metrics for determining whether two projects were matches. Regular expressions can be used to compare strings in a simple fashion, while Hamming distances and Levenshtein distances (Levenshtein, 1966; Black, 2007) are more complex algorithms used to compare the similiarity of two strings. With Levenshtein distances, the higher the calculated distance value, the less similar the strings are. Distance is calculated based on the number of deleted, inserted, or swapped characters it takes to turn one string into another.

Disjoint Sets

The next improvement we considered was to use the notion of a disjoint set, as in 2.2. by listing which attribute values would likely never coexist. Initial ideas included the following possible disjoint sets: {op_sys = linux, prog_lang = asp}, {date_regist < 2001, prog_lang = C#}. Not only are these rules fairly weak insofar as there are plenty of examples of projects that would violate them for various reasons, but unlike the age/salary information in the example case in 2.2, the number of records in FLOSSmole which match these disjoint sets is likely to be quite small. We conclude that in the FLOSS domain, it is more likely to be the case that matches can be found through simpler methods than disjoint sets. This is due to three factors: the low number of valid disjoint set rules we would be able to construct, the difficulty of applying disjoint set rules to our data when so many of the pairs are missing metadata on which these disjoint sets would be based, and the low number of duplicates that would not be identified by other, simpler methods.

APPLICATION

To apply entity matching methods to project data in FLOSSmole, we assumed a set of heuristics and associated weights for calculating whether the items in a pair are a match (Table 4). In Trial One, match modifiers were initially based on an intuitive sense of which matching criteria were important. In Trials Two, Three, and Four, we attempted various alternative scoring systems, and

Table 4. Trial one sample scoring table

	Modifier
Home Page URLs match	+3.00
Short names match	+2.00
--if yes, is short name in the dictionary	-1.00
--if not, does Partial Name match?	+0.50
-- if partial name matches, is partial name in dictionary?	-0.25
Textual descriptions tokens match, per token match	+0.10
Long names match	+0.50
Programming language matches, per token match	+0.50
License matches, per token match	+0.50
Other project metadata matches, per token match	+0.50

there is a description of these in Section 4.1.2. We are keenly aware of the limitations of this method; in the future (see also Section 5), we may wish to expand our methodology a bit by using statistical or information theoretical models for a more effective scoring system.

Application Example

A short example of a table designed to hold the FLOSSmole pairs with their matching scores across multiple repositories might look like Table 5. Higher scores mean the pair is more likely to be a match, but it will be up to an individual analyst to decide where to "draw the line" for what score indicates a match. The highest score is around 8; the lowest score is 0. As shown in the table, the highest score could be higher if more attributes were added. Attributes included are programming language, operating system, and license because these are the fields whose values were most available and easiest to standardize over a variety of repositories. (Table 2 showed that attributes like "environment", "interface", or "topic" are harder to standardize.)

Pair 1 shows Sourceforge project phpmyadmin matching an identically-named Freshmeat project. These projects share a short name (with low fre-

Table 5. Sample scores for matching project pairs, Trial One

Pair ID	Project Name	Src.A	Project Name	Src.B	Score
1	phpmyadmin	SF	8001 (phpmyadmin)	FM	6.9
2	octopus	SF	octopus	OW	1.0
3	octopus-ge	SF	octopus	OW	2.6
4	16120 (octopus)	FM	octopus	OW	1.5
5	13902 (ant)	FM	152 (ant)	FSF	4.1
6	sqlite-ruby	SF	sqlite-ruby	RF	6.9

quency count when compared to a dictionary word: +2), long name (+.5), URL (+3), and license type (+.5). Several key tokens are the same in each description (+.9: The matching tokens are 'MySQL', 'PHP', 'Web', 'administration,' 'alter', 'drop', 'database', 'delete', 'SQL').

Pair 2 shows Sourceforge project *octopus* with ObjectWeb project *octopus*. The short project names match (+2), but urls are different. The long project names are also different ('Octopus' and 'Enhydra Octopus'). Additionally, because the Sourceforge project *octopus* does not list any project metadata, it can't be matched very well with the ObjectWeb project of the same name using these additional attributes. Finally, these two entities share the dictionary word name 'octopus' (-1).

Pair 3 shows the project *octopus-ge* on Sourceforge and project *octopus* on ObjectWeb. These projects share a beginning partial string match, *octopus** (+1), but that string is a dictionary word (-.5). They share one programming languages (+.5), a license type (+.5), and one operating system (+.5). The textual description of the projects increases the score, since both use the token strings 'Enhydra Octopus', 'extraction', 'transformation', 'load*', 'ETL', and 'XML' (+.6). However, a closer read of the textual description field by a human being reveals that the Sourceforge project is actually a graphical editor for the ObjectWeb project. They are related projects, but not the same project. The combination of no URL score and

low scores for the textual matches has (accurately) kept this project from a high score.

Pair 4 shows the attempted match between that same *octopus* project at ObjectWeb but now paired with the *octopus* project at Freshmeat. The projects have the same short name (+2 for similarity, -1 for dictionary), but different URLs, totally different textual descriptions, and share only the license type in common (GPL, +.5). Indeed, manual checking of this result shows that these two projects are not related.

Pair 5 shows the Freshmeat project *ant* matching with the Free Software Foundation project *ant* as follows: short name (+2), url (+3). However, the display names for this project are different ('ant' on FSF and 'apache ant' on FM). In addition, the common dictionary name 'ant' lowers the score somewhat (-1). Note that while there is only one significant matching token in the textual description (the word "Java", +.1), the entire first sentence of the two projects is identical. This indicates a strong need to refactor the scoring algorithm for textual descriptions.

Pair 6 shows that *SQLite-ruby* projects listed nearly identical information on both Sourceforge and Rubyforge. They share: the project home page (+3), short name (+2), the display name (+.5), one programming language (+.5), the operating system (+.5), and 4 significant text tokens (+.4), yielding a total score of 6.9.

Table 6. Trial two sample scoring table

	Modifier
Home Page URLs match	+3.00
Short names match	+2.00
--if yes, is short name in the dictionary?	-1.00
Long names match	+0.50
Programming language matches, per token match, but only if score > 0	+0.50
License matches, per token match, but only if score > 0	+0.50

Table 7. Trial four sample scoring table

	Modifier
Top of chart same as for Trial Two: URLs, Names...	
If score = 0, measure Levenshtein distance between names, giving 0.5 if <25% difference	+0.25
Programming language matches, per token match, but only if score > 0	+0.50
License matches, per token match, but only if score > 0	+0.50

Comparison and Evaluation

The problems with the Trial One scoring system seem obvious: first, calculating probably-insignificant token matching on completely unrelated projects takes up an enormous amount of processing time, and second, there is no "memory" for matching likelihoods based on the calculations that have already taken place. Trials Two, Three, and Four attempt to solve some of these problems. Tables 6 and 7 show the scoring systems used for these additional trials.

In Trial Two, we made two changes. First, we simply reduced the number of small-scoring attributes, while leaving the most decisive attributes in the scoring system. This was decidedly faster for processing, and eliminated some of the irrelevant "false positives" generated by cumulative low scores. We also introduced the notion of phased scoring by major and minor attributes. The remaining token match attributes (programming languages and licenses) were only scored *if* the project pair already had some sort of positive correlation from one of the other three major attributes (URL, short name, or long name). This seemed to solve the problem of trivial token matching, and solved some of the problems of processing time.

In Trial Three, we decided to explore solutions for the speed-of-processing issues caused by our massive Cartesian product generation (all projects in one forge times all projects in another

forge). To do this, we considered what we know about how disjoint sets work (Section 2.2 and 3.4.2). We decided to invert our program logic a bit: instead of building up a huge list of projects and comparing all projects in forge A against all projects in forge B, we instead attempt to identify likely sets immediately (or eliminate disjoint sets immediately) and thus we can *discount* projects that are unlikely to be related. This will serve to reduce the size of the sets being compared. For example, we built a list of projects that used Java on forge A and another list of projects that use Java on forge B, then only compare these projects along the other attributes. This method didn't actually reduce the number of comparisons, since every project had one or more programming languages, but it did serve to reduce the size of the in-memory hashes being built.

In Trial Four we wanted to improve the accuracy of our partial name matches. We decided to use Levenshtein distances to measure the similarity between two tokens, such as between two short names. (In Trial One we had used simple regular expression-based partial string matches, so for example, *starfish* and *xstarfish* would match but *andychat* and *andyschat45* would not match.) Levenshtein distances are calculated for each string pair based on the smallest number of characters that must be deleted, replaced, or inserted to make one string into another string. In our case, we choose to set an arbitrary threshold for similarity at 25%. The Levenshtein distance between *andychat* and *andyschat45* is 3 (or 25% of the longest string), which is (barely) enough to warrant token matching in programming languages and license types according to our threshold of 25% or less.

LIMITATIONS AND FUTURE WORK

Based on the experiments described in Section 4, entity matching is an interesting exercise, but is certainly problematic. One of the most obvious problems is that the scoring modifiers given in Tables 4, 6, and 7 are completely arbitrary and based on trial and error and an intuitive sense of the data. In the case of Trial One, there is a distinct possibility that a pair of projects could achieve a score of 4.0 by having a partial non-dictionary name match (+.5), five attributes in common (+2.5), and a handful of well-chosen tokens in the textual description (+.5), and yet these projects could be completely unrelated. Tweaking the scores to reduce false positives and false negatives in this way is tedious and inefficient.

In the subsequent trials, we attempted to reduce processing time and false positives/false negatives, but there are many other routes we could have taken to accomplish this. For instance, in the case of token matching, we look at the case of *ant*, for which there were very few singularly meaningful tokens in the textual descriptions, but the description as a whole matched perfectly. The use of dictionary word definitions for frequency matching may need to be refactored also. The *ant* match lost points because of this. We also recognize that open source developers and projects are a decidedly global population, and more languages than just English are used, so perhaps English dictionary matching is an arbitrary solution. Would other dictionaries be effective? Should non-dictionary strings that are also common in software development ("lib", "db", "php") be added to the dictionary?

Next, what about multi-way matches? We have given little attention to the problem (as presented

in Howison, et al. 2006) of how to merge multiple confidence scores after they've been created. Consider a project such as *sqlite-ruby* that appears on Sourceforge, Rubyforge, Freshmeat, and the FSF directory. What is the appropriate way to integrate its multiple scores? *Sqlite-ruby* is likely to have high scores on all 6 pair combinations, so a simple average might work, but what about a project like *ant* whose scores may vary more?

Section 3 mentioned the possibility of matching projects based on the lists of developers on each project. Before doing this, it would be necessary to use similar entity matching methods to actually match developer entities as well. As is described in Robles and Gonzalez-Barahona (2005), matching developers also leads to a few additional complexities: "real" emails are most often not available for public lists of developers on code repositories, name matching with developers could be even more complex than matching on names for projects because of similarities in names and spellings, and of course, developer privacy is always a concern when integrating personal data points.

One final recommendation for future work is to remember some of the work being done on sites like Krugle, Ohloh, Swik, DOAPSpace and the Galactic Project Registry to standardize the notion of a project name. Krugle is a source code search engine that actually uses some FLOSSmole data to populate its list of projects. Swik and Ohloh are user-driven directories of information about individual open source projects; Swik gets some of its initial information from FLOSSmole as well. DOAPSpace and the Galactic Project Registry are two different efforts to put together the DOAP (description of a project) metadata for all open source projects. Each of these efforts probably would benefit from this discussion about entity matching and duplicate identification across repositories, and perhaps they can contribute to the conversation about the best way to achieve this goal.

REFERENCES

Algorithms and Theory of Computation Handbook. CRC Press LLC, 1999, "Levenshtein distance", in Dictionary of Algorithms and Data Structures [online], Paul E. Black, ed., U.S. National Institute of Standards and Technology. 11 June 2007. (Accessed 15 June 2007) Available from: http://www.nist.gov/dads/HTML/Levenshtein.html

Batini, C., Lenzerini, M., & Navathe, S. (1986). A comparative analysis of methodologies for database schema integration. *ACM Computing Surveys, 18*(4), 323–364. doi:10.1145/27633.27634

Bitton, D., & David, J. (1983, June). DeWitt, Duplicate record elimination in large data files [TODS]. *ACM Transactions on Database Systems, 8*(2), 255–265. doi:10.1145/319983.319987

Conklin, M. Beyond low-hanging fruit: seeking the next generation of FLOSS data mining. In Proc. 2nd Intl. Conf. on Open Source Systems. (Como, Italy, June 2006). Springer, New York, NY, 2006. 47-56.

Doan, A., Domingos, O., & Halevy, A. Reconciling schemas of disparate data sources: A machine learning approach. In Proc. of the SIGMOD conference. (Santa Barbara, CA, USA, 2001). ACM Press, New York, NY, 2001, 509-520.

Doan, A., Lu, Y., Lee, Y., & Han, J. Object matching for information integration: A profiler-based approach. In Proc. of the IJCAI Workshop on Information Integration and the Web. (Acapulco, Mexico, 2003). 53-58.

Garcia-Molina, H. 2006. Pair-Wise entity resolution: overview and challenges. In Proceedings of the 15th ACM international Conference on information and Knowledge Management (Arlington, Virginia, USA, November 06 - 11, 2006).CIKM '06. ACM, New York, NY, 1-1.

Hernandez, M. A. and Stolfo, S. J. 1995. The merge/purge problem for large databases. SIGMOD Rec. 24, 2 (May. 1995), 127-138.

Howison, J., Conklin, M., & Crowston, K. OSSmole: A collaborative repository for FLOSS research data and analyses. In Proc. 1st Intl. Conf. on Open Source Systems. (Genova, Italy, June 2005). 54-59.

Levenshtein, V. I. (1966). Binary codes capable of correcting deletions, insertions, and reversals. *Soviet Physics, Doklady, 10*, 707–710.

On, B.-W., Lee, D., Kang, J., & Mitra, P. Comparative study of name disambiguation problem using a scalable blocking-based framework. In Proc. of 5th ACM/IEEE-CS Joint Conf. on Digital Libraries. (Denver, CO, USA, 2005). 344-353.

Rahm, E., & Bernstein, P. (2001). A survey of approaches to automatic schema matching. *The VLDB Journal, 10*, 334–350. doi:10.1007/s007780100057

Robles, G., & Gonzalez-Barahona, J. Developer identification methods for integrated data from various sources.In Proc. of Mining Software Repositories Workshop (MSR 2005) (St. Louis, MO, USA, 2005). 1-5.

Winkler, W. (1999). *The State of Record Linkage and Current Research Problems. Technical Report, Statistical Research Division*. US Bureau of the Census.

This work was previously published in International Journal of Open Source Software and Processes (IJOSSP), edited by Stefan Koch, pp. 46-57, copyright 2009 by IGI Publishing (an imprint of IGI Global)

Chapter 4
Bridging the Gap between Agile and Free Software Approaches:
The Impact of Sprinting

Paul J. Adams
Sirius Corporation Ltd., UK

Andrea Capiluppi
University of Lincoln, UK

ABSTRACT

Agile sprints are short events where a small team collocates in order to work on particular aspects of the overall project for a short period of time. Sprinting is a process that has been observed also in Free Software projects: these two paradigms, sharing common principles and values have shown several commonalities of practice. This article evaluates the impact of sprinting on a Free Software project through the analysis of code repository logs: sprints from two Free Software projects (Plone and KDE PIM) are assessed and two hypotheses are formulated: do sprints increase productivity? Are Free Software projects more productive after sprints compared with before? The primary contribution of this article is to show how sprinting creates a large increase in productivity both during the event, and immediately after the event itself: this argues for more in-depth studies focussing on the nature of sprinting.

INTRODUCTION

Agile and Free Software development have received rapid growth in popularity, both as development paradigms and as research topics. In theory they are very different concepts; the latter,

strictly speaking, being just a licensing paradigm with implications for code reuse and redistribution.

The interface between Agile and Free Software is very interesting and a fertile area in which not much rigorous research has been carried out to date. Some comparative studies have been made in the past, but given the scarcity of data from Agile processes, most of the studies have remained

DOI: 10.4018/978-1-60960-513-1.ch004

on the surface of theoretical discussions (Koch, 2004)(Warsta and Abrahamsson, 2003). Empirical attempts have been also made to measure, on an empirical basis, the degree of *agility* within other development paradigms (Adams, Capiluppi and deGroot, 2008).

This article examines and compares the Free Software and Agile approaches by observing typical Agile practices when deployed within Free Software teams: in particular, it reports on the Plone and KDE PIM projects, where sprinting (Beck, 1999) is commonly used by developers to focus the activity for a limited period of time. Sprinting allows developers to meet in person, get to know each other and create the basis for collaborating more effectively in a distributed environment (During, 2006). In previous works, the PyPy and the Zope projects have been reported to use sprinting regularly within their projects (Sigfridsson, Avram, Sheehan and Sullivan, 2007), and its use is advocated as an *"applied (...) idea of Agile development to the very difficult problem of distributed software development"* (Goth, 2007).

What past literature has not provided yet is a quantitative evaluation of the impact of sprinting on productivity of developers: what has instead been reported is that traditional productivity metrics could fail in capturing the effects of the interactions among developers within sprints (Goth, 2007). In order to tackle this issue, this article explores the use of automatic measures to determine the productivity of developers both before and after the sprinting efforts. A research hypothesis has been formulated as follows: when quantitatively evaluating sprinting, the productivity of developers will display higher values after a sprint than before it. If the null hypothesis can be rejected, this result could prove useful to others in the Free Software communities, encouraging them to adopt this practice and to focus their efforts within a constrained period of time to increase their productivity.

This article is structured as follows: Section 2 introduces the context of the work, explaining how the Agile and Free Software paradigms share some of their process characteristics. Section 3 reports on the methodology, the attributes and the definitions used throughout the article. Section 4 describes how sprinting is accomplished within the two reported case studies, while Section 5 summarises the main findings of measuring the effects of sprinting on developers productivity. Since this work reports on empirical analysis of public data, Section 6 will report on the threats to validity. Finally Section 7 will conclude the article, and illustrate avenues of further research.

SPRINTS WITHIN THE AGILE DEVELOPMENT

As an activity, sprinting has its roots within the Agile development, specifically the SCRUM development model (Schwaber and Beedle, 2001). The SCRUM model is not a method per se, in that it does not prescribe specific practices to be followed in the release cycle. Within SCRUM, the principal period of development is focused during the sprints. Typically, a sprint would be a short period of development, typically 4 to 6 weeks (although they can be shorter). Within this period, developers would work to solve a specific and well-focused problem, such as the addition of a new set of functionality. Normally a sprinting team is collocated, with a dedicated manager who monitors progress on a daily basis in a short stand-up meeting.

As described, this model is in great contrast to the open development approach, as found within many Free Software projects. Again, the Free Software model does not prescribe specific practices, just how contributions should be handled. Originally Eric Raymond argued for what he called the "bazaar" model of development (Raymond, 1999). In this model contributions to the code

Figure 1. The open development model

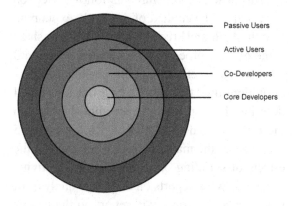

Passive Users

Active Users

Co-Developers

Core Developers

may be made by anyone whilst concurrently this openness leads to many people discovering and fixing bugs. In practice this is not what is found (Crowston, Annabi, Howison and Massango, 2004). Instead it is more common to have a model with a "cathedral" component at its center, managed by core developers. This model is shown in Figure 1. It has been also shown that some Free Software projects show transitions between one stage to the other, and that this transition can be started by explicit actions of the core developers of a Free Software project (Capiluppi and Michlmayr, 2007).

At the centre of the model are the core developers, who are typically long-term contributors to a project and drive its development. They are the *de facto* management of Free Software developments. Other contributors to a project typically move in towards the centre of the model from the outside, where they began as users of the software.

Despite the commercial nature of the Agile approach, sprinting practices have been adopted by Free Software teams: given the differences as described above, and due to the unique nature of this model, Free Software developers have so far preferred to maintain the Free Software name instead of using the much more structured "Agile" term to define their approach (Goth, 2007), even when blended with tools coming from other development approaches.

EMPIRICAL APPROACH

The following concepts and attributes have been used to extract data from the two Free Software projects, and used to compare the effectiveness of their sprinting practices:

- **Commit:** the atomic action of developers checking in one or more files (being source code or other) into a central repository. Both the Plone and the KDE PIM projects store the source code and other artifacts within similar Configuration Management Systems (subversion), therefore the same scripts were used to extract the relevant information out of each project.
- **Lines of code (LOCs):** in this study, the number of lines of code (LOCs) of each commit is also recorded. They will be used in conjunction with the commits to describe the output produced by Free Software developers.
- **Productivity:** in its most basic definition, it evaluates the amount of work produced during an observed period. Considering the information stored in configuration management systems, the productivity was in first instance evaluated by taking the amount of commits in a day. Secondly, the LOCs of the commits were also extracted, to provide a clearer picture of the productivity of developers during sprints.
- **Sprint duration:** since their inception, sprints are considered one of the core practices within the SCRUM development model (Beck, 1999). Short periods of focused development work, preceded by a precise set of requirements both by stakeholders and final users, are at the core of the practice. Within this work, the sprints are characterised by evaluating the time (in days) when the sprints were held. The measurement of productivity was evaluated not only in each of the sprint periods,

but also one week (*i.e.*, 7 days) before and one week after those events.

KDE PIM and Plone

The KDE website[1] hosts a large number of Free Software projects under a common name which together form both a desktop environment and associated application software, primarily for Unix-like operating systems. The complete project repository is roughly 50GB large and has grown steadily, along with contributors, since the project's launch over ten years ago. The KDE repository has somewhere in the order of 300 projects, ordered by application domain, one of which is Personal Information Management (PIM). KDE as a whole lists more than 1500 developers as committers in its Subversion CMS; considering the KDE PIM project alone, an overall of 380 committers are traceable in its evolution history.

Plone[2] is a Free Software content management system based upon the Zope web application server. Written in Python, it can run on all major platforms. As a project it is much smaller than KDE with 163 accounts in the project repository. Although Plone is focussed on one particular product, development is subdivided into teams working on specific issues within the system: css, programmed logic, work flow management, etc.

GQM: Goal Question Metric

The Goal-Question-Metric (GQM) method evaluates whether a goal has been reached, by associating that goal with questions that explain it from an operational point of view, and providing the basis for applying metrics to answer these questions (Basili, Caldiera and Rombach, 1994). The aim of the method is to determine the information and metrics needed to be able to draw conclusions on the achievement of the goal.

In the following, we applied the GQM method to first identify the overall goal of this research; we then formulate a number of hypotheses related

to the two Free Software projects and their sprinting methods; and finally we collected adequate productivity metrics to determine whether the goal was achieved.

- **Goal:** The long-term objectives of this research are both to assess the presence, and to evaluate the efficacy of Agile processes within a Free Software development paradigm. If confirmed on these initial case studies, the results should be made public to other Free Software projects, in order to take advantage of Agile practices and tools.
- **Question:** The aim of this study is to establish the efficacy of an Agile practice (sprinting) within the Free Software paradigm. The productivity of the two Free Software systems will be studied: based on the "productivity" and "sprint duration" attributes defined above, two research hypotheses were formulated:
  - **HP1:** *There is a difference between the average productivity of Free Software projects and the productivity as achieved during the sprints.*
  - **HP2:** *In the presence of sprinting, there is a difference in the productivity of Free Software developers between the periods immediately before and immediately after the selected sprints.*
- **Metrics:** based on the number of sprints actually performed during the lifecycle of the two projects, 6 sprints were selected from each project, and the productivity evaluated during the week before the sprint, during the sprint duration, and during the week after the sprint.

A summary of the research hypotheses is displayed in Table 1: the null and the alternative counterparts are formulated, as well as the metrics used to assess the hypothesis, and the type of test conducted to evaluate the hypothesis.

Table 1. Summary of the research hypotheses and the applied tests

Hypo	Null	Alternative	Metrics	Test
HP1	Productivity during sprints is larger than the baseline productivity	Productivity is larger during sprints	Commits-per-day (C)	$C_{sprints} > C_{baseline}$
HP2	Productivity after the sprints is larger than productivity after the sprints	Productivity after the sprints is equal to before	Commits-per-day (C)	$C_{after} > C_{before}$

Sprinting in Free Software Projects

As one might expect, the implementation of sprinting varies between different Free Software projects. Even when the activities are similar, the frequency and motivation can be very different. A common value for all the observed sprints in the Free Software approach has been the location of these sprints: being it a distributed development, the face-to-face meetings have been typically run alongside main Free Software conferences, or developers meet-ups (During, 2006). In this section the sprinting practices of Plone and KDE PIM are described: one of the authors has been involved in the development of the KDE PIM, while directly collaborating with several developers from the other.

Sprinting in Plone

Since early 2003 there have been 32 Plone project sprints. Typically these involve less than 10 developers. However, as sprints have become more regular, so has the number of sprinters increased with meetings growing to be as large as 120 registrants[3]. These larger meetings are a-typical in that they are not, in themselves, one sprint alone. Instead, they are a gathering of many sprint meetings. Here, this larger type of meeting is described based upon observation of a sprint held in October 2007.

Each team, within the larger event, works on an individual subcomponent of the entire system: work flow, cascading style sheets, ZODB, etc. These teams set their own daily targets and share them with the entire sprint team in a short meeting at the beginning of the day. A similar meeting is held at the end of the day in order to convey progress made. In general, these Plone sprints are focused on the rapid introduction of new functionality to the system and optimisation of existing functionality. Some Plone sprints have also had a shared focus on system documentation. Six sprints (out of 32) were randomly selected between 2003 and 2007, with sprint durations varying from 3 to 8 days. A summary of the sprints' dates (in ISO format) and their durations is displayed in Table 2.

Sprints in KDE-PIM

The sprints of this project have been held annually since 2003. As with the Plone sprints they are generally larger than an Agile sprint, typically with around 15 developers. However, unlike Plone sprints, there is no structure (explicit or otherwise) to each day and the primary focus of the event is not on coding, although this is one of the activities[4].

The annual KDE PIM plays a specific role within the product release cycle. KDE PIM development, like KDE as a whole, is based upon a 6 month release cycle for major releases. Minor releases for bug fixing and small amounts of new functionality happen monthly. The KDE PIM sprints occur at the beginning of one of these release cycles and is primarily focused with planning the next release.

In order to be consistent with the Plone case, six sprints were selected between 2003 and 2008, with reported shorter sprint durations, varying from 3 to 4 days. This corresponds to all of the

Table 2. Summary of the dates of the sprints in Plone and KDE PIM

Project / Event		Start Date	End Date	Duration (days)
Plone	Sprint 1	2003-05-09	2003-05-11	3
	Sprint 2	2004-09-16	2004-09-19	4
	Sprint 3	2005-02-20	2005-02-27	8
	Sprint 4	2005-03-24	2005-03-27	4
	Sprint 5	2006-04-23	2006-04-29	7
	Sprint 6	2007-02-17	2007-02-20	4
KDE PIM	Sprint 1	2003-01-03	2003-01-05	3
	Sprint 2	2004-01-02	2004-01-05	4
	Sprint 3	2005-01-06	2005-01-09	4
	Sprint 4	2006-01-06	2006-01-08	3
	Sprint 5	2007-01-12	2007-01-15	4
	Sprint 6	2008-02-01	2008-02-03	3

sprints happened within the KDE PIM project: details of these sprint dates are in Table 2.

Sprint Impact: Setting Base Rates

The impact that a particular event may have on the development cycle is inevitably hard to assess without insider knowledge of what may be happening within that project at that time. There are, however, simple metrics that can be applied to public data sources in order to produce results which are indicative of the impact of an event (*i.e.*, sprinting) without needing to know specifi-

cally what has occurred. As reported above, the Configuration Management servers of the two studied projects have been analysed to extract the amount of commits recorded in the development activities. The number of commits per day was then used as a means of assessing productivity before and after development sprints, as well as within the sprint period.

As a start, a simple means of establishing any trends in commit rates is to plot the commit rates for the entire project history. Example for KDE PIM and Plone development are given in Figure 2 and Figure 3.

Figure 2. Growth of commits-per-day in plone

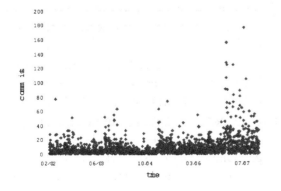

Figure 3. Growth of commits-per-day in KDE PIM

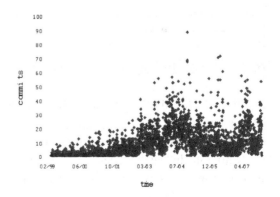

Table 3. Different base rates of commits-per-day for the two projects

Base Rates	Plone			KDE PIM		
	Year	Median	Average	Year	Median	Average
Sprint 1	2003	4	5,97	2003	12	12,9
Sprint 2	2004	4	4,75	2004	20	20,57
Sprint 3	2005	6	7,97	2005	11	13,26
Sprint 4	2005	6	7,97	2006	7	9,67
Sprint 5	2006	7	8,32	2007	12	16,42
Sprint 6	2007	12	19,1	2008	15	20,37

Figure 2 shows the distribution of commits-per-day in the Plone project. From this distribution, it is also possible to evaluate an overall average commit rate of 10 commits per day, and a median value is 6. Since the distribution of Figure 2 is clearly not uniform, using the global average and median as base rates could produce spurious results. It was therefore decided to use different base rates of productivity for the various sprints: the base rates were in fact computed only during the year when the sprint happened, and are summarised in Table 3.

Similar to the Plone plot of commits, Figure 3 shows that largely due to an increase in activity between late 2003 and early 2006, KDE PIM has an average commit rate of 10 (31,214 commits assessed over 2,853 days), with a median value of 8. As there have only ever been 6 KDE PIM sprints, they were all assessed in the same manner as the Plone sprints. The dates are shown in Table 2. As seen above for the Plone system, different base rates were used to assess whether the effect of sprinting could be visible on the productivity of developers (Table 3).

Productivity During the Sprints

In order to tackle the first research hypothesis (HP1), an approach to measuring the impact of sprints upon project development is to compare the commit rate during the sprints to the base rate established in the previous section. In the next subsections, the productivities of the two selected projects are evaluated during the six sprints, and compared to the base rates of the appropriate year. The test of the hypothesis HP1 is based on the principle of majority: if the majority of sprints achieve a larger productivity with respect to the yearly base rate, the null hypothesis will be rejected.

Effects of Sprinting – Plone

Figure 4 shows the commits per day for the 6 randomly selected sprints and the context weeks before and after: a vertical line divides the context week before the sprint from the sprint itself. Since the sprints have different durations, no common vertical line is displayed between the end of the sprint and the context week after it. As an example, the data for sprint 4 in Figure 4 displays 18 points: 7 points for the week before the sprint, 4 for the sprint duration, and 7 for the week after.

For each sprint, the average productivity and the median were recorded during each sprint duration, and compared with the base rates of the productivity within Plone. A summary of these results is shown in Table 4. As visible, in general the productivity during the six sprints in Plone has not increased, when compared with the base rates (depicted in bold within the Table), apart from two events where the values are greatly larger. One of the possible explanations is that Plone sprints have a large amount of participants

Figure 4. Commits during plone sprints

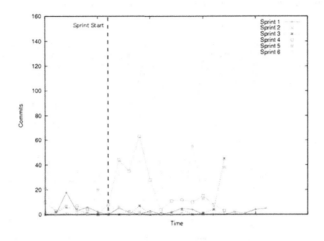

turning up for the meetings, and coordination problems could arise which could make the productivity decrease.

The amount of lines of code in a day (i.e., LOCs-per-day) was also evaluated during the sprints of Plone, in order to test whether the commits-per-day and the LOCs-per-day trends followed the same pattern. Table 5 summarises the results: the Plone case shows that the average LOCs-per-day metrics follow the same pattern also seen in commits-per-day: in the presence of

more commits, the Plone system experienced an increased productivity in LOCs, as compared to the week immediately after the sprint.

Effects of Sprinting: KDE PIM

Shows the commits per day for the 6 randomly selected sprints and the context weeks before and after. As done above, the productivity of KDE PIM developers was recorded during the sprints, and evaluated against the base rates (Table 4). As

Table 4. Average commits-per-day during plone and KDE PIM Sprints

		Median		Average		Test of HP1 – Commits-per-day	
		Baseline	**Sprint**	**Baseline**	**Sprint**		
Plone	Sprint 1	**4**	3,5	**5,97**	3.5	x	x
	Sprint 2	**4**	2,5	**4,75**	2,5	x	x
	Sprint 3	**6**	2.5	**7,97**	3.25	x	x
	Sprint 4	**6**	39.5	**7,97**	42.5	√	√
	Sprint 5	**7**	1	**8,32**	2.25	x	x
	Sprint 6	**12**	117.5	**19,1**	105.5	√	√
KDE PIM	Sprint 1	**12**	13	**12,9**	14	√	√
	Sprint 2	**20**	18.5	**20,57**	18.25	x	x
	Sprint 3	**11**	68,5	**13,26**	63.75	√	√
	Sprint 4	**7**	35	**9,67**	29.33	√	√
	Sprint 5	**12**	20	**16,42**	19	√	√
	Sprint 6	**15**	28	**20,37**	28.71	√	√

Table 5. LOCs-per-day in the sprints, as compared with the seven days immediately after the sprints. For the first three KDE PIM sprints, and the fifth Plone sprint, no LOCs data is available from the SVN servers

		Average		
		During the sprint	**7 days after the sprint**	**Test of HP2 – LOCs per day**
Plone	Sprint 1	0.63	8.29	x
	Sprint 2	3.33	0	√
	Sprint 3	32.18	28.83	√
	Sprint 4	458.84	0	√
	Sprint 5	N/A	N/A	-
	Sprint 6	70.22	55.59	√
KDE PIM	Sprint 1	N/A	N/A	-
	Sprint 2	N/A	N/A	-
	Sprint 3	N/A	N/A	-
	Sprint 4	173.92	84.87	√
	Sprint 5	151.05	95.92	√
	Sprint 6	102.61	17.24	√

visible in the table, the majority of the sprints in KDE PIM achieve a larger productivity (either as medians, averages, or both) than the base counterparts. Differently from the Plone case, KDE PIM sprints tend to gather the same developers to work on the selected requirements, and this could be reflected on the improved productivity during these events. KDE PIM sprints are generally starting with a commit rate lower than that of the project base rate. However a crucial difference between the KDE PIM and Plone sprints is that KDE PIM sprints are not only more consistent at improving productivity, but they are also successfully raising the commit rate above the base.

As done for the Plone case, the amount of LOCs-per-day in KDE PIM was evaluated during the sprints, as compared to the week immediately after the sprint, and the results reported in Table 5. The KDE PIM case shows that the LOCs-per-day metric follows the same pattern of commits-per-day: the three sprints where data of LOCs was available (sprint 4, 5 and 6) achieved a higher rate of LOCs-per-day than the weeks immediately after them. Sprints 1, 2 and 3, due to the recent

conversion to Subversion, have no data available regarding the LOCs involved in the commits.

Productivity after the Sprints

The study of the first research hypothesis above showed a mixed picture: the development of Plone does not achieve (overall) an increased productivity during sprints with respect to its base rates of effort. Instead, the KDE PIM productivity during sprints largely differs from its average, showing a very focused development process during certain periods of the project's lifecycle.

The second research hypothesis was designed in order to assess how the process of development reacted after the sprinting event, and to ascertain whether the productivity before was impacted by the event itself, showing a clear increase after the event. For each sprint the average commits per day, and their medians, were noted for the week immediately before and immediately after the sprint. As a base line for this hypothesis, one would expect an increased productivity after the event, when compared with the period just before it. The results of this analysis are shown in Table 6.

Table 6. Summary of results for the test of hypothesis 2

		Before		After		Test of HP2	
		Median	Average	Median	Average		
Plone	Sprint 1	4.5	7.25	3.5	3.5	x	x
	Sprint 2	1	1.25	0	0	x	x
	Sprint 3	3	3.25	2	2.71	x	x
	Sprint 4	7	6.5	11	15	√	√
	Sprint 5	7	5	5	13.5	x	√
	Sprint 6	20	31	38	57	√	√
KDE PIM	Sprint 1	7	7.71	12	12	√	√
	Sprint 2	7	7.29	8	8.43	√	√
	Sprint 3	24	18.71	21	20.57	x	√
	Sprint 4	6	10	19	16.71	√	√
	Sprint 5	7	6.57	5	8.57	x	√
	Sprint 6	11	13.14	28	28.71	√	√

Productivity after the Sprints: Plone

Comparing the base rate medians and averages with the sprints' achievements, Table 6 shows that the productivity has not steadily increased after the event, as compared with the period before the event: sprint 1, 2 and 3 clearly show that the overall activity, in terms of commits per day, not only dropped after the sprints, compared to just before; but it also decreased to lower levels than the overall base rates for the Plone project itself.

By analysing the remaining sprints, two additional findings were instead revealed: first, the high productivity accomplished during the sprints 4 and 6, was not paired to a similar productivity after the sprint effort (see Table 4). Second, in either the median or average, or both the measurements, an increase of productivity is detected after the event. An explanation for that was given by Plone insiders, revealing that sprints were more and more effective, as long as the use of this practice became clearer and more diffused. In summary, these results are indicative of sprints improving the productivity of the project as a whole, but the null hypothesis of HP2 could not be rejected for Plone: in the majority of cases, the productivity of

developers is not larger after sprints as compared to before the sprints.

Productivity after the Sprints: KDE PIM

Table 6 confirms for KDE PIM what was already learned from the analysis of the sprint effort. All the studied sprints experienced an increase of either the median or the average productivity, or both. In the majority of the sprints, differently from the Plone case, the week after these sprints also accomplished a higher productivity than the observed base rates for the project itself.

An interpretation for that is the increased focus of the development work as a result of the sprint events. Therefore the null hypothesis could not be rejected: in the majority of cases, the productivity of KDE PIM developers after the sprints was higher than before.

As a more general message, Plone and KDE PIM share the same pattern: after the sprints developers increase their efforts as compared to before the sprints. Also, the sprinting events serve as gatherings of exceptional productivity: even simple metrics like the one proposed in this

Figure 5. Commits during KDE PIM Sprints

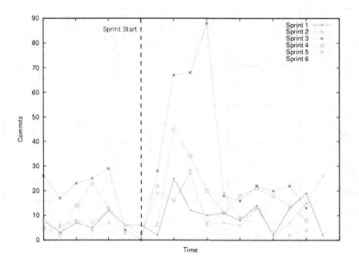

article can be used to share knowledge, motivate and reinforce standard rates of effort.

Threats to Validity

The following aspects have been identified which could lead to threats to validity of the present empirical study:

- **Productivity:** This metric as discussed above (number of commits per day) is limited by its fragility; there are a large series of events which may affect this figure. The major consideration in the applicability of this metric is the requirement of other community knowledge in order to provide qualitative explanation for the measurements. Commit-per-day is a sensitive measurement and can be affected by many external forces, e.g.~lower commit rates are probable on public holidays. Commits-per-day can also be affected by many internal forces, e.g.~reaction to a security flaw in the codebase may increase the commit rate. As a result the observer must be careful to understand the full context of com-

mit rates within the project and around the dates of the events being assessed.

- **Context Periods:** The commit examination period, *i.e.*~one week before and one week after the sprint, could be problematic. Some developers could skew the distribution with many exogenous causes: they could profuse very little effort just before the sprint as they prepare for travel, or on the other hand, some developers might do a lot beforehand to make their code look better.

- **KDE PIM Timings:** The evaluation of KDE PIM sprints is problematic due to their timing. Each KDE PIM sprint occurs within around the first week of a new year. It is possible that the productivity for the week before a KDE PIM sprint is reduced in this new year period.

FURTHER WORK AND CONCLUSION

This article provided a research study into the increasing phenomenon of mixed software development paradigms, when blending together some aspects, practices or shared tools. From the theoretical standpoint, both the Agile and Free Software methodologies have been studied in the past, and several shared concepts have been identified. The Agile paradigm has been deemed as the "commercial" counterpart of the Free Software approach in many respects, and Free Software developers have been reported in the past to have adopted Agile techniques and practices. Still, no rigorous studies have been carried out to evaluate the results and the effects when a development approach (*i.e.*, Free Software) incorporate a practice (sprinting) belonging to another paradigm (*i.e.*, Agile).

Recent empirical research has looked beyond the usual data sources for indicators of quality within Free Software development projects. As such, measuring aspects of the developer community has become of interest (SQO-OSS, 2008). Within this article, commits-per-day was presented as a simple metric for developers productivity and it was shown how it can be used to measure the impact of events within the release cycle, specifically developer sprints. Through this metric, it was also possible to characterise an Free Software project based on its "base rates", *i.e.* the global average and median of the accomplished productivity.

Two Free Software projects were selected for study, Plone and KDE PIM: the rationale of this selection was based on a reported use of the sprinting practices in the two projects, and insider knowledge was available due to one author being part of one of the projects. The first project had a larger number of sprinting events, attended by an increasing amount of developers. The second had sprint events just once in a year, and overall only 6 events have been recorded. Two research hypothesess were formulated: first, the productivity during the sprinting events increases with respect to the base rates observed in a Free Software project. Second, the sprinting event has a follow-up effect on productivity, and the amount

of commits per day increases after the events, compared to the period before.

Results and insider knowledge showed a composite picture: the Plone project had just 2 sprints during which the productivity increased over the base rates, whereas all the KDE PIM events produced a larger amount of commits per day than the average. It was reported also that Plone meetings hosted an increasing numbers of developers, which could hint a higher cost of coordination of efforts. On the other hand, results showed that within Plone, the sprint events have lately started to show an increasing productivity after the event (compared to before), whereas the earlier meetings did not achieve the same levels. The sprints in KDE PIM, instead, always increased the rate of commits per day: less frequent, and more focused meetings have been deemed responsible for this pattern.

Further work has been identified in further studying the quality of the alleged increased productivity: the code committed during the events should be analysed in order to assess its quality compared to the average baseline within the project. Its complexity should also be assessed: Free Software developers should consider whether to commit large amounts of new code, but with higher complexity, or to commit smaller portions, but with an overall lower complexity. assessed: Free Software developers should consider whether to commit large amounts of new code, but with higher complexity, or to commit smaller portions, but with an overall lower complexity.

REFERENCES

Adams, P., Capiluppi, A., & de Groot, A. Detecting agility of Free Software projects through developer engagement. In Proceedings of the 4th International Conference on Open Source Systems, 2008.

Beck, K. Extreme Programming Explained: Embrace Change. Addison-Wesley Professional, October 1999. A. Capiluppi and M. Michlmayr. From the cathedral to the bazaar: An empirical study of the lifecycle of volunteer community projects. In J. Feller, B. Fitzger- ald, W. Scacchi, and A. Silitti, editors, Open Source Development, Adoption and Innovation, pages 31–44. International Federation for Information Processing, Springer, 2007.

Cameron, L. (2003). Challenges for ELT from the expansion in teaching children. *ELT Journal, 57*, 105–112. doi:10.1093/elt/57.2.105

Crowston, K., Annabi, H., Howison, J., & Massango, C. Effective work practices for software engineering: Free/libre open source development. In ACM Workshop on Interdisciplinary Software Engineering Research, 2004. B. During. Sprint driven development: Agile methodologies in a distributed open source project (pypy). In P. Abrahamsson, M. Marchesi, and G. Succi, editors, XP, volume 4044 of Lecture Notes in Computer Science, pages 191–195. Springer, 2006.

Goth, G. (2007). Sprinting toward open source development. *IEEE Software, 24*(1), 88–91. doi:10.1109/MS.2007.28

Koch, S. Agile principles and open source software development: A theoretical and empirical discussion. In Extreme Programming and Agile Processes in Software Engineering: Proceedings of the 5th International Conference XP 2004, number 3092 in Lecture Notes in Computer Science (LNCS), pages 85–93. Springer Verlag, 2004. E. Raymond. The Cathedral and the Bazaar, chapter The Cathedral and the Bazaar. O'Reilly & Associates, Inc., 1999.

Schwaber, K., & Beedle, M. Agile Software Development with Scrum. Prentice Hall, October 2001. A. Sigfridsson, G. Avram, A. Sheehan, and D. K. Sullivan. Sprint-driven development: working, learning and the process of enculturation in the pypy community. In J. Feller, B. Fitzgerald, W. Scacchi, and A. Sillitti, editors, OSS, volume 234 of IFIP, pages 133–146. Springer, 2007.

The, S. QO-OSS Project Consortium. D7 – Novel Quality Assessment Techniques, February 2008. J. Warsta and P. Abrahamsson. Is open source software development essentialy an agile method? In 3rd Workshop on Open Source Software Engineering, 2003.

Wilcoxon, F. (1945). Individual comparisons by ranking methods. *Biometrics Bulletin, 1*(6), 80–83. doi:10.2307/3001968

ENDNOTES

[1] http://www.kde.org/

[2] http://plone.org/

[3] Plone Naples sprint: http://www.openplans.org/projects/plone-conference-2007/sprint

[4] The details here are based upon information derived from an interview held in 2008 with Adriaan de Groot, Vice President of KDE e.V.

This work was previously published in International Journal of Open Source Software and Processes (IJOSSP), edited by Stefan Koch, pp. 58-71, copyright 2009 by IGI Publishing (an imprint of IGI Global).

Chapter 5
Teaching Software Engineering with Free/Libre Open Source Projects

Ioannis Stamelos
Aristotle University of Thessaloniki, Greece

ABSTRACT

One of the major problems in software engineering education is the involvement of students in real world software projects. Industry projects are a solution, but in many cases they are hard to find and student participation can be problematic due to cultural, familiarization and other practical reasons. The abundance of Free / Libre Open Source Software (FLOSS) projects is a neat solution, offering multi-lingual, multi-cultural environments in virtually every application domain, at different levels of project size, maturity, organization etc. The paper analyzes how acquisition of practical experience on several basic and advanced software engineering topics can be achieved by working in a FLOSS project. The kind of skills that can be acquired are those requested by the Overview Report for Computing Curricula by ACM and topics examined are those of the Software Engineering Body of Knowledge, by IEEE. Also software engineering areas that require special care or that may not prove suitable for such treatment are identified. Various isolated teaching cases pertaining to this approach are presented and discussed.[1]

INTRODUCTION AND RELATED WORK

FLOSS projects often provide excellent examples of well-organized, successful projects producing highly effective systems. Moreover, FLOSS projects are based on open, self organized communities of volunteers, that manage to support software development, support and maintenance in an unprecedented way. This unique kind of virtual community provides an excellent environment for

DOI: 10.4018/978-1-60960-513-1.ch005

learning how to communicate with, cooperate with and ultimately learn from other members of the community. Knowledge generation and sharing (Sowe, 2006c) is implicit in the everyday operations of FLOSS communities.

FLOSS world is growing constantly. As an example, SourceForge[2] projects grew in number from approximately 30.000 in 2005 to 177.000 in mid 2008. However, FLOSS is not a synonym for success. Most of the new projects are one, two or three developer projects with little or no activity at all and unknown future. These, and many other bigger projects, fail mainly because they do not manage to build a large, self sustained community.

A very interesting evolution of FLOSS in the last few years is the appearance of hybrid projects, i.e. projects that are run in a FLOSS way but at the same time sponsored by private companies. One recent study reported that one third of the 300 most active FLOSS projects nowadays are sponsored by private companies (Bonnacorsi, 2007).

From the above, it is evident that the FLOSS ecosystem provides a unique environment of numerous, open software projects and corresponding communities, building and maintaining not only software applications but also incredible amounts of knowledge. FLOSS has an evident impact on education, a fact that is already subject of analysis, investigation and discussion. FLOSS has already produced highly successful tools related to education, e.g. the course management system MOODLE[3]. Many reports are available on the use of FLOSS tools at various levels of education and education management, and significant experience has been already acquired (e.g. the Extremadura case reported in Bulchand, 2007). Major FLOSS distributions, such as the education version of UBUNTU (EDUBUNTU[4]) specialize on education. The on-going worldwide project of One Laptop Per Child[5] is currently under development and will potentially change the way education of new generations is achieved on this planet. Finally, Tigris[6] is one FLOSS forge with a special focus on student projects.

However, this paper does not deal with the use of FLOSS tools while educating. Moreover, the paper does not present an approach to teach FLOSS, although by following the proposed approach, students become very knowledgeable about and familiar with various FLOSS products and processes. The paper is meant to explore the use of the FLOSS world (communities, projects) to improve higher level education, in particular Software Engineering (SE) education. Using FLOSS projects with that purpose in higher education in general is already a reality up to some extent. Therefore, we briefly review some sporadic cases of such usage of FLOSS reported in the literature. We will use knowledge from these cases to build later a full scale model. However, most probably there are many other cases that are not yet published. For example, research on the Internet[7] has revealed that in one case, students at a part time Masters Degree in Computing have been asked to investigate FLOSS code and detect design patterns that were used in it. Presumably, in the close future there will be more cases of systematic FLOSS usage in software education and they will be given more visibility.

In (Jaccheri, 2007) FLOSS possibilities for empirical software engineering and software education are discussed. The paper reports on a course at the Norwegian University of Science and Technology, that is based on the involvement of students in the NetBeans project and their interaction with its community. At the Athens University of Economics and Business (Greece), in the context of a master level course titled "Advanced Topics in Software Engineering", students are asked to participate and produce code in FLOSS projects (Spinellis, 2006). Staring et al. (Staring, 2005; Staring, 2006) also claim that "involving students in large scale, international open source projects has a potential for transformation of the relationship between students, educational institutions and society at large". Lundell et al. (Lundell, 2007) report their experience from a practical assignment "designed to give students on an Open Source Masters course an insight into real involvement in Open Source projects" at the University of Skövde (Sweden). They also report on a reduced exercise for undergraduate students related to FLOSS. The authors found out that "the learning experience was both positive and valuable in that it gave real insight into Open Source participation". They also report that students were further encouraged to keep on participating in Open Source projects even after their course was completed.

In (Petrenko, 2007) the issue of teaching evolution of large software systems at the Wayne State University (U.S.) is proposed to be resolved through the use of open source software and through "a software change process model that can narrow this gap without imposing excessive demands on students or instructors". As we will see later in this paper, the approach in (Petrenko, 2007) is really to the point: use of FLOSS projects to involve students in the real world of software engineering, but with a carefully designed process to avoid overload and other practical problems, both for students and instructors. Finally, during the last three years, a consistent attempt is being made at the Department of Informatics of the Aristotle University of Thessaloniki, Greece by the author and his teaching assistants, to introduce FLOSS in the practical training of SE undergraduate students. The ideas in this paper are based on the experience gained from these endeavor and further details will be provided later in the paper.

A project that focuses on the use of FLOSS in higher education has been recently funded by EU, namely FLOSSCom (www.flosscom.net). The project focuses on identifying the factors that contribute to successful knowledge construction in informal learning communities, such as the FLOSS communities and intends to analyze the effectiveness of FLOSS-like learning communities in formal educational settings (Meiszner, 2008).

This paper examines the many opportunities that FLOSS provides for SE education. First, necessary requirements for effective SE educa-

tion are discussed and a brief description of major content that is expected to be found in a SE curriculum is given, based on ACM and SWEBOK reports. Next, each sub-area of a SE curriculum is analyzed, providing hints about plausible involvement of students in FLOSS projects as part of their practical exercise. Next, it is briefly discussed how ACM requirements are met and experiences from teaching with FLOSS, both at the undergraduate and graduate level are described. Finally, potential issues and problematic situations when FLOSS is used as a practice field are discussed and conclusions are provided along with certain future research topics.

OPEN SOURCE OPPORTUNITIES FOR FORMAL SOFTWARE EDUCATION

Software education requires theoretical instruction and practical training of some kind. It is not clear yet how FLOSS could help in teaching directly traditional SE theoretical concepts, since there is an abundant FLOSS literature but obviously it focuses on FLOSS. However, FLOSS projects often provide excellent examples of effective, successful projects producing qualitative software. Beside this, there are many FLOSS projects in which private software industry is already involved. FLOSS can have a significant contribution in SE education by helping students to exercise practical SE aspects.

At this point, it is interesting to remind the reader what ACM considers as Common Requirements of Computing Degrees in its *Computing Curricula 2005: The Overview Report (ACM, 2005)*[8] for every type of computing curriculum (i.e. either focusing on Computer Engineering, Computer Science, Information Technology, Informations Systems, or Software Engineering). That report requests initially six, mostly theoretical, requirements and then proceeds with the following four:

- "Identification and acquisition of skill sets that go beyond technical skills. Such skill sets include interpersonal communication skills, team skills, and management skills as appropriate to the discipline....
- Exposure to an appropriate range of applications and case studies that connect theory and skills learned in academia to real-world occurrences to explicate their relevance and utility.
- Attention to professional, legal, and ethical issues so that students acquire, develop, and demonstrate attitudes and priorities that honor, protect, and enhance the profession's ethical stature and standing.
- Demonstration that each student has integrated the various elements of the undergraduate experience by undertaking, completing, and presenting a capstone project."

We believe that these requirements can be effectively met by combining formal SE education with FLOSS. It is interesting to note that FLOSS participants reported during a survey at high percentages (35-47%) that they acquired basic/introductory programming, managing complex software systems, testing etc skills in a period of two years (Ghosh, 2005). We evangelize full-scale deployment of the involvment of SE students in FLOSS projects as part of their practical training, after they are taught SE theory according to a standard formal training process. Such approach is not meant to be deployed only in avanced SE courses as has been done occasionally up to now. It is meant to be used mainly in SE undergraduate curricula, taking sufficient precautions. Under this point of view the basic teaching scheme would be as shown in Fig. 1.

According to this scheme, students are given basic, theoretical knowledge on any SE topic in class lectures and provided with examples from their books and other reading material as usual. Next, examples picked from FLOSS projects introduce students to the real SE world. Students

Figure 1. Basic teaching scheme

Stage 1: Theoretical concepts (in class)
↓
Stage 2: Book examples (in class)
↓
Stage 3: Real case examples (taken from FLOSS projects, in class)
↓
Stage 4: Real case investigation (in FLOSS projects)
↓
Stage 5: Lab / Project exercise (participation in FLOSS, lab)

are prompted to investigate SE materials (documentation, code, discussion materials, etc) that are abundant in FLOSS projects. As practical training, students are asked to fulfill predefined tasks by entering a FLOSS project (and community) and reporting back the artefacts they produced, feedback from the community and the overall contribution they made to the project. We now proceed by implementing the last two stages of the proposed approach in a hypothetical SE Curricilum.

AN ENHANCED SOFTWARE ENGINEERING EDUCATION CURRICULUM

According to the IEEE Guide on Software Engineering Body of Knowledge[9], major software engineering knowledge areas are shown in Table 1 along with their potentiality for and suitability to the proposed approach. A comprehensive SE teaching module should include all of these subareas. In addition, modern SE Curricula include knowledge areas that are common with other disciplines, e.g. business modeling that is akin to Information Systems.

We now proceed with examining each area to determine educational opportunities that FLOSS offers. At the end a comprehensive template is provided for each sub-area, identifying the tasks that may be assigned to students and the way students' results may be assessed. Common items in student grading are community feedback and

Table 1. Software engineering knowledge areas according to SWEBOK and degree of educational opportunities in FLOSS on a 1 to 5 scale

Software engineering knowledge area	Degree of FLOSS Educational opportunities
Software requirements	3
Software design	3
Software construction	3
Software testing	4
Software maintenance	3
Software configuration management	2
Software engineering management	2
Software engineering process	2
Software engineering tools and methods	3
Software quality	4

peer review. Community feedback is of paramount importance: if project participants consider the work of a student useful, the assignment has been accomplished with success. Community feedback can take the form of e-mails or messages to discussion lists, thanking students for their contribution or commenting on their work. However, there is still room for assessment by teachers, e.g. judgment on degree of adherence to pre-specified standards. On the other hand, because typically each student would be assigned to a different project, assessment of many different assignments would be necessary, a cumbersome and time demanding task for the instructor. Peer review (each student assesses at least one other student assignment) can help to reduce this overload.

Software Requirements

Requirements specifications are scarce in FLOSS (Scacchi, 2001). It is reasonable to presume that requirements specifications would be found only for big FLOSS projects. However because of the lack of requirements documents for most of its projects, FLOSS does provide an interesting field for practice: its unspecified thousands of projects can be a target for practical exercise by the students. Therefore the following topics apply as candidates for student assignments:

1. Requirement Document Assessment: students may inspect available requirement documentation of any kind in major FLOSS projects. They may apply typical rules of requirement quality inspection, ensuring that requirement documentation is detailed enough and updated with current release features. They can also check whether requirements are correct, complete and consistent by downloading and executing the program. Students are asked to inform the community on the outcome of their analysis, proposing improvements and amendments to the existing requirements as appropriate. Students are graded according to community feedback and extent of requirement improvement.

2. Requirement Document Production: students are asked to prepare a requirement document for a project that does not possess one or that is partially specified. In the latter case they may produce requirements for non-specified features or non-functional requirements that have been already implemented. Alternatively they may be asked to select requested features from project forums, discussion lists or wish-lists and specify them to help in their better and faster implementation by the community. Students are asked to inform the community on the outcome of their analysis, proposing improvements and amendments to the existing requirements as appropriate. Students are graded according to community feedback (acceptance of requirement documents as official project documents, number of features specified, quality of their work, community feedback on the amount of interesting information they produced).

3. Peer review of other students' work on requirements: identify missed, incorrect, inconsistent requirements. This may be a partial assignment, complementing one of the previously proposed tasks. Students are graded by community feedback on their comments and answers from the original requirement authors.

Students are graded according to acceptance of requirement documents as official project documents, number of features specified, quality of their work, community feedback on the amount of interesting information student produced and review from peers.

Software Design

Teaching software architecture and design with FLOSS has a lot of common characteristics with teaching software requiremens. Software design documents, such as software architecture documents and detailed designs are hard to find in FLOSS. For large projects there is some documentation, typically a high-level architectural block diagram[10]. FLOSS projects rely heavily on code as a means of documenting software architecture at various levels. As with requirements, students may be asked to contribute towards filling this gap. Therefore, the following topics apply as candidates for student assignments:

1. Design Document Assessment: students may inspect available requirement documentation in major FLOSS projects. They may apply typical rules of design quality inspection, ensuring that design documentation is detailed enough and updated with current release features. They can also check whether design information is correct, complete and consistent by downloading and executing the program. Students are asked to inform the community on the outcome of their analysis, proposing improvements and amendments to

the existing architecture / design blueprints. Students are graded according to community feedback and extent of design improvement.

2. Design Document Production: students are asked to prepare an architecture or detailed design document for a project that possesses partial or no such documentation at all. They may produce high level block designs, UML diagrams or detailed algorithm descriptions. Because it is possible that the amount of documentation can require significant more work than expected in a typical student semester project, it is essential that the student proposes an outline of what he intends to do and get teachers' approval before proceeding. Applying all possible UML diagrams for example may be just too much. Fortunately, lightweight software processes are available, such as ICONIX (Rosenberg, 2007) that may help in rightsizing students' workload. As before, students are asked to inform the community on the outcome of their analysis, proposing improvements and amendments to the existing designs whenever appropriate. Students are graded according to community feedback (acceptance of design documents as official project documents, depth of analysis, quality of their work, community feedback on the amount of interesting information they produced).

3. Peer review of other students' work on designs: identify missing, incorrect, inconsistent design elements w.r.t. to requirements (if there are any) and/or system execution. This may be a partial assignment, complementing one of the previously proposed tasks. Students are graded by community feedback on their comments and answers from the original document authors.

An interesting alternative would be to ask students to study FLOSS design pattern libraries, such as the one by the FLUID project[11].

Software Construction

This is probably the most delicate SE area since because it is the first SE course where students will have to develop their basic programming skills. Participation in a FLOSS project for novice programmers can be very painful and frustrating if not organized well. In certain cases, weak students should avoid this task and maybe given alternative, old fashioned programming tasks. Nevertheless, for students who have acquired basic programming skills, FLOSS may also become their exercise field. As an example, consider the teaching of basic algorithms, in particular sorting algorithms. According to the proposed approach (Fig 1.) such module would consist of:

1. Presentation and discussion in class of various types of sorting algorithms (bubblesort, quicksort, etc). Exercises on sorting algorithms with book examples.
2. Presentation and discussion of examples of implementations of sorting algorithms taken from FLOSS code (a recent search on www.code.google.com produced 48 occurrences of the single term bubblesort only). Students are presented with real world application of the topic studied (stage 3 in Fig 2).
3. Students (possibly organized in teams) are invited to search for implementations of sorting algorithms within FLOSS code. After locating such pieces of code they are asked to study and understand them, and comment the code if necessary. They need to understand and describe only the data sorted, not the context of use of the algorithm. In this way they are also trained in understanding implementations of other programmers, a basic skill in modern software engineering.
4. Students are next asked as a weekly assignment to produce implementations in different algorithms, operating on the same data as the original one. They have to analyze the suitability and performance of each

implementation. They need to obtain basic information from the FLOSS project they are working in. This means that they might have to interact with community members, ask for assistance etc. Ideally, although not necessarily, they would obtain such help from the author of the code. Instructor acts basically as a mentor during the week.

5. Students present their solution in lab sessions. Instructor and students vote for the best solution and decide whether to commit it as an improvement to the project.

There is an important note to make here: the Curriculum must contain teaching of basic programming languages in its very first semester. This is the only way to ensure that students will be able to understand FLOSS code in C, C++ and Java, which are the most popular languages in FLOSS. Other languages such as Python and Perl have a significant share in FLOSS as well.

Software Testing

There is already practical experience with students practicing software testing in the context of a SE semester course (Sowe, 2006a; Sowe, 2006b). Students are asked to act as FLOSS participants, assuming one of the most frequent and critical roles in FLOSS, namely the role of tester. Students are prompted to choose a suitable FLOSS project/release. Suitability depends on the liveliness of the project and the maturity of the release. The project should be active (otherwise there is no community feedback) and the release should not be stable / mature (or there will be no bugs). Relevant information is often provided by the forges themselves. For example, SourceForge provides information for each project status, with predefined categories, such *as alpha, beta, production, stable, mature*, etc.

Student assignment here is rather uniform and consists of the following stages:

1. Bug detection
2. Bug reporting to the project
3. Assistance to the community for understanding the operation conditions that produced the bug, possibly providing hints for bug location
4. Monitoring of bug removal actions
5. Preparation of a comprehensive report on their activities

More details are given later, in Section 4.1

Software Maintenance

Typically, software maintenance costs have been reported to be much higher (up to four times) than software development costs. As a consequence, SE education needs to address carefully software evolution if SE students are supposed to be prepared to work in real software operation environments. While teaching software evolution to undergraduate students typically covers theoretical aspects, normally actual implementation related to system maintenance is not sufficiently addressed (Postema, 2001). FLOSS projects are maintenance projects to a large extent right from their very beginning. A FLOSS community typically develops and maintains the core of a system proposed by one or more individuals. As such, FLOSS projects are highly suitable for practicing software maintenance. As mentioned above, FLOSS is already used for such purposes and the reader should refer to (Petrenko, 2007) for one already implemented approach in this area.

Typical practice of software maintenance would require impact analysis, change propagation, refactoring, regression testing, etc. In brief, student assignments for learning software maintenance could be as follows: Initially students should select a target FLOSS system release (preferably the most recent one) and locate changes w.r.t. previous release(s) using appropriate tools and project's version control system (i.e. CVS or SVN) information. Then plausible assignment areas, based on the above mentioned software maintenance topics, are:

1. Impact analysis and Change propagation reporting. Students should examine the target release and previous release(s) and report on the impact that changes on the newest release have had on previous release(s).
2. Refactoring. Students should identify problematic areas in the code of the target release and attempt to refactor it accordingly. This assignment may be combined with assignments of the same or different students concerning software quality (see later in the paper).
3. Regression testing. This task is similar to the tasks proposed for Software Testing (see Section 3.4). One difference is that students focus on system faults that have been induced to previous release code because of newly inserted code.

Software Configuration Management

Configuration management is about managing successive versions of software artifacts as they become available throughout the FLOSS development cycle. Versioning in FLOSS is extremely important for at least two very good reasons: rapid succession of code releases, following the moto "release early, release often" (Raymond, 1998) and distributed, concurrent, around the clock development by a multitude of programmers. Tools such as CVS and SVN are the milestones of FLOSS projects and collect a wealth of information that makes FLOSS so interesting for empirical software engineering research.

This area has common characteristics with Software Maintenance. However, student practicing is not easy because configuration management is in the hands of the coordinators of FLOSS projects. Students should select FLOSS releases as described in Section 3.5. Then, practical student exercises may include:

1. Examination of configuration management policies in their FLOSS project: when new software is released, which are the release request mechanisms, who is responsible for releasing, etc. Students compare with closed source configuration management practices.

2. Examination of CVS/SVN contents. Students report on release contents and on the delta w.r.t. to previous release

3. Release emulation. Students may emulate the generation of a subsequent release of their FLOSS project in lab (stage 5 in Fig.1).

Software Engineering Management

FLOSS provides relatively few opportunities for software engineering (project) management w.r.t. to other areas. Practicing software project management involves activities such as studying the feasibility of implementing an idea, planning and scheduling the activities to implement the project, finding, selecting and deploying resources, monitoring project evolution, making decisions and reporting. While many of these activities are present in FLOSS projects, other are almost meaningless or non existent at all. In the following, we examine each one of these project management activities, and attempt to identify how FLOSS projects could be exploited:

1. Feasibility study: a FLOSS project rarely requires an extensive feasibility study. A feasibility study is a detailed investigation and analysis of a proposed development project to determine whether it is viable technically and economically. Before initiating a FLOSS project some technical analysis may be necessary. However, if the idea behind the project is interesting, there is hope that experienced programmers will be attracted and project implementation will become a reality. Economical analysis is not critical because of the volunteering

of project participants, availability of free hosting services by FLOSS forges etc.

2. Planning and scheduling: the need for planning and scheduling in FLOSS is also quite limited. Typically there is no deadline for project delivery as in closed source, although there might be some informal commitment by members of the community.

3. Resource management: major FLOSS resources are its programmers and resource management in FLOSS means mainly coordination of the efforts of volunteers. Configuration management has been discussed in Section 3.6.

4. Monitoring project evolution, Decision making, Reporting: these activities are made in rather informal ways w.r.t. the rigid management procedures that are followed in closed source development

As in the case of Software Configuration Management, control is exercised by FLOSS project coordinators. As a conclusion, FLOSS provides few opportunities for practicing most of typical project management activities. Even if such activities are present to some extent in a FLOSS project, it is not straightforward to guide SE students in applying traditional project management methods and tools on FLOSS projects. However, it is easy to instruct students on how to effectively manage themselves FLOSS projects! An assignment of this kind might be appropriate for a group capstone project, and might involve the following:

1. Propose an idea for a FLOSS project

2. Prepare the core of the system (this might necessitate significant design and coding work). Can be part of their assignment for Software Construction.

3. Initiate the project (on a forge), coordinate it and make the project become a success. Such a task would require the student group to exercise project coordination and monitoring,

and participate as users and/or developers in the project themselves. Other management activities such as decision making (e.g. when to release) will also become necessary as the project evolves.

In this particular task, student performance is assessed according to their project success (size of community, number of downloads, etc).

Software Engineering Process

Much of what has been said on project management applies to software engineering process as well. It is not reasonable for students to acquire experience on process models such as waterfall, the spiral model, or RUP when such processes are not practiced in FLOSS. However, there are a couple of SE process areas in which students may gain practical knowledge:

1. Study and understand FLOSS processes. Not all FLOSS projects are run following the same process (Capiluppi, 2002). Students may be asked to study successful FLOSS project processes and describe them in detail.
2. Model FLOSS processes using process modeling tools and languages. This is an exercise of research interest, since there is little work on formal FLOSS process desciption.

Software Engineering Tools and Methods

Teaching SE tools involves investigation of the taxonomy of such tools and their possible architectures. Practical training requires the application of such tools on the development and management of software. FLOSS has produced a number of successful, widely used software engineering tools in many areas. One example of successful software development tool is ECLIPSE[12], while an example of FLOSS tool for software manage-

ment is Subversion (SVN[13]). Students may acquire knowldge about SE tools by:

1. Analysing the families of SE tools e.g. on SourceForge or Tigris. Studens should report on the kinds of tools they encounter, their success and degree of use, detect trends in tooling, etc.
2. Examining and reporting on FLOSS SE tools. Students should download, execute the FLOSS tools they choose and report on their characteristics, comparing them with other known tools.
3. Applying SE tools in combination with other assignments such as those mentioned in software design or construction.

Software Quality

Software quality is a critical SE issue, and it is often neglected while developing closed source software, mainly because of the need to respect strict deadlines. On the other hand, in many cases, specific quality levels are required by contract, and quality control is intense for particularly demanding software applications such as safety critical systems. In FLOSS, quality is optional: there are no contracts that impose specific quality requirements, since often there are no detailed requirements at all. However, many FLOSS projects manage to achieve impressive quality levels because of the rather informal but effective quality assurance procedures imposed by the communities. One recent development is the availability of FLOSS repositories, observatories and quality assessment web based systems (e.g. SQO-OSS[14], QUALOSS[15], FLOSSMETRICS[16]). Such systems provide or will provide in the close future free services for the quantified assessment of the quality of FLOSS code, based on structural metrics and other relevant information (such as strength of community). In particular, the SQO-OSS system provides a plug-in architecture that can easily accommodate new measurement tools.

After being taught in class software quality theory and formal quality procedures and tools, such as quality models, formal checklist based inspections and audits, students may be asked to accomplish the following tasks:

1. Study and report quality procedures in selected FLOSS projects, in which the communities or coordination teams have imposed specific quality related rules and guidelines. Coding standards are of particular interest. Compare with analogous closed source procedures.
2. Apply quality tools in their own assignments (e.g. those mentioned in software construction)
3. Perform measurements of FLOSS software quality using relevant FLOSS tools or the quality measurement systems mentioned above. Compare FLOSS products of similar functionality. If possible, compare FLOSS with closed source software quality. Report on the effectiveness and usefulness of FLOSS quality assessment systems.
4. Develop plug-in tools for FLOSS quality assessment systems, as part of their assignment for software construction

As a conclusion we may state that FLOSS is not suitable for teaching formal quality procedures, but is highly suitable for providing an environment where students may experience and apply effective software quality practices.

Table 2 summarizes the types of assignments and proposed kinds of assessment per each SE area when using FLOSS for practical training. Types of assessment are given in order of preference. Note that Community feedback, whenever exists, normally prevails on instructor assessment and student peer review is always given the lowest preference. In certain cases (e.g. impact analysis) IA is preferred to CF because it is considered that FLOSS communities do not practice often such SE tasks in a formal way.

EXPERIENCES FROM TEACHING SE AND INFORMATION SYSTEMS WITH FLOSS

As mentioned above, at the Department of Informatics of the Aristotle University of Thessaloniki, we have been trying to implement one version of the approach proposed in this paper for three consecutive years. Such trial application was on the course of Introduction to Software Engineering (5th semester in a 8-semester undergraduate Curriculum) and on the Course of Enterprise Information Systems (Information and Management Master Program).

Introduction to Software Engineering

The course covers basic concepts of software life cycle, requirements, design, testing and coding. Students were asked to volunteer for the first two years. FLOSS project participation became obligatory in third year, which is still incomplete. Table 3 reports some figures on this trial application. Initially, the proposed project consisted of only software testing activities, but in the third year students were offered the possibility to choose among requirements, testing and coding. Most of them preferred requirements (23) to testing (13) and coding (3). Out of some 150 students, 11 volunteered during first and 21 during second trial year, while 39 assignments have been completed in the third year up to now. A detailed report on students' performance and assessment can be found in (Sowe, 2006a) and (Sowe, 2006b). Initially, students were afraid to embark in what they considered to be an adventure, but they gradually gained confidence when they realized that their assignment was feasible and discussed it with their previous years' colleagues.

One tool for assisting students in their task was the preparation of a user guide (and a slide presentation) based on it. Among other information, the guide provided:

Table 2. Types of assignments and assessment per SE area

SE area	Type of assignment	Type of assessment
Software Requirements	Requirement Document Assessment Requirement Document Production	IA CF, IA, SPR,
Software design	Design Document Assessment Design Document Production	IA CF, IA, SPR
Software construction	Research for Algorithm/Problem Solving Implementation Implementation of Algorithms/Problem Solutions	IA CF, IA, SPR
Software testing	Bug Finding Bug Reporting Bug fixing	CF, IA, SPR CF, IA, SPR CF, IA, SPR
Software maintenance	Impact/ change analysis Refactoring Regression Testing	IA, CF, PR CF, IA, SPR CF, IA, SPR
Software configuration management	CM Process analysis Release Content Analysis Release Emulation	IA IA IA, SPR
Software engineering management	FLOSS Project Proposal FLOSS Project Coordination FLOSS Project Implementation	IA, SPR CF, IA CF, IA, SPR
Software engineering process	Process Analysis Process Modeling	IA IA
Software engineering tools and methods	SE Tool Family Analysis SE Tool Analysis SE Tool Application	IA IA, SPR IA, SPR
Software quality	FLOSS Quality Procedure Analysis Quality Measurements (activities common with Software Construction)	IA IA, SPR

IA = Instructor Assessment, CF = Community Feedback, SPR = Student Peer Review

Table 3. Student activity report

	2005-2006 only volunteers	2006-2007 only volunteers	2007-2008 obligatory project
SE areas	Software Testing	Software Testing	Software Testing Software Requirements Software Construction
No of Student projects completed	11	21	39 (on-going, partial results)
Results	involved in 16 FLOSS projects, reported 68 bugs, received 43 replies	involved in 24 FLOSS projects, reported 105 bugs, received 218 replies	N/A

1. a short explanation of the FLOSS world
2. a description of the assignment
3. short user guides for basic FLOSS tools (e.g. CVS/SVN, Bugzilla)
4. guidelines for choosing the correct project
5. pointers to useful material (e.g. similar successful student projects, FLOSS documents)

Note that this guide not only provided technical information, but implicitly provided psychological support aiming to raise the morale of suspicious, low motivated students, demonstrating to them that their assignment is feasible. Another important help for students was the availability of a dedicated lab for accessing FLOSS projects and implementing their assignment under the supervision and help of teaching assistants. A standard course assessment questionnaire was filled by the students at the end of the lectures (project was still on-going). The students still considered their assignment hard (compared to other, traditional, assignments) but they collectively appreciated the help they were given by their teachers and the availability of the lab facility.

Teaching Enterprise Information Systems

Teaching of Enterprise Information Systems is one Computer Science area that is also appropriate for exploiting FLOSS. In recent years, FLOSS has shifted from building operating systems and desktop software (utilities, e-mail clients etc) to developing vertical, end-user applications, such as finance software, ERP/CRM systems etc. This creates an interesting opportunity for students to explore a wealth of business applications spanning different business functions of a modern enterprise: marketing, finance, accounting, production, human resource management.

The assignment that is described here is given to students of an introductory Enterprise Information Systems course at the Master level (Master course on Informatics and Management). Students have a background in Finance and Management (they are not Computer Scientists) and only theoretical knowledge about Enterprise Information Systems. Their assignment is meant to show them both the way the FLOSS world is structured and functions and the variety of FLOSS solutions provided to enterprises nowadays.

Through a short introduction in class about FLOSS, the students receive information about basic FLOSS concepts, ways of organization of FLOSS projects, available forges, FLOSS tools and FLOSS applications in general. Next, the following steps are taken:

1. Students are directed to one or two consultant sites for enterprise application systems[17]. Such sites provide white papers and experience reports coming from consultants, companies and vendors. Students become familiar with available system taxonomies and market terms used to describe modern business applications offered to enterprises. They are asked to choose a class of Information Systems they find interesting and prepare a short presentation of it, along with the presentation of a white paper or report of their choice.

2. Students are given a list of forges and they are asked to locate FLOSS products that belong to the class of systems of step 1. Then they are asked to choose one or two "interesting" FLOSS products. Interest of a FLOSS product depends on the size of the community, the number of downloads, the lifetime of the project, commit rate, code growth, amount of positive comments and assessments found on forums and discussion lists, etc.

3. After choosing their target FLOSS projects, the students have to read any available documentation on them (descriptions, reports, user manuals, etc) to understand the functionality they offer, and must register basic facts about the growth of the project. Optionally, students may download and experiment with their product (this is not always feasible, since sometimes students choose large systems).

4. Students have to assess functionality and quality of their target by using the available web tools for FLOSS assessment from business point of view (QSOS[18], Open_BRR[19], etc). These models require input data from

their users, therefore students have to use the data they collected in previous step.

5. Finally, students have to compile a comprehensive report, containing any interesting information they have gathered on their target, the results of any assessments they have performed, judgments of third parties they have encountered and their overall opinion. They must also present their work in class, receive questions and discuss their findings with their classmates and teacher. During fall semester of year 2007-2008, 20 students worked on this project, producing reports on a range of FLOSS applications. Most of them were about successful projects (MOODLE, Openbravo, etc) but in a couple of cases, "baby", almost inactive, FLOSS projects were also analyzed and reported

While FLOSS provides an incredible range of business applications, one must keep in mind that Enterprise Information Systems are not just complicated software and some hardware to run it on: they are users and business processes as well. There are many reported failed attempts of introducing advanced and promising information systems in enterprises, without taking care of user implications and business requirements. In addition, one potential problem of FLOSS is the lack of sufficient support. Therefore, practical student exercises such as the one described above, should be integrated with careful study of both FLOSS and closed source business cases, describing experiences with implementing, operating and maintaining Information Systems in an enterprise. Students that participated in the Information System exercise described above, were also provided with access to a Case Based Learning System, namely e-CASE (Papadopoulos, 2006), which, among other content, contains successful and unsuccessful cases of such implementations, packaged in a learning-oriented shell. Students comments were very positive for this type of assignment. Although it does not contain practical

training on a system in a real enterpise environment, it does provide a wealth of information from real world information systems.

HOW ACM REQUIREMENTS ARE MET BY THE PROPOSED APPROACH

Referring back to the four ACM requirements mentioned above:

*   Identification and acquisition of skill sets that go beyond technical skills: involvement in FLOSS projects and participation in a FLOSS community enhances interpersonal communication skills, since students have to exchange information, formulate interesting, non-trivial questions and manage feedback from the community. In addition they must develop and exercise their team skills, because in many cases they will have to enter a small team or cluster that deals with a specific problem (e.g. maintenance of a FLOSS module). Occasional sprint meetings will further enhance this type of skill. They will also develop their management skills when they will initiate and coordinate a FLOSS project of their own.
*   Exposure to an appropriate range of applications and case studies that connect theory and skills learned in academia to real-world occurrences: During stage 3 in Fig.1, students will explore and become familiar with real world applications and be given the opportunity to assess themselves the knowledge they have received during the first two stages of Fig 1. During stages 4 and 5 they produce practical results related to real world systems.
*   Attention to professional, legal, and ethical issues: FLOSS projects have their own rules of behavior, demanding their partici-

pants to be sincere, useful volunteers and respect each other. Yet, most interaction occurs in the context of a virtual, open community with little or no bureaucracy at all. However, FLOSS ecosystems are different than software industry settings in many ways, and students may need additional instruction on this topic (e.g. code ownership may be an issue in closed, non agile, software development).

- Demonstration that each student has integrated the various elements of the undergraduate experience by undertaking, completing, and presenting a capstone project: With the proposed scheme, students may start and finish their studies working on the same FLOSS project, their capstone project. Significant gains stem from such continuity in project assignments, since students build upon their previous knowledge of their project and the bonds they have made with the community.

POTENTIAL PROBLEMS OF THE FLOSS BASED EDUCATION APPROACH

However the FLOSS education approach evangelized in this paper is not without pitfalls. Such problems must be addressed before starting using the approach because they may cause practical problems (difficulty in accessing the FLOSS projects and communities, ineffective cooperation with community, etc) and worst of all, early student disappointment and frustration. For example, during the Software Testing assignment described above, certain students reported problems in finding a suitable project, in finding sufficient number of bugs and in their interaction with the community. Potential problems and plausible solutions to them are the following:

- Student personality and temperament may not be appropriate for participation to FLOSS. For instance, extrovert types may be favored over introvert personality types, since communication with the community is of paramount importance. Personality and temperament tests (Keirsey, 1998) are already used in SE development and education situations (Sfetsos, 2004) and may help in determining students that might experience problems.

- Students may experience language problems when trying to participate actively in a FLOSS community. Typically, English is used in FLOSS communities, but other languages are also common, especially in "national" discussion lists. FLOSS communities tolerate non native English speakers but nevertheless instructors should take care of this problem by orientating their students either to projects using familiar languages or by avoiding to assign them tasks requiring heavy use of texts, such as documentation or specification. Alternatively, texts may be written in the student's preferred language. FLOSS projects still welcome such contributions, which are then translated to English or other languages by volunteers.

- Students may experience intimidation problems due to insulting behavior or flame throwing that may (rarely) occur when intermixed with an open, multicultural and multinational community. An alleviation to this problem is to instruct students on how to approach the community, how to discuss and how not to react in case they are provoked in some way.

- Not all FLOSS projects may be appropriate for educational purposes (e.g. projects with no activity, very few member community, no significant knowledge sharing taking place). Students should be guided on how to select their projects but more concrete methods and tools for such kind of project assessment are needed (see Conclusions and Further Research).

- Single or group student assignments? Some of the assignments proposed above may be suitable for one student (e.g. coding), while others may be more appropriate for groups of students (e.g. software maintenance assignments are assigned to groups of students in Petrenko, 2007). Instructors should choose the correct kind of assignment from this point of view, trading off between better student assessment (single student assignment) and better assessment effort balance (group projects).

We have already described two ways for assisting students in their quest, namely the guide and the lab facility mentioned above. One particular role found in FLOSS communities, namely *mentors*, may help to further alleviate many of those problems. Students that have successfully accomplished a FLOSS based assignment in one of their previous courses may serve as mentors for the students that are asked to do a similar kind of assignment during the current edition of the course. As an example, an experienced student may become mentor of students involved in requirements specification or students that have to do some task in the context of the same FLOSS project. Project participants may also undertake such role: if needed, instructors might approach project members and ask for mentorship. Finally, it must be noted that most of the above problems are inevitable if students are supposed to be immersed in a real world SE environment, whether it is a FLOSS or a software industry project. Nevertheless, in extreme cases, a safe choice for the instructor would be to provide his/her students with an alternative, old fashioned "toy" project as a practical assignment.

CONCLUSION AND FUTURE RESEARCH

This paper has proposed the consistent involvment of SE students in FLOSS projects to fulfill the requirements of a modern SE Curriculum for practical training. Few, known sporadic cases of such employment of FLOSS in SE education have been reviewed and a detailed proposal for such a consistent approach across all major SE areas has been presented and discussed. However, caution is necessary because of various potential problems students might encounter when actively involved with FLOSS communities. First impression is that students, although often worried about a potential failure to meet the assigned tasks, find this kind of endeavor interesting and challenging. On the other hand, FLOSS communities always wellcome students that approach them to fulfill their assignments and take profit of the results (documents, reports, code). We believe that with sufficient care, a SE academic teacher can easily shape a course on one of the SE topics examined.

Various opportunities for further research and improvement of what has been proposed in this paper exist. Many of the proposed tasks and ways of student assessment are subjective and academic instructors may take different paths while implementing a FLOSS based course. Wide aplication is the only way to provide broad, convincing field evidence about the potentiality of the proposed approach. Teaching advanced topics such as software component reuse with the use of formal methods is also another area worth of investigation, probably posing even more challenges. Empirical studies that will investigate the kind of combination of student mentality, personality type, temperament and skills that are appropriate for FLOSS based education are also necessary.

Further research is also necessary for FLOSS project pre-assessment. This tasks requires inspection of forge project classification indicators, but will probably require the use of more detailed analyses (e.g. through the use of FLOSS observatories such as SQO-OSS, that specialise on FLOSS quality assessment), and knowledge management specific indicators (e.g. metrics that denote the knowledge sharing activity of the project). In general, evaluation criteria for FLOSS projects, that will discriminate between suitable and to-be-avoided FLOSS projects must also be clearly defined and validated. There is a lot of space for reasearch and application of techniques (e.g. text mining) that will allow the identification of FLOSS material (pieces of code of every type and size, documentation, e-mails with high information content, etc) that is suitable for education purposes. One final point worth investigating is how FLOSS can help in teaching theoretical concepts, although at first sight it seems that there is no such straightforward approach.

As a final conclusion, SE courses in countries where software industry is not sufficiently developed to host all students for their practical training, may benefit from the proposed approach. Moreover, in the challenging and demanding area of Software Engineering education, advanced learning organizations offering FLOSS based courses and Curricula might obtain a competitive advantage over organizations offering traditional, better understood but with known limitations, SE education.

ACKNOWLEDGMENT

Sincere thanks to S. Sowe, A. Karoulis, E. Constantinou, and K. Moustaka for helping me to implement the student project part of the course on Software Engineering that is described in the paper. Many thanks to MERIT (R. Ghosh, R. Glott and K. Haaland) for hosting me during the preparation of this paper and for their many useful studies and surveys on FLOSS.

REFERENCES

Bonaccorsi, A., Lorenzi, D., Merito, M., & Rossi, C. (2007). Business Firms' Engagement in Community Projects. Empirical Evidence and Further Developments of the Research. In the Proceedings of First International Workshop on Emerging Trends in FLOSS Research and Development, 2007

Bulchand, J., Osorio, J., & Rodríguez, J. (2007). Information Technology for Education Management and Open Source Software: Improving Education Management through Open Source. In *Knowledge Management for Educational Innovation* (pp. 115–122). Boston: Springer. doi:10.1007/978-0-387-69312-5_15

Capiluppi, A., Lago, P., & Morisio, M. (2002). Characterizing the OSS Process. In Proceedings of the 2nd Workshop on Open Source Software Engineering, Orlando, FL, May 2002.

Ghosh, R., & Glott, R. (2005). FLOSSPOLS Skill Survey Report, available from: http://flossproject.org/papers/20050415/RishabGHOSH-padua-skills.pdf

Keirsey, D. (1998). *Please Understand Me II*. Del Mar, CA: Prometheus Nemesis Book Company.

Lundell, B., Persson, A., & Lings, B. (2007). Learning Through Practical Involvement in the OSS Ecosystem: Experiences from a Masters Assignment. In Proceedings of the Third International Conference on Open Source Systems 2007, 289-294

Meiszner, A., Sowe, S., & Glott, R. (2008). Preparing the Ne(x)t Generation: Lessons learned from Free/Libre Open Source Software. Fourth International Barcelona Conference on Higher Education: new challenges and emerging roles for human and social development, 2008. Jaccheri, L., Osterlie, T. (2007). Open Source Software: A Source of Possibilities for Software Engineering Education and Empirical Software Engineering. First International Workshop on Emerging Trends in FLOSS Research and Development, 2007.

Papadopoulos, P., Demetriadis, S., & Stamelos, I. (2006). Online Case-Based Learning: Design and Preliminary Evaluation of the eCASE Environment. Sixth IEEE International Conference on Advanced Learning Technologies, ICALT, 2006.

Petrenko, M., Poshyvanyk, D., Rajlich, V., & Buchta, J. (2007). Teaching Software Evolution in Open Source. *IEEE Computer*, *40*(11), 25–31.

Postema, M., Miller, J., & Dick, M. (2001). Including Practical Software Evolution in Software Engineering Education. In Proceedings of the 14th Conference on Software Engineering Education and Training, CSEET 2001, 127-135.

Raymond, E. (1998). The Cathedral and the Bazaar. *First Monday*, *3*(3). http://www.firstmonday. org/issues/issue3_3/raymond/index.html.

Rosenberg, D., & Stephens, M. (2007). *Use Case Driven Object Modeling with UML: Theory and Practice*. New York: Springer-Verlag.

Scacchi, W. (2001). Understanding the Requirements for Developing Open Source Software Systems. *IEE Proceedings. Software*, *149*(1), 24–39. doi:10.1049/ip-sen:20020202

Sfetsos, P., Stamelos, I., Angelis, L., & Deligiannis, I. (2006). Investigating the Impact of Personality Types on Communication and Collaboration-Viability in Pair Programming - An Empirical Study. In *Proceedings of eXtreme Programming (XP) 2006* (pp. 43–52). Springer-Verlag. doi:10.1007/11774129_5

Sowe, S., Angelis, L., & Stamelos, I. (2006c). Identifying Knowledge Brokers that Yield Software Engineering Knowledge in OSS Projects. *Information and Software Technology, Elsevier*, *48*(11), 1025–1033. doi:10.1016/j.infsof.2005.12.019

Sowe, S., Angelis, S., & Stamelos, I. (2006b). An Empirical Approach To Evaluate Students Participation In Open Source Software Projects. In the Proceedings of IADIS Cognitive and Exploratory Learning in the Digital Age (CELDA) 2006, 304-308.

Sowe, S., & Stamelos, I. (2006a). A Framework for Teaching Software Testing using F/OSS Methodology. In Proceedings of the 2nd International Conference on Open Source Systems 2006, Springer Verlag, 261-266.

Spinellis, D. (2006). Prof. Diomidis Spinellis, Personal communication, Athens, 2006.

Staring, K., & Titlestad, O. H. (2006). Networks of Open Source Health Care Action. In the Proceedings of the 2nd International Conference on Open Source Systems, Springer-Verlag, 135-141.

Staring. K., Titlestad, O. H., Gailis, J. (2005). Educational transformation through open source approaches, IRIS'28 Meeting. http://wwwold.hia. no/iris28/Docs/IRIS2028-1106.pdf

ENDNOTES

[1] Part of the work described in this paper has been supported by the EU funded FLOSS-Com Project, Reference: 229405 - CP -1- 2006-1- PT - MINERVA - M

[2] SourceForge, the world's largest development and download repository of Open Source code and applications, http://sourceforge.net

[3] MOODLE, Modular Object Oriented Dynamic Learning Environment, http://moodle.org/

[4] EDUBUNTU, Linux-based operating system for classroom use, http://www.edubuntu.org/

[5]   OLPC, One Laptop Per Child, a learning tool created expressly for children in developing countries, http://www.laptop.org/en/index.shtml

[6]   TIGRIS, Open Source Software Engineering Tools forge, www.tigris.org

[7]   http://forum.java.sun.com/thread.jspa?threadID=691833&messageID=4021508

[8]   ACM Computing Curricula 2005: The Overview Report (www.acm.org/education/curric_vols/CC2005-March06Final.pdf)

[9]   SWEBOK, Guide to the Software Engineering Body of Knowledge. IEEE Computer Society Press, 2004, http://www.bilkent.edu.tr/~bakporay/ctis_459/SWEBOK_Guide_2004.pdf

[10]   see for example http://wiki.zmanda.com/index.php/Software_architecture

[11]   FLUID (2008). http://wiki.fluidproject.org/display/fluid/Open+Source+Design+Pattern+Library

[12]   http://www.eclipse.org/eclipse/

[13]   http://subversion.tigris.org/

[14]   SQO-OSS, Software Quality Observatory for Open Source Software, http://www.sqo-oss.eu/

[15]   QUALOSS, QUALity in Open Source Software, http://www.qualoss.eu/

[16]   FLOSSMETRICS, Free/Libre Open Source Software Metrics, http://flossmetrics.org/

[17]   e.g. http://www.technologyevaluation.com

[18]   QSOS, Qualification and Selection of Open Source Software, http://www.qsos.org/

[19]   Open BRR, Open Business Readiness Rating, http://www.openbrr.org/wiki/index.php/Home

This work was previously published in International Journal of Open Source Software and Processes (IJOSSP), edited by Stefan Koch, pp. 72-90, copyright 2009 by IGI Publishing (an imprint of IGI Global).

Section 2

Chapter 6

What Makes Free/Libre Open Source Software (FLOSS) Projects Successful?
An Agent-Based Model of FLOSS Projects

Nicholas P. Radtke
Arizona State University, USA

Marco A. Janssen
Arizona State University, USA

James S. Collofello
Arizona State University, USA

ABSTRACT

The last few years have seen a rapid increase in the number of Free/Libre Open Source Software (FLOSS) projects. Some of these projects, such as Linux and the Apache web server, have become phenomenally successful. However, for every successful FLOSS project there are dozens of FLOSS projects which never succeed. These projects fail to attract developers and/or consumers and, as a result, never get off the ground. The aim of this research is to better understand why some FLOSS projects flourish while others wither and die. This article presents a simple agent-based model that is calibrated on key patterns of data from SourceForge, the largest online site hosting open source projects. The calibrated model provides insight into the conditions necessary for FLOSS success and might be used for scenario analysis of future developments of FLOSS.

Although the concept of Free/Libre Open Source Software (FLOSS) has been around for many years, it has recently increased in popularity as well as received media attention, not without good

reason. Certain characteristics of FLOSS are highly desirable: some FLOSS projects have been shown to be of very high quality (*Analysis of the Linux Kernel*, 2004; *Linux Kernel Software*, 2004) and to have low defect counts (Chelf, 2006);

DOI: 10.4018/978-1-60960-513-1.ch006

FLOSS is able to exploit parallelism in the software engineering process, resulting in rapid development (Kogut & Metiu, 2001); FLOSS sometimes violates Brooks' law (Rossi, 2004), which states that "adding manpower to a late software product makes it later" (Brooks, 1975); and FLOSS development thrives on an increasing user- and developer-base (Rossi, 2004).

As open source has become a prominent player in the software market, more people and companies are faced with the possibility of using open source products, which often are seen as free or low-cost solutions to software needs. However, choosing to use open source software is risky business, partly because it is unclear which FLOSS will succeed. To choose an open source project, only to find it stagnates or fails in the near future, could be disastrous, and is cited as a concern by IT managers (T. Smith, 2002). Accurate prediction of a project's likelihood to succeed/fail would therefore benefit those who choose to use FLOSS, allowing more informed selection of open source projects.

This article presents an initial step towards the development of an agent-based model that simulates the development of open source projects. Findings from a diverse set of empirical studies of FLOSS projects have been used to formulate the model, which is then calibrated on empirical data from SourceForge, the largest online site hosting open source projects. Such a model can be used for scenario and sensitivity analysis to explore the conditions necessary for the success of FLOSS projects.

BACKGROUND

There have been a limited number of attempts to simulate various parts of the open source development process (Dalle & David, 2004). For example, Dalle and David (2004) use agent-based modeling to create SimCode, a simulator that attempts to model where developers will focus their contribu-

tions within a single project. However, in order to predict the success/failure of a single FLOSS project, other existing FLOSS projects, which are vying for a limited pool of developers and users, may need to be considered. This is especially true when multiple FLOSS projects are competing for a limited market share (e.g., two driver projects for the same piece of hardware or rival desktop environments such as GNOME and the KDE). Wagstrom, Herbsleb, and Carley (2005) created OSSim, an agent-based model containing users, developers, and projects that is driven by social networks. While this model allows for multiple competing projects, the published experiments include a maximum of only four projects (Wagstrom et al., 2005). Preliminary work on modeling competition among projects is currently being explored by Katsamakas and Georgantzas (2007) using a system dynamics framework. By using a population of projects, it is possible to consider factors between the projects, e.g., the relative popularity of a project with respect to other projects as a factor that attracts developers and users to a particular project. Therefore, our model pioneers new territory by attempting to simulate across a large landscape of FLOSS with agent-based modeling.

Gao, Madey, and Freeh (2005) approach modeling and simulating the FLOSS community via social network theory, focusing on the relationships between FLOSS developers. While they also use empirical data from the online FLOSS repository SourceForge to calibrate their model, they are mostly interested in replicating the network structure and use network metrics for validation purposes (e.g. network diameter and degree). Our model attempts to replicate other emergent properties of FLOSS development without including the complexities of social networking. However, both teams consider some similar indicators, such as the number of developers working on a project, when evaluating the performance of the models.

In addition, there have been attempts to identify factors that influence FLOSS. These have ranged from pure speculation (Raymond's (2000) gift giving culture postulates) to surveys of developers (Rossi, 2004) to case studies using data mined from SourceForge (Michlmayr, 2005). Wang (2007) demonstrates specific factors can be used for predicting the success of FLOSS projects via K-Means clustering. However, this form of machine learning offers no insight into the actual underlying process that causes projects to succeed. Therefore, the research presented here approaches simulating the FLOSS development process using agent-based modeling instead of machine learning.

To encourage more simulation of the FLOSS development process, Antoniades, Samoladas, Stamelos, Angelis, and Bleris (2005) created a general framework for FLOSS models. The model presented here follows some of the recommendations and best practices suggested in this framework. In addition, Antoniades et al. (2005) developed an initial dynamical simulation model of FLOSS. Although the model presented here is agent-based, many of the techniques, including calibration, validation, and addressing the stochastic nature of the modeling process, are similar between the two models. One difference is the empirical data used for validation: Antoniades et al.'s (2005) model uses mostly code-level metrics from specific projects while the model presented here uses higher project-level statistics gathered across many projects.

IDENTIFYING AND SELECTING INFLUENTIAL FACTORS

Factors which are most likely to influence the success/failure of FLOSS must first be identified and then incorporated into the model. Many papers have been published in regards to this, but most of the literature simply speculates on what factors might affect the success and offers reasons why. Note that measuring the success of a FLOSS project is still an open problem: some

metrics have been proposed and used but unlike for commercial software, no standards have been established. Some possible success indicators are:

- Completion of the project (Crowston, Howison, & Annabi, 2006)
- Progression through maturity stages (Crowston & Scozzi, 2002)
- Number of developers
- Level of activity (i.e., bug fixes, new feature implementations, mailing list)
- Time between releases
- Project outdegree (Wang, 2007)
- Active developer count change trends (Wang, 2007)

English and Schweik (2007) asked eight developers how they defined success and failure of an open source project. Answers varied for success, but all agreed that a project with a lack of users was a failure. Thus having a sufficient user-base may be another metric for success.

Papers that consider factors influencing success fall into two categories: those that look at factors that directly affect a project's success (Michlmayr, 2005; Stewart, Ammeter, & Maruping, 2006; S. C. Smith & Sidorova, 2003) and those that look for factors that attract developers to a project (and thus indirectly affect the success of a project) (Bitzer & Schröder, 2005; Rossi, 2004; Raymond, 2000; Lerner & Tirole, 2005). A few go a step further and perform statistical analyses to discover if there is a correlation between certain factors and a project's success/failure (Lerner & Tirole, 2005; Michlmayr, 2005), and Kowalczykiewicz (2005) uses trends for prediction purposes. Wang (2007) demonstrates that certain factors can be used for accurate prediction using machine learning techniques. Koch (2008) considers factors affecting efficiency after first using data envelopment analysis to show that successful projects tend to have higher efficiencies.

In general, factors affecting FLOSS projects fall into two categories: technical factors and

Table 1. Agent properties

Property	Description	Type/Range
Consumer number	Propensity of an agent to consume (use) FLOSS.	Real [0.0, 1.0]
Producer number	Propensity of an agent to contribute to (develop) FLOSS.	Real [0.0, 1.0]
Needs vector	A vector representing the interests of the agent.	Each scalar in vector is real [0.0, 1.0]
Resources number	A value representing the amount of work an agent can put into FLOSS projects on a weekly basis. A value of 1.0 represents 40 hours.	Real [0.0, 1.5]
Memory	A list of projects the agent knows exist.	

social factors. Technical factors are aspects that relate directly to a project and its development and are typically both objective and easy to measure. Examples of technical factors include lines of code and number of developers.

The second category is social factors. Social factors pertain to aspects that personally motivate individuals to engage in open source development/use. Examples of social factors include reputation from working on a project, matching interests between the project and the developer/user, popularity of the project with other developers/users, and perceived importance of the code being written (e.g., core versus fringe development (Dalle & David, 2004)). Most of the social factors are subjective and rather difficult, if not impossible, to measure. Despite this, it is hard to deny that these might influence the success/failure of a project and therefore social factors are considered in the model. Fortunately, the social factors being considered fall under the domain of public goods, for which there is already a large body of work published (e.g., Ostrom, Gardner, & Walker, 1994; Jerdee & Rosen, 1974; Tajfel, 1981; Axelrod, 1984; Fox & Guyer, 1977). Most of this work is not specific to FLOSS, but in general it explores why people volunteer to contribute to public goods and what contextual factors increase these contributions.

The findings of this literature are applied when designing the model, as are findings from publications investigating how FLOSS works,

extensive surveys of developers asking why they participate in FLOSS (e.g., Ghosh, Krieger, Glott, & Robles, 2002), and comments and opinions of FLOSS users (e.g., T. Smith, 2002).

INITIAL MODEL

The model universe consists of agents and FLOSS projects. Agents may choose to contribute to or not contribute to, and to consume (i.e. download) or not consume FLOSS projects. At time zero, FLOSS projects are seeded in the model universe. These initial projects vary randomly in the amount of resources that will be required to complete them. At any time, agents may belong to zero, one, or more than one of the FLOSS projects. The simulation is run with a time step (t) equal to one (40 hour) workweek.

Table 1 contains the properties of agents. Table 2 contains the properties of projects.

At each time step, agents choose to produce or consume based on their producer and consumer numbers, values between 0.0 and 1.0 that represent probabilities that an agent will produce or consume. Producer and consumer numbers are statically assigned when agents are created and are drawn from a normal distribution. If producing or consuming, an agent calculates a utility score for each project in its memory, which contains a subset of all available projects. The utility function is shown in Box 1.

Table 2. Project properties

Property	Description	Type/Range
Current resources	The amount of resources or work being contributed to the project during the current time interval.	Real
Cumulative resources	The sum, over time increments, of all resources contributed to the project.	Real
Resources for completion	The total number of resources required to complete the project.	Real
Download count	The number of times the project has been downloaded.	Integer
Maturity	Six ordered stages a project progresses through from creation to completion.	{planning, pre-alpha, alpha, beta, stable, mature}
Needs vector	An evolving vector representing the interests of the developers involved in the project.	Each scalar in vector is real [0.0, 1.0]

Each term in the utility function represents a weighted factor that attracts agents to a project, where w_1 through w_5 are weights that control the importance of each factor, with $0.0 \leq w_1, w_2, w_3, w_4, w_5 \leq 1.0$ and. Factors were selected based on both FLOSS literature and our own understanding of the FLOSS development process. Keeping it simple, a linear utility equation is used for this version of the model. The first term represents the similarity between the interests of an agent and the direction of a project; it is currently calculated using cosine similarity between the agent's and project's needs vectors. The second term captures the current popularity of the project and the third term the size of the project implemented so far. The fourth term captures the popularity of a project with consumers based on the cumulative number of downloads a project has received. The fifth term captures the maturity stage of the project. Values with the subscript "norm" have been normalized (e.g., $downloads_{norm}$ is a project's download count divided by the maximum number of downloads that any project has received). The discreet function f maps each of the six maturity stages into a value between 0.0 and 1.0, corresponding to the importance of each maturity stage in attracting developers. Since all terms are normalized, the utility score is always a value between 0.0 and 1.0. Both consumers and producers use the same utility function. This is logical, as most FLOSS developers are also users of FLOSS. For consumers that are not producers, arguably the terms represented in the utility function are still of interest when selecting a project. There is relatively little research published on users compared to developers of FLOSS, so it is unclear if selection criteria are different between the two groups.

It is possible that some of the terms included in the utility function are redundant or irrelevant. Part of the model exploration is to determine which of these factors are relevant. See the Calibrating the Model and Results sections below.

Box 1.

```
utility = w₁ similarity (agentNeeds, projectNeeds)
        + w₂currentResources_norm
        + w₃cumulativeResources_norm
        + w₄downloads_norm
        + w₅ f(maturity)                        (1)
```

Agents use utility scores in combination with a multinominal logit equation to probabilistically select projects. The multinominal logit allows for imperfect choice, i.e., not always selecting the projects with the highest utility.

There is no explicit formulation of communication between agents included in the model; implicitly it is assumed that agents share information about other projects and thus agents know characteristics of projects they are not currently consuming/producing. At each time step, agents update their memory. With a certain probability an agent will be informed of a project and add it to its memory, simulating discovering new projects. Likewise, with a certain probability an agent will remove a project from its memory, simulating forgetting about or losing interest in old projects. Thus, over time an agent's memory may expand and contract.

Projects update their needs vector at each iteration using a decaying equation, where the new vector is partially based on the project's previous vector and partially on the needs vectors of the agents currently contributing to the project. An agent's influence on the project's vector is directly proportional to the amount of work the agent is contributing to the project with respect to other agents working on the same project. This represents the direction of a project being influenced by the developers working on it. Finally, project maturity stages are computed based on percent complete threshold values.

VALIDATION METHOD

Creating a model that successfully predicts the success or failure of FLOSS projects is a complicated matter. To aid in the iterative development process, the model is first calibrated to reproduce a set of known, emergent properties from real world FLOSS data. For example, Weiss (2005) surveyed the distribution of projects at SourceForge in each of six development categories: planning, pre-

alpha, alpha, beta, stable, and mature. Therefore, the model will need to produce a distribution of projects in each stage similar to that measured by Weiss. In addition, two other emergent properties were chosen to validate the initial model:

- Number of developers per FLOSS project.
- Number of FLOSS projects per developer.

By creating a model that mimics a number of key patterns of the data, confidence is derived about the model.

CALIBRATING THE MODEL

The model has a number of parameters that must be assigned values. A small subset of these can be set to likely values based on statistics gathered from surveys or mined from FLOSS repository databases. For the remaining parameters, a search of the parameter space must be performed to find the combination that allows the model to most closely match the empirical data. Since an exhaustive search is not practical, the use of genetic algorithms from evolutionary computation is used to explore the parameter space (Kicinger, Arciszewski, & De Jong, 2005). This is done as follows: an initial population of model parameter sets is created randomly. The model is run with each of the parameter sets and a fitness score is calculated based on the similarity of the generated versus empirical data. The parameter values from these sets are then mutated or crossed-over with other parameter sets to create a new generation of model parameter sets, with a bias for selecting parameters sets that resulted in a high fitness; then the new generation of parameter sets are evaluated and the process repeated. In this case, a genetic algorithm is being used for a stochastic optimization problem for which it is not known when a global optimum is found. Genetic algorithms are appropriate for finding well-performing solutions in a reasonably brief amount of time. Reviewing

Box 2.

$$fitness = 1 - \frac{sum\ of\ square\ of\ errors}{maximum\ possible\ sum\ of\ square\ of\ errors} \qquad (2)$$

the values of the best performing parameters will help identify which factors are important/influential in the open source software development process.

The fitness function chosen for the genetic algorithm is based on the sum of the square of errors between the simulated and empirical data, as shown in Box 2.

Since there are three fitness values calculated, one per empirical data set, the three fitness values are averaged to provide a single value for comparison purposes.

RESULTS

Since the model includes stochastic components, multiple runs with a given parameter set were performed and the results averaged. In this case, four runs were performed for each parameter set after initial experimentation showed very low standard deviations even with small numbers of runs. The averaged model results were then compared to the empirical data.

As empirical investigations of FLOSS evolution note, it takes approximately four years for a project of medium size to reach a mature stage (Krishnamurthy, 2002). Thus, the model's performance was evaluated by running the model for 250 time steps, with a time step of one week, for a total simulated time equivalent of a little over five years. All metrics were gathered immediately following the 250th time step.

The averaged data (over 4 runs) from the simulator's best parameter set, along with the empirical data, is shown in Figs. 1, 2, and 3.

Figure 1 shows the generated percentage of projects in each maturity stage is a similar shape to the empirical data, with the main difference being the highs are too high and the lows are too low in the simulated data. This disparity may be a result of initial model startup conditions. At time 0, the model starts with all projects in the planning stage. This is obviously different than SourceForge, where the projects were gradually added over time, not all at once in the beginning. While the model does add new projects each time step, with a growth rate based on the rate of increase of projects at SourceForge, it may take more than 250 time steps for maturity stages to stabilize after the differing initial condition. At the end of the simulation run, just short of 60% of the projects were created sometime during the simulation while the remaining 40% were created at time 0.

As shown in Figure 2, the number of developers per projects follows a near-exponential distribution and the simulated data is similar, especially for projects with fewer than seven developers. Note that the data in Figure 2 uses a logarithmic scale to

Figure 1. Percentage of FLOSS projects in maturity stages. Empirical data from (Weiss, 2005)

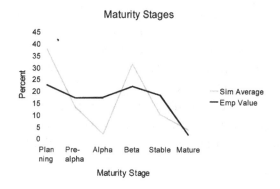

Figure 2. Percentage of projects with N developers. Empirical data from (Weiss, 2005)

Figure 3. Percentage of developers with N projects. Empirical data from (Ghosh et al., 2002)

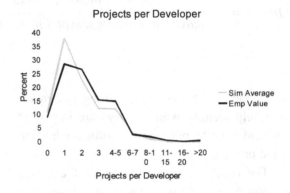

help with a visual comparison between the two data sets. Beyond seven developers, the values match less closely, although this difference is visually amplified as a result of the logarithmic scale and is actually not as large as it might initially appear. Since there are few projects with large numbers of developers in the empirical data, the higher values may be in the noise anyhow and thus focus should be on the similarity of the lower numbers.

Figure 3 shows the number of projects per developer is a relatively good match between the simulated and empirical data, with the main difference being the number of developers working on one project. It is likely that this could be corrected via additional experimentation with parameters.

Table 3 contains the average fitness scores for each of the emergent properties for the top performing parameter set. These values provide a quantitative mechanism for confirming the visual comparisons made above: the maturity stage fitness score is indeed lower than the other two properties. The combined fitness is simply the mean of the three fitness scores, although this value could be calculated with uneven weights if, say, matching each property was prioritized. Doing so would affect how the genetic algorithm explored the parameter space. It may be the case that certain properties are easy to reproduce in the model and work over a wide range of pa-

rameter sets, in which case these properties may be weighted less than properties that are more difficult to match. Properties which are always matched should be discarded from the model for evolution purposes as they do not discriminate against different parameter sets.

Finally, examining the evolved utility weights of the top 10 performing parameter sets provides insight into what factors are important in the model for reproducing the three properties examined. Table 4 contains the averages and standard deviations for each of the weights. It appears that the cumulative number of resources and download counts are not important in reproducing the examined properties in the model. This conclusion is reached by observing these weights' small values (low mean and small variance) in comparison to the other weights (high means and

Table 3. Averaged fitness scores for the best performing parameter set for the three emergent properties

Emergent Property	Fitness Score
Maturity stage	0.9679
Devs per project	0.9837
Projects per dev	0.9938
Combined	0.9818

Table 4. Utility function weights from the 10 best performing parameter sets

Weight	Mean	Std. Dev.
w_1 (similarity)	0.1849	0.1137
w_2 (current resources)	0.3964	0.1058
w_3 (cumulative resources)	0.0003	0.0003
w_4 (downloads)	0.0022	0.0039
w_5 (maturity)	0.4163	0.1534

Table 5. Evolved producer/consumer number distributions parameters

Producer/Consumer Number		Parameter statistics from top 10 parameter sets	
		Mean	Std. Dev.
Producer number	Mean	0.9801	0.0079
	Std. Dev.	0.1104	0.0101
Consumer number	Mean	0.6368	0.1979
	Std. Dev.	0.3475	0.3737

larger variance). Unfortunately, the high variance of the remaining three weights makes it difficult to rank them in order of importance. Rather, the conclusion is that similarity, current resources, and maturity are all important in the model.

Another interesting set of values evolved by the system are the parameters for the producer and consumer numbers. While the producer and consumer numbers are drawn from normal distributions bounded by 0.0 and 1.0 inclusive, neither the mean nor standard deviations of these distributions are known. Therefore, these values are evolved to find the best performing values. Table 5 contains the evolved mean and standard deviation for the producer and consumer numbers averaged from the top 10 parameter sets. Notice that the mean producer number is very high at 0.9801 and very stable across the top 10 parameter sets, with a standard deviation of 0.0079. Likewise, the standard deviation is relatively low at 0.1104 and also stable with a standard deviation of 0.0101. This indicates that the top performing model runs had agents with high propensities to develop. In other words having most agents produce frequently (i.e., most agents be developers) produces better matching of the empirical data. This is in alignment with the notion that FLOSS is a developer-driven process. The evolved consumer number mean is much lower and standard deviation is much higher compared to the producer number. Neither one of these parameters is particularly stable, i.e., both have large standard deviations over the top 10 parameter sets. This

indicates that the consumer number distribution has little effect on matching the empirical data for the top 10 parameter sets. Note that this is in alignment with the evolved weight for downloads approaching 0.0 in the utility functions. Consumers are not the driving force in matching the empirical data in the model.

DISCUSSION

Once developers join a project, it is likely that they will continue to work on the same project in the future. This is especially evident in the case of core developers, who typically work on a project for an extended period of time. Currently, the model attempts to reproduce this characteristic by giving a boost (taking the square root) of the utility function for projects worked on in the previous time step. In effect, this increases the probability of an agent selecting the same projects to work on in the subsequent time step. Improvements to the model might include adding a switching cost term to the utility function, representing the extra effort required to become familiar with another project. Gao et al. (2005) address this issue by using probabilities based off data from SourceForge to determine when developers continue with or leave a project they are currently involved with in their FLOSS model.

The model's needs vectors serve as an abstraction for representing the interests and corresponding functionalities of the agents and projects respectively. Therefore, the needs vector is at the crux of handling the matching of developers' interests with appropriate projects. For simplicity, initial needs vector values are assigned via a uniform distribution, but exploration of the effects of other distributions may be interesting. For example, if a normal distribution is used, projects with vector components near the mean will have an easy time attracting agents with similar interests. Projects with vector components several standard deviations from the mean may fail to attract any agents. A drawback of a normal distribution is that it makes most projects similar; in reality, projects are spread over a wide spectrum (e.g., from operating systems and drivers to business applications and games), although the actual distribution is unknown and difficult to measure.

Currently, needs vectors for projects and agents are generated independently. This has the problem of creating projects which have no interest to any agents. An improvement would be to have agents create projects; when created, a project would clone its associated agent's needs vector (which would then evolve as other agents joined and contributed to the project). This behavior would more closely match SourceForge, where a developer initially registers his/her project. By definition, the project matches the developer's interest at time of registration.

For simplicity's sake, currently the model uses a single utility function for both producers and consumers. It is possible that these two groups may attach different weights to factors in the utility function or may even have two completely different utility functions. However, analysis of the model shows that developers are the driving force to reproduce the empirical data. Exploration of a simplified model without consumers may show that concerns about using multiple utility functions are irrelevant.

One final complication with the model is its internal representations versus reality. For example, a suggested strategy for success in open source projects is to release early and release often (Raymond, 2000). Using this method to determine successful projects within the model is problematic because the model includes no concept of releasing versions of software. Augmenting the model to include a reasonable representation of software releases is non-trivial, if possible at all. Likewise, it is difficult to compare findings of other work on conditions leading to success that map into this model. For example, Lerner and Tirole (2005) consider licensing impacts while Michlmayr (2005) consider version control systems, mailing lists, documentation, portability, and systematic testing policy differences between successful and unsuccessful projects. Unfortunately, none of these aspects easily map into the model for comparison or validation purposes.

CONCLUSION

A better understanding of conditions that contribute to the success of FLOSS projects might be a valuable contribution to the future of software engineering. The model is formulated from empirical studies and calibrated using SourceForge data. The calibrated version produces reasonable results for the three emergent properties examined. From the calibrated data, it is concluded that the similarity between a developer and a project, the current resources going towards a project, and the maturity stage of a project are important factors. However, the cumulative resources and number of downloads a project has received are not important in reproducing the emergent properties.

The model presented here aids in gaining a better understanding of the conditions necessary for open source projects to succeed. With further iterations of development, including supplementing the model with better data-based values for parameters and adding additional emergent properties for validation purposes, the model could move into the realm of prediction. In this case, it would be possible to feed real-life conditions into the model and then observe a given project as it progresses (or lack of progresses) in the FLOSS environment.

REFERENCES

Analysis of the linux kernel. (2004). Research report. (Coverity Incorporated)

Antoniades, I., Samoladas, I., Stamelos, I., Angelis, L., & Bleris, G. L. (2005). Dynamical simulation models of the open source development process. In Koch, S. (Ed.), *Free/open source software development* (pp. 174–202). Hershey, PA: Idea Group, Incorporated.

Axelrod, R. (1984). *The evolution of cooperation.* New York: Basic Books.

Bitzer, J., & Schröder, P. J. (2005, July). Bug-fixing and code-writing: The private provision of open source software. *Information Economics and Policy*, *17*(3), 389–406. doi:10.1016/j.infoecopol.2005.01.001

Brooks, F. P. (1975). *The mythical man-month: Essays on software engineering.* Reading, MA: Addison-Wesley.

Chelf, B. (2006). *Measuring software quality: a study of open source software. Research report.* Coverity Incorporated.

Crowston, K., Howison, J., & Annabi, H. (2006, March/April). Information systems success in free and open source software development: Theory and measures. *Software Process Improvement and Practice*, *11*(2), 123–148. doi:10.1002/spip.259

Crowston, K., & Scozzi, B. (2002). Open source software projects as virtual organizations: competency rallying for software development. *IEE Proceedings. Software*, *49*, 3–17. doi:10.1049/ip-sen:20020197

Dalle, J.-M., & David, P. A. (2004, November 1). *SimCode: Agent-based simulation modelling of open-source software development* (Industrial Organization). EconWPA.

English, R., & Schweik, C. M. (2007). Identifying success and tragedy of FLOSS commons: A preliminary classification of Sourceforge.net projects. In *FLOSS '07: Proceedings of the first international workshop on emerging trends in FLOSS research and development* (p. 11). Washington, DC, USA: IEEE Computer Society.

Fox, J., & Guyer, M. (1977, June). Group size and others' strategy in an n-person game. *The Journal of Conflict Resolution*, *21*(2), 323–338.

Gao, Y., Madey, G., & Freeh, V. (2005, April). Modeling and simulation of the open source software community. In Agent-Directed Simulation Conference (pp. 113–122). San Diego, CA.

Ghosh, R. A., Krieger, B., Glott, R., & Robles, G. (2002, June). 4: Survey of developers. In *Free/libre and open source software: Survey and study. Maastricht, The Netherlands: University of Maastricht.* The Netherlands: Part.

Jerdee, T. H., & Rosen, B. (1974). Effects of opportunity to communicate and visibility of individual decisions on behavior in the common interest. *The Journal of Applied Psychology*, *59*(6), 712–716. doi:10.1037/h0037450

Katsamakas, E., & Georgantzas, N. (2007). Why most open source development projects do not succeed? In *FLOSS '07: Proceedings of the first international workshop on emerging trends in FLOSS research and development* (p. 3). Washington, DC, USA: IEEE Computer Society.

Kicinger, R., Arciszewski, T., & De Jong, K. A. (2005). Evolutionary computation and structural design: A survey of the state of the art. *Computers & Structures*, *83*(23-24), 1943–1978. doi:10.1016/j.compstruc.2005.03.002

Koch, S. (2008). Exploring the effects of Source-Forge.net coordination and communication tools on the efficiency of open source projects using data envelopment analysis. In Morasca, S. (Ed.), *Empirical Software Engineering*. Springer.

Kogut, B., & Metiu, A. (2001, Summer). Open-source software development and distributed innovation. *Oxford Review of Economic Policy*, *17*(2), 248–264. doi:10.1093/oxrep/17.2.248

Kowalczykiewicz, K. (2005). Libre projects lifetime profiles analysis. In *Free and open source software developers' European meeting 2005*. Brussels, Belgium.

Krishnamurthy, S. (2002, June). Cave or community?: An empirical examination of 100 mature open source projects. *First Monday*, *7*(6).

Lerner, J., & Tirole, J. (2005, April). The scope of open source licensing. *Journal of Law Economics and Organization*, *21*(1), 20–56. doi:10.1093/jleo/ewi002

Linux kernel software quality and security better than most proprietary enterprise software, 4-year Coverity analysis finds. (2004). Press release. (Coverity Incorporated)

Michlmayr, M. (2005). Software process maturity and the success of free software projects. In Zielinski, K., & Szmuc, T. (Eds.), *Software engineering: Evolution and emerging technologies* (pp. 3–14). Krakow, Poland: IOS Press.

Ostrom, E., Gardner, R., & Walker, J. (1994). *Rules, games and common pool resources*. Ann Arbor, MI: University of Michigan Press.

Raymond, E. S. (2000, September 11). *The cathedral and the bazaar* (Tech. Rep. No. 3.0). Thyrsus Enterprises.

Rossi, M. A. (2004, April). *Decoding the "Free/Open Source (F/OSS) Software puzzle" a survey of theoretical and empirical contributions* (Quaderni No. 424). Dipartimento di Economia Politica, Università degli Studi di Siena.

Smith, S. C., & Sidorova, A. (2003). Survival of open-source projects: A population ecology perspective. In *ICIS 2003. Proceedings of international conference on information systems 2003*. Seattle, WA.

Smith, T. (2002, October 1). *Open source: Enterprise ready – with qualifiers*. theOpenEnterprise. (http://www.theopenenterprise.com/story/TOE20020926S0002)

Stewart, K. J., Ammeter, A. P., & Maruping, L. M. (2006, June). Impacts of license choice and organizational sponsorship on user interest and development activity in open source software projects. *Information Systems Research*, *17*(2), 126–144. doi:10.1287/isre.1060.0082

Tajfel, H. (1981). *Human groups and social categories: Studies in social psychology*. Cambridge, UK: Cambridge University Press.

Wagstrom, P., Herbsleb, J., & Carley, K. (2005). A social network approach to free/open source software simulation. In *First international conference on open source systems* (pp. 16–23).

Wang, Y. (2007). *Prediction of success in open source software development*. Master of science dissertation, University of California, Davis, Davis, CA.

Weiss, D. (2005). Quantitative analysis of open source projects on SourceForge. In M. Scotto & G. Succi (Eds.), *Proceedings of the first international conference on open source systems (OSS 2005)* (pp. 140–147). Genova, Italy.

Chapter 7

Open Source Software Governance Serving Technological Agility:
The Case of Open Source Software within the DoD

Thomas Le Texier
GREDEG – UMR 6227 CNRS and University of Nice - Sophia Antipolis, France

David W. Versaille
EconomiX, University Paris 10 Nanterre, France

ABSTRACT

The development of open source software is currently arousing increasing interest in the IT world. This research inquires some specific paths enlarging the traditional view over open source software in inquiring the US Department of Defense (DoD) and the dynamics associated its front- and back-office activities. We explain how distinguishing basic administration from operational constraints and weapon R&D dynamics introduces specific governance concerns among public and private stakeholders. By no longer defining open source solutions as mere goods, but as services characterized by a flow of knowledge, we particularly highlight new emerging strategies of technological acquisition. Our analysis leads to revise the traditional role focusing mainly on cost issues and introduces open source software with distinctive properties serving the management of innovation and technological agility at the level of complex systems, exemplified here with the constraints associated to weapon systems and the Network centric warfare doctrine.

DOI: 10.4018/978-1-60960-513-1.ch007

INTRODUCTION

The development of open source software, the use of which used to be peripheral and anarchical, is currently arousing increasing interest in the IT world from both practitioners and theorists. Although extensive academic research has been carried out into the subject, this research mostly focuses on commercial implications at both market-based and organizational levels and yields few concrete analyses with applications to the public sector. Open Source Software differ from proprietary ones, since these are usually distributed under commercial license agreements. Open source software development, which previously constituted a marginal and merely ideological phenomenon, today corresponds to an emerging production model that draws increasing attention. Yet, one key research field would be yet to measure to what extent the open source software development model may be perceived differently under the scope of the various missions associated to public administrations.

This article focuses on the case of open source software adoption by the American Department of Defense (DoD). Following the end of the Cold War, the American Department of Defense is currently turning to a new model redefining its resources, structures and capabilities in order to fit in with a new framework where major uncertainty prevails, where military operations are running on all continents and where public budgets need to be refocused on specific civilian purposes. The end of the Cold War had already introduced an important shift at the time of President Clinton's administration; new constraints associated to the Global War against Terrorism have been introduced during President G. W. Bush's administration. Appraising the tenants of the adoption of open source software solutions by the Pentagon requires to nuance the evolution managed by the US DoD over the last twenty years.

We analyze the specificity of the activity of Defense in its national security mission purposes and in the shaping of the industrial relations within the sector. By no longer defining software solutions as mere goods, but as services characterized by a flow of knowledge, we particularly highlight new emerging strategies of technological acquisition, notably knowledge sourcing and outsourcing, for the American Department of Defense. The implementing of such new strategies can consequently entail a reshaping of the industrial environment, as it alters the existing competitive relations between the various agents of the American Defense sector. Our analysis thus leads us to revise the role of the DoD as a program manager and to measure how the adoption of open source software by the military stimulates innovation.

The paper focuses is organized as follows. Section 2 surveys prior open source software related analyses. We show that the 'libre' development model is nowadays appraised as a pattern improving productivity and software quality. In this context, an increasing number of firms run their activity upon 'hybrid' business models. We present the way open source software development is currently perceived by most governmental administrations. We underline that traditional cost cut concerns prevail over innovation. Open source software tend to be apprehended as a pure substitute to proprietary ones. Section 3 highlights that the US Department of Defense endorses the converse way. Our demonstration distinguishes between the various missions – back office vs. front office – performed by the Pentagon and explain how the main dimensions associated to software quality apply in reality to the system as a whole, from which it turns out that software are impossible to separate. Section 4 focuses on governance issues. It explains first how the Pentagon main driver focuses on innovation and technology management in order to achieve at the required technological "agility". The recent trends introducing service oriented architectures methodologies and the Open Technology Development project are situated in this process. Section 5 concludes.

FROM OPEN SOURCE SOFTWARE DEVELOPMENT TO HYBRID BUSINESS MODEL. THE CASE OF FIRMS AND PUBLIC ADMINISTRATIONS

The 'open' nature of open source software tends to make them public goods (Lerner & Tirole, 2002; Johnson, 2002), since they are defined by non-rivalry in consumption (Baldwin & Clark, 2006) as well as non-excludability (Osterloh & Rota, 2007). Open properties of 'libre' software thus open new fields of research that analyze the way open source project participants contribute to the public provision of the source code, then describing new models of both software production and collaborative work (von Krogh & von Hippel, 2003). The scope of potential contributors to open source software projects being extended, the overall outcome of the open source software development model may be better and more suited to any user's needs. As a model of 'private-collective' innovation, the openness of the source code has to be interpreted as a new way to create software.

Contrasting to the previous studies analyzing the way open source software stand as potential incumbents on the software market, recent trends in the scientific literature open new research paths. Bonaccorsi and Rossi (2003) have explained how open source software development and proprietary software development may co-exist on a same market. Dahlander and Magnusson (2005) underline that firms producing proprietary software for commercial purposes may also benefit from the activity of the surrounding communities producing open source software solutions. By enhancing sponsorship strategies, commercial software producers may benefit from the growing number of open source software development initiatives by taking part and driving in some cases such 'libre' projects (Shah, 2006). Open source software development can then be seen as a new opportunity for commercial software producers

to cut their production costs (Krishnamurthy, 2003) and to acquire new types of knowledge that cannot be developped inside the boundaries of the firm. Specific firms bringing to the market proprietary software encourage their developers to spend a lot of time in being present with open source software communities and in contributing to them. Such developers are often told to drive open source software communities to solve complex problems in the firms' initial interest, along trends which open source software developers would not spontaneously manage. These strategies thus represent new opportunities to take benefit from innovative activities standing outside the traditional boundaries of the firms, and show that open source software can be perceived as a complementary asset for commercial software producers (Dahlander & Wallin, 2006).

The benefits commercial software producers may derive from open source software initiatives naturally incite them to set up activities relying on hybrid business models (Bonaccorsi & al., 2006). IBM, Hewlett-Packard and Sun Microsystems have for instance adopted such new types of business-models and have succeeded in comforting their product portfolio by mobilizing new forms of knowledge developed "outside". Implementing hybrid business models is made easy by the modular architecture of open source software code structure (MacCormack & al., 2006). Producers may therefore take advantage from the efforts initiated by open source software communities, and internalize new knowledge assets produced by community-based dynamics. The firm sponsorship phenomena – as it is observed within open source software development projects – can thus be interpreted as a means for both open source software communities and commercial software firms to share knowledge enabling them either to improve software development in accordance with outsourcing and sourcing schemes (von Hippel, 1987; Howells, 1996; Tsoukas, 1996), or to improve the systems software are integrated into, without customers and end-users to be able to discriminate between proprietary and open source software. As a 'collective-private' innovation model in which both non-commercial and commercial actors may participate, the emergence of hybrid business models shows that open source software development is likely to enhance both software production models and commercial product quality. The properties of open source software development and the activity of open source software communities therefore open new fields for news business potentialities.

As opposed to both private market-based and managerial-based literatures, open source software research has yielded fewer analyses with applications to the public sector; these mainly aim at producing guidelines for adoption and seek for sharp cost-reductions. In many cases, open source software diffusion is not effective yet. Governmental reports introduce general guidelines to adopt 'libre' software for public administrative tasks, or leave the implementation of dedicated applications at the initiative of specific offices. In practice open source software adoption is not as popular as it might, which holds for the operating systems and the software as well. Even though concrete instances remain not as numerous as official decisions and discourses may advertise for it, a large number of countries have decided to support open source software initiatives in a public administrative framework.

It remains uneasy to delineate the very content of public policies in favour of open source software, which are supposed to improve social welfare and foster specific innovation paths. Research has been developed to stress the importance of encouraging new standards and stimulating the convergence between standards; other scholars (e.g. Mustonen, 2003) acknowledge the promotion of open source software initiatives in informing about the true content of what "libre" implies. In this framework, Schmidt and Schnitzer (2003) have stressed that incentives in favour of contributions to open source software development may even divert from specific customers' needs

which cannot be addressed but in the framework of proprietary development models, and for which GPL licence terms are irrelevant. Training and learning initiatives for civil servants remain quite efficient in order to orient towards open source software development. Yet it presupposes to focus on specific domains and applications, the choice of which remains precisely difficult to anticipate. Biases to competition and innovation mechanisms on the software market may be even introduced in that way.

Surveys commissioned by governments to inquire whether open source software models apply to public administrations remain basically focused on economical relevance and cost cuts. For obvious reasons, a growing number of governments see in open source software adoption a new opportunity to reallocate public budgets. Other advantages open source software adoption may provide (e.g., reliability and flexibility, see Cremer & Gaudeul (2004) are generally regarded as secondary. Major public concerns are therefore not open source software acquisition costs as such, since these are generally null, but the costs that would result from such adoption (i.e., switching costs, including both the technical and learning costs required to turn to 'libre' software). Supporting such functioning costs has become the focus point of specific policies, which also engage in training and educational programs. Administrative workers need to learn how to use software that are sometimes less convenient that proprietary ones (e.g., adaptation to new interfaces, to new time-saving procedures, to long-lasting and transferable applications over the various versions of the software). Evidence has shown that switching costs do not represent unsuperable obstacles, since the support interruption from Microsoft to its public customers for Windows NT have incited both the German and Taiwanese governmental authorities to adopt functionally-equivalent – Linux – open source software. Public administrations remain also concerned that the transition occurs in a limited time horizon (continuity of public services), and that perfect substitutability between proprietary and open source software remains on the long run (reversibility). Surveys do not really focus on the repercussions in the framework of innovation policies and sector-based industrial policies, aimed at preserving innovative properties and the creation of specific capabilities. So are the decision-making processes, where the arguments mainly reflect the appreciations of the administration only as an "end-user".

OPEN SOURCE SOFTWARE DEVELOPMENT IN US MILITARY AFFAIRS

From the recent years, one may easily observe attempts to somewhat integrate the open source software development model in the American DoD's one. In this section we first present the environment in which the US DoD has to evolve and we secondly present the critical aspects of cost savings in its daily mission.

The American Department of Defense is a large administration, in charge of conducing military operations on several continents. It turns out that such a complex structure endorses several motivations as regard the adoption of open source software. It behaves as a normal administration, managing 2 million military and civilian people in 2007[1] (NATO statistics). It implements weapons on the battlefield under the scope of an operational doctrine which was totally reshaped by the Network Centric Warfare[2] (NCW) doctrine (Mérindol & Versailles, 2007). It also drives R&D programs when it prepares for the forthcoming weapons to be used on the battlefield. At the level of the increasing complexity of the Defense environment and of the various constraints ruling over the R&D decision making processes or with the administration of the DoD and the weapons, open source software may be introduced in order to bring now opportunities into the various processes. Globally stated, it remains important to divide

the analysis among three different framesets, corresponding respectively to "back office" and general administration of the Pentagon; to military operations and "front" office activities; to R&D programs and weapons production. Reshaping industrial activities through the development and the introduction of open source software remains sharply different in each case. The introduction of a such diversity on the basis of the US DoD missions helps improving the examination of the open source software adoption into the public sector.

When dealing with the various missions associated to the administration of the US DoD, it remains first and foremost important to remember that the various services do maintain a strong independence as regard software acquisition. The Pentagon used to adopt software very pragmatically, in focusing on the opportunity to lower-level decision-makers to procure and implement the solutions they requested for their day-to-day administration and operational responsibilities. For software management and procurement, the strategy of the Pentagon focuses on flexibility and reliability. It stresses the importance of local adaptation (i.e., flexibility) to the various tenants of the mission and an important part of decision-making associated to software therefore remains decentralized at the level of local mission commanders. It underlines the necessity to constantly improve the effectiveness of software in relation with the success of the mission, on the long run (i.e., reliability). As a counterpart, this situation has come to introduce competitive solutions inside the various services (US Navy, US Marines, US Air Force, US Army) and among the services, which also testify for discrepant strategies as regard their interactions with the industry and as regard the management of innovation. Cost-related concerns have now arisen and take into account these divergences in the management of technology in order to foster the introduction of some operational "joint-ness" between services.

Discriminating support and administrative tasks from the "front office" remains therefore important. When it deals with administration and logistics management, the minimization of procurement and maintenance costs represents an important target, which remains totally consistent with the objectives of flexibility and reliability when considering this process under the prism of long-lasting processes. Transitioning to open source software might be of budgetary relevance even though switching costs do exist, because the Pentagon itself experienced the rupture in upgrades and support Microsoft was providing for Windows NT (Dombrowski & al., 2003, p.27). As a matter of fact, the US DoD does not behave exactly along the model described in the previous section when it deals with open source software: It cares much more about the warranty of supplies associated to the reliability of the service (qualitatively and quantitatively) than about the various technological aspects associated to software solutions, provided that specific standards and clearances are respected. Key variables remain here functional autonomy, flexibility and reliability; budget considerations are never subordinated to the requirements of reliability and of permanence of services software serve. This pragmatic attitude contrasts therefore with public management options described in the previous section.

The main logic described here has come to an increasing complexity with the end of the 1990s, which did not balance the flexibility it was intended to serve. The Pentagon was then confronted to sharply diverging strategies among its various services. A reform process seeking for a new consistency with the various constraints associated to the requirements of joint operations has been therefore installed. It deals first and foremost with front line operations and does not affect but indirectly the aspects of basic administration. This reform is aiming at introducing the consequences of the Network centric warfare doctrine in the management of information technologies, and therefore at reorganizing "front office" activities dealing with information technologies in the US Air Force, the US Navy, the US Marines and the US Army. When dealing with interoperability issues at NATO-wide level, one often forgets that the most important concerns deal with the actual "joint-ness" of the various American services. The NCW doctrine thus represents an important organizational challenge. It becomes reality with the transformation of the 1960-established Defense communications agency (DCA) into the Defense information systems agency (DISA), which was initiated in 1995. This agency devotes now 80% of its budget to the implementation of information systems linking together the various systems existing in the different DoD services. The DISA organizes this revolution with "service-oriented" governance rules where efficient returns of experience acknowledged in one of the services end with DoD-wide generalization of the corresponding software and information systems. The objective is to create value from information with speed, in order to command and control from anywhere. When the DCA was created, communications were relying on three technologies: wire, radio and radar. Today's requirements cannot remain terrain-focused and enemy-focused as warfare used to be. They require software and hardware technologies allowing for network-enabled capabilities to be constantly adapted to missions requirements. Under this perspective, hardware, software, applications, services, data, etc. cannot be separated from each other and their integration only may be appraised as efficient – or not – in the realm of real time missions. It turns out that the impact of software systems remains distinctively appraised when working for back-office activities only, while they cannot be separated from the evaluation of the global efficiency of weapon systems when dealing with R&D or front-office systems.

The issue of costs represents here a distinctive situation for the Pentagon. Public decision making as it was described in the previous section mainly focused on procurement costs and does not cope with the issue of the integration of software – or of information technologies – into complex systems. When focusing on basic administration, the main important costs may be obviously limited to the procurement of licences and to switching costs. End-users can check directly the kind of software they use and manipulate as they know the name of the software they use. When focusing on the operational service software contributes to, the relevant concern relates to total ownership costs associated to the system itself (Gholz, 2003, p. 280). End-users only deal with man-machine interfaces providing dedicated functionalities. Singularizing software appears therefore as irrelevant. The implementation of code lines remains the result of a trade-off among various required functionalities and development costs associated to each part of the whole system. Scholars usually measure software quality by underlining five dimensions, namely reliability, maintainability, flexibility, usability and security (Varian & Shapiro, 2003). All these dimensions apply, yet at the level of the whole system. As for the other aspects of system integration (Prencipe & al., 2003; Versailles, 2005), the optimization of specifications and the arbitrage between costs, functionalities and efficiency is to occur only at the level of the system and the management of costs remains impossible at the level of software only.

Instances of the Pentagon's interest in the open source software development model may be testified by applications which have been adopted or implemented within US military services. Security Enhanced Linux (SELinux) is an application developed and used by the National Security Agency (NSA) since 2001. SELinux is a version of Linux which aims at meeting a number of security-related objectives critical for the activities of the NSA. It is also setting up security mechanisms encouraging flexibility for complex systems security requirements. According to its license terms, SELinux's source code and documentation are available for free downloading[3] on the website of the NSA. This clearly manifests the willingness of the NSA to take benefit from external open source communities in order to improve security-based functionalities.

Another instance exists with the NASA, which is currently using a specific dynamic updating internet information system based upon MySQL architecture. The NAIS (NASA Acquisition Information Service) case study shows that it is possible to switch to open source software solutions for military tasks in cases where users are highly skilled potential developers (Weinstock & Hissam, 2005). The U.S. Navy is also using open source software based applications with the DISA-managed Global Command and Control System Maritime (GCCSM), which is a critical application licensed upon 'libre' terms and whose goal is to coordinate both ships and airplanes control movement (Lechner & Kaiser, 2005). This is another instance where the DoD switches to open source software applications, even for major tactical tasks. Evidence has exhibited that such switch to 'libre' solutions may be beneficial for external vendors at two levels. Indeed, market opportunities may emerge, and reputation effect may improve the global image of companies able to address the Pentagon's requirements.

Open source software adoption is likely to become popular for US Defense purposes, yet it is both mobilized at the level of specific applications and of system components. An increasing number of Defense-related units are implied in open source software diffusion initiatives. Life cycle cost management and technology readiness remain major issues, which are typically addressed during the R&D processes.

OPEN SOURCE SOFTWARE DEVELOPMENT AS AN INSTANCE OF OPEN ARCHITECTURES PROCESSES: IMPLICATIONS FOR THE DOD AND THE SOFTWARE INDUSTRY

As widely analyzed in the litterature dealing with open source software adoption (Gaudeul, 2003; Nonneke & Preece, 2000; van Wendel de Joode

& Egyedi, 2005; Kuk, 2006), the autonomy and flexibility properties that the Pentagon currently intends to enhance require a specific governance model for software development. Fact is that the Government accountability office[4] highlights (GAO, 2004; 2008) that 63% of the weapons programs had changed requirement once system development began, and experienced significant cost increases; roughly half the programs testified for a 25% increase in the expected lines of software code since starting the respective development programs. Even though the issue of costs is not significant as such[5], it might be interesting to remind that DoD in FY03 spent as much as $bn 8 to rework software because of quality-related issues, which is enough to procure two nuclear carrier vessels of the forthcoming generation (CVN 21). GAO assessed also that DoD will spend nearly $bn 14 in software changes during FY06 alone, to be divided into enhancements of the legacy systems and the development of forthcoming programs. This is an issue in the management of technology and in the convergence between the various parts of complex weapon systems.

From the early 2000s, the R&D structures associated to the DoD started appraising the relevance of a convergence with open source software. The Mitre Corp. issued for instance in 2003 a report praising the virtues of technology transfers with open source communities. In 2004, the Office of management and budget published a memorandum calling on agencies to exercise the same procurement procedures for open source as would be done for commercial software. The same texts explain that open source software should not be assimilated to freeware or shareware, which are discarded by the DoD because the government does not have any access to the original source code. The DISA's missions and duties represent another answer provided by the Pentagon. As software are goods whose use can be complex and vary from one user to the other, DISA is asked to take into account the users' heterogeneity (i.e., their abilities to use and/or to

implement new technologies) in military software acquisition, as well as the degree of specialization of the mission for which the use of software is required. Information technologies represent a major concern in the broad framework of the implementation of the Network centric warfare doctrine, yet the very difficulty relates here to the various R&D paths leading to the integration into the military platforms and systems. Interoperability between systems and services remain the main important goal.

In 2006 this process went some steps further as the Advanced Systems and Concepts (ASC) agency launched the Open Technology Development (OTD) project within the DoD (Scott, Lucas & Herz, 2006). The goal of this project is to set up a technological platform that gathers all types of software already in use within the DoD, and to facilitate the development of appropriate software solution. The OTD project aims at encouraging the development of military software according to open standards development schemes. In practice, it intends to take benefit from both proprietary and open source software development initiatives. Collaborative software development is supposed to cut R&D costs and achieve at greater system development and acquisition flexibility. The goal of the OTD project is not to oust traditional commercial actors from military software activities but to improve technological agility (as opposed to technological autonomy) of the US services. As such, this project would lead military organizations to empower the software industry with open source software development model and to question the leadership of some traditional supplying firms in the software sector. The OTD project opens the paths for modular architectures for software solutions, as it states that DoD should share programming code and standards with the open source community. It clearly recommends the use of service oriented architectures. No wonder that the US Navy remains very active in this process. Dombrowski, Gholz and Ross explain (2003, p. 27) that Microsoft's omnipresence within the DoD occurred with the development of Windows NT along the military requirements associated to the implementation of military information networks. Microsoft then installed a dedicated office spreading out commercial off-the-shelves version of Win NT over the DoD. This office progressively downsized over time, up to become virtual when coming to the new early R&D phases of the frigate program DD(X) and of the DD-21 demonstrator project. The authors report that Microsoft was totally committed to the elaboration of new 'Windows' versions suited to commercial markets and did not engage in the emerging military programs. Starting from 2003, the US Navy decides to become highly proactive in open architectures dynamics, and starts to officially communicate[6] about the "end of proprietary technology". Top executives clearly state no longer to accept "systems that couple hardware, software and data" and the US Navy engages in a path where dependencies towards such a crucial provider vanish progressively.

The OTD project leads the DoD to consider both open source and proprietary software development to build an appropriate military software development model. This project applies for all services and subparts in the DoD. The open technology platform the DoD is likely to set up can rely on open source or on proprietary solutions with open standards and interfaces that enable to easily implement new capabilities. This is the kernel of a new organisation based upon open interfaces, where users are no longer isolated in technology stovepipes and captive to (locked-in) technology providers. 'Stovepipe' may represent here a system built along proprietary dynamics or provided by a system integrator. The reference to open architectures enables the integration of components from any supplier that implement the open interfaces specifications, and makes it possible to directly interoperate with other systems architected along the same interfaces (which means without the step of an 'integration' process). In this context, the OTD project would

help the DoD to increase the number of specific functionalities without facing previously met coordination constraints. The R&D strategy now associated to software clearly focuses on the agility required to provide the war fighters with the latest functionalities and therefore constantly adapt the systems. Software life cycles do not seem to be suited to proprietary technology anymore, as updating the whole systems has to follow new time schedule constraints. Indeed, software upgrades never end and system implementation remains a constant driver led by operations requirements. At the level of the US DoD services, the main important issue relates to the legacy systems, that is to say articulating together hardware and software from various weapons generations which need to be made together consistent. In service legacy IT systems represent a tremendous drain on the R&D budgets and prevent the DoD services from being more agile.

Software behind servers, networks, man-machine interfaces are now to be considered as commodities that are obtainable from whoever is willing to offer the best delivery schedule, price, service and quality. This means that commercial-off-the-shelves products may be quickly adapted to and adopted in the DoD services. This means also that suppliers need to commit to the process of constantly improving and upgrading code lines. In this new process, the competence of DoD personnel remains crucial for the interaction with the suppliers committed to "open" architectures contributions. Accumulating knowledge inside the services over time and over the various programs remains compulsory for the global efficiency of open technology policies. The setting up of open technology platforms therefore leads to change the way both US services and external vendors ought to deal together, since it aims at breaking away from traditional deterministic market-based relationships. Software-related knowledge held by external vendors remains obviously essential to meet DoD requirements and expectations, as these actors remain at the origin of the drivers of innovation. Yet the openness of architectures requires two essential points to be met. First, the appraisal of the various propositions has to be performed – at least partly – by in-house experts who maintain an accurate big picture of the whole system in order to perform efficiently the various improvements and updates. One of the main priorities of the DoD is therefore to develop internal military-based competence sets – and eventually acquiring external ones – in order to perform the various interfaces of military organizations with the other stakeholders to the process. Second, the interfaces with potential suppliers should also deliver the various information and data relevant for them to make propositions. Failures in capitalizing knowledge and a global picture about each system would therefore induce automatically that National Defence concerns are not met anymore. In this context, imposing military open technology development models appears as a way to introduce more agility. At the same time it disseminates knowledge among a larger number of actors. Centralization of data and information about the development process occurred previously on the sides of the integrator and of the final user. If the integrator disappears, it becomes compulsory to extend the knowledge base military organizations maintain on the issue of software and systems. Setting up the OTD project requires therefore a complex re-organization of the reference model on which the DoD used to rely, and goes beyond purely military software procurement matters. In this perspective, there are numerous challenges to overcome.

First, the DoD has to overcome its bureaucratic historical inertia and to adopt a more dynamic technological adoption policy. Military organizations have to consider that turning to open technology adoption should be apprehended as continuity but not as a technological break.

Second, the DoD has to turn to an organizational model in which community-based dynamics prevail in order to fully address appropriate military-oriented use. Such an expectation re-quires to challenge current preventions against joint examinations of operational issues and to introduce governance mechanisms stimulating the participation of military and industry-related program managers and developers. Furthermore, the governance issue needs to address the content of knowledge flows between stakeholders, which should occur during the various program phases with all potential suppliers (on the long run). The focus is put here on the heterogeneous nature of the core competences held by all actors who might take part in open technology development initiatives (Hamel & Prahalad, 1990) and on the various requirements for them to introduce proposals.

Third, the DoD has to manage new boundaries between military organizations, open source software contributors and commercial software suppliers (Howells et al, 2003; Azoulay, 2004). Software development can be apprehended as a collective knowledge-based storage and creation process (Bessen, 2002; Nuvolari, 2002; Narduzzo & Rossi, 2003) where knowledge sourcing and outsourcing are likely to introduce new interactions between the various actors of innovation networks. The various DoD services still testify for different governance modalities inherited from their respective history and relationships with major industry players. The US Air Force still manages its major programs in a framework where decision making is shared with a lead-system integrator. The US Navy now explicitly turns towards open architectures environments where it endorses an integration activity. No doubt that the drivers of the open architecture governance will affect the stability of their respective governance models.

In this emerging framework, it remains obvious that specific security issues will have to be managed in order to protect Defence and military missions. This will lead to the definition of specific license terms for the DoD's strategic asset not to be unwisely widespread worldwide. Military knowledge base needs to be extended by the participation of external vendors in open technology platforms while being heavily protected in order to maintain the US Forces supremacy. The "opening vs obscurity" dilemma therefore remains, even if transposed onto other arguments within military affairs.

CONCLUSION

This article has focused on the way to appraise open source software in the public sector. It has developed some paths to enlarge and refine this analysis thanks to the examination of the dynamics associated to the US Department of Defense. It explains that the DoD does not have any prevention against open source software and clearly favours its introduction in the framework of service oriented architectures. Drivers for the Pentagon relate first to the implementation of a dedicated R&D strategy suited to address the constraints of technology management, and do not but indirectly deal with cost issues. Distinguishing "back-office" administration from military operations ("front-office") and the R&D processes associated to weapon systems production makes it possible to understand this situation and to overcome the considerable focus put on cost management (and on switching costs) when investigating the adoption of open source software by the public sector.

The US DoD aims at achieving the technological agility requested by current military operations, as these are now driven by the Network centric warfare doctrine. The related software base is now associated to upgrade and implementation specifications which remain hardly consistent with the proprietary model endorsed in the past. Reliability, maintainability, flexibility, usability and security do not only apply at the level of software, but at the level of the whole weapon systems software contribute to. We have explained how the introduction of open source software development can become an asset suited to the improvement of the contribution of software to the efficiency of the systems. We also have insisted on the impossibility to separate the assessment of software and code

lines from the assessment of the global efficiency of weapon systems. This holds for all activities but back-office and basic administration tasks and might be easily transposed onto other domains.

Our findings have led us to address some issues related to the governance of R&D processes when dealing with open architectures, open source software and the various actors associated to the contributing communities. It explains how the Pentagon has come to the current situation and the issues at stake. The complexity of weapon systems R&D has been proven to represent an interesting investigation field for such an issue. The US DoD is based on a particular hybrid development model which differs from that currently adopted by commercial vendors, since modular software development model enables the DoD to integrate and combine competences available among external vendors and the existing US military software-related knowledge base. As their R&D management and culture differ, the various DoD services experiment different governance options. They meet on several points and issues. This procurement model develops rather dynamic knowledge-based approaches than a reference to static assets. Concerns associated to knowledge sourcing and coordination constraints prevail and the implementation of new governance paths will follow in reality the failure or success of the ongoing programs.

We believe that the case of the US DoD – once again – illustrates how the open source software development model may be beneficial for public purposes. One key issue to focus on is related to the way the US DoD may participate within open source projects. Another relevant key aspect to analyze would also to see armies (i.e., US and non-US armies) differ in their willingness to adopt the open source way of developing. Although evidence today shows fewer evidence of such 'libre' patterns within non-US armies, further analyses will lead us to study the scope of positioning strategies public actors may adopt to meet national security needs.

REFERENCES

Azoulay, P. (2004). Capturing Knowledge within and across firm boundaries: Evidence from clinical development. *The American Economic Review*, *94*(5), 1591–1612. doi:10.1257/0002828043052259

Baldwin, C., & Clark, K. (2006). The architecture of participation: Does code architecture mitigate free riding in the open source development model? *Management Science*, *52*(7), 1116–1127. doi:10.1287/mnsc.1060.0546

Bessen, J. (2002). What good is free software? In Hahn, R. W. (Ed.), *Government policy toward open source software* (pp. 12–33). Washington, DC: Brookings Institution Press.

Bonaccorsi, A., Giannangeli, S., & Rossi, C. (2006). Entry strategies under competing standards: Hybrid business models in the open source software industry. *Management Science*, *52*(7), 1085–1098. doi:10.1287/mnsc.1060.0547

Bonaccorsi, A., & Rossi, C. (2003). Why open source software can succeed. *Research Policy*, *32*(7), 1243–1258. doi:10.1016/S0048-7333(03)00051-9

Command and Control Research Program (The). CCRP, www.dodccrp.org.

Cremer, J., & Gaudeul, A. (2004). Some economics of the open-source software. *Reseaux*, *22*(124), 111–139.

Dahlander, L., & Magnusson, M. G. (2005). Relationships between open source software companies and communities: Observations from nordic firms. *Research Policy*, *34*(4), 481–493.

Dahlander, L., & Wallin, M. W. (2006). A man on the inside: Unlocking communities as complementary assets. *Research Policy*, *35*(8), 1243–1259. doi:10.1016/j.respol.2006.09.011

Defense industry daily, DID, online information service at www.defenseindustrydaily.com.

Defense information systems agency (the), DISA, www.disa.mil, and more specifically the information letter *The Grid*, volume 7 number 1, June 2008.

Dombrowski, P., Gholz, E., & Ross, A. L. (2002). *Military transformation and the Defense industry after next, The Defense industrial implications of Network Centric Warfare*. Naval war college Newport papers #18, New Port (RI): Naval war college.

Federal computer week, FCW, www.fcw.com, section dedicated to "Stories".

Gaudeul, A. (2003). The (La)TeX project: a case study of open source software. *TUGboat*, *24*(1), Proceeding of the 2003 Annual Meeting, (pp. 132-145).

Gholz, E. (2003). In Prencipe, A., Davies, A., & Hobday, M. (Eds.), *Systems integration in the US Defence industry: who does it and why is it important?* (pp. 279–306).

Government accountability office, GAO, (2004). *Defense acquisition, Stronger management practices are needed to improve DoD's software intensive weapon acquisitions*, Report to the committee on armed services, US Senate, reference GAO-04-393. Available from www.gao.gov.

Government accountability office, GAO, (2008). *Defense acquisitions, Assessment of selected weapon programs*, Report to congressional committees, reference GAO-08-467SP. Available from www.gao.gov.

Government computer news, GCN, www.gcn.com, sections dedicated to "Hot topics" and "White papers".

Hamel, G., & Prahalad, C. K. (1990). The core competence of the corporation. *Harvard Business Review*, *68*(may-june), 79–91.

Henderson, R. M., & Clark, K. B. (1990). Architectural innovation: The reconfiguration of existing product technologies and the failure of established firms. *Administrative Science Quarterly, 35*(1), 9–30. doi:10.2307/2393549

Herz, J. C., Lucas, M., & Scott, J. (2006). Open technology development – Roadmap plan. http://www.acq.osd.mil/actd/OTDRoadmapFinal.pdf

Hissam, S., Weinstock, C. B., Plakosh, D., & Asundi, J. (2001). *Perspectives on open source software*, Carnegie Mellon Software Ingineering Institute, Technical report CMU/SEI-2001-TR019, november 2001.

Howells, J. (1996). Tacit knowledge, innovation and technology transfer. *Technology Analysis and Strategic Management, 8*(2), 91–106. doi:10.1080/09537329608524237

Howells, J., James, A., & Malik, K. (2003). The sourcing of technological knowledge: distributed innovation and dynamic change. *R & D Management, 33*(4), 395–409. doi:10.1111/1467-9310.00306

Johnson, J. P. (2002). Open source software: Private provision of a public good. *Journal of Economics & Management Strategy, 11*(4), 637–662. doi:10.1162/105864002320757280

Krishnamurthy, S. (2003). A managerial overview of open source software. *Business Horizons, 9-10,* 47–56. doi:10.1016/S0007-6813(03)00071-5

Kuk, G. (2006). Strategic interaction and knowledge sharing in the KDE developer mailing list. *Management Science, 52*(7), 1031–1042. doi:10.1287/mnsc.1060.0551

Lechner, D., & Kaiser, H. (2005). The fortress and the bazaar: Open-source and DoD software. *Defense Acquisition Review Journal*, december, (pp. 374-391).

Lerner, J., & Tirole, J. (2002). Some simple economics of open source. *The Journal of Industrial Economics, 50*(2), 197–234. doi:10.1111/1467-6451.00174

MacCormack, A., Rusnak, J., & Baldwin, C. Y. (2006). Exploring the structure of complex software designs: an empirical study of open source and proprietary code. *Management Science, 52*(7), 1015–1030. doi:10.1287/mnsc.1060.0552

Mérindol, V., & Versailles, D. W. (2007). Towards a re-interpretation of ICT impact on command and control. *Defence Studies, 7*(2), 232–237.

Military information technology online edition, available at www.military-information-technology.com online archives volumes 7 (2003) to 12 (2008).

Mitre corporation (The). (2003). *Use of Free and Open source software (FOSS) in the US Department of Defence*, version 1.2.04, January 2nd, 2003, prepared for the DISA, report number MP W 02 0000101; approved for public release yet unpublished; downloaded in pdf format on October 16th, 2008, from http://terrybollinger.com/.

Mustonen, M. (2003). Copyleft - The economics of Linux and other open source software. *Information Economics and Policy, 15*(1), 99–121. doi:10.1016/S0167-6245(02)00090-2

Narduzzo, A., & Rossi, A. (2003). Modularity in action: GNU/Linux and Free/Open source software development model unleashed. Working paper.

Nonneke, B., & Preece, J. (2000). Lurker demographics: Counting the silent. *Proceedings of the SIGCHI conference on Human factors in computing systems*, New York: ACM Press, (pp. 73-80).

Nuvolari, A. (2002). Collective invention ancient and modern: A reappraisal. ECIS working paper.

Osterloh, M., & Rota, S. (2007). Open source software development – Just another case of collective invention? *Research Policy, 36*(2), 157–171. doi:10.1016/j.respol.2006.10.004

Prencipe, A., Davies, A., & Hobday, M. (Eds.). (2003). *The business of systems integration*. Oxford: Oxford university press. doi:10.1093/0199263221.001.0001

Schmidt, K., & Schnitzer, M. (2003). Public subsidies for open source? Some economic policy issues of the software market. *Harvard Journal of Law & Technology, 16*(2), 473–505.

Scott, J., Lucas, M., & Herz, J.-C. (2006). *Open technology development Roadmap plan*. version 3.1 (final), prepared for the Deputy Under Secretary of Defense, Advanced Systems and Concepts, cleared for open publication on June 7th, 2006, available from www.acq.osd.mil/asc/.

Shah, S. (2006). Motivation, governance and the viability of hybrid forms in open source software development. *Management Science, 52*(7), 1000–1014. doi:10.1287/mnsc.1060.0553

SIPRI. (2006). *SIPRI Yearbook 2006, Armaments, disarmaments and international security*. Stockholm: SIPRI.

Tsoukas, H. (1996). The firm as a distributed knowledge system: a constructionist approach. *Strategic Management Journal, 17*(winter), 11-25.

van Wendel de Joode, R., & Egyedi, T. M. (2005). Handling variety: the tension between adaptability and operability of open source software. *Computer Standards & Interfaces, 28*(1), 109–121. doi:10.1016/j.csi.2004.12.004

Varian, H. R., & Shapiro, C. (2003). Linux adoption in the public sector: An economic analysis. Working paper.

Versailles, D. W. (2005). La nouvelle gouvernance des programmes de Défense: les relations entre l'Etat et l'industrie. *Revue d'économie industrielle, 112*(4), 83-105.

von Hippel, E. (1987). Cooperation between rivals: informal know-how trading. *Research Policy, 16*(6), 291–302. doi:10.1016/0048-7333(87)90015-1

von Krogh, G., & von Hippel, E. (2003). Special Issue on Open Source Software Development [Editorial]. *Research Policy, 32*(7), 1149–1157. doi:10.1016/S0048-7333(03)00054-4

Weinstock, C. B., & Hissam, S. A. (2005). Making lightning strike twice. In Feller, J., Fitzgerald, B., Hissam, S. A., & Lakhani, K. R. (Eds.), *Perspectives on Free and Open Source Software* (pp. 143–159). Cambridge: The MIT Press.

West, J. (2003). How open is open enough? Melding proprietary and open source platform strategies. *Research Policy, 32*(7), 1259–1285. doi:10.1016/S0048-7333(03)00052-0

ENDNOTES

[1] In 2005, US military expenditures amount for $bn 478,3 representing 1 604$ per capita. Other world top five countries (assessed under purchasing power parity) are China with $bn 188,4, India with $bn 105,8, Russia with $bn 64,4 and France with $bn 45,4. The US figure corresponds to 3,64% of the US 2005 GDP. The global amount for 2005 subdivides into $bn 147,844 for personnel expenditures, which are part of $bn 346,1 associated to functioning costs; and 123,6 of capital expenditures. Functioning expenditures have decreased to $bn 317,1 in 2007 while capital expenditures increased to $bn 139,4. Source: NATO statistics and SIPRI, 2006, p. 302.

[2]   The Network centric warfare doctrine focuses on the informational superiority of the US Armed forces and massively integrates information technologies in the strategy and the military tactics.

[3]   http://www.nsa.gov/selinux/

[4]   GAO is known as "the investigative arm of Congress" and "the congressional watchdog." GAO supports the Congress and helps improve the performance and accountability of the federal government in investigating federal policies and programs.

[5]   Especially as compared to the global evaluation of more than $tn 1 700 of total procurement and acquisition costs associated to currently scheduled weapon programs.

[6]   Vice Adm Mark Edwards, deputy chief of naval operations for communications, on March 5, 2008, at the Navy IT Day audience in Vienna, VA, USA. Other elements were previously published in *Chips* (Dec. 2006), the Department of the Navy Information technology magazine, or in Military information technology (online edition available from http://www.military-information-technology.com).

This work was previously published in International Journal of Open Source Software and Processes (IJOSSP), edited by Stefan Koch, pp. 14-27, copyright 2009 by IGI Publishing (an imprint of IGI Global).

Chapter 8
Innovation, Imitation and Open Source

Rufus Pollock
University of Cambridge, UK

ABSTRACT

An extensive empirical literature indicates that, even without formal intellectual property rights, innovators enjoy a variety of first-mover advantages and that 'imitation' is itself a costly activity. There is also accumulating evidence that an 'open' approach to knowledge production can deliver substantial efficiency advantages. This article introduces a formal framework incorporating all of these factors. We examine the relative performance of an 'open' versus a 'closed' (proprietary) regime, and explicitly characterise the circumstances in which an open approach, despite its effect on facilitating imitation, results in a higher level of innovation.

INTRODUCTION

The last decade or so have seen an explosion in the level of 'open'[1] information production not only in traditional areas such as software (e.g. Linux, Firefox) but also in areas ranging from online encyclopaedias (Wikipedia) to genomic databases (the Human Genome Project). Such developments suggest that, at least in some important cases, open models of knowledge production can do as,

or even better, than closed[2] ones. As we discuss further below, this is somewhat surprising and it is important to investigate carefully how and why this could be the case.

It is important to note here that we are focused on the rate of innovation and not the level of welfare. After all it is well-accepted that being more 'open' (having weaker intellectual property rights) can improve welfare by improving access. But this is certainly not the case in relation to innovation. In fact most of the traditional literature on innovation would support, implicitly or explicitly, reasoning

DOI: 10.4018/978-1-60960-513-1.ch008

along the following lines: the level of innovation is a function of the value that innovators (that is the original creators of a work or invention) obtain, V, and the cost they incur, F. Furthermore, it is clear that the level (or likelihood) of innovation is increasing in the value and decreasing in cost. Label the closed and open regimes by C and O respectively then it is usual to assume that the proprietary regime results in higher returns than in the open one: $V^P > V^O$, while costs are unchanged: $F^P = F^O$.[3] This necessarily implies that innovation must be higher in the proprietary regime than in the open one. Furthermore, suppose imitation has cost F^{IMM} but is 'fast'.[4] Then, simple competitive free entry arguments would suggest that the common returns (common because imitation is fast) must be driven down to costs so the innovator receives $V = F^{IMM}$. Since an innovator must cover her costs innovation can only occur if imitation is at least as costly as innovation: $F^{IMM} \leq F$. But, at least in the open case, imitation is certain to be cheaper than innovation and hence no innovation will occur!

This brief sketch of the standard approach already indicates why the level of 'open' production is rather surprising. It also points us to where we must look if we are to explain the success, or simply survival, of open approaches: either we can examine costs $F()$ or income/value V. At this point it is worth recalling that repeated surveys, such as Levin et al. (1987), Mansfield (1985), Cohen et al. (2000), and Arundel (2001), show that firms appropriate returns from innovation using a variety of methods other than exclusive rights (IP) such as secrecy, lead time, marketing and sales, learning curve advantages. Not only does this indicate that there are a variety of first-mover advantage for an innovator, but this work also shows that imitation is a costly process both in terms of time and money even when no exclusive rights are used (or available). Of course, the major alternative to IP is often secrecy. In the case of `open' (`open source') knowledge production both secrecy and the traditional exclusivity of IP are foregone. Nevertheless, even in this case,

imitation costs and first-mover advantage will still exist -- though perhaps much reduced in size.

This article takes this empirical evidence 'seriously' and we explicitly model imitation as costly (though still as cheaper than innovation usually) and the innovator as having some form of first-mover advantage. Our framework provides a simple, and novel, way to conceptualize 'innovation' space, which allows one to compare innovation under a proprietary and an 'open-source' regime in a straightforward and intuitive manner. We show that, even in the baseline case where 'open-sourcing' simply reduces imitation (copying) costs, some innovation will still take place under the open-source regime – albeit substantially less than in the proprietary case. The crucial point here is that, at low innovation costs, 'allowable' imitation costs (that is imitation costs that still result in the innovation being made) can be even lower. Thus, even for large large reductions in the cost of imitation some innovations remain feasible.

Our next step is to consider the possibility that an 'open' approach reduces both innovation and imitation costs. A variety of authors (e.g. Lakhani and von Hippel (2003); Bessen (2006)) have pointed out that an `open-source' approach may offer substantial efficiency advantages – for example by allowing users to participate directly in adding features and fixing `bugs' – and this is particularly true where the information good is complex and (hence) transaction costs are high. While the initial arguments in favour of the efficiency of open approaches were based on anecdotal or case study evidence, recent empirical work on a larger scale, such as Koch (2008), have provided strong empirical support for his view. Thus, we explicitly model the move to `open-source' as resulting in a simultaneous reduction in *both* innovation and imitation cost. This clearly makes an open approach more attractive. However, the real question is not whether it is more attractive but to what extent this is so. After all the outcome under an open regime may still be (far) inferior to that under a closed one. Here, we are able to analyse the effect of a change of regime within a single overarching, but simple, framework. Using it, we can compare, clearly, and formally, different assumptions about what going 'open' entails, and derive specific (sufficient) conditions under which a move to an open regime results in an increase in innovation.

THE MODEL

There is some information good, the 'innovation',[5] which can be created at fixed cost F_i – the innovation cost. Once created, it may be imitated with cost F_m (implicitly assumed to be common across all imitators).[6]

What does this imitation cost, F_m, represent? The empirical literature discussed above suggests two main options: either it represents the cost of imitation in money or the cost in time.[7] In general we need not be too concerned with whether it is one of these, or the other – or some combination of both. Rather what will matter for our purposes is that the imitation 'cost' a) affects the income of the innovator b) is itself affected by the regime (open or proprietary) under which the information good is produced.

Specifically, define Π to be *gross* profits of the innovator (that is revenues net of all expenses other than the main innovation cost – note that throughout this article, unless otherwise stated, when referring to profits we shall mean *gross* profits). Following our just stated presumption that imitation 'cost' affects the innovator's income we have that Profits are a function of imitation cost: $\Pi = \Pi(F_m)$. Furthermore as imitation costs rise innovator's profits are non-decreasing: $\Pi' \geq 0$. Finally, though infrequently needed, it will be useful to define $\Pi m(F_m)$ as the (gross) profits of the imitators.[8]

In what follows, we will rarely go beyond this reduced form approach to specify the exact mechanism by which imitation costs impact on the innovator's income as this allows us to proceed with greater generality. For our purposes, all we will require is that costs and profits are all denominated in comparable terms – for example, in terms of a numeraire good 'money'. Nevertheless, it may be useful for the reader to have in mind some concrete examples of the underlying strategic interactions by which an innovator's (gross) profits are determined.

One possibility is that F_m represents pure monetary cost and the innovator and imitators compete to supply a homogenous good in Stackelberg fashion (the innovator being the first-mover).[9] In that case, since imitators must cover their own fixed cost, F_m defines, via a zero profit free-entry condition, the total number of imitators who enter and hence the price level. Lower imitation costs lead to more entry and hence lower prices.

Another possibility is that F_m represents time, that is, the delay before imitators are able to produce a competing product. In this case the innovator enjoys a monopoly prior to imitator entry followed by some subsequent competitive game. Again it is clear that a lower imitation 'cost' corresponds to lower (gross) profits for an innovator. Yet another possibility is to have competition between innovators and imitators but with differentiated products (whether vertically or horizontally differentiated). Here, F_m would be some measure of the proximity of imitators to the innovator in product space and as F_m rises innovator's enjoy a larger/stronger local monopoly and hence once again have larger (gross) profits.

A Normalization

Let M be (gross) monopoly profits of the innovator (i.e. gross profits without any imitative entry). No agent's revenues can be greater than monopoly profits M. Hence, it makes sense to simplify by normalizing profits and innovation fixed costs by dividing them by M:

$$f_i = \frac{F_i}{M}$$

$$f_m = \frac{F_m}{M}$$

$$\pi = \frac{\Pi}{M}$$

We can also take (normalized) profits π to be a function of f_m rather than F_m. It is also useful to define the proportional imitation cost

$$\phi = \frac{F_m}{F_i} = \frac{f_m}{f_i}.$$

Note, in what follows, in order to avoid constant repetition, we will usually omit the statement that a term is 'normalized', and the reader should remember that, by default, when referring to 'profits', 'innovation cost' etc we mean normalized (gross) profits, normalized innovation cost etc.

The Space of Innovations

In this model an innovation (under a particular regime – see next section) is specified by the tuple consisting of its 'innovation' cost and its 'imitation' cost: (f_i, f_m). This conveniently allows us to visualize innovation space in a two dimensional graph (see the figures below for examples). Specifically, innovation and imitation costs are non-negative, $f_i, f_m > 0$ and, without loss of generality, under our normalizations must lie between 0 and 1.[10]Thus, under the assumptions given and using normalized variables the space of innovations is $IS = \{(f_i, f_m) \in [0,1] \times [0,1] \}$, that is the unit square.

In addition, we note that if imitation cost is less or equal to innovation cost, as is often assumed, we have: $f_m \leq f_i$. In this case no innovation will ever lie above the 'diagonal' in the unit square and $IS = \{(f_i, f_m) \in [0,1] \, s \, [0,1]: f_m \leq f_i \}$. Under the intuitive equation of area with amount, using f_i, f_m coordinates gives the impression that the number of (potential) innovations is dropping as

innovation cost drops (since the height under the diagonal is falling with innovation costs). This is rather misleading and to correct this it is natural to change to (f_i, ϕ) coordinates in which case innovation space is again the full unit square: $IS = \{(f_i, \phi) \in [0,1] \times [0,1]\}$. Obviously there is a one-to-one mapping between these coordinate systems and so it does not strictly matter which we use. However, in what follows it will frequently be more convenient to work with (f_i, ϕ) rather than (f_i, f_m).

Proprietary and Open Regimes

We shall be interested in comparing different regimes under which a given innovation (or set of innovations) may be produced. A regime (R) can have two distinct effects. First, it can affects the innovation and imitation costs (f_i, f_m), that is, the location of an innovation in 'innovation space' (IS). In particular, location of an innovation (or set of innovations) can be represented by some density function on IS, say k, which is a function of the regime – so $k = k^R$.[11] Second, the regime may alter the profit function itself π, that is, the manner in which imitation cost affects the (gross) profits of the innovators.

Here, we focus on the first of these effects only and assume that the regime has no impact on the profit function itself – of course, it will affect profits since these are a function of imitation costs. We will be interested in comparing and contrasting two particular regimes: a closed/proprietary one – based on some combination of secrecy and exclusive rights (e.g. patent or copyright) – and an open one. These two regimes, via their impact on imitation and innovation cost will lead to the same innovation (or set of innovations) being located in different positions in innovation space. This is illustrated in Figure 1 for the case where the move from closed to open results in a drop in both innovation costs f_i and a reduction in proportional imitation costs ϕ (which corresponds to an even larger drop in imitation costs since $f_m = \phi f_i$).

Figure 1. Effect of different regimes on the location of an innovation or innovation set. As shown, an open regime results in both lower innovation and lower imitation costs (both absolutely, f_m, and proportionately φ).

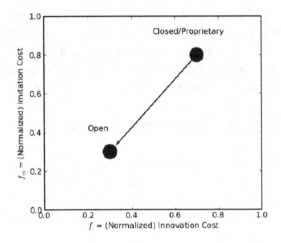

ANALYSIS

Our analysis proceeds in stages. First, we define the feasible set, that is the subset of innovations in innovation space that would occur with a particular (normalized, gross) profits function. Next, we deduce some basic properties and structure of this feasible set. Given a particular set of (potential) innovations a regime determines their location in innovation space. Intersecting that location with the feasible set we have the set of innovations that occur under that particular regime. Since, as just discussed above, we take an approach where the profit function is assumed not to change across regimes the feasible set remains constant. Thus, finally, we look out how a change in regime affects the level of innovation by examining how the regime alters the location of (potential) innovations within innovation space, and thereby alters the intersection of these innovations with the feasible set. In particular, we can provide non-trivial conditions on the size of the reductions in innovation and imitation cost under which a move to an open regime increases the level of innovation.

The Feasible Set

Take a particular regime R. This has associated with it some (gross) profits function: $\pi(f_m)$. A (potential) innovation, (f_i, f_m), is feasible if, and only if, it generates a non-negative net surplus for its associated innovator: $\pi(f_m) - f_i \geq 0$ – that is if, and only if, its fixed cost is less than its (gross) profits. We may then define the 'feasible set' as the subset of IS consisting of all (potential) innovations which are feasible:

Definition 1 *(The Feasible Set). The 'Feasible Set', F for a regime R is the subset of innovation space whose corresponding innovations occur under R:*

$$F = \text{FeasibleSet} = \{(f_i, f_m) \in IS : f_i \leq \pi(f_m)\}$$
$$= \{(f_i, \phi) \in IS : f_i \leq \pi(\phi f_i)\}$$

As discussed above, a regime affects the distribution of innovation within innovation space and/or the profit function π itself. In the latter case (but not the former) the feasible set will then depend on the regime: $F = F^R$. As also discussed above, by default we focus only on the former case – where the regime is taken only to affect the distribution of innovations. In this situation the feasible set is independent of the regime. Thus, in what follows we will talk simply about 'the' feasible set F, independent of the particular regime.

What can we say about the structure of the feasible set? First, observe that the feasible set is closed and hence it includes its boundary. Next note that, with innovation cost on the x-axis in the IS diagram, the feasible set will simply be the space lying to the left of the line $f_i = \pi(f_m)$. Since f_i is plotted on the x-axis it is natural to transform this to a function of innovation cost: F is then the set lying above the line $g(f_i)$ where $g = \pi^{-1}$. In terms of proportional imitation cost coordinates (f_i, ϕ) this is the line given by $h(f_i)$ where $h = g(f_i)/f_i$, and the feasible set are those points lying above this line.[12]

Figure 2. An example of a feasible set corresponding to π (f_m) = ⇒ g(f_i) =, h(f_i) = f_i. The functions shown conform to the restrictions described in the text (in fact they derive from the Stackelberg example already discussed in the section 2).

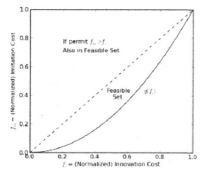 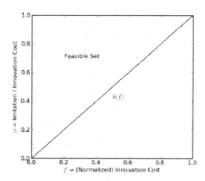

Thus, what is needed is to characterise how (gross) profits, $\pi (f_m)$, vary with imitation costs. First recall that we have $\pi' > 0$ that is (gross) profits are increasing in imitation cost. Next, observe that as we are using renormalized variables $lim (f_m \to) \pi (f_m) = 1$ and so $g(f_i, 1) \in F \forall f_i \in (0,1)$ (in particular, (1,1) is in F). Similarly, the limit of (gross) profits as imitation costs go to zero must be non-negative: $\pi(0) \geq 0$. Figure 2 shows a graphical rendering of one possible feasible set conforming to these restrictions together with a labelling of the main features (e.g. g, h curves). To go beyond these basic observations we need to introduce a condition on the profit function. First a definition:

Definition 2. *A function H,(x) is super-linear if $H(kx) \geq kH(x)$ and sub-linear if $H(kx) \leq kH(x) \forall k \in (0,1)$. That is H lies below (above) any ray from the origin to x.*

Note that a sufficient condition for H to be super-linear (sub-linear) is that (a) $H(0)$ is non-negative (b) H is quasi-concave (quasi-convex) (Pf: take $0, x$ as the endpoints of an interval and apply the usual definition of convexity/concavity). With this definition in place we may make our main assumption regarding the profit function $\pi (f_m)$:

Assumption 3. *The profit function is super-linear in imitation cost f_m.*

This has several important implications. However, before discussing these we should ask whether this assumption is reasonable. Our answer is a clear yes. For example, in the Stackelberg case discussed above, and analyzed at length in Pollock (2006), (gross) profits are concave in imitation costs: $\pi (f_m) = \sqrt{f_m}$ (remember here that all values are normalized to lie in 0, 1 so $\sqrt{f_m} \geq f_m$). Taking another of the examples mentioned previously, if f_m measures time before imitative entry then simple discounting again implies that π is concave and hence that π is super-linear. To take another example, suppose f_m represent the mark-up over (variable) costs the innovator is able to charge,[13] then for all 'normal' models of demand one again has that $f_m \pi$ is (quasi-) concave in f_m. Lastly, suppose the innovator has some fixed first mover advantage π_A over imitators so $\pi = \pi_m + \pi_A$. With a standard free-entry assumption imitator (gross) profits π_m will be driven down close to f_m. Then $\pi (f_m) \approx f_m + \pi_A$ and so π is super-linear in f_m.[14] To summarize, in any situation where (gross) profits are concave in imitation 'costs' π will be super-linear. In most normal cases (e.g. several of those just discussed) concavity follows from classic diminishing returns arguments and hence π is super-linear. We therefore feel this is a natural, and reasonable, assumption to impose. We now return to the implications of this assumption for the structure of the feasible set.

First, take any point in the feasible set (f_i, f_m) and $k \in (0,1)$. Now, by super-linearity, $(f_m) \geq f_i$ hence $\pi(kf_m) \geq k\pi(f_m) \geq kf_i$ and hence the point (kf_i, kf_m) is in the feasible set. In particular, for any point on the boundary of the feasible set (i.e. $\pi(f_m), f_m)$ or, equivalently, $(f, g(f))$ the entire ray from that point to the origin must be in the feasible set. This immediately implies that $g(f_i)$, the function defining the boundary of the feasible set in terms of innovation cost, is sub-linear. Changing to f, ϕ coordinates this equates to the following proposition:

Proposition 4. *If an innovation (f, φ) is in the feasible set then all points on the horizontal line to its left lie within the feasible set. Equivalently, h, which defines the boundary of the feasible set, is non-decreasing in innovation cost.*

Proof. *Take a point on the boundary of the feasible set: $(, \varphi^0)$, $\varphi 0 = h()$. Then $\pi() = \pi(\varphi 0) \geq$. Consider a horizontal line from this point to the φ axis, i.e. points of the form $(, \varphi)$, $\varphi = \varphi^0$, $= k \in (0,1)$. Then (gross) profits at a point on this line $(, \varphi 0)$ are:*

$$\pi(f_m^k) = \pi(\phi^0 k f_i^0)$$
$$= \pi(\frac{f_m^0}{f_i^0} k f_i^0)$$
$$= \pi(k f_m^0)$$

By super-linearity of π, $\geq k\pi()$ which we have already shown is $\geq kf_i =$. Hence $(, \varphi)$ is in the feasible set. Thus, the entire horizontal line is in the feasible set. This in turn implies that h is non-decreasing (if not we would have a point on the boundary of feasible set with not all of

the associated horizontal line within the feasible set – contradiction).

The implications of this result, together with the previous remarks, may be summarized in the following proposition:

Proposition 5. *Take an innovation $X = (f_i, f_m) = (f_i)$ and another innovation $Y = (f_i, f_m)$. For some λ, μ we may write $f_i = \lambda f_i$, $f_m = \mu f_m$ and, without loss of generality, $\mu < 1$. If X is in the feasible set, a sufficient (though not necessary) condition for Y to be feasible is $\mu \geq \lambda$, that is, the (proportional) drop in imitation cost is less than the drop in (proportional) innovation cost. In addition, if X is not in F and $\mu \geq \lambda$ then for μ sufficiently small (and hence λ sufficiently small) Y is feasible – that is if we reduce innovation cost and imitation costs at a proportional rate then for a sufficiently great reduction the innovation becomes feasible.*

Proof. *X is feasible so $\pi(f_m) \geq f_i$. Now, $\pi(f_m) = \pi(\mu f_m) \geq \mu\pi(f_m) \geq \mu f_i$. If $\mu \geq \lambda$ then $\mu f_i \geq \lambda f_i = f_i$ and we are done. Note that a more intuitive, geometrical version, of this proof is provided using the IS diagram in the next section (see Figure 3).*

Changing Regimes

We now consider the effect of a change of regime on whether an innovation is feasible – or more generally, for a given set of innovations what subset of them are feasible. In particular, we examine what happens if an open regime is adopted instead of a closed, proprietary, one. As discussed in Section 2.3, the change in regime is naturally modelled as a change in the innovation and imitation costs associated with an innovation. Thus, take a particular innovation or technology X, and define $X^C = (,)$ to be its location in innovation space under a closed regime and $X^O = (,)$ its location under an open regime (see Figure 1). It will be useful to write X^O in terms of the coordinates of X^C by defining λ, μ, κ as:

Figure 3. Examples of different 'trajectories' in innovation space under a change from a closed to an open regime. Cases are numbered to correspond to those enumerated in text. Two different feasible sets are illustrated. The first illustrates perhaps the simplest profit function satisfying super-linearity viz μ $(f_m) = kf_m$ (here k = 2). The second is that arising from the Stackelberg model.

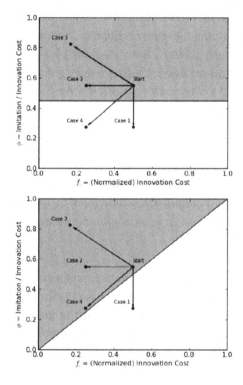

$$f_i^O = \lambda f_i^C$$
$$f_m^O = \mu f_m^C$$
$$\phi^O = \kappa \phi^C \quad \kappa = \frac{\mu}{\lambda}$$

λ, μ, measure the *relative* drop in innovation and imitation costs (respectively) when moving from a closed to an open regime while κ is the ratio of these (relative) changes in imitation cost to innovation cost. A large κ correspond to a situation where innovation costs have fallen much more (relatively) than imitation costs, a small κ

corresponds to the reverse, that is innovation costs have dropped (relatively) much less than imitation costs, and $\kappa = 1$ corresponds to the case where both costs have fallen relatively by the same amount.

Clearly we have λ, $\mu \geq 0$ as innovation and imitation costs cannot be negative. In addition we have:

Assumption 6. *Under a move to an open regime imitation and innovation costs either fall or remain unchanged, that is λ, $\mu \leq 1$.*

This has been stated as an 'assumption' however this statement appears to us so self-evident from the definition of openness as to hardly merit justification. Certainly, it seems clear that by making one's work open one can only reduce the costs of 'imitation' (after all reproduction and reuse are now expressly permitted), while it seems hard to think of any circumstance in which innovation costs increase (they may stay the same – more on this below).

Given this 'assumption', we always have λ, $\mu \in [0,1]$ (and hence $\kappa \in [0, \infty]$) irrespective of the type of the innovation and its initial location under the closed regime. This provides one of the main reasons for using relative values rather than absolute ones (e.g. $\Delta f_i = -$), for, with them, we would have that the change in a variable such as innovation cost was limited by its initial value (e.g. $f_i \geq 0 \Rightarrow \Delta f_i \leq$). Furthermore, relative values fit naturally with the previous results on the structure of the feasible set. We turn now, to the main question of this section. It should already be clear that the impact of a move to openness on feasibility will depend on how innovation and imitation costs change, that is on the values of λ, μ. We shall consider several distinct cases in turn.

The 'Traditional' View

The 'traditional' theoretical view discussed in the introduction equates to:

Relative Change in Innovation Cost = $\lambda = 1$

Relative Change in Imitation Cost = $\mu \ll 1$

That is, a move to openness, by depriving an innovator of the use of exclusive rights or secrecy,[15] must necessarily reduce imitation costs – and reduce them significantly (hence $\mu \ll 1$ not simply $\mu < 1$). Furthermore, though usually more implicit, it is also assumed that innovation costs are unaffected by a change a regime – that is, openness has no impact on the innovator's cost of producing the initial innovation.

The implications of such assumptions are clear. Reducing imitation costs reduces an innovator's (gross) profits while costs are unchanged. Thus, an innovation that is feasible under the closed regime may become infeasible under the open one (while any innovation that is initially infeasible remains so).[16] Hence, moving to an open regime makes it less likely a given innovation is feasible and, thus, on average, reduces the level of innovation that occurs. Furthermore, with the drop in imitation costs being large ($\mu \ll 1$) it is very likely that an innovation feasible under the closed regime is infeasible under the open one.[17]

Changes in Innovation Cost

As discussed in the introduction there is accumulating evidence that an open regime can reduce the innovators cost either by simply making production more efficient or by allowing the innovator to share some of the costs with the wider user community. Letus therefore consider the more general case where a move to openness reduces innovation costs *in addition* to imitation costs:

RelativeChangeinInnovationCost = $\lambda < 1$

RelativeChangeinImitationCost = $\mu < 1$

Here it will be useful to work primarily with

$\lambda, \kappa = \frac{\mu}{\lambda}$

rather than λ, μ – that is in (f_i, ϕ) coordinates rather than (f_i, f_m) coordinates.

Proposition 7. *Irrespective both of the initial location of the innovation in IS and λ, if $\kappa \geq 1$, ($\mu \geq \lambda$) that is the relative reduction in innovation cost is greater than the relative reduction in imitation cost, then an open regime is 'better' than a closed one. 'Better', here, meaning that the level of innovation under that regime is greater than or equal to that under the alternative.*

Proof. *Proposition 5 shows that, irrespective of the initial costs and λ, if $\kappa \geq 1$ any feasible innovation remains feasible. Furthermore, it also shows that, at least for some values of λ (and/or the initial location of the innovation), a innovation infeasible under a closed regime becomes feasible under an open one.*

This is the most general statement we can make without further information about the form of the feasible set (i.e. the structure of the underlying competition model) and/or details of the location of the innovation within that space. Nevertheless, it is important to realize that an open regime may be 'better' under much weaker conditions than $\kappa \geq 1$. For example, in the Stackelberg case discussed above $\pi (f_m) = \sqrt{f_m}$ and hence the boundary of the feasible set has the particularly simple form: $h(f_i) = f_i$, $(g(f_i) = f_i^2)$ Thus, in this case an open regime is better if $\kappa \geq \lambda$. So, for example, if innovation costs drop significantly under the move to an open regime, $\lambda \ll 1$, then the open regime will be better for all but very small κ (to be precise it will be better if imitation costs have fallen by less than $\mu = \lambda^2 \ll \lambda$ since $\lambda \ll 1$). To illustrate this point suppose, under the closed regime, that innovation costs were $1 million imitation costs $750k and that the innovation was feasible. Furthermore, suppose an open approach reduced innovation costs to $200k, a fifth of their original value, then imitation costs could have gone down to any amount above $30k (one 25th of their original value) and the innovation would still be feasible.

In addition to this 'algebraic' proof, it is useful to consider an alternative equivalent geometrical approach based on IS diagrams as this easier to understand and provides a more intuitive presentation of the results. In IS space using (f,ϕ) coordinates a change in costs given by (λ, κ), $\lambda,<1$, equates to a translation of a point in the following ways, each of which is illustrated on the IS diagrams in Figure 3:

$(\lambda, \kappa) = (1,<1)$: vertically downwards. This is the 'traditional case': innovation costs are unchanged and imitation costs $\kappa = \mu$ with fixed innovation costs) have dropped.

$(\lambda, \kappa) = (\lambda,1)$: horizontally left. Innovation and imitation costs have dropped by equal proportions.

$(\lambda, \kappa) = (\lambda,> 1)$: diagonally to the left and upwards. A reduction in innovation costs with a less than proportional drop in imitation costs. One (extreme) example is the case of a reduction in innovation costs with no drop in imitation costs which corresponds to $(\lambda, 1/\lambda)$

$$\frac{1}{\lambda}$$

(i.e. moving left along the hyperbola).

$(\lambda, \kappa) = (\lambda, < 1)$: diagonally to the left and downwards. A reduction in innovation costs with a more than proportional drop in imitation costs.

As just mentioned, Figure 3 illustrates these trajectories together with two examples of feasible sets both satisfying the (minimal) 'horizontal-line' condition. Not only is the basic result clear but we can easily deduce various other simple properties. For example, (for most feasible sets and most innovations) as $\kappa \to 0$ (imitation costs fall much more than innovation costs) a closed regime is 'better' than an open one (the 'tradi-

tional' result). Similarly, one can easily see how conditions on λ, κ will vary with the form of the feasible set (as given by its boundary function h) as well as with (initial) location of an innovation relative to that boundary.

To conclude, if we allow, as the evidence suggests, that openness results in a fall in innovation costs as well as imitation costs then an open regime may be superior to a closed one (for innovation). Whether this is so, depends on the relative rates at which costs of innovation have fallen relative to imitation costs. It was shown that, at a minimum, with equiproportional reductions in costs openness was always preferable (and therefore was also better for any situation in which innovation costs fell less rapidly relative to imitation costs). Thus, contrary to the 'conventional wisdom', openness need not always result in a decline in innovation – in fact it might sometimes increase it. Furthermore, as was illustrated by the use of an IS diagram, stronger results could be obtained if one imposed more structure on the feasible set and/or the initial location of the innovation under the closed regime.

On this last point, it is worth observing that producers of information goods may derive some benefit from their efforts, whether monetary or otherwise, that is not affected by imitation of the original work. For example, they may be able to supply an associated complementary item – e.g. support services – which are not open to easy imitation (perhaps they are rival or proprietary), or, alternatively, they may simply derive intrinsic satisfaction from their creative endeavours.[18]

The existence of such an alternative, but related, source of 'income', has three significant implications. First, and most obviously, it ensures a certain minimum level of 'income' even if openness has sharply reduced imitation costs and hence innovator's (gross) profits from the original information good. Second, opening up the underlying information good is likely to increase usage thereby stimulating demand for the complementary one.[19] Third, and least obvious, since knowledge of the original innovation is needed to supply the complementary one, 'open-sourcing', by increasing the gap between imitation and innovation costs, is likely to increase an innovator's income on the complementary good by reducing the number of competitors.

Crucially, all three of these effects act a) to increase the size of the feasible set, and b) to increase it more at low levels of the imitation cost. In terms of the IS diagram this is an increase in the feasible set in the lower left-hand quadrant. Cursory examination of the IS diagram shows that it is precisely these sort of changes in the structure of the feasible set which make openness (more) attractive (e.g. compare top and bottom diagrams in Figure 3). They therefore make it more likely that an open regime is superior to a closed one.

CONCLUSION

In this article we have presented a simple framework with which to understand the interaction of innovation and imitation. Using it, we discussed how a move from a closed to an open regime could be represented in 'innovation space'. The approach also allowed one, at the same time, to represent (simultaneously) the set of feasible innovations – as determined by the underlying model of competition between 'innovators' and 'imitators'.

It was shown that, when innovators enjoy first-mover advantages, innovation may still occur even when imitation is (substantially) cheaper than innovation. Going further we proposed a basic condition, which if satisfied by underlying model of competition(as encapsulated in the innovator's profit function), allowed us to derive important features of the feasible set. With a regime determining the location of innovations in 'innovation space' one could use properties of the feasible set to make specific predictions about how changes in regime (e.g. closed to open) affected the level of innovation.

Starting from the accumulating anecdotal and empirical evidence that openness may confer significant efficiency advantages, we examined the situation where a move to open production resulted in a reduction in *both* innovation costs as well as in imitation costs – not simply a reduction in imitation costs alone as is usually assumed by the more traditional literature.

Precise sufficient conditions on the relative reductions in the two types of cost were derived under which a move to an open regime would actually increase innovation. These conditions had a particularly simple form: if the proportional reduction in innovation cost was a least as large as that in imitation cost then an open regime was better. We discussed the sufficiency aspect of this result and pointed out that in many situations it was likely that much stronger results would hold. Here however, though we provided some explicit examples to illustrate this point, we wished to remain at as general level as possible and therefore did not go further in examining specific cases – this may be a fruitful area for future work.

Nevertheless, we did observe that the ability of an innovator to sell some form of complementary good would be one major example where stronger results could be obtained. A cursory examination of current 'real-world' practice reveals that this possibility is more the norm that the exception. For example, the author of a piece of software is often able to supply support services or additional 'plugins'. Similarly a musician gives live performances in addition to writing the music itself, and engineers may charge for consultancy as well as access to any inventions they make.[20]

Thus, it is likely that in a variety of areas open approaches are a sustainable form of operation and, at least in some cases, may be superior to proprietary ones. However, as should be clear, we are not suggesting that this will always be the case. It is therefore important for society to have some method for deciding for which industries, or technologies, it is so, and for which it is not. One of the primary contributions of this article has been precisely to provide a simple, intuitive, yet rich, framework in which, by reference to an overarching 'innovation space', one can go about doing this.

REFERENCES

Arundel, A. (2001). Patents in the Knowledge-Based Economy. *Beleidstudies Technology Economie, 37*, 67–88.

Bessen, J. (2006). Open Source Software: Free Provision of Complex Public Goods. In Bitzer, J., & Schraeder, P. J. H. (Eds.), *The Economics of Open Source Software Development*. Elsevier B. V.doi:10.1016/B978-044452769-1/50003-2

Cohen, W., Nelson, R., & Walsh, P. (2000). Protecting Their Intellectual Assets: Appropriability Conditions and Why U.S. Manufacturing Firms Patent (or Not). NBER Working Paper No. W7552.

Hopenhayn, H. A., & Mitchell, M. F. (2001). Innovation Variety and Patent Breadth. *The Rand Journal of Economics, 32*(1), 152–166. doi:10.2307/2696402

Klemperer, P. (1990). How Broad Should the Scope of Patent Protection Be? *The Rand Journal of Economics, 21*(1), 113–130. doi:10.2307/2555498

Koch, S. (2008). Effort Modeling and Programmer Participation in Open Source Software Projects. *Information Economics and Policy*.

Lakhani, K. R., & von Hippel, E. (2003). How open source software works: "free" user-to-user assistance. *Research Policy, 32*(6), 923–943. doi:10.1016/S0048-7333(02)00095-1

Levin, R., Klevorick, A., Nelson, R., Winter, S., Gilbert, R., & Griliches, Z. (1987). Appropriating the Returns from Industrial Research and Development. *Brookings Papers on Economic Activity, 3*, 783–831. doi:10.2307/2534454

Macleod, C. (1988). *Inventing the Industrial Revolution: The English Patent System, 1660-1800*. Cambridge.

Mansfield, E. (1985). How Rapidly Does New Industrial Technology Leak Out? *The Journal of Industrial Economics, 34*(2), 217–223. doi:10.2307/2098683

Nordhaus, W. (1969). *Invention, Growth and Welfare: A Theoretical Treatment of Technological Change*. M.I.T. Press.

Pollock, R. (2006). *The Value of the Public Domain*. Published by the Institute for Public Policy Research as part of a series on IP and the Public Sphere.

Rossi, M. A. (2004). *Decoding the "Free/Open Source (F/OSS) Software Puzzle" a survey of theoretical and empirical contributions. Department of Economics University of Siena 424*. Department of Economics, University of Siena.

Scherer, F. (1972). Nordhaus' Theory of Optimal Patent Life: A Geometric Reinterpretation. *The American Economic Review, 62*(3), 422–427.

Scotchmer, S., & Green, J. (1990). Novelty and Disclosure in Patent Law. *The Rand Journal of Economics, 21*(1), 131–146. doi:10.2307/2555499

Teece, D. J. (1986). Profiting from technological innovation: Implications for integration, collaboration, licensing and public policy. *Research Policy, 15*(6), 285–305. doi:10.1016/0048-7333(86)90027-2

ENDNOTES

[1] For the purposes of this paper a work is 'open' or 'open-source' if it can be used, redistributed and reused freely. Here, freely means without monetary or other substantial restriction though, for example the requirement of attribution or even that derivative

works be re-shared, does not render a work unfree. However it does exclude the requirement of payment or that explicit permission be sought, or the imposition of restrictions on the type of use (such as limiting it to research or non-commercial activities). Furthermore, since, without access, a piece of knowledge cannot be used it also excludes the use of secrecy – 'open' knowledge must be publicly available.

2   Hat is those based on on secrecy, exclusive rights (IP) or some combination thereof.

3   Proprietary regime gives the innovator an exclusive monopoly right. As such, in the traditional view, an innovator should make at least as much – and probably substantially more – under the closed regime than under the open one. On the costs points, as we shall discuss in great detail below this assumption is not necessarily accurate. However, here we are simply illustrating a 'standard' view common in the literature.

4   It is noteworthy that much of the existing theoretical literature has tended to assume 'perfect' nonrivalry, that is, that an innovation (or creative work) once made may be costlessly, and instantaneously, reproduced if not protected by IP or hidden from others via secrecy. For example, Nordhaus (1969) (and following him Scherer (1972)), in what is considered to be one of the founding papers of the policy literature, implicitly assume that without a patent an innovator gains no remuneration. Similarly, Klemperer (1990) in his paper on patent breadth makes clear his assumption of costless imitation as do Scotchmer and Green (1990). For a more recent example see e.g. Hopenhayn and Mitchell (2001).

5   Throughout we will use the term innovation and imitation rather than alternatives such as creator and copier. Though the former are usually more associated with (patentable) 'ideas' while the second are more associated

with (copyrightable) expressions no such distinction is intended here.

6   This model can easily be generalized to allow variations in imitation costs – for example imitation costs could fall as more and more imitators enter, or it could fall with time etc.

7   There are clearly other possibilities, for example imitation may be limited by the availability of skilled labour, or access to other necessary complementary assets – see e.g. Teece (1986). However, these are both more complex to model and, we believe, of lesser importance than the main factors of time and money.

8   If profits vary across imitators define this as the maximum of the profits earned by imitators.

9   Pollock (2006) considers this particular model in detail.

10   Clearly the maximum revenue an innovator – or an imitator – can obtain is. Hence, no innovation with an innovation cost above will ever occur and thus we may, without loss of generality, ignore such a possibility.

11   This distributional approach gives us a natural way to represent not only a single innovation or technology but a whole set of innovations – for example at the industry or economy wide level – as well to represent uncertainty with respect to the location of a particular innovation or technology.

12   Note that while was increasing – as innovations cost rise so the feasible imitation cost must rise – may not be.

13   This would be a natural outcome of a model where imitators locate in relation to an innovator in quality 'space' and is some measure of their 'proximity' to the innovator – cf. 'breadth' in standard patent models.

14   For $k \in (0,1)$ we have. $\pi(kf_m) \approx kf_m + \pi_A \geq k(f_m + \pi_A) = k\pi(f_m)$

15   In fact secrecy is usually ignored and it is simply the lack of exclusive rights that is considered sufficient to justify this result.

[16] In IS space we can visualize this change as move vertically downwards (note this trajectory is the same whether in (f_i, f_m) or $(f_i,$ coordinates). Since the feasible set lies above the line defined by a non-decreasing function gh (or h) a move vertically downwards can only make it more likely a given point is not in the feasible set.

[17] Alternatively, suppose the drop in imitation costs is not large but (as is often also implicitly assumed) first-mover advantages are small then (gross) profits, , are close to imitation costs. Assuming that a given innovation is initially feasible we must have that its cost is close to (initial) imitation costs () and hence any reduction in profits is likely to make it infeasible.

[18] See e.g. Rossi (2004) for a review of these sorts of possibilities.

[19] Increased imitation and dissemination may also be positive effect for the more 'intrinsic' motivations. For example, a scientist may gain enhanced prestige (and citations) as a result of their work being more widely reused and disseminated when released openly (it is important to emphasize here that openness is perfectly compatible with a strong attribution requirement – in fact many 'open' licenses explicitly require clear attribution).

[20] This last case is inspired by the 18th century engineer John Rennie, one of the most famous engineers of the industrial revolution. In 1789 he worked on the Albion Mills for Watt and Boulton. To Watt's horror, upon completion, Rennie, rather than patenting his new design, was eager to demonstrate it to others. "[F]ar from ruining him [Rennie] as Watt predicted, [this] established his reputation and led to a flood of commissions"[?] [p. 104]macleod 1988

This work was previously published in International Journal of Open Source Software and Processes (IJOSSP), edited by Stefan Koch, pp. 28-42, copyright 2009 by IGI Publishing (an imprint of IGI Global).

Chapter 9
Consumer Welfare and Market Structure in a Model of Competition between Open Source and a Model of Proprietary Software

Alexia Gaudeul
University of East Anglia, UK

ABSTRACT

I consider a Vickrey-Salop model of spatial product differentiation with quasi-linear utility functions and contrast two modes of production, the proprietary model where entrepreneurs sell software to the users, and the open source model where users participate in software development. I show that the OS model of production may be more efficient from the point of view of welfare than the proprietary model, but that an OS industry is vulnerable to entry by entrepreneurs while a proprietary industry can resist entry by OS projects. A mixed industry where OS and proprietary development methods coexist may exhibit large OS projects cohabiting with more specialized proprietary projects, and is more efficient than the proprietary model of production from the point of view of welfare.

INTRODUCTION

There is a variety of mixed industries; industries where for-profit and non-profit coexist. In the present model, I will focus on the decision by consumers between contributing to collective projects, or buying goods that are produced by independent entrepreneurs and sold for profit. The model will be particularly adapted to the study of competition in the software industry between software developed under proprietary license terms and software developed under open source ('OS') license terms. However, it is also adapted to the wide range of areas in which open development methods are used concurrently with proprietary methods. This includes genetic and biological research, which among other research areas has benefited from the use of open source methods. For example, the publicly financed and open Human Genome Project competed with the privately financed Celera Genomics. Other projects have been set up to further the use of OS methods in this area (www.bioforge.net, www.bioinformatics.org, www.genome.wustl. edu). This also includes blogs (Raynes-Goldie (2004), Gaudeul, Mathieu, and Peroni (2008)), which link spontaneously generated independent contributions together in a complex system of relations and have emerged as an alternative and/ or complement to established news media. Online databases that can be openly edited by anybody (Wikis) generate alternative repositories of knowledge also compete with established dictionaries and encyclopedias. Online communities and other group communication mechanisms, such as Facebook or LinkedIn compete with established search and coordination infrastructures provided by firms and in markets. Knowledge production in the academia, which can be described as an open source process (Bezroukov (1999), Raymond (2001)), competes with the research output produced from within firms. Finally, non profits in the health sector, the provision of services to the poor, museums, job training, etc...compete with their private counterparts. The domains of application of this article are therefore extensive.

The current literature on the patterns of competition and cooperation between open source and proprietary projects and methods is already rather well developed. However, there is little work on how the cohabitation of open source and proprietary models of production affects consumer welfare and market structure at the industry level. I find that an industry where only the OS development model is used is more efficient from the point of view of welfare than an industry where proprietary development is used to the exclusion of other development methods. However, an OS industry will be vulnerable to entry by entrepreneurs that use proprietary development methods, while an industry that uses the proprietary mode of development will be able to resist entry by

OS projects. A mixed industry where OS and proprietary development methods coexist may exhibit large OS projects cohabiting with more specialized proprietary projects, and this pattern of coexistence will improve on a proprietary industry from the point of view of welfare.

CONTEXT

I have conducted two main empirical studies to analyze the patterns of cohabitation between open source and proprietary software. In the first project (Gaudeul (2003), Gaudeul (2007)), I consider the evolution of the patterns of competition between LATEX, an open source typesetting software, and its proprietary alternatives and complements. In a second project (Gaudeul (2008)), I consider empirical data to explain when and why open source software does not attract users. There are very few other empirical studies of the patterns of competition between OS and proprietary software ('PS') and of the influence of open source software ('OSS') on PS production and vice-versa. Bitzer and Schröder (2006) assert from case studies that OSS encourages innovation from proprietary software – even though Klincewicz (2005) report that OSS itself may not be very innovative, and Harison and Koski (2008) report that firms that develop OSS as part of their business model are less productive than those that provide only proprietary applications. Franke and von Hippel (2003) consider the development of security functionalities in Apache, the web server, and show its success comes from being able to address the heterogeneous needs of those users who are dissatisfied with the proprietary offering. Mockus, Fielding, and Herbsleb (2005) compares the development of Apache and Mozilla and underlines how Mozilla may have benefited from maintaining much of the machinery of its past commercial development.

LITERATURE REVIEW

The above empirical studies have inspired a number of models of competition between OS and PS. I will neglect in this review all the papers that compare the performance of OS and proprietary development methods from the point of view of efficiency (see for example Johnson (2002) or Kuan (2002)). The models of competition that have been devised up to now essentially consider mixed market duopolies, where one OS software/platforms competes with one proprietary alternative. In Bitzer (2004), proprietary developers can survive entry by OSS as long as they differentiate enough from the OS offering. In Darmon, le Texier, and Torre (2006), proprietary firms can adopt a "low price and/or high quality" strategy and dominate the market, or a "high price and/or low quality" strategy and risk losing the market to OSS. In Lambardi (2007), the proprietary developer may want to lower the price charged to users-developers in order to deter entry and prevent the development of an open source alternative. In Gaudeul (2005), I show that competition favors the use of the BSD license terms rather than the GPL. This is because potential competitors will contribute to BSD software with the hope of integrating it in their own proprietary software. In Economides and Katsamakas (2006), proprietary developers can base their development on an open-source or a proprietary platform. Proprietary platforms are shown to attract a bigger share of users. Sen (2007) considers the choice between developing proprietary software and developing a commercial version of OSS. Casadesus-Masanell and Ghemawat (2006) consider a dynamic mixed duopoly model and analyze the dynamics of diffusion of OSS in a market dominated by proprietary software. PS is shown to resist entry by OSS by exploiting network effects strategically. Leoncini, Rentocchini, and Marzetti (2008) consider a technology diffusion model and confirm coexistence is possible.

Quite apart from those models of competition, another strand of literature, presented in a special issue of Organization Science (von Hippel and von Krogh (2003)) offers a number of reflections on the emergence of a 'private-collective' innovation model that combines the strengths of both OS and proprietary production models. Hybrid development models are analyzed in Mustonen (2005) where firms may support OS development if network effects are small in order to encourage compatibility of OSS with their product, but also in Bonaccorsi and Rossi (2006) and Wichmann (2002) which survey the motivations for proprietary involvement in OS development. Finally, O'Mahony (2005) considers the role of non-profit foundations in fostering collaboration between the OS community and firms.

Darmon, le Texier, and Torre (2006), along with Schmidt and Schnitzer (2003) or Bessen (2006), are among the few articles to consider explicitly the consumers' welfare issues that are brought about by the adoption of OSS. Darmon, le Texier, and Torre (2006) argue that the development of OSS can lead to consumers mis-coordinating on the wrong sort of software if the objectives of commercial developers are not aligned with those of consumers. Schmidt and Schnitzer (2003) argues that OSS lower profits and therefore incentives for innovation from the part of proprietary developers. Comino and Manenti (2005), however, show that governments would be well advised, if not to subsidize OSS, at least to advertise its availability. Bessen (2006) argues that in the case of complex products, concurrent provision of software as OSS improves welfare as it saves on development costs for specialized needs. von Engelhardt and Swaminathan (2008) show that coexistence of OS and PS spurs innovation and improve growth.

Less directly related to this article, there are a few papers that analyze competition between for-profit and non-profits. However those papers focus on different aspects of this coexistence, such as ownership effects (Ballou (2005)), motivations and objectives in non-profit provision (Brhlikova (2004), Brhlikova (2006)), or the taste of some consumers for non-profit provision (Besley and Ghatak (2001)). In Sloan (2000), consumers might prefer non-profit provision of services such as health care because they fear that for-profit provision might lead to inadequate incentives for hospital managers and physicians. In Glaeser (2002), competition from for-profits will discipline managers in non-profit firms. Rose-Ackerman (1990) analyzes more generally the patterns of coexistence between non-profits and for-profits and considers when non-profits will successfully enter the commercial sector. The influence of government policies is analyzed in the context of the competition between public (State) and private (Public) schools (Epple and Romano (1998)),[1] and in the context of public financing for the arts, which can crowd out private provision (Frey (1999)). It is important to notice that there is no role for the State or charitable institutions in the present article, as I focus on a process of private provision of a public good (Bergstrom, Blume, and Varian (1986)). I will however be able to draw out some public policy implications from this article.

THE MODEL

I adapt a model offered in Alesina and Spolaore (1997) ('A&S') to consider a circular city location model where consumers differ in their preferences over one dimension of a specific good (the software they use), and have the choice between a variety of competing products located along the preference circle. Each product costs K to produce, and has value g to the consumer that is closest to its location. A consumer i that is located at distance i from the location of the product derives utility i from the product, with a measuring the extent to which products are differentiated – the higher is a, the more important it is for the good to be close to the consumer's preferred location.

The model is thus a Vickrey-Salop (circular city) model of spatial product differentiation with

quasi-linear utility functions (Vickrey (1964), which was reprinted in Vickrey (1999), and Salop (1979)). As in most of the literature using that type of model, I will consider equilibria where firms are evenly spaced, even though other types of equilibria may exist in theory (Braid (2004)). I consider free-entry equilibrium such that there is no profit to be made by an additional firm entering the market when firms do not react strategically to entry by either changing location or changing prices.

I consider two modes of production. Under the open source model, portion s of consumers decide to produce the good collectively, with each consumer contributing equally to the cost K of production. Under the proprietary model, an entrepreneur, j, decides to produce the good, at cost K, and then sells the good at price j, the same for all consumers. In a first section, I reproduce the results by A&S and extend them to consider potential entry by a proprietary entrepreneur. I show that this potential entry puts additional constraints on how big OS projects can become, and I also show that if OS contributors anticipate entry, then OS projects cannot resist entry by proprietary developers. In a second section I apply A&S's model to the context of proprietary production. I compare that situation with that obtained in the open source ('OS') production model and show that welfare obtained in a proprietary industry is lower than that obtained in an OS industry, and worse, that it is robust to entry by the potentially more efficient OS model. After having analyzed those two situations, where a single production method, collective or entrepreneurial, is used, I analyze a mixed industry model where both methods are used in the same market for different products. The analysis of this specific context allows me to determine the share of users of OS vs. proprietary software when all users are also potentially developers, and whether a mixed industry provides higher or lower welfare than an industry with a single production model. This mixed industry context also leads me to offer a number of ideas for extensions to the model at the end of the article.

OS INDUSTRY

In this part, I give out and interpret the main results of interest from Alesina and Spolaore (1997), and examine the effect of potential entry by proprietary software in an OS industry.

A world population of mass 1 is composed of a continuum of individuals whose ideal points are distributed uniformly over a circle of circumference 1. Each individual may contribute to the production of a public good, an Open Source Software ('OSS') project. There may be a number of such projects, $N \geq 1$, and it costs K for any such project to be completed. This cost may be expressed in monetary terms, but does not necessarily reflect monetary contributions, but rather the money equivalent of the time and effort devoted by each contributing individuals to the project. An individual i that contributes t_i to a project that is located at distance l_i from her ideal point derives from that project utility $U_i = g(1 - al_i) - t_i$.

The location of the project is determined by the average of the locations of individual contributors to the project. I will assume that each individual does not consider the impact of her contribution on the location of the project (a contributor 'to the right' of the project would presumably change its position to the right, even if by an infinitesimal amount); that is, contributors take the position of the projects as given.

The contributions of the developers must sum up to K for the project to exist, that is, if s is the mass of contributors, and they all contribute t to the project, then I must have $st = K$ for the project to be achieved successfully. I will assume all developers contribute equally to the project they participate in and they contribute to only one project.

The proposition below sets out the optimal size s^* and number N^* of software projects from

the point of view of a benevolent social planner who seeks to maximize social welfare.

Proposition 1. *A social planner seeking to maximize welfare will choose to establish N^* projects of equal size s^*, such that $s^* = 2\sqrt{K/ag}$ and $N^* = \sqrt{ag/K}/2$.*

Proof. *Consider N projects equally spaced in the location circle. The social planner maximizes the sum of all individual utilities. Denoting project numbers as $x = 1,...,N$ and $\bar{l}_x$ the average distance from the project for each of its individual contributors, then social welfare SW will be*

$$SW = \sum_{x=1}^{N} s_x[g(1 - a\bar{l}_x) - t_x] \qquad (1)$$

In a symmetric equilibrium, each project x covers space $s_x = 1/N$ and therefore, the farthest a consumer can be from her preferred location is $1/2N$, so that on average consumers will be located at distance $1/4N$ from their preferred location. Furthermore, the contribution that is required of each consumer must be such that $t_x = K/s_x$, which is equal to KN by the expression of s_x above. Therefore, the expression for social welfare can be simplified to

$$SW = g - KN - ag/4N \qquad (2)$$

which is concave and is maximized for $N^* = \sqrt{ag/4K}$. SW will then be:

$$SW^* = g - \sqrt{Kag}$$

A detailed proof including the cases where N^* is not an integer is in A&S, proposition 1. QED

The following proposition sets out the number N_{OS} and size s_{OS} of projects in a symmetric equilibrium that occurs as the result of the competition between projects organized along open source principles. Projects must be at least larger than a minimum size for contributors not to defect to the adjoining project where they would be asked for a lower contribution.

Proposition 2. *If developers are free to choose the project they want to contribute to, but are not able to coordinate their decisions with other developers, then a stable equilibrium of the contribution game must be such that there will be N_{OS} projects of equal size such that*

$$s_{OS} > \sqrt{2}\sqrt{K/ag} \text{ and } N_{OS} < \sqrt{ag/2K}.$$

Proof. *Consider project 1 and 2, of size s_1 and s_2 respectively. The user developer at the border between the two projects is located at distance $s_1/2$ of project 1 and $s_2/2$ of project 2 and must be indifferent between the two for the projects' border to be stable. Therefore, I must have:*

$$g(1 - as_2/2) - K/s_2 = g(1 - as_1/2) - K/s_1$$

which is solved in two cases, either $s_1 = s_2$ or $s_1 s_2 = 2K/ag$. The case where $s_1 = s_2$ (= s by definition) is stable only if, supposing project 2 increases in size by ε at the expense of project 1, then the individual at the new border at distance $(s-\varepsilon)/2$ of project 1 prefers contributing to project 1 rather than project 2, that is:

$$g(1-a(s+\varepsilon)/2)-K/(s+\varepsilon)<g(1-a(s-\varepsilon)/2)-K/(s-\varepsilon)$$

which simplifies to $s^2 > 2K/ag$ as ε tends towards 0.

The other case, where $s_1 s_2 = 2K/ag$, will not be stable according to the logic above. There is therefore a unique stable symmetric equilibrium as exposed in the proposition. More details are provided in A&S, proposition 2. QED

The above proposition sets a minimum size for an OS project. The threat of forking, that is, developers within a project striking on their own and establishing a separate project, will put a upper limit to how big a project can be. This is because an OS project that becomes too big will see a significant number of marginal contributors

(contributors far from the center of the project) who, while not being required to put up high contributions to the project, will be dissatisfied with its central direction. Those developers may then decide to 'fork' and set up their own project.[2] The following proposition states that any equilibrium of the OS contribution game such that $s_{OS} \le (\sqrt{6}+2)\sqrt{K/ag}$ will be robust to forking.

Proposition 3. *Symmetric equilibria of the OS contribution game are robust to forking only $s_{OS} \le (\sqrt{6}+2)\sqrt{K/ag}$.*

Proof. *In A&S, proposition 5.*

I can therefore conclude from this section that in a stable symmetric equilibrium of the contribution game, then the size of OS projects will be anywhere between $\sqrt{2K/ag}$ and $(\sqrt{6}+2)\sqrt{K/ag}$. I will show in the following that the threat of forking is not as strong as the threat of entry by proprietary software, and thus imposes additional limits on the size of OSS projects. In the discussion of welfare, I will show that the threat of entry by PS may improve welfare by preventing the emergence of welfare inefficient 'overgrown' OSS projects.

Proprietary Entry

Consider the possibility of entry by proprietary firms in a situation where there are only OS projects. This is a situation of interest when OSS has been the development method of choice in one development area, and proprietary developers try to enter that area with their software. A situation where this would hold would for example be proprietary developers providing specialized applications that cater for the needs of those who are not satisfied with such OSS as Apache, TEX or Sendmail.[3]

I will analyze here whether the pure OS equilibrium is robust to entry by proprietary firms. I will consider entry as follows: a proprietary firm sets up between two OS projects and seeks to attract a portion of those who would have been developers of one or the other project – that is, those developers, instead of participating in OS production, choose to buy from the proprietary developer. As stated previously in the exposition of the model, I assume that OS location does not change as a strategic reaction to the entry of PS.

The timing is as follows:

1. OS projects, who do not anticipate entry, set their location and recruit contributors.
2. Before planned contributors start contributing, a proprietary project locates between two projects and offers software at price p.
3. Contributors choose between fulfilling their commitment to the OS project or buying the proprietary software.

There are then two cases, **case A**, with 'naïve users', where OS contributors assume all other contributors will fulfill their commitment to the OS project, and **case B**, with 'savvy users', where OS contributors assume that some contributors will buy proprietary software instead.

Case A: Consider **case A** first. Under **case A** then the size of projects will be limited further than with the threat of forking, as only a subset of symmetric equilibria of the OS contribution game that are robust to forking are robust to entry under **case A**:

Proposition 4. *Only symmetric equilibria such that $s_o \leq (\sqrt{2}+2)\sqrt{K/ag}$ will be robust to entry under* **case A** *where users are naïve.*

Proof. *In appendix 5.*

Case B: Consider now **case B** where a contributor anticipates that if she decides not to contribute to an OS project and buys proprietary software instead, then other likely contributors that are closer to the proprietary project than she is herself are likely to do so as well. This makes entry by

a proprietary firm easier than in **case A**. Indeed, those developers who would not have bought PS if others kept on contributing to OSS will be tempted to buy PS as the contribution required of them to sustain the project in the absence of those who fled will be higher. This is confirmed in the following proposition:

Proposition 5. *The equilibrium of the development game played by competing open-source projects is not robust to entry by a proprietary firm under* **case B** *where users are savvy.*

Proof. *In appendix 6*

This means that what makes entry possible for the entrepreneur under **case B** is the fact that any OS user taken away from the OS project increases contributions needed from other OS developers remaining in the project. Proprietary entry thus works by a domino effect.

In the following, I discuss how proprietary entry under **case A** limits the size of OS projects in a way that is beneficial for welfare compared to the case where the only threat to OS projects was the possibility of forking:

Welfare

The optimum of the social planner is achievable under the OS system and is robust to forking. However, there is a wide range of equilibria that may occur under the OS mode of production, and there is therefore no guarantee that the optimum will be achieved. In the following, I define lower bounds for welfare under the open source model.

The expression of social welfare in equation 2 can be expressed as a function of s by exploiting the fact that in a symmetric equilibrium, $N = 1/s$, so social welfare will be

$$SW = g - K/s - ags/4 \qquad (3)$$

which is a concave function of s. Therefore, the minimum possible welfare in an OS industry that is not subject to entry by proprietary software will be either when $s = \sqrt{2K/ag}$ (minimum stable size) or when $s = (\sqrt{6}+2)\sqrt{K/ag}$ (maximum size without forking).

In the first case, total welfare is

$$SW = g - \frac{3\sqrt{2}}{4}\sqrt{Kag} \qquad (4)$$

to be compared to optimal welfare of $SW^* = g - \sqrt{Kag}$, so welfare is reduced by at most 6.07% of $\sqrt{Kag}$ in the smallest size OS equilibrium.

In the second case, total welfare is

$$SW = g - \frac{3\sqrt{6}-2}{4}\sqrt{Kag} \qquad (5)$$

which is less than optimal welfare by 33.71% of $\sqrt{Kag}$. This is therefore the highest possible loss compared to optimal welfare that can occur under an OS equilibrium when there is no threat of entry by PS.

Now, when the OS industry is subject to entry by proprietary software, and one is under case A (naïve users), then s_o cannot be higher than $(\sqrt{2}+2)\sqrt{K/ag}$ which puts a new lower bound to the loss in welfare as this limits overgrowth in OS projects. From equation 3, social welfare will be

$$SW = g - (\frac{6-\sqrt{2}}{4})\sqrt{Kag} \qquad (6)$$

so the loss of welfare compared to the social optimum will be limited in case A to 14.64% of $\sqrt{Kag}$ compared to 33.71% of $\sqrt{Kag}$ when the threat of forking was the only factor limiting the size of OSS projects. Threat of entry by PS under case A may thus improve welfare by limiting the size of OSS projects.

Under case B however the optimum of the social planner is not achievable as it will not be robust to entry by proprietary firms.

In conclusion to this part, potential competition by proprietary software imposes additional constraints for the existence and stability of the OS model of production. In cases where OS developers anticipate correctly the effect of entry by proprietary firms, then proprietary firms will enter. This will justify later on the study of mixed models where OS and PS coexist. From a policy point of view, as we will see, the OS model of production can achieve higher social welfare than the proprietary model, but open-source projects are at risk of overgrowth, which might lead to an OS industry being very inefficient. However, potential entry by proprietary software can limit the size of OSS in such a way that the loss from overgrowth of OS project can be limited. All this means that a social planner might want to encourage the use of the OS model but let open the possibility for proprietary software to enter by maintaining copyright protection for software.

PROPRIETARY INDUSTRY

In this part, I consider the situation where all projects are proprietary. As stated in the introduction, A&S reduces to a standard Vickrey-Salop model in that case, with well known results. What is original in this part is to analyze whether the proprietary equilibrium is robust to OS entry, and also to compare welfare under the proprietary system and that under the OS system.

Consider thus an individual (the entrepreneur) who develops a project j at cost K and sells it to consumers at price p_j. I consider a free entry equilibrium whereby no new projects can be set up between other projects and turn up any strictly positive profit (as before, I consider entry without strategic reaction from established firms).

Proposition 6. *The free entry equilibrium of the development game played by competing profit motivated entrepreneurs is such that there will be N_p projects of equal size s_p such that*

$$N_p = \sqrt{ag/K} \text{ and } s_p = \sqrt{K/ag}.$$

Proof. *In appendix 7.*

There will thus be more proprietary firms than in even the equilibrium with the smallest stable projects of the OS development game. There is excess entry compared to the welfare optimal market structure because size is limited by the zero profit condition. Since the sum of all payments made by consumers to a specific entrepreneur must cover development costs K, and less consumers use a specific proprietary software than would use an OS software, then each consumer has to contribute more, in terms of price to pay, than they would contribute in kind in terms of development in an OS industry.

OSS Entry

Consider now if OSS can make a successful entry in a domain that is dominated by proprietary software. A situation of interest would be that of GPL software such as Linux entering the field of operating systems vs. Apple or Microsoft.

The timing of entry is as follows:

1. Proprietary developers, who do not anticipate entry, set their location and price p.
2. Before consumers choose which software to buy, an open source project locates between two projects and seeks contributors.
3. Consumers choose between contributing to the open source project or buying proprietary software.

Proposition 7. *The equilibrium of the development game played by competing proprietary entrepreneurs is robust to entry by an open-source project.*

Proof. *In appendix 8.*

Contrary to the case of entry by a proprietary firm into an OS equilibrium, the proprietary developers can choose to maintain their price p at the same level as without entry by the OS project;

therefore, the contribution needed from consumers to obtain the proprietary good does not increase in the same way as contributions required from OS developers increased when there was entry by a proprietary firm in the OS equilibrium and contributors were savvy. This makes entry by OSS in a proprietary equilibrium more difficult than entry by PS in an OS equilibrium. Indeed, while entry by PS was always possible when OS contributors were savvy, entry by OSS is never possible in a proprietary industry.

Welfare

As seen previously in the calculation of the social welfare generated when a social planner chooses N optimally to maximize welfare, I found in equation 2 that the expression for social welfare could be simplified to $SW = g - KN - ag/4N$. In the equilibrium of the proprietary industry, I will have $N_p = \sqrt{ag/K}$, which is double the optimal number of projects, so

$$SW_p = g - \frac{5}{4}\sqrt{Kag},$$

to be compared with optimal welfare of $SW^* = g - \sqrt{Kag}$. Welfare is thus reduced by 25% of $\sqrt{Kag}$ compared to the optimum. Said in another way, and since $\sqrt{Kag}$ is the price of PS in the proprietary equilibrium, welfare is reduced by 25% of the total sales of proprietary firms in the proprietary equilibrium. This loss in welfare is more than in any of those equilibria of the OS industries that are robust to entry by proprietary entrepreneurs when contributors are naïve in their expectations (case A). This would mean the OS model is more efficient than the proprietary model as long as it is subject to entry by PS but contributors do not anticipate entry. As seen previously however, OS production will not be robust to entry by PS in case B, where OS contributors anticipate entry, which means that the OS model may not be sustainable and I need to examine the situation where both production models coexist.

MIXED INDUSTRY

I will now consider competition between OS and proprietary projects. Competition will be considered at the level of the user/developer, who chooses either to develop software or buy software developed by someone else. The mixed industry case corresponds to a number of market configurations (Gaudeul (2008)) where OS and PS coexist. The model applies specifically to some areas in software development where users are or can be also developers (for example, professional applications such as web server software). I will speak later on in this article of how the model could be adapted to correspond to the type of markets where most users are not developers, and may not even know how to use OSS.

I will consider the case where OS and proprietary projects alternate in location. This is not the only possible configuration, but it is the simplest to consider. I will be interested in the relative size of open source and proprietary projects (how many users do they attract), and I will make the usual robustness checks: robustness to entry to either OS or proprietary competitors, and robustness to forking for OS projects. Figure 1 illustrates the type of configuration I will be considering. Note that in a symmetric equilibrium, open source and proprietary software will be evenly spaced and equal in number, so if there are N projects in total, half of them will be open source and half of them will be proprietary, and they will be at distance $1/N$ of each other.

The following proposition outlines the properties of the two possible equilibria of the mixed industry where OS and PS alternate in the preference space:

Proposition 8. *There are two possible equilibria of the mixed industry model where open-source and proprietary projects alternate in the consumer's preference space:*

Figure 1. Symmetric equilibrium with open-source and proprietary software alternating in the location circle

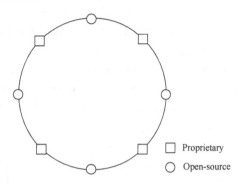

- *The first equilibrium is such that open-source and proprietary projects are of the same size, that size being the size of proprietary projects in a proprietary industry.* Each type of software gains half of the market.
- *The second equilibrium is such that open-source projects are twice bigger (attract more consumers/developers) than proprietary projects, and therefore gain two third of the market. Open-source projects are of the optimal size from the point of view of welfare, while proprietary projects are the same size as in a proprietary industry.*

Proof. *In appendix 9.*

The proposition above can be expanded further as follows:

- In the first equilibrium with equal sized open-source and proprietary software, the proprietary projects will take up $N_p s_p$ of the space, with

$$N_p = \frac{1}{2}\sqrt{ag/K} \text{ and } s_p = \sqrt{K/ag},$$

so the space will be divided half and half between PS and OS. Since OS projects will be of the same size as proprietary projects, then each OSS user will contribute the same to OS development as each PS users pays for PS. Total expenses for private and public provision of goods will be equally shared in the economy (half will be made of in-kind contributions by OS users, half will be made of monetary contributions by proprietary users). Total expenses and contributions in kind will be $\sqrt{Kag}$, the same as was expended in a proprietary industry.

• In the second equilibrium, with asymmetric size proprietary and open source projects, proprietary projects will take up $N_p s_p$ of the space with

$$N_p = \frac{1}{3}\sqrt{ag/K} \text{ and}$$

$$s_p = \sqrt{K/ag},$$

so the space will be divided one third/two third between PS and OS projects respectively. This means there will be twice more users of OSS than of PS. Since the size of OSS projects will be $s_o = 2\sqrt{K/ag}$, that is, twice the size of PS projects, then each OSS user will contribute to OS development half of what each PS users pays for PS. However, total expenses and contributions for private and public provision of goods will be equally shared in the economy, in the same way as it was equally shared in the first equilibrium. However, expenses and contributions will total only

$$\frac{2}{3}\sqrt{Kag},$$

which is one third less than what was expended in a proprietary industry.

In the second equilibrium, with unequal sized projects, proprietary software is more specialized than OS software, in the sense that its users will be closer to their ideal points, than the average user in the OS projects. In the first equilibrium,

where OS and PS projects are of the same size, they are of the equilibrium size in the proprietary industry, while in the second equilibrium, where OS and PS projects are of different sizes, then the size of the OS projects will be equal to the size that would have been chosen by a social planner. This leads to an analysis of welfare:

Welfare

If OS and proprietary projects are of the same size in a mixed-industry model, then total welfare will be the same as in the pure proprietary model, which thus represents a lower bound to welfare.

In the equilibrium with asymmetrically sized proprietary and open-source projects, where OS and proprietary projects alternate in the preference space, the average size of a project will be

$$(s_o + s_p)/2 = \frac{3}{2}\sqrt{K/ag},$$

which is more than $\sqrt{2K/ag}$, the minimum stable size of an open source project in the pure OS model. The difference is small, but would indicate that overall welfare might be higher in a mixed industry model with different sized OS and proprietary projects, than in some pure OS industries.

Proposition 9. *Total welfare in the mixed industry model with asymmetric sized open-source and proprietary projects may be higher than in some open source industries, and will be significantly higher than welfare in the pure proprietary model.*

Proof. *In appendix 10.*

This means that an industry where both production models coexist is more efficient than an industry where only proprietary software is developed. Competition from OSS thus improves the situation for the society as a whole. To give an idea of how much of an improvement mixed industries can represent compared to pure proprietary models, one can take as a reference point the total sales of firms in a pure proprietary industry. The loss of welfare compared to the optimum is 25% of those sales in the proprietary model, compared to 8.33% of those sales in the mixed industry with asymmetric sized open-source and proprietary projects.

Figure 2 represents total welfare as a function of project sizes in the economy. I take as an example $g = 8$, $a = 10$ and $K = 0.2$. In that setting, the optimal number of projects is 10, in which case social welfare is and the size of projects is $s^* = 0.1$. OS equilibria achieve a range of outcomes, from s_o^{min} which prevents contributors from switching projects, to s_o^{fork} which prevents contributors from forking and establishing their own project within a project. This range includes s_o^{entry}, which denotes the maximum size for OS that are robust to entry by PS when contributors are naïve and do not anticipate flight from other developers. Proprietary projects in both a proprietary and a mixed industry are of size s_p and are too small to achieve efficiency so a proprietary industry achieves social welfare of $SW_p = 3$ only, that is, 25% less than optimal. In a mixed industry with asymmetric sized OS and PS, total welfare

$$SW^{mixed} = \frac{2}{3} * 4 + \frac{1}{3} * 3 = 3.67$$

is the average from two third of consumers using optimally sized OS projects and from one third of consumers using software from proprietary projects that are too small. As seen graphically, this equilibrium achieves higher welfare than most OS equilibria and than the equilibrium in a proprietary industry.

From a public policy point of view, and as long as one can assume that all software users can be developers, the State may want to encourage the emergence of large open-source software projects that would be used by the majority of users, while proprietary entrepreneurs would fulfill more specialized needs. This type of ideal market structure would become more relevant as software users become more experienced and more able to make their own contributions to the development of software they use.

A further possible public policy, to be explored in future versions of the article, would be to encourage the use of BSD licenses so entrepreneurs can make use of OS source into specialized applications for 'marginal' consumers of OSS – consum-

Figure 2. Social welfare under different industry configurations

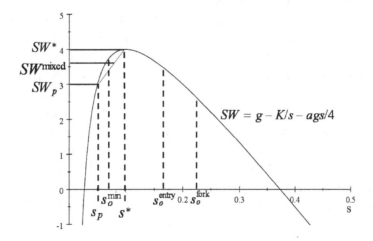

ers that have priorities (preferences) that differ from the average user of a specific OSS project.

CONCLUSION AND EXTENSIONS

I analyzed in this article the patterns of competition between open source and proprietary software by adapting standard models of product differentiation and public good production in a novel way. This article provides some insights on how open-source and proprietary production systems can be expected to cohabit, and why cohabitation of OS and proprietary systems of production is desirable. In an industry where consumers can choose between contributing to open source software development or buying proprietary software, situations may occur where a majority of users would choose to contribute to open-source projects, while a minority would buy from proprietary projects. Each of the proprietary projects would be more specialized than OS projects in so far as they would cover the needs of a smaller range of users.

There is some indication that this would be what is indeed observed in markets in which users can choose between a private and a public sector. For example, Apache dominates the market for web server software, and TEX was the dominant typesetting software in the early days of its development. More generally, OSS will gain a large share of the market when most of its users are also developers. The conclusions of the article do not hold however when most users are not or cannot be developers.

The conclusions from the article in its present state could also be used to analyze cohabitation of private and public provision of health care. Propper and Green (2001) report that the public share of total expenditure on health has been stable around 75% in OECD countries since the 1970s. However, in this case, users of private services usually also have to contribute to the public services, which

differs from the model in this article. The case is different again in education. The UNESCO Institute for Statistics (2007) compares public and private expenditure on education in a variety of countries and shows that public provision is highest in primary and secondary education, but is much lower in tertiary education. For example, only 70% of expenditures in tertiary education in the UK are publicly funded, compared to 87% in primary and secondary education. Without paying too much attention to the precise share of private vs. public funding, it is however apparent that a number of countries find it optimal to combine a dominant public sector with a marginal private sector. This would seem to confirm the efficiency properties of a mixed model of production in some industries.

The model will need to be adapted to correspond to a wider variety of settings, and I indicate below several ways in which this could be done in the case of open source software provision:

Users and Developers

There is no central authority that can require equal contributions from each participant in OSS development. In effect, Mockus, Fielding, and Herbsleb (2005) show that development of the code base is characterized by a high concentration of contributions among a few, while other tasks such as defect repair are more equally distributed among contributors. Lakhani and von Hippel (2003) emphasize further how disparate the type of contributions to OSS projects can be, ranging from programming to user-assistance. Fershtman and Gandal (2004) show that contributions will depend on the type of license used, while Krishnamurthy (2002) and Healy and Schussman (2003) show that most OSS projects are the work of an individual rather than of a community. The model would therefore need to be adapted to take account of those empirical findings.

An easy way to do this would be to examine what happens when a portion of the users are not able to develop software on their own and/or are not able to use OSS. In this article, I considered that all users were able to develop and use OSS, while in reality, only a fraction may be able to use OSS, and a fraction of that fraction would be able to develop. Considering this extension may bring about ambiguous results. On the one hand, users who cannot develop OSS (or do not want to and prefer to free-ride) would essentially get OSS for free and thus obviously prefer it to PS. On the other hand, OS projects would have to extend further in order to attract sufficient contributions, and would thus possibly become even more fragile and vulnerable to competition by PS than before. In future extensions to this article, I will argue that PS may improve welfare if PS is more accessible to some users than OSS is.

Imperfect Competition

It is probably not reasonable to assume as in this article that there is free entry into a proprietary industry. Sunk costs are important in the software industry. Branding is very important, which allows Norton, Microsoft or Apple to cover a wide range of applications. Consumer inertia is also a factor, not only due to network but also learning effects – consumers may understandably be loathe to switch to possibly better alternatives because of the trauma of their early experience with learning how to use Microsoft software! One would therefore have to consider the effect of introducing sunk costs in the model. Total profit in the market would then be equal to the value of the sunk costs an entrant needs to incur to enter it. This would reduce welfare as there would be less firms, each charging more than in a perfectly competitive market, so consumers would have to pay more and would obtain software that is further from their own preferences.

Core and Extensions

Open-source development occurs over time, and developers may be involved into either the development of the core or of extensions of the

program that are designed to adapt it to specific uses. Core and extensions may be developed simultaneously, but the development of the core will usually determine what extensions of the program can be made. The development of the core could be modeled as in the present article as a collective enterprise, involving many entrepreneurs into a common project. The development of the extensions on the other hand could be modeled as a private enterprise, whereby a developer can choose to develop an extension to the program at some cost, and the extension would allow the developer to move the point of gravity of the project from its original point to a point closer to the developer's own preferred point. Under the GPL, a developer could borrow from an OS project and develop on it for her own private uses and goals without contributing back to it, as long as she does not sell it for profit, while under the BSD, she would be able to sell software that includes OS code. This leads me to a further possible extension:

Proprietary Extensions

What if a BSD licensFe was used in OS production, so proprietary developers could borrow from OS software for use in their own proprietary applications? Consider an OS project that is under the Berkeley Software Distribution ('BSD') licensing scheme. In that case, proprietary developers can extend the software and sell the extension to the public. I could suppose as above that there is a cost to developing an extension to the OS program, that this allows the developer to move the location of the project to some extent and that the proprietary developer may sell the extension. The extension would have to be developed on an element of the core, that is, its location would have to be within the boundaries of the original project. The proprietary extension would extend the number of users of the open source software and may also increase motivation in participating in the open-source project since proprietary exploitation of the project may be made further down the line.

Further work on that line would examine competition between independently developed proprietary projects and proprietary extensions on open-source products. This would differ from the previously explored competition between proprietary projects and open-source projects that were developed under the General Public License ('GPL'). This extension would be relevant as there is ongoing debate over whether to use restrictive (GPL) or permissive (BSD) licenses.[4]

Dynamics

A mixed industry was shown to possibly occur when proprietary software enters an industry dominated by OS software, but the opposite was shown not to be possible. Which equilibrium will occur in the mixed-industry model thus depends on the way the OS equilibrium will converge to the mixed industry equilibrium after entry by proprietary software. This will be the subject of further inquiry.

ACKNOWLEDGMENT

I would like to thank Yossi Spiegel and other participants at the F/LOSS 2007 Workshop in Nice Sophia-Antipolis for their comments and suggestions. The support of the ESRC is gratefully acknowledged.

REFERENCES

Alesina, A., & Spolaore, E. (1997). The number and size of nations. *The Quarterly Journal of Economics, 112*(4), 1027–1056.

Ballou, J. P. (2005). An Examination of the Presence of Ownership Effects in Mixed Markets. *Journal of Law, Economics, & Organization, 21*(1), 228–255.

Bergstrom, T., Blume, L., & Varian, H. (1986). On the Private Provision of Public Goods. *Journal of Public Economics, 29*(1), 25–49.

Besley, T., & Ghatak, M. (2001). Government Versus Private Ownership Of Public Goods. *The Quarterly Journal of Economics, 116*(4), 1343–1372.

Bessen, J. (2006). Open source software: Free provision of complex public goods. In J. Bitzer & P. J. H. Schröder, (Eds.), The economics of open source software development. (pp. 57–81). Elsevier: Amsterdam.

Bezroukov, N. (1999). Open Source Software Development as a Special Type of Academic Research (Critique of Vulgar Raymondism). *First Monday, 4*(10).

Bitzer, J. (2004). Commercial versus open source software: the role of product heterogeneity in competition. *Economic Systems, 28*, 369–381.

Bitzer, J., & Schröder, P. J. H. (2006). The impact of entry and competition by open source software on innovation activity. In J. Bitzer & P. J. H. Schröder (Eds.), The Economics of Open Source Software Development (pp. 219–246). Elsevier: Amsterdam.

Bonaccorsi, A., & Rossi, C. (2006). Comparing Motivations of Individual Programmers and Firms to Take Part in the Open Source Movement: From Community to Business. *Knowledge, Technology, and Policy, 18*(4), 40–64.

Braid, R. M. (2004). Uneven spacing in free-entry equilibrium for spatial product differentiation. *Economics Letters, 84*(2), 155–161.

Brhlikova, P. (2004). Models of competition between one for profit and one non profit firm. CERGE-EI Working Paper no. 240.

Brhlikova, P. (2006). Mixed Competition and Welfare Under Various Nonprofit Objectives. Mixed Competition Under Various Cost Configurations. CERGE-EI Working Paper No. 310.

Casadesus-Masanell, R., & Ghemawat, P. (2006). Dynamic mixed duopoly: A model motivated by Linux vs. Windows. *Management Science, 52*(7), 1072–1085.

Comino, S., & Manenti. F. M. (2005). Government Policies Supporting Open Source Software for the Mass Market. *Review of Industrial Organization, 26*(2), 217–240.

Darmon, E., le Texier, T., & Torre, D. (2006). Commercial or Open Source Software? Winner-Takes-All Competition, Partial Adoption and Efficiency. Discussion paper, University of Nice-Sophia Antipolis, CREA and University of Rennes.

Economides, N., & Katsamakas, E. (2006). Two-sided competition of proprietary vs. open source technology platforms and the implications for the software industry. *Management Science, 52*(7), 1057–1071.

Epple, D., & Romano, R. E. (1998). Competition Between Private and Public Schools, Vouchers and Peer-Group Effects. *American Economic Review, 88*(1), 33–62.

Fershtman, C., & Gandal, N. (2004). The Determinants of Output per Contributor in Open Source Projects: An Empirical Examination. Discussion paper, Tel-Aviv University, Michigan State University, and CEPR.

Franke, N., & von Hippel, E. (2003). Satisfying heterogeneous user needs via innovation toolkits: the case of Apache security software. *Research Policy, Special Issue on Open Source Software, 32*(7), 1199–1215.

Frey, B. S. (1999). State Support and Creativity in the Arts: Some New Considerations. *Journal of Cultural Economics, 23*(1), 71–85.

Gaudeul, A. (2003). The LATEX project: A case study of open-source software. *TUGBoat, 24*(1), 66–79.

Gaudeul, A. (2005). Public Provision of a Private Good: What is the Point of the BSD License? . SSRN eLibrary, http://ssrn.com/paper=933631.

Gaudeul, A. (2007). Do Open Source Developers Respond to Competition? : The LATEX case study. *Review of Network Economics, 6*(2), 239–263.

Gaudeul, A. (2008). Open Source Licensing in Mixed Markets, or Why Open Source Software Does Not Succeed. CCP Working Paper No. 08-2.

Gaudeul, A., Mathieu, L., & Peroni, C. (2008). Blogs or the economics of reciprocal (in)attention. Discussion paper, School of Economics and ESRC Centre for Competition Policy, University of East Anglia, Norwich.

Glaeser, E. L. (2002). The governance of not-for-profit firms. Harvard Institute of Economic Research, Paper No. 1954.

Harison, E., & Koski, H. (2008). Does open innovation foster productivity? Evidence from open source software firms. Discussion paper 1135, University of Groningen and ETLA.

Healy, K., & Schussman, A. (2003). The Ecology of Open-Source Software Development. Discussion paper, Department of Sociology, University of Arizona.

Johnson, J. P. (2002). Open Source Software: Private Provision of a Public Good. *Journal of Economics & Management Strategy, 11*(4), 637–662.

Klincewicz, K. (2005). Innovativeness of open source software projects. Discussion paper, Tokyo Institute of Technology and Warsaw University.

Krishnamurthy, S. (2002). Cave or Community? An Empirical Examination of 100 Mature Open Source Projects. First Monday, 7(6).

Kuan, J. (2002). Open Source Software as Lead User's Make or Buy Decision: A study of Open and Closed Source Quality. Discussion paper, Stanford Institute for Economic Policy Research.

Lakhani, K., & von Hippel, E. (2003). How open source software works: "free" user-to-user assistance. *Research Policy, 32*(6), 923–943.

Lambardi, G. D. (2007). Code development: Open vs. proprietary source. Discussion paper, GREMAQ, University of Toulouse.

Leoncini, R., Rentocchini, F., & Marzetti, G. V. (2008). You won the battle. What about the war? A model of competition between proprietary and open source software. University of Trento, Discussion paper 2008.11.

Mockus, A., Fielding, R. T., & Herbsleb, J. D. (2005). Two case studies of open source software development: Apache and Mozilla. In J. Feller, B. Fitzgerald, S. A. Hissam, & K. R. Lakhani (Eds.), Perspectives on free and open source software, (pp. 163–210). The MIT Press: Cambridge, MA.

Mustonen, M. (2005). When Does a Firm Support Substitute Open Source Programming? *Journal of Economics & Management Strategy, 14*(1), 121–139.

O'Mahony, S. (2005). Non-Profit Foundations and their Role in Community-Firm Software Collaboration. In J. Feller, B. Fitzgerald, S. A. Hissam, & K. R. Lakhani Perspectives on Free and Open Source Software, (pp. 393–414). The MIT Press: Cambridge, MA.

Propper, C., & Green, K. (2001). A Larger Role for the Private Sector in Financing UK Health Care: the Arguments and the Evidence. *Journal of Social Policy, 30*(4), 685–704.

Raymond, E. (2001): *The Cathedral and the Bazaar: Musings on Linux and Open Source by an Accidental Revolutionary.* O'Reilly Media, Inc.

Raynes-Goldie, K. (2004). Pulling sense out of today's informational chaos: LiveJournal as a site of knowledge creation and sharing. *First Monday, 9*(12).

Rose-Ackerman, S. (1990). Competition between non-profits and for-profits: entry and growth. *Voluntas, 1*(1), 13–25.

Salop, S. (1979). Monopolistic competition with outside goods. *Bell Journal of Economics, 10*(1), 141–156.

Schmidt, K. M., & Schnitzer, M. (2003). Public Subsidies for Open-Source? Some Economic Policy Issues of the Software Market. *Harvard Journal of Law & Technology, 16*(2), 473–505.

Sen, R. (2007). A strategic analysis of competition between open source and proprietary software. *Journal of Management Information Systems, 24*(1), 233–257.

Sloan, F. A. (2000). Not-for-profit ownership and hospital behavior. In A. Culyer, & J. Newhouse Handbook of Health Economics, (pp. 1141–1174). Elsevier Science B.V.

UNESCO Institute for Statistics (2007). What do societies invest in education? Public versus private spending. UIS/FS/07/04.

Vickrey, W. (1964): Microstatics. Harcourt, Brace and World: New York, USA.

Vickrey, W. S. (1999). Spatial competition, monopolistic competition, and optimum product diversity. *International Journal of Industrial Organization, 17*(7), 953–963, with foreword by S.P. Anderson & R.M. Braid.

von Engelhardt, S., & S. Swaminathan (2008). Open source software, closed source software or both: Impacts on industry growth and the role of intellectual property rights. Discussion paper 799, FSU Jena and DIW Berlin.

von Hippel, E., & von Krogh, G. (2003). Open Source Software and the "Private-Collective" Innovation model: Issues for Organization Science. *Organization Science, 14*(2), 209–223.

Wichmann, T. (2002). Firms' open source activities: Motivations and policy implications. Free/

Libre and Open Source Software Final Report, Part II, International Institute of Infonomics.

ENDNOTES

[1]   'Public' being private in the UK of course…

[2]   Note that in practice, modular development can overcome part of the problem, as developers are then able to develop their own module without separating from the project altogether.

[3]   I do not consider here those developers who extend BSD software with their own proprietary packages, in the way Scientific Workplace provides an interface to LATEX. Rather, I consider the case of developers who develop proprietary applications from scratch to compete with a dominant OSS.

[4]   See 'controversy' in http://en.wikipedia.org/wiki/Free-software_licence

This work was previously published in International Journal of Open Source Software and Processes (IJOSSP), edited by Stefan Koch, pp. 43-66, copyright 2009 by IGI Publishing (an imprint of IGI Global).

APPENDIX

PROOF OF PROPOSITION 4

The proprietary project will set up in the middle of the distance between two OS projects, where the marginal contributor, who obtains the lowest utility of all contributors, is located. Suppose OS projects are of size s_o which as explained above is the result of stage 1 where the size of each project is that of a symmetric equilibrium with no anticipated entry by proprietary software. Here (case A), I suppose developers are naïve and do not take into account that if they flee the OS project, then others are likely to do so too. Then the marginal consumer will be such that

$$g(1 - as_p / 2) - p = g(1 - a(s_o - s_p) / 2) - K / s_o$$

Indeed, $(s_o - s_p)/2$ is the distance of the marginal developer to the location of the OS project. Since the marginal consumer does not anticipate flight, then it anticipates that the required contribution will still be K/s_o.

Profit for the entrepreneur will be

$$\pi_p = ps_p - K$$

with $p = ag(s_o / 2 - s_p) + K / s_o$ by the equation above.

For profit made through entry to be positive, I must have p^3K/s_p which translates through the expression of p into $ag(s_o/2-s_p)+K/s_o{}^3K/s_p$ (i.e. price must be more than average costs).

Denoting $T=ags_o/2+K/s_o$, this translates in terms of s_p into

$$ags_p^2 - Ts_p + K \le 0$$

which is not possible if $\Delta=T^2 - 4agK<0$ and is possible if $\Delta=T^2 - 4agK>0$ s.t. $s_p \in s_p^1, s_p^2]$ with

$$s_p^1 = (T - \sqrt{\Delta}) / 2ag$$

and

$$s_p^2 = (T + \sqrt{\Delta}) / 2ag.$$

Therefore, entry is not possible s.t.

$$(ags_o / 2 + K / s_o)^2 - 4agK < 0$$

which translates in $s_o^2 \in [(6 - 4\sqrt{2})K / ag, (6 + 4\sqrt{2})K / ag]$.

In the symmetric equilibria, I will have $s_o^2 \in [2K / ag, (10 + 4\sqrt{6})K / ag]$, which means that only symmetric equilibria such that $s_o^2 \le (6 + 4\sqrt{2})K / ag$ will be robust to entry under the case A. This translates in the condition expressed in the proposition.

PROOF OF PROPOSITION 5

The proprietary project will set up in the middle of the distance between two OS projects, where the marginal contributor, who obtains the lowest utility of all contributors, is located. Suppose OS projects are of size s_o which as explained above is the result of stage 1 where the size of each project is that of a symmetric equilibrium with no anticipated entry by proprietary software. Here (case A), I suppose developers are naïve and do not take into account that if they flee the OS project, then others are likely to do so too. Then the marginal consumer will be such that

$$g(1\ as_p/2) - p = g(1 - a(s_o - s_p)/2) - K/(s_o - s_p/2)$$

Indeed, $(s_o - s_p)/2$ is the distance of the marginal developer to the location of the OS project. Since the marginal consumer anticipates flight, then she anticipates that the required contribution will still be $K/(s_o - s_p/2)$ as half of the buyers of the PS will come from her own project.

Profit for the entrepreneur will be

$$\pi_p = p s_p - K$$

with $p = ag(s_o/2 - s_p) + K/(s_o - s_p/2)$ by the equation above.

For profit made through entry to be positive, I must have $p^3 K/s_p$ which translates through the expression of p into $ag(s_o/2 - s_p) + K/(s_o - s_p/2)^3 K/s_p$ (i.e. price must be more than average costs). Note already that this condition is easier to fulfill than in case A.

This translates in terms of s_o into

$$ags_p s_o^2 - (\frac{5}{2} ags_p^2 + 2K)s_o + ags_p^3 + 3Ks_p^3 >= 0$$

(equation 1) Denote Δ the determinant of this function;

$$\Delta = 4K^2 - 2Kags_p^2 + \frac{9}{4} a^2 g^2 s_p^4,$$

which is a function of s_p^2. The determinant of Δ is always negative, which means that $\Delta > 0$ for any s_p so that for any s_p there are always solutions to the equation 1. For any s_o the proprietary developer need only set s_p such that either or in order for entry to be successful. Therefore, entry is always possible. One can check for example that in the pure OS equilibrium where $s_o = \sqrt{2K/ag}$ (the equilibrium with the smallest possible OS project size) then the proprietary entrepreneur can set $s_p = s_o$ and then the condition for entry is verified (indeed, in that case,

$$s_o \leq (\frac{5}{2} ags_p^2 + 2K - \sqrt{\Delta})/2ags_p).$$

PROOF OF PROPOSITION 6

Consider a configuration with firms i, j and k located in this order on the preference circle, with distance measured clockwise from an arbitrary point of reference. With a shortcut in notation, say that $i<j<k$ is the location of firm i, j and k respectively. The utility of individual A situated at distance l_{Aj} from firm j is $U_A = g(1 - al_{Aj}) + y - p_j$ when buying from firm j, situated between i and k.

The profit of the firm j, if l_j and L_j are the distance to the right and to the left of the consumer that is indifferent between i and j and j and k respectively, is $\pi_j = p_j(L_j + l_j) - K$, with K the cost of development.

l_j will be such that $g(1 - al_j) + y - p_j = g(1 - aL_i) + y - p_i$ with $L_i = j - i - l_j$ while L_j is such that $g(1 - aL_j) + y - p_j = g(1 - al_k) + y - p_k$ with $l_k = k - j - L_j$.

I find that

$$\frac{1}{2}(j - i) - \frac{p_j - p_i}{2ag} = l_j$$

while

$$\frac{1}{2}(k - j) - \frac{p_j - p_k}{2ag} = L_j$$

so the firm maximizes

$$\pi_j = p_j(\frac{1}{2}(k - i) - \frac{2p_j - p_i - p_k}{2ag}) - K \tag{7}$$

This is maximized for

$$\frac{1}{4}(ag(k - i) + p_i + p_k) = p_j.$$

Consider a symmetric equilibrium, and denote p the equilibrium price for all firms. Then I have

$$p_j = \frac{1}{4}(ag(k - i) + 2p) \tag{8}$$

and $p_j = p$ s.t. $p = \frac{1}{2}ag(k - i)$.

Replacing the above into the zero profit condition, I obtain $k - i = 2\sqrt{K / ag}$, which is the space taken up by two symmetric firms, so any one firm is of size $s = \sqrt{K / ag}$, which is less than the maximum size of OS projects in a pure OS model. The number of firms is then the closest integer to $\sqrt{ag / K}$, which is more than the number of OS projects in a pure OS model. Note also that $p_j > t$, the contribution needed to sustain OS (assuming contributions are expressed in monetary terms). The situation will be robust to entry by an additional proprietary firm.

PROOF OF PROPOSITION 7

I want to show that any entry of any size s_o by open-source software is not possible. Suppose the entrant locates in the middle of two proprietary software (the best entry position as it targets the consumers who are most dissatisfied with the proprietary offering), and there is no strategic change in price or location as a competitive measure by the entrepreneur, then the marginal consumer will be such that:

$$g(1-\frac{a}{2}(s_p - s_o)) - p \le g(1 - a\frac{s_o}{2}) - \frac{K}{s_o}. \tag{9}$$

For such a s_o to exist, I must have

$$gas_o^2 - (\frac{ag}{2}s_p + p)s_o + K \le 0 \tag{10}$$

Remember that $p = \sqrt{Kag}$ in the proprietary equilibrium, while p replacing this in the above, this means I must find s_o such that:

$$gas_o^2 - (\frac{3}{2}\sqrt{Kag})s_o + K \le 0 \tag{11}$$

but the determinant of this function is

$$\Delta = \frac{9}{4}Kag - 4Kag < 0$$

so there is not solution to the equation. This means that there is no o that would make the marginal consumer prefer contributing to the OS project rather than buy from the proprietary entrepreneur in the equilibrium of the proprietary industry development game.

PROOF OF PROPOSITION 8

First note that projects will be at distance $1/N$ of each other. Indeed, in equilibrium, proprietary projects will locate in the middle of two adjoining OS projects to maximize differentiation and thus profit. Similarly, in a symmetric equilibrium where all *PS* is of the same price, OS projects will locate in the middle of proprietary projects. In a symmetric equilibrium, projects will thus be equally spaced. Consider a consumer who has a choice between paying p for proprietary software that is at distance l from her preferred point, or contributing t to an OS project which is at distance $1/N-l$ from her preferred point.

She will be indifferent between the two if

$$g(1-al)-p=g(1-a(1/N-l))-t$$

which means that l^*, the location of the indifferent consumer, will be such that

$$l^* = [1/N - (p-t)/ag]/2 \tag{12}$$

Profit for the proprietary developer will be

$$\pi_p = 2l^* p - K$$

and profit maximizing price will be such that

$d\pi_p/dp = 0$

so optimal price will be

$$p^* = \frac{1}{2N}(ag + Nt)$$

and therefore, from equation 12,

$$l^* = (ag + Nt)/4Nag \qquad (13)$$

In a zero profit equilibrium, I will have $\pi_p = 0$, that is, $2l^*p^* = K$, which translates in $(Nt + ag)^2 = 4N^2 agK$ which obtains only one solution with positive contributions, $t^* = 2\sqrt{agK} - ag/N$, so that from equation 13,

$$l^* = \frac{1}{2}\sqrt{K/ag}.$$

This means that the size of the proprietary projects is $s_p = \sqrt{K/ag}$ in any mixed strategy equilibrium of the development game. This is equal to their equilibrium size in a proprietary industry.

Now, to find N^*, remember that the OS project will require contribution t such that $2(1/N - l^*)t = K$ (total contributions equal the cost of the project, so that replacing t with its optimal level t^*, that I find that N^* must be a solution to $3KN^2 - 5\sqrt{Kag}N + 2ag = 0$. The two solutions are

$$N^* = \left\{ \sqrt{ag/K}, \frac{2}{3}\sqrt{ag/K} \right\}.$$

If $N^* = \sqrt{ag/K}$, then $p^* = \sqrt{Kag}$ and $t^* = \sqrt{Kag}$.

If $N^* = \frac{2}{3}\sqrt{ag/K}$, then $p^* = \sqrt{Kag}$ and

$$t^* = \frac{1}{2}\sqrt{Kag}.$$

I have to check the *stability of the first equilibrium*, since OSS projects are smaller in the first equilibrium than was stable in the pure OS industry. In equilibrium, I have

$$g(1 - as_p/2) - p = g(1 - as_o/2) - K/s_o$$

(indifferent consumer condition). Here (first equilibrium), $s_o = s_p$. This case where $s_o = s_p$ is stable only if, supposing the OS project increases in size by ε at the expense of proprietary projects, then the individual at the new border at distance $(s-\varepsilon)/2$ of the proprietary projects prefers paying the (unchanged) p rather than contributing to the OS project, that is:

$g(1-a(s+\varepsilon)/2)-K/(s+\varepsilon)<g(1-a(s-\varepsilon)/2)-p$

that is, $K - p\varepsilon - ps + ag\varepsilon^2 + ags\varepsilon > 0$ which simplifies to $K>ps$ as ε tends to 0, which is indeed verified in equilibrium since this is the free entry condition (zero profit for the proprietary developer).

PROOF OF PROPOSITION 9

The expression for social welfare in equation 1 can be expressed as

$$SW = g - \sum_{x=1}^{N} ag\frac{s_x^2}{4} - NK \tag{14}$$

In the mixed equilibrium with asymmetric sized OS and proprietary projects, $s_o = 2\sqrt{K/ag}$ and $s_p = \sqrt{K/ag}$ and there is an equal number of OS and proprietary projects. The total number of projects is

$$N = 2/(s_o + s_p) = \frac{2}{3}\sqrt{ag/K}.$$

Denote $N_o = N_p = N/2$ the number of open source and proprietary projects respectively.
Total welfare will then be

$$SW = g - \frac{N}{2}(ag\frac{s_o^2}{4} + ag\frac{s_p^2}{4}) - NK \tag{15}$$

$$= g - \frac{13}{12}\sqrt{agK} \tag{16}$$

Welfare in the mixed model is thus lower than welfare in the minimum sized stable equilibrium of the pure OS model ($13/12 > 3\sqrt{2}/4$ but higher than in the maximum sized forking-proof equilibrium of the pure OS industry ($13/12 < (3\sqrt{6}-2)/4$), and also higher than in the maximum sized entry-proof equilibrium of the OS industry ($13/12 < (6-\sqrt{2})/4$). The mixed model is a clear improvement on total welfare in the pure proprietary equilibrium which was

$$g - \frac{5}{4}\sqrt{agK}.$$

There is a loss of 8.33% of $\sqrt{agK}$ in welfare compared to the optimum, compared with a loss of 25% of $\sqrt{agK}$ in the pure proprietary model.

Chapter 10

Open Source and Commercial Software Platforms:
Is Coexistence a Temporary or Sustainable Outcome?

Eric Darmon
Université de Rennes 1 and CREM-CNRS, France

Dominique Torre
GREDEG-CNRS and University of Nice - Sophia Antipolis, France

ABSTRACT

In this article, we consider the dynamics and competition between two software platforms (Open Source and proprietary software). Potential user-developers can adopt one of the two platforms in order to develop and sell new applications based on the platform. We consider the static issue first and then use a simple dynamic system where the dynamics comes from the development efforts (spillovers) made on each platforms. In this context, we first identify the conditions for the two platforms to coexist in the long run. From this baseline, we then consider different strategies for the editor. A first strategy is for the editor to "show the code" of its software, so as to develop more compatible products. A second strategy is to strategically monitor the compatibility degree between the proprietary and OS platform. In both cases, we analyse whether a mixed industry may be sustainable in the long run.

INTRODUCTION

Open Source (OS) Software have attracted much attention in the last decade. From an economic point of view, the initial focus was on the original

DOI: 10.4018/978-1-60960-513-1.ch010

production and distribution modes of Open Source Software (see e.g. Bitzer and Schröder, 2006 for a survey) and the public good properties and their direct impacts – developers' motivations to engage in OS communities (see e.g. *Lerner & Tirole, 2002*) were stressed. As a second step, the original competition between an OS (non profit motivated) organization and a proprietary/commercial (profit motivated) software editor has been studied (see e.g. Bonnacorsi and Rossi [2002], Darmon, Le Texier and Torre [2007], see also Gaudeul and Pollock in this issue). Now, OSS seems to impose in many sectors so that interactions between the commercial and OS software production mode have taken new forms and both actors need to reconsider their strategies.

On the one hand, OS seems to have obtained large market shares in many different areas so that incumbent software editors need now to change their attitude towards OS. Looking at Microsoft's strategy as some anecdotic evidence, one can observe how Microsoft's strategy towards OS has tremendously evolved from a competition strategy to a somewhat more cooperative approach (see e.g. Galoppini [2008]). Conversely, while many firms now think of "going open source", many OS projects consider the reverse way and now think of going "business". These two simultaneous trends lead to new types of "hybrid models" within the software industry. Such models may take very diverse forms. Dual licences can also be considered as a first hybrid strategy where a firm chooses to distribute two differentiated products: one is released under proprietary licence terms while the other is OS (see e.g. Comino and Manenti [2008] for an economic analysis). Another strategy goes through a better interoperability between each OS and Proprietary platforms or software. Many OS developers are firms that are users-developers à la Von Hippel [2005]. They decide to use OS primarily because of the higher utility they can derive from it. Besides, it should be kept in mind that many open-source developers are directly employed by firms to contribute to OS communities (see Henkel [2006 a, b] for an illustration to embedded Linux). Considering the case of a platform software (i.e. a software that other firms/users adopt to build new pieces of software under that platform), the commercial

editor of such software platform may think of "opening" its code in order to increase the utility of its users and increase its market share when confronted to an OS competitor.

In a framework close to this article, Economides and Katsamakas [2007] compare a situation where the software platform is proprietary to another where it is OS. They show the OS outcome may be socially more efficient depending on users' preference for application variety. Parker and Van Alstyn [2008] investigate a close situation where the firm can maximize the development and network externalities when it selects an open source-based strategy. These papers yield interesting results as regards with welfare and firms strategy. Yet, they do not explicitly consider the rivalry between two competing platforms and the long term effects of such competition.

As Casadesus-Masanell and Ghemawat [2006], we consider in this article a situation where proprietary and OS platforms are simultaneously active on the market. While their paper focuses much on demand-side externalities, we here focus on knowledge externalities. In our model, there are two platforms that can then be adopted by independent developers and by end users to build new pieces of software and to introduce new functionalities. When confronted to an OS competitor, the proprietary platform may have an incentive to go open. It can first "show the code" to its users. This would enable users to build more compatible applications thus leading to a higher utility of the proprietary platform. Second, the editor can decide to rearrange its compatibility strategically so that it may capture larger spillovers. In both cases, we study the incentive for a software editor to implement such strategy in the short term. Using a simple dynamical system, we determine in each case, the set of conditions for which such competition would lead to a sustainable hybrid industry in the long run.

THE BENCHMARK MODEL

There are four categories of agents. The two first agents are the editor (or publisher) of the proprietary software and the Open Source community/project. These two agents develop two competing software platforms. Rights to use this platform are defined according to the licence terms of the two software. OS licence terms are here General Public Licence (GPL). In the basic model, the publisher uses a standard proprietary model (closed source code, copyright product). The two other agents are "final" users and "developers" respectively. Users have heterogeneous preferences and needs for new applications. They can build these new applications either on the proprietary platform or on the OS one. We will further assume that users do not develop themselves and buy the services of small independent developers[1].

Statics

The Editor of the Proprietary

Software

The proprietary editor is a monopoly producing software without cost. When adding new lines of code, it can decide whether to open or not its source code and which kind of openness it will consider. In the benchmark model, we assume that the proprietary editor chooses a closed the source code. In this case, users can neither access to the source code nor modify this code. The profit of the proprietary editor is given by Π^P with

$$\Pi^P = m^P (A, B, p)p \tag{1}$$

where $m^P(.)$ figures the demand for proprietary software coming from developers and p the price paid by developers for the use of proprietary software as an input. The demand depends on this price but also on A and B which represent respectively the knowledge base of the proprietary

software and that of the software maintained by the OS community (see the definition of A and B hereafter).

Users and Independent Commercial Developers

There are n heterogeneous users labelled i, ($i = 1, 2...n$) with different needs associated to their respective locations (uniformly distributed on the unit circle). These needs can be fulfilled by adequate solutions customized by independent commercial developers from proprietary software (proprietary solutions) or from the OS platform (OS solutions)[2].

Proprietary and OS Solutions

Given that the source code of proprietary software is closed, the proprietary solutions provide different levels of utility to users according to their needs (i.e. location over the circle). Since the OS source code is open (GPL licence), using the OS platform offers the same potentialities (e.g. adaptability) and disadvantages (e.g. time spent to try and find adapted modules for the developer...) for all users. Let S represent any arbitrary location over the circle (see Figure 1). Without any loss of generality, we suppose that, whatever the size of the two bases, the more the user i is close to the point S on the circle, the more adapted are for him (or her) the proprietary solution. If d_i figures the distance of agent i from S on the unit circle, let Δu_i denote the difference between gross utility expressed in monetary unit of the proprietary solution and that of the OS solution. Δu_i is linked to the location of the user first and to the respective sizes of the two bases second. Let us take A/B as the relevant variable. We then suppose that for all users, the difference in utility between a proprietary solution and an OS solution is an increasing function of A/B. For user i, the increment of utility of a proprietary

Figure 1. Market share of the two platforms

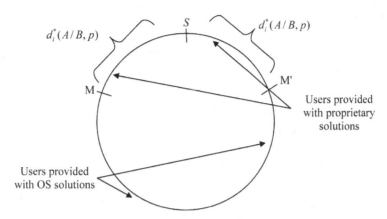

solution on an OS software is then given by $\Delta u_i = d(A/B) - \gamma d_i$ with,, , $d(1) = 0$ and $\gamma > 0$.

For developers, different costs are also associated to the use of the two bases. The cost advantage of the proprietary Platform over the OS Platform depends positively on A/B. The larger is the size of the proprietary Platform, smaller are the relative cost noted $c(A/B)$ of using the proprietary platform instead of the OS platform. The licence cost of the editor generates conversely an advantage for the OS Platform. For developers, the total advantage in term of costs of the proprietary Platform over the OS basis is then given by $\Delta c = c(A/B) - p$ where , , and $c(1) = 0$.

Thus, the net benefit when using the proprietary software and not the OS one is given by (2)

$$\Delta u_i + \Delta c = d(A/B) - \gamma d_i + c(A/B) - p \tag{2}$$

For some given levels of the licence cost p and of the two bases A and B, we suppose without loss of generality that each user i and its independent solution provider select jointly the best solution and share the gain from trade[3]. If (2) is positive, a proprietary solution is selected by user i; if (2) is negative, an OS solution is implemented.

Short-Term Sequence

Inside one period of time, the short term sequence of the game is as follows:

- **Step 1:** The editor chooses a level of the licence cost p able to maximise its profit (1); doing so, the editor supposes that in each implementation the best solution will be chosen rationally by each pair user / independent developer.
- **Step 2:** Given the licence cost set by the monopoly, independent developers and users select for each implementation the best choice between proprietary and OS solutions
- **Step 3:** Licences are sold by the editor to the developers interested by proprietary software. Independent developers and users share the gain associated to the solution they have chosen.

Inside each period, the game is solved by backward induction.

Dynamics

Let us define as $2d^*$ the market share of market for the proprietary platform. The increment of the two bases is the joint result of different forces.

Accumulation of Knowledge Inside the Platforms

From one period to the other, the increment of the proprietary basis (A) is in proportion the result of three terms:

The first term $A_1 = \alpha_1$, $\alpha_1 > 0$ is autonomous and determined by the long term R&D policy of the editor.

The second term is induced by the competitive pressure coming from the OS platform. Beside the long term R&D policy, the editor may increase its R&D effort in the short term greater is the competitive pressure, larger is the effort of R&D. We suppose that this term A_2 is proportional to the share of market $(1 - 2d^*)$ of OS solutions, $A_2 = \alpha_2 (1 - 2d^*)$ with $\alpha_2 > 0$.

The third term A_3 is a joint effect of the level of activity of independent developers using proprietary software. The contribution of these developers to the knowledge included in the proprietary basis depends positively on the share of market of proprietary solutions. This term is such that $A_3 = 2\alpha_3 d^*$ with $\alpha_3 > 0$.

The dynamic equation of the proprietary platform is then given by

$$\dot{A} / A = \alpha_1 + \alpha_2(1 - 2d_i^*) + 2\alpha_3 d_i^* \qquad (3)$$

In the same time, the net increment of the OS software has only two components[4]:

The first term $B_1 = \beta_1$, $\beta_1 > 0$ is autonomous and depends on the 'vitality' of the OS community (incentive to contribute to the OS project, quality of the management of the OS community notably).

The second term B_3 is the result of the activity of the independent commercial developers using OS software. This induced term can be written as $B_3 = \beta_3(1 -)$.

The dynamic equation of the OS platform is then given by (4):

$$\dot{B} / B = \beta_1 + \beta_3(1 - 2d_i^*) \qquad (4)$$

In the benchmark case, the dynamical system is then expressed as (5):

$$\begin{cases} \dot{A} / A = \alpha_1 + \alpha_2(1 - 2d_i^*) + 2\alpha_3 d_i^* \\ \dot{B} / B = \beta_1 + \beta_3(1 - 2d_i^*) \end{cases} \qquad (5)$$

Dynamic Equilibrium Concept

We are mainly interested in the type of outcome arising in the long run (coexistence of the two bases or exclusion of one of the two bases). That is captured by the relative size of the two bases in the long run. Consequently, the relevant dynamic equilibrium concept corresponds to the time stationary relative sizes of the two software platforms, i.e. formally to .

Results

Inside each period the size of the software basis is given. The short term sequence defines a Stackelberg equilibrium where the editor plays leader. Independent developers and users take as given the level of the fees determined by the editor and select cooperatively whatever i the best choice between the implementation of a proprietary and an OS solution. From one period to the other, the sizes of the bases then move according the dynamics represented by (5).

The Static Outcome

The market share of the proprietary platform 2 (A/B, p) depends on the size of the bases A,B and on the editor control variable p. Solving backwardly, we first observe that whatever the sizes of A and B and p, (A/B, p) is obtained as the value of d_i vanishing (2), i.e. (A/B, p) = [$d(A/B)$ +

$c(A/B) - p]$ /g when this expression is included in the closed interval [0, 1/2]. When the value of d_i solving (2) is smaller than 0 or larger than 1/2, $(A/B, p)$ is obtained as a corner solution i.e., $(A/B, p) = 0$ or $(A/B, p) = 1/2$

Since the editor plays leader, it maximises its profit given by (1) once taken into account the consequences of its strategy on the decisions of users/developers. Three cases can be distinguished. To the corner solutions $(A/B, p) = 0$ corresponds the case where whatever the price chosen by the editor its profit cannot be positive. As some starting conditions, we do not consider this case as relevant since it would fully exclude proprietary software. The same applies for the opposite case $(A/B, p) = 1/2$ where the OS is not used. In the standard case (interior solution), the profit of the editor can be expressed as $\Pi^P = 2n (A/B, p)p$. The optimal price p is then given by the FOC from which we deduce $p^* = [d(A/B) + c(A/B)]/2$ from which we deduce the optimal profit and the market share of the proprietary editor. In static terms, we observe that the level of the licence fees, the profit of the editor and the market share of the proprietary editor always increase with the relative size of the proprietary basis A/B.

Dynamics

The dynamics of the relative size of the platforms can be formulated as (6):

$$\left(A/B\right)^{\cdot} = \left(\frac{A}{B}\right)\left|\frac{\dot{A}}{A} - \frac{\dot{B}}{B}\right| \tag{6}$$

This dynamics has two first equilibria $A = 0$ and $B = 0$. These correspond to situations where one of the two platforms no longer exists on the market. Since one platform gets the whole market in these equilibria, let us denote these equilibria as WTA-equilibria (for Winner-Takes-All equilibria). Other equilibria solve the equation and libria). Other equilibria solve the equation and correspond to the coexistence of the two platforms (further C-equilibria).

Proposition 1: *There exists at most one C-equilibrium for the relative size of the two bases. The existence of this equilibrium is conditioned by a sufficient autonomous level of development of the OS platform. Its level then depends i) on the relative weight of the competitive pressure and of the joint effects of the activity of the developers, and ii) on the difference of weight of the long term R&D policy of the editor and of the vitality of the OS community.*

Proof: from (5), C-equilibria solutions of (6) correspond to values of (A/B) solving the equation (A1) $/B = (\alpha_1 + \alpha_2 - \beta_1 - \beta_3) + 2(\alpha_3 + \beta_3 - \alpha_2) (A/B, p) = 0$ with $0 \le (A/B, p) \le 1/2$. Consider first the condition $0 \le (A/B, p) \le 1/2$. This condition implies that i) $\{\alpha_1 + \alpha_2 \le \beta_1 + \beta_3$ and $\alpha_2 \le \alpha_3 + \beta_3\}$ or $\{\alpha_1 + \alpha_2 \ge \beta_1 + \beta_3$ and $\alpha_2 \ge \alpha_3 + \beta_3\}$ and ii) $\{\beta_1 - \alpha_1 \ge \alpha_3\}$. After substitutions, these conditions reduce to the last one $\{\beta_1 - \alpha_1 \ge \alpha_3\}$. Consider now the question of the number of C-equilibrium solutions when one C-equilibrium solution exists. Given the short term equilibrium values of p and the static expression of $(A/B, p)$, (A1) reduces to (A2)$(\alpha_1 + \alpha_2 - \beta_1 - \beta_3) + (\alpha_3 + \beta_3 - \alpha_2)[d (A/B) + c (A/B)] = 0$. Given the continuity of $d(A/B)$ and $c(A/B)$ and their limit properties, there exists one single value $(A/B)^*$ of A/B solving this equation, *i.e.* only one C-equilibrium for the dynamics represented by (6) when $A \ge 0$ and $B \ge 0$. The analytical expression of $(A/B)^*$ is such that $d(A/B) + c (A/B) = -\gamma(\alpha_1 + \alpha_2 - \beta_1 - \beta_3)/(\alpha_3 + \beta_3 - \alpha_2)$. Q.E.D.

Given that $d(\cdot)$ and $c(\cdot)$ are strictly increasing functions of (A/B), we verify that when $(\alpha_3 + \beta_3 - \alpha_2) \le 0$, *i.e.* when the weight of competitive forces is greater the joint effects of the activity of the developers, the relative size of the proprietary basis $(A/B)^*$ increases with the difference in weight of the long term R&D policy of the editor and of the vitality of the OS community $\alpha_1 - \beta_1$. When $(\alpha_3 + \beta_3 - \alpha_2) \le 0$, *i.e.* when the weight of the competitive forces is smaller than the joint effects of the activity of developers, the difference in weight of the long term R&D policy of the editor and of the vitality of the OS community $\alpha_1 - \beta_1$ play in the opposite way.

Proposition 1 has important implications with respect to the existence of a mixed (both OS and proprietary) industry in the long run. The dynamics of the two software platforms exhibits different kinds of externalities. In particular, the two software platforms exhibit adoption externalities: as more developers base their new products on one of the two bases, they generate positive effects (compatibility or development externalities) that increase their propensity to reuse the same platform for developing further products. Such feedbacks lead to one of the two winner-takes-all equilibria, where one of the two platforms ends up with the whole market share. Unlike these equilibria, *Proposition 1* defines some conditions for which the dynamics of the two platforms leads to the coexistence of the two platforms in the long run. The condition for such situation to occur is about the vitality of the OS community. This emphasizes the role played by the management of OS community since the vitality of the OS community is defined by the ability of OS community-management to induce high levels of contributions inside the community. All other things being equal, such management is a necessary condition for OS to sustain in the long run.

Proposition 2: *The C-equilibrium is locally stable (so the two WTA-equilibria are unstable) if the influence of the competitive pressure is greater than the joint effects of the level of activity of developers. Conversely, the WTA-equilibria are stable when the C-equilibrium is locally unstable.*

Proof: we introduce the following notations, $m = \gamma(\alpha_1 + \alpha_2 - \beta_1 - \beta_3)$, $n = (\alpha_3 + \beta_3 - \alpha_2)$, $x = A/B$ and $f(x) = d(x) + c(x)$. Condition (A1) can then be expressed as (A2) $m + nf(x) = 0$ where $f(\cdot)$ is a continuous increasing function of x such that

$\lim_{A/B \to \infty} f(x) = +\infty$, $\lim_{A/B \to 0} f(x) = -\infty$ and $f(1) = 0$. The value of x^* solving (A2) is such that $f(x) = -(m/n)$ with, in all cases $x^* > 0$.

To consider the conditions for local stability, we express the derivative of (6) for the C-equilibrium x^* such that $f(x^*) = -(m/n)$. (6) can be rewritten as (A3) $x = x[m + nf(x)]$ and . The equilibrium x^* is then locally stable if and only if $/dx < 0$ for $x = x^*$. Given that $\forall x, f'(x) > 0$ and $x^* > 0$, the sign of $/dx$ for $x = x^*$ depends only on the sign of n. We conclude that the local stability is verified if and only if $n < 0$, i.e. $\alpha_2 > \alpha_3 - \beta_3$. For the equilibrium $x^{**} = 0$, we note that $/dx \sim nf(x)$. We verify that the local stability of x^{**} is obtained only if $n > 0$. The same result holds for the C-equilibrium x^{***} such that $1/x = 0$. Q.E.D.

Proposition 1 was about the existence of different types of equilibria. Yet, Proposition 2 gives us some insights about the convergence towards these equilibria. It clearly shows the role played by the competitive pressure i.e. the reaction of the editor in the short run to counterbalance the loss in market share as the OS project becomes more attractive. The greater is this competitive pressure, the greater is the probability that the two bases coexist at long term. Once this equilibria is reached, the (relative) magnitude of the OS community given by β_1 in comparison to the level of the R&D policy of the editor α_1, increases the relative size of the OS platform at a coexistence equilibrium.

OPENING STRATEGY

We here introduce the possibility for the editor to open its source code[5]. Opening has short term and long term consequences.

Statics

All things being equal, opening the proprietary code (or part of it) decreases the costs incurred by developers when providing solutions based on the proprietary software. Yet, opening the code also increases the propensity for developers using OS solutions to copy some sequences of code. These sequences may be reused into the OS base and thus benefit also to the OS platform. It is natural to consider that if the editor decides to open some lines of code, it can first choose to open those lines which are the most important for developers using the proprietary platform (or those who bring the highest utility to them). In this case, the advantage is greater for solutions using proprietary software than for solutions developed from the OS basis. Hence, when the relative part of the open code increases in the proprietary basis, opening more presents less and less benefits for developers using the proprietary platform (since the most strategic part of the code is already opened). At the same time, the benefit from opening more increases developers' utility when using OS. To keep things simple, let us suppose that the marginal benefit from opening more is constant. With this simplifying assumption, we can deduce the existence of an interior optimal level of openness.

Let μ $(0 \leq \mu \leq 1)$ represent the part of the proprietary code that the editor chooses to open. When μ is small, increasing μ amplifies marginally the advantages in terms of costs of the proprietary solutions. Yet once reached a critical level of μ, the marginal advantages of open lines for the developers of proprietary solutions are overcome by the advantages drawn from the use of the open lines of the proprietary basis for the developers in OS basis. Let $\chi(A/B, \mu)$ be the function depicting the cost advantage other than that associated to the fees for developers using the proprietary basis. $\chi(A/B, \mu)$ is defined in the following way: $\chi(A/B, \mu)$ is two time continuous on every variables and such that: $\forall A/B$, $\chi(A/B, 0) = c(A/B)$, $\lim_{A/B \to 0} \chi(A/B, \mu) = -\infty$, $\lim_{B \to 0} \chi(A/B, \mu) = +\infty$ and $\forall A,B,(B \neq 0)$, μ^*, $(0 < \mu^* < 1)$, such that $\chi(A/B, \mu)$ increases with μ for $\mu < \mu^*$ and decreases for $\mu > \mu^*$. In order to simplify the analytical expression of the cost, consider also the following specification of the effect of μ: $\chi(A/B, \mu) = c (A/B) + (a\mu - a'\mu^2)$

$h(A/B)$ with $0 < a < 2a'$ and $h(A/B)$ an increasing generic function such that $h(0) = 0$ where coefficients a and a' capture the sensibility of users to a more or less open code. One can easily check that in this simple form, $\mu^* = a/2a'$ whatever A/B.

The editor's objective is then to select a pair (p, μ) maximising its profit (8):

$$\Pi^P = m^P \left(A, B, p, \mu \right) p \tag{8}$$

The short term sequence is unchanged and determines the level of fees, openness and market share at each time step.

Dynamics

Opening the code increases the quality of the contribution of independent developers. System (5) then modifies to (9):

$$\begin{cases} \dot{A} / A = \alpha_1 + \alpha_2(1 - 2d_i^*) + 2\alpha_3'(\mu)d_i^* \\ \dot{B} / B = \beta_1 + \beta_3'(\mu)(1 - 2d_i^*) \end{cases} \tag{9}$$

where and are increasing functions of μ such as $(0) = \alpha_3$ and $(0) = \beta_3$. The rest of the dynamics remains unchanged.

Results

The static outcomes are deduced from the introduction of μ into the cost functions. The dynamic outcomes then integrate the effect of μ on $(\cdot)$ and $(\cdot)$.

Static Outcome

The market shares of each platform depend now on the size of the bases A and B, on the fees of proprietary software p and of the rate of openness μ. From the new definition of $c(A/B, \mu)$, we solve backwards (and limit to interior cases) and obtain $p = [d(A/B) + \chi(A/B, \mu^*)] / 2\gamma$ where μ^* is such that $(A/B, \mu^*) = 0$. With the chosen specification, the short term solutions are $\mu^* = a/2a'$ and $p = [d(A/B) + \chi(A/B, a/2a')]/2$. Note that $(A/B, p) = [d(A/B) + \chi(A/B, a/2a')]/2\gamma$. Whatever A/B, $\chi(A/B, a/2a') > c(A/B)$, *i.e.* when the editor of the proprietary software decides to open, its current share of market increases.

Dynamic Outcomes

On a dynamic point of view, 'opening' part of the code increases the attractiveness of the proprietary technology and thus stimulates the dynamics of the knowledge base A. This intuition is confirmed by *Proposition 3*.

Proposition 3: *Opening the proprietary basis reduces the range of variation of the parameters compatible with the existence of a C-equilibrium. When it exists, the C-equilibrium may or not correspond to a larger relative size of the proprietary platform.*

Proof: the C-equilibrium solution of (9) is the value of A/B such that $[\alpha_1 + \alpha_2 - \beta_1 - (\mu^*)] + 2[(\mu^*) + (\mu^*) - \alpha_2](A/B, p, \mu^*) = 0$. Its conditions of existence still reduce to $\{\beta_1 - \alpha_1 \geq (\mu^*)\}$. In the general case, μ^* depends on A/B in such a way that the conditions of existence of the C-equilibrium are not independent from the short term components of the model, *i.e.* on the shape of the functions $\chi(\cdot)$ and $d(\cdot)$. However, except when the optimal solution is $\mu^* = 0$, $(\mu^*) > \alpha_3$. We conclude that the conditions of existence of the C-equilibrium are more restrictive. When it exists, the C-equilibrium analytical expression of $(A/B)^*_{\text{open code}}$ is such that $d(A/B) + \chi(A/B, \mu^*) = -\gamma[\alpha_1 + \alpha_2 - \beta_1 - (\mu^*)]/[(\mu^*) + (\mu^*) - \alpha_2]$ and the incidence of opening on the equilibrium solution is not easy to analyse. According to the form of the functions (μ^*), (μ) and $\chi(A/B, \mu)$, the new stationary equilibrium can be more at the advantage of the proprietary platform or not. Even with our specification and more generally if we suppose

that the optimal level of openness does not depend on the level of A/B, this ambiguity is maintained since the equilibrium $(A/B)^*_{\text{open code}}$ depends not only on short term functions but also on (μ) and (μ). Q.E.D.

In order to analyse whether the long run effect of opening confirms or not its short term benefits for the editor, we then has to consider the stability issues.

Proposition 4: *When the optimal level of 'openness' does not depend on the relative size of the two software bases and when a C-equilibrium exists, opening the code of the proprietary software increases the range of the parameters that correspond to WTA-equilibria and reduces the range of stability conditions of the parameters that correspond to the local stability of the C-equilibrium.*

Proof: as in the proof of Proposition 2, one expresses the dynamical system under the form $= x[m(x) + n(x)f(x)]$ and $/dx = m(x) + xm'(x) + xn(x) f'(x) + xn'(x) f(x) + n(x) f(x)$. When we express this condition at the C-equilibrium $x^*_{\text{open core}}$, it reduces to $x^*_{\text{open code}}[m'(x^*_{\text{open code}}) + n(x^*_{\text{open code}}) f'(x^*_{\text{open code}}) + n'(x^*_{\text{open code}}) f(x^*_{\text{open code}})]$. The C-equilibrium $x^*_{\text{open code}}$ is still locally stable if and only if $/dx(x = x^*_{\text{open code}}) < 0$. Given that $\forall x$, $f'(x) > 0$ and $x^*_{\text{open code}} > 0$, the sign of $/dx$ for $x = x^*_{\text{open code}}$ depends only on the sign of the bracket. The variations of μ^* according to A/B play a part in the signs of the terms $m'(\cdot)$ and $n'(\cdot)$ and do not provide easily interpretable stability conditions. Consider now our specification. Given that $\forall A, B, \mu^* = (a'/2a')$, in this case $m'(\cdot) = 0$ and $n'(\cdot) = 0$, *i.e.* the stability condition reduces to $n = (a'/2a') + (a'/2a') - \alpha_2 < 0$. In comparison to the previous condition, *i.e.* $\alpha_3 + \beta_3 - \alpha_2 < 0$, this condition is more restrictive since $\forall (a'/2a') > 0$ $(a'/2a') > \alpha_3$, $(a/2a') > \alpha_3$ and $(a'/2a') > \beta_3$ $(a/2a') > \beta_3$. More generally, if μ^* does not depend on A/B, the stability condition reduces to $n = (\mu^*) + (\mu^*) - \alpha_2 < 0$ which is a more restrictive condition than $\alpha_3 + \beta_3 - \alpha_2 < 0$. In this case, for the equilibrium $x^{**} = 0$, we still verify that $/dx \sim nf(x)$. We note that the local stability of x^{**} is still obtained only if $n > 0$. The same result holds for the other WTA-equilibrium x^{***} such that $1/x = 0$. Opening the code then decreases the range of values of the parameters involving the stability of the WTA-equilibria and the instability of the C-equilibria one. Q.E.D.

To illustrate the content of Propositions 3 and 4, let us consider the following simplifying illustration. Suppose first that at time *0*, the situation of the software industry is balanced with respect to the two software bases. This means here that the industry has reached a locally stable equilibrium $(A/B)^*$ where the two software platforms coexist and grow at the same rate. Now, suppose that at time 1, the editor decides to open partially the code. Such strategy would have two effects. First, it would increase the market share and the profit of the proprietary platform in the short run. Second (according to *Proposition 3*), the industry should switch to another equilibrium. This new equilibrium would be characterized by a new ratio $(A/B)^*_{\text{open code}}$ such that $(A/B)^*_{\text{open code}} < (A/B)^*$ or $(A/B)^*_{\text{open code}} > (A/B)^*$. This indeterminacy has important implications for the software editor. It means that after opening its code, the editor cannot assess with certainty the effects of this strategy in the long run. Put differently, opening part of its code generates some complex dynamical effects that the commercial editor cannot anticipate and manage with certainty. In the long run, it may then be better off (larger $(A/B)^*_{\text{open code}} < (A/B)^*$) or less off, depending on the generated dynamical effects.

COMPATIBILITY STRATEGY

Beside the opening strategy, the degree of compatibility between the two platforms is another strategic variable for the editor of the proprietary platform. When jointly implemented with an opening strategy, this would consist in reorganizing the code of the proprietary platform software before it is open so as to increase the compatibility of its platform with that of the OS software. Yet, unlike the previous strategy, a strategy based on a higher compatibility enables the editor to benefit partly from the development efforts of the OS community. Conversely, the OS community also benefits from a higher compatibility of the proprietary platform. This effect could negatively impact the proprietary platform since this could increase the substitutability between the two platforms and lead to a fiercer competition.

Statics

Let us assume that the editor decides to make a proportion $\lambda(0 \leq \lambda \leq 1)$ of its code compatible with the OS platform. This introduces a new strategic variable for the editor. For the sake of simplicity, let us assume that this compatibility decision incurs no specific costs[6]. One can however expect that increasing the compatibility of software allows developers of proprietary solutions to integrate lines of OS into the solution they propose. Conversely, increasing the compatibility allows developers of OS solutions to use code in the reverse way. The effect of λ is twofold: i) it reduces the negative consequences of having specific needs (i.e. needs that are imperfectly filled by the proprietary platform) when using the proprietary platform; ii) it decreases the cost of the developers' effort. To keep things simple, let us assume the first effect to be linear. The second increases more than proportionally the advantage of developers providing OS solutions.

The total gain from the implementation of a proprietary hybrid solution over an OS hybrid one is then given by (10)

$$\Delta u_i + \Delta c = d(A/B) - \gamma(1 - \lambda) d_i + \psi(A/B, \lambda) \tag{10}$$

where $\psi(A/B, \lambda)$ is two times continuous on every variables and such that: $\forall A/B, \psi(A/B, 0) =$

$c(A/B)$, $\lim_{A/B \to 0} \psi(A/B, \lambda) = -\infty$, if $\lambda \neq 0$, $\lim_{B \to 0} \psi(A/B, \lambda) = (\lambda)$,, and $\forall A,B$, $\psi(A/B, 1) = \psi_{-} < 0$. It seems also reasonable to consider that if the proprietary code is open and fully compatible with the OS code, there will remain no advantage for an independent commercial developer to propose a proprietary solution. This assumption can as well be formulated in the following way: $\forall A,B$, $d(A/B) + \psi(A/B, 1) \leq 0$.

Consider also the following specification of the effect of λ: $\psi(A/B, 1) = c(A/B) - b\lambda^2 k(A/B)$ where $b > 0$ and $k(A/B)$ is an increasing function of A/B such that $k(0) = k$. The editor objective is then to select a pair (p, λ) maximising its profit (11):

$$\Pi^P = m^P\left(A, B, p, \lambda\right) p \qquad (11)$$

The short term sequence still determines the short-term fees, level of compatibility and market share of the two software platforms.

Dynamics

Making the two software more compatible also increases the quality/quantity of developers' contributions. System (5) then modifies to (9):

$$\begin{cases} \dot{A}/A = \alpha_1 + \alpha_2(1 - 2d_i^*) + 2\alpha_3''(\mu)d_i^* \\ \dot{B}/B = \beta_1 + \beta_3''(\mu)(1 - 2d_i^*) \end{cases}$$

where (μ) and (μ) are increasing functions of μ such as $(0) = \alpha_3$ and $(0) = \beta_3$. The rest of the dynamics remains unchanged.

Results

The static outcomes are deduced from the introduction of λ in the short term part of the model. The dynamic outcomes then integrate the effect of λ on $(\cdot)$ and $(\cdot)$

Static Outcome

The market shares of each platform depend on the size of the bases A and B, on the fees of proprietary software p and of the level of compatibility λ. Solving backwards and focussing again on interior solutions, one obtains the two following conditions: $p = [d(A/B) + \psi](A/B, \lambda^*)] /2$ and $(A/B, \lambda^*)\gamma(1 - \lambda) + \gamma[d(A/B) + \psi (A/B,\lambda^*) - p] = 0$ which jointly determine p and λ^*. Given our assumptions on the form of $\psi(A/B, \lambda)$, an interior value of λ^* always exists with the corresponding optimal price p. As in the previous cases, we will suppose the current sizes of the two bases A and B are such that $(A/B, p, \lambda^*)$ determines positive shares of market for the two solutions. Even if there is no possibility to provide an analytical expression of p and λ^* in the general case, one can deduce from the first and second order conditions on ψ $(A/B, \lambda)$ that larger is A/B, smaller is λ^*.

Dynamic Outcomes

On a dynamic point of view, higher compatibility stimulates the growth of the two software platforms. It is then important to compare their respective level of development and to evaluate the potential long term outcomes.

Proposition 5: *Making the two software bases more compatible reduces the parameter set for which the two software platforms coexist in the long run. When it exists, this C-equilibrium may or not correspond to a larger relative size of the proprietary software platform.*

Proof: the reasoning is the same as that of *Proposition 3*. The C-equilibrium solution of (9) is the value of A/B such that $[\alpha_1 + \alpha_2 - \beta_1 - (\lambda^*)] + 2(\lambda^*) + (\lambda^*) - \alpha_2]$ $(A/B, p, \lambda^*) = 0$. Its conditions of existence still reduce to $\{\beta_1 - \alpha_1 \geq (\lambda^*)\}$. Since $(\lambda^*) \geq \alpha_3$, the condition of existence of a C-equilibrium with a compatibility strategy is more restrictive than without compatibility. For the same reasons as for proposition 3, no general conclusion can here be deduced from the comparison of $(A/B)^*_{\text{compatible}}$ to $(A/B)^*$. Q.E.D.

Proposition 5 shows that when the editor has an incentive to make its platform more compatible with the OS platform, it may do so in order to increase its short term profit. Yet, such compatibility generates dynamical effects parallel to the opening strategy. Two effects need to be stressed. First, after the two software are made more compatible, the market share of the proprietary platform increases in the short run, and not that of the OS, whenever the software industry switch to a coexistence equilibrium. Yet, in the long run, this increase in market share and profit is no longer guaranteed and the dynamical effects generated by the initial compatibility strategy may either benefit to the editor or harm it. Besides, the probability of switching to a C-equilibrium decreases with the introduction of the compatibility strategy, making it less likely for the two software to coexist in the long run.

There is in this case no relevant support for a proposition parallel to Proposition 4. In general, even with simple specifications of $\psi\,(A/B, \lambda)$, the static value of λ^* is not independent from A and B. The conditions of stability of the C and WTA-equilibria then depend on some complex relation between the static and dynamic part of the model. The static analysis reveals that λ^* is rather large when $(A/B)^*_{\text{compatible}} > (A/B)^*$ and that λ^* is rather small when $(A/B)^* > (A/B)^*_{\text{compatible}}$. Since the size of λ^* has a direct influence on (λ^*) and (λ^*), defining how the conditions on the parameters vary is totally dependant from the case $(A/B)^*_{\text{compatible}} > (A/B)^*$ or $(A/B)^*_{\text{compatible}} < (A/B)^*$. Therefore, taken independently, the effect of the coefficients (λ^*) and (λ^*) tends to involve less local instability for the C-equilibrium when $(A/B)^*_{\text{compatible}} > (A/B)^*$ than when $(A/B)^*_{\text{compatible}} < (A/B)^*$.

CONCLUSION

In this article, we were interested in the long term effects of the competition between two software platforms (where one is released upon Open Source licence terms and the other is proprietary). Since the software is a platform, new applications are built on that platform and developers need to choose the platform on which they want to operate. We built a theoretical model to study the short and long run effects of the competition between the two platforms. In the short term, the characteristics of the two software are considered as given. In the long run, these are dependant from the "knowledge base" of each software (which in turn depends on developers' contributions and use of the platform). In that framework, we studied different situations. In the benchmark case, we determined the different types of outcome that would occur in the long run. In one case, the long run outcome is a winner-takes-all situation where one platform only remains active in the long run. In the other case, the coexistence of the two platforms is sustainable in the long run. The condition for this last situation to occur relates partly to the management of the OS community (ability of OS community-management to induce high levels of contributions inside the community and more generally to attract core developers). Besides, the competitive pressure – i.e. the reaction of the editor in the short run to counterbalance the loss in market share as the OS project becomes more attractive – plays an important role for this simplified 'industry' to converge towards a coexistence outcome. Grounding on this benchmark, we then introduced two strategies for the editor of the commercial platform. The first one is to "open" (i.e. make it visible in a non-compiled file to user, without giving them the possibility to reuse and redistribute freely the code). In that case, we showed that the editor has a short term incentive to open its code so as to attract more developers. Yet, the effects in the long run of such strategy are not *ex ante* predicable. Opening part of the code induces a switch from one equilibrium outcome to another, and generates many dynamical effects. Some of these effects cannot be perfectly integrated by the commercial editor, so that the convergence can be towards a less favourable outcome in the long run. A second strategy would be to reconsider its degree of compatibility while opening part of its code. We showed that such strategy would generate dynamical effects analogous to those of the opening strategy. Besides, the probability of switching to a coexistence outcome decreases with the introduction of the compatibility strategy, making it even less likely for the two software to coexist in the long run.

These results could be extended in two different ways. A first direction would be to reconsider the choices of the editor. In this article, we considered that the editor was maximizing its instantaneous profit. Indeed, because of the existence of numerous dynamical effects, it seems quite difficult to assume that the editor would be able to maximize a discounted profit up to an infinite time horizon. Yet, a multi-stage decision game could be introduced to analyse further the short term/long term trade off identified in this article. A second direction would be to introduce other types of hybridization. In the present article, part of the code is open, yet such opening is not sufficient to become "Open Source". A less conservative strategy would be to allow for such reuse and distribution, thus creating more "hybrid" models.

REFERENCES

Bitzer, J., & Schröder, P. J. H. (Eds.). (2006). *The Economics of Open Source Software Development*. Elsevier Science Publishers.

Bonaccorsi, A., & Rossi, C. (2003). Why Open Source software can succeed . *Research Policy*, *32*(7), 1243–1258.

Casadesus-Masanell, R., & Ghemawat, P. (2006). Dynamic Mixed Duopoly: A Model Motivated by Linux vs. Windows. *Management Science*, *52*, 1072–1084.

Comino, S., & Manenti, F. M. (2008). *Dual licensing in open source software markets*. Communication to the 2nd International Workshop on FLOSS Rennes, June.

Darmon, E., Le Texier, T., & Torre, D. (2007). *Commercial or Open Source Software? Winner-Takes-All Competition, Partial Adoption and Efficiency*. GREDEG Working paper.

Economides, N., & Katsamakas, E. (2006). Two-sided Competition of Proprietary vs. Open Source Technology Platforms and the Implications for the Software Industry. *Management Science*, *52*(7), 1057–1071.

Galoppini, R. (2008). *Open Source at Microsoft: an analysis of Microsoft Open Source Strategy*, http://robertogaloppini.net/2008/03/20/open-source-at-microsoft-an-analysis-of-microsoft-open-source-strategy/

Henkel, J. (2006a). Selective revealing in open innovation processes: the case of embedded *Linux*. *Research Policy*, *35*(7), 953–969.

Henkel, J., & Gruber, M. (2006b). New ventures based on open innovation - an empirical analysis of start-up firms in embedded Linux. *International Journal of Technology Management*, *33*(4), 256–372.

Lerner, J., & Tirole, J. (2002). Some Simple Economics of Open Source. *The Journal of Industrial Economics*, *50*(2), 197–234.

Parker, G., & Van Alstyn, M. (2008). *Innovation through Optimal Licensing in Free Markets and Free Software*. Available at SSRN: http://ssrn.com/abstract=639165.

Von Hippel, E. (2005). *Open Source Software Projects as User Innovation Networks* (pp. 267–278). Cambridge, London: Perspectives on Free and Open Source Software.

ENDNOTES

[1] It may be argued that some users may develop themselves instead of outsourcing software development. As it will be seen later, our model allows for such reinterpretation.

[2] See Henkel [2006 a] and Henkel & Gruber [2006 b] for an empirical illustration of such framework

[3] Since the objective of users and developers are the same, the model can be also interpreted without development outsourcing.

[4] We could also assume that OS communities may react in the short term to editors' strategy. Formally, this would lead to $B_2 = \beta_2(d^*)$. This may be an extension of the current model. Yet, the ability of OSS communities to react may be less than that of a commercial editor (since e.g. OSS projects have less financial and human resources to invest in the short run. That is why we normalized this effect to 0.

[5] To some extend, the opening strategy might recall Netscape's strategy when Netscape 5.0 has been relaunched under OS licence terms. Yet, the context (standard war, end-user oriented software) is here different from that of the model and the model better illustrates Microsoft's strategy when opening part of MS Windows' code.

[6] Increasing software compatibility may induce some costs (code reengineering). Yet, assuming that such reengineering involves no cost enables us to isolate the strategic reasons for the firm to increase compatibility.

This work was previously published in International Journal of Open Source Software and Processes (IJOSSP), edited by Stefan Koch, pp. 67-80, copyright 2009 by IGI Publishing (an imprint of IGI Global).

Section 3

Chapter 11

Simulation-Based Study of Community Governance and Conflict Management in Emerging Global Participatory Science Communities

Levent Yilmaz
Auburn University, USA

ABSTRACT

Despite significant research in open innovation, much less is known about why and how collective creativity emerges in open source scientific communities, as relatively little is known about organizing processes in such cyber-enabled Global Participatory Science (GPS) communities. One of the significant problems in understanding emergence of innovation involves how GPS communities govern and coordinate to maximize innovation output. We conduct an agent simulation study to examine the impact of culture and conflict management styles on collective creativity. Findings suggest that decentralized coordination schemes such as emergent selection such as found in utility communities and moderate degrees of assertiveness and cooperation for conflict management result in higher incidence of innovation.

INTRODUCTION

The practice of science is more open and global, as the access to knowledge, as well as its production is becoming increasingly transparent. Service ori-

ented science (Foster, 2005) and e-Science (David and Spence, 2003) initiatives lead to scientific communities, where shared domain knowledge is no longer exclusively documented in the scientific literature or patents, but is also documented in software, simulations, and databases that represent an evolving collective knowledge-base

DOI: 10.4018/978-1-60960-513-1.ch011

that is governed and maintained by community members. Just like open source software communities, "SourceForge for science" style in scientific production and collaboration provide the requisite infrastructure that encompass community membership services, catalogs, storage services, and workflow orchestration service.

Recently a number of virtual scientific collaboratories emerged and continue to successfully bring together scientists over the globe to collaborate to not only share and aggregate data, but also create new knowledge. We call these groups Global Participatory Science (GPS) communities. For instance, OBO Foundry (Smith et al., 2007), the testbed that influenced and inspired this study, is collaboration among a group of communities that are active in developing ontologies to standardize data acquisition and use in the health sciences community. As collaboratories over the cyberinfrastructure become sophisticated in terms of capabilities that support remote access, collaboration, and cooperative activity management, virtual organizations as open science socio-technical systems are becoming prominent and increasingly central to science and engineering projects. Despite significant innovation research, much less is known about why and how innovation emerges in open science communities, as relatively little is known about organizing processes in cyber-enabled open science communities. Therefore, discovering optimal levels of connectivity, diversity, and interactivity at which scientific production and innovation can be optimized in open science socio-technical systems become a critical problem. One of the challenging problems involving such open science communities is to understand how and why such communities form and evolve as a result of interaction and collaboration among individuals in accord with their governance mechanisms.

We choose virtual GPS communities as a testbed to study, develop, and explore models of innovation in virtual innovation communities. GPS communities may experience reduced

production loss through production blocking (Diehl and Stroebe, 1991; Gallupe et al., 1991) because all team members can contribute ideas simultaneously. They reduce problems with social influence such as evaluation apprehension and anonymity (Dennis and Valacich, 1993; DeRosa et al., 2007). Also, GPS communities, which often communicate through electronic media, reduces cognitive failures (Nijstad et al., 2006) and enhances the synergistic effects of group brainstorming because access to the data is unrestricted by individual recall (Dennis and Valacich, 1993). Traditional organizational archetypes are hierarchical organizations, in which employees have little or no control over their jobs (Lawler, 1992). In contrast, GPS communities accentuate emergent selection because individuals are given some control, which stimulates and motivates them (Von Hippel, 2005), so that individuals are adaptive as opposed to optimizing. Contributions compete for adoption and unanticipated innovations emerge as a result of interactions between the culture, organization, and the technology. Given these observations, the objective of this study involves using a computational model

- *to explore and improve our understanding of the structural and behavioral assumptions for the emergence and sustainment of creativity in GPS communities under alternative community cultures and **conflict managementstyles**.*

Methodology – Agent Simulation: Each research method has its strengths and weaknesses. Empirical studies such as case studies, surveys, and similar inductive are useful and powerful in discovering empirical regularities and gaining empirical insight they are not as powerful in revealing underlying mechanisms and exploring the impact of normative strategies under hypothetical scenarios. On the other hand, computer simulation facilitates not only understanding the socio-technical systems under consideration as they are (e.g., empirical insight), but also provides a computational laboratory to ask questions such "what should be" and "what might be". As such a research methodology that takes advantage of computer simulation enables analysis of the impacts of alternative mechanisms and policies to discover normative strategies, while also improving our ability to conduct exploratory analysis over the full range of plausible behaviors. Therefore, an agent simulation model of knowledge creation is developed to test hypotheses regarding the innovation potential of open innovation communities.

Objective: To this end, the focus of this study is to use plausible and conceptually grounded operational GPS community mechanisms to discover structural community constraints (e.g., size, organization) and behaviors (e.g., conflict management style) that confer incidence of innovation. Using the conceptually grounded, yet hypothetical GPS community we test propositions and generate hypotheses pertaining to the impact of (1) community cultures and (2) conflict management styles of project leadership. This ongoing line of inquiry is first concerned with the following questions to identify proper abstractions to study GPS communities:

- Can complex systems theory and generative modeling provide a sound formal basis to study the dynamics of GPS communities? If they do, how can we represent co-evolution of the community dynamics and project growths as they reinforce each other?
- What are the underlying structural and behavioral patterns of the mode of production in GPS communities, and how can we model them as self-organizing systems of agents?

Based on the developed model of the hypothetical GPS community, we examine the impact of variation of GPS community culture in terms of their decision-making and coordination styles.

Three alternative styles that are considered: (a) exploration-oriented, (b) utility-oriented, and (c) service-oriented (Ye et al. 2005). Using the model, we address the following questions: What types of coordination and decision-making styles are associated with higher innovation output in GPS community projects and which specific conflict management styles improve the incidence of innovation?

Observed results reinforce and extend earlier findings on the wisdom of collectives, which suggest that aggregation of decisions of focused individuals in collectives consistently outperform experts in terms of prediction accuracy concerning likely outcome of future events. When they become stable, utility-oriented communities lend themselves to a climate with higher degrees of boldness and receptivity as compared to exploratory and service-oriented communities, which utilize central or council style decision-making styles. In both the exploratory and service communities, the avoidance (low assertiveness and low cooperation) style in conflict management leads to higher degrees of differentiation in project structure. In the case of low assertiveness and high cooperation style (i.e., accommodation) the project structure becomes well integrated. On the other hand, the integrating style, which is characterized by moderate to high levels of cooperation and assertiveness, performs better in achieving integrated differentiation.

The rest of the paper is structured as follows. In section 2, we overview the perspective, background, and related work on conceptual models of GPS communities and substantiate the analogy between systems model of creativity and mode of production in GPS communities. Section 3 presents the basis for the model by means of paradox of conflict and the mechanism underlying evolutionary innovation. Section 4 outlines the proxy metrics used to measure potential for incidence of collective creativity. Section 5 presents the issues involving the design and implementation of the model. In section 5, we also delineate the experiments and preliminary results in terms of the observed emergent archetypal patterns. Section 6 concludes by summarizing findings and discussing potential avenues of further research.

RELATED WORK

Open source innovation communities such as GPS are suitable candidates for exploring models of innovation, as their mode of production and dynamics align with the characteristics of innovation systems (Edquist, 1997). Individual and collective activities in an innovation system give rise to an evolutionary pattern of technical change (McKelvey, 1996). Similarly, Nelson (1995) argued that evolutionary theories of innovation are predicated on three principles: retention and transmission of information; generation of novelty leading to diversity; selection among alternatives.

Systems Model of Creativity

Creativity is the production of novel and useful ideas by an individual or group of individuals working together (Amabile, 1988). Innovation is an extension of creativity, as it is the successful implementation, adoption, and transfer of creative ideas, products, processes, or services (West and Farr, 1990). From a process perspective, creativity involves social, cognitive, and technical processes situated in individual, team, and organization contexts that repeatedly produce innovative products. This work answers the call for new methods of studying organizational creativity and innovation (Anderson et al., 2004) in community forms of organizations.

To this end, we focus on contributing to the socio-psychological understanding of innovation in open and virtual innovation communities. The mode of production in such communities involves autonomous contributions, while maintaining the necessary adjustments to common subject matter of work. For instance, GPS communities consist of members that not only work on a common product, but they are also aware of this collective work and adjust their actions to new information. Such community forms, in which organizational creativity and innovation rates are high, appear to be increasingly important to solving problems and sharing knowledge (van Maanen and Barley 1984; Brown and Duguid 1991, 2000, 2001; Hargadon and Bechky 2006), and they are well suited for an information economy that relies upon the production and diffusion of knowledge.

As depicted in Figure 1, collective innovation communities not only exhibit behavior that is similar to Nelson's principles (Nelson, 1995), but also align with Csikszentmihalyi's (1999) systems model of creativity. The components shown in Figure 1 are useful in conceptualizing the processes of creativity and innovation output in open innovation socio-ecologies. The first component, called the *individual*, pertains to technical contributions made by individuals that produce creative solutions to domain-specific problems. Such technical factors induce novel variations in the domains that constitute the technical context. However, acceptance of variations and innovations in a domain requires the community of scientists and engineers (i.e., the field) to confirm the appropriateness of the contribution. The systems view of creativity (Csikszenthmihalyi, 1999) advocates

Figure 1. Systems Model of Creativity

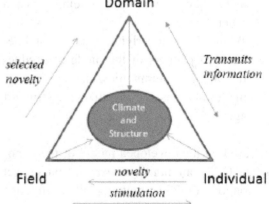

the role of cultural and social environment, as well as psychological dimension in defining creativity. According to the model, for creativity to occur, a set of domain-specific rules and practices must be adopted for an individual to produce a novel and appropriate contribution. The contribution results in a variation in the *domain*, and it must be selected by the *field* for inclusion in the domain.

The project presents to participants opportunities to make contributions and enable them to adjust their actions based on the evolving code base that defines the domain knowledge. The proposals are evaluated by the project leader along with a small group of core contributors (i.e., the field) on the basis of technical merits and elegance of the contributions. Selected contributions are then rejected on the project. The actions of the leader and the core group influence the intrinsic motivation of the participants of projects by affecting the joy and reputation they gain in the process. This strong similarity between the systems model of creativity and GPS mode of production suggests GPS community dynamics and software development process as a useful testbed to study organizational creativity and innovation.

Virtual GPS Communities: The OBO Foundry Case

The loss of richness in communication, diversity in membership, and increased mobility in virtual communities pose unique challenges. Traditions of scientific independence, difficulties in sharing knowledge, and formal organizational barriers are considered among the challenges that influence the sustainability of such communities. On the other hand, recently a number of virtual scientific collaboratories emerged and continue to successfully bring together scientists over the globe to collaborate to not only share and aggregate data, but also create new knowledge. The following are among such growing and increasingly active active open science collaboratories.

- OBO Foundry- Open Biomedical Ontologies
- NanoHUB - Simulation, Education, Technology for Nano Technology
- NEES Grid - Network for Earthquake Engineering Cyberinfrastructure
- CABIG - Cancer Biomedical Informatics Grid

OBO Foundry (Smith et al., 2007) is collaboration among a group of communities that are active in developing ontologies to standardize data acquisition and use in the health sciences community. OBO now comprises over 60 ontologies, and its role as an ontology information resource is supported by the NIH Roadmap National Center for Biomedical Ontology (NCBO). OBO Foundry serves as a hub for a network of communities to foster interoperability and to align and integrate their efforts. Some of the participating communities such as Open Biomedical Invesitigations (OBI), which is an international, collaborative effort to build an ontology to be used for annotation of Biomedical Investigations.

The OBO Foundry was initiated by Michael Ashburner and Suzanne Lewis (Smith et al., 2007) in 2001 to provide an infrastructure for authoring, maintenance, and evaluation of scientific ontologies in the biomedical and biological systems domain. The Foundry is an attempt to apply the scientific method to the task of ontology development, with the objective that the data generated through biomedical research should form a single, consistent, cumulatively expanding and algorithmically tractable knowledge structure. Hence, coordinated evolution of conceptual knowledge through the efforts of the members of the OBO consortium is aimed to support efficient and effective biomedical data integration, as well as incremental, empirical, accumulative, and collaborative knowledge construction OBO Foundry along with its related and affiliated communities constitute an open innovation network. Figure 2 illustrates a conceptual architecture of a global

Figure 2. Network of Communities

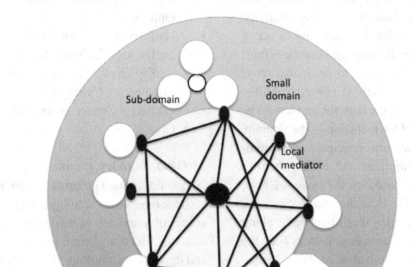

network of innovation communities that are coordinated via a group of local mediators and the hub coordinator that orchestrate the overall network.

As a hub, the OBO Foundry serves to align ontology and service development efforts carried out by separate communities that are active in research on various model organisms. For instance, since the establishment of OBO foundry, communities that focus on Gene Ontology (GO) and Foundational Model of Anatomy (FMA) have reformed their strategy and activities, so that conceptual knowledge can be formalized, documented, and evaluated using principles advocated by the core group of the OBO Foundry. As a collaborative experiment based on the voluntary acceptance by its participants of an evolving set of principles (available at http://obofoundry.org), OBO consortium is a unique example of a network of open innovation communities. Participants of the consortium vary from small communities that concentrate on specific targeted problems to large

domains that incorporate multiple sub-communities. For instance, The Ontology for Biomedical Investigations (OBI), addresses the need for controlled vocabularies to support integration of experimental data. OBI aims to facilitate coordinated representation of designs, protocols, instrumentation, materials, processes, data and types of analysis in various areas of biological and biomedical investigation. Twenty-five groups are now involved in building OBI (http://obi.sf.net/community), and the Foundry discipline has proven essential to its distributed development.

NanoHub is a community comprised of scientists, engineers, and educators that share and exchange resources related to Nano techology. NanoHub is based on an NSF-funded initiative that aims to establish a virtual organization and network for computational nanotechnology. Shared resources include simulations, learning modules such as course materials, publications, presentations, and tools. Similarly **NEESGrid**, which is an active consortium of earthquake engineering centers, institutes, researchers, and practitioners in United States and around the world and is the result of a collaboration effort led by the National Center for Supercomputing Applications (NCSA). As collaboratories over the cyberinfrastructure become sophisticated in terms of capabilities that support remote access, collaboration, and cooperative activity management, virtual communities are becoming prominent and increasingly central to science and engineering projects.

A Provisional Taxonomy of GPS Community Cultures

The culture of a GPS community can have a significant impact on the evolution of the project and the innovation potential of the community (Furst et al., 1999). Table 1 depicts the classification of cultures using Ye et al.'s (2005) categorization of virtual communities based on the degree of openness of their processes. The objective of an *exploration-oriented community* is to co-produce and share innovations and knowledge under the guidance of a central project leader. One example of exploration community is the OBO foundry (Smith et al, 2007), whose goal is to create a suite of orthogonal interoperable reference ontologies in the biomedical domain, thereby enabling scientists and their instruments to communicate with minimum ambiguity. In this way the data generated in the course of biomedical research will form a single, consistent, cumulatively expanding whole.

The objective in *utility-oriented communities* is to satisfy individual needs of scientists and

educators. The structure of such communities is decentralized and lacks a core project management. NanoHUB, for instance, is a utility-oriented community with a vision to pioneer the development of nanotechnology. The members in NanoHUB are developing resources to help others learn about nanotechnology while making use of these resources in their own research and education.

The purpose of *service-oriented communities* is to provide stable services under the leadership of a core group of active members. Ontology Lookup Service (OLS) subcommunity of the OBO Foundry is one such collaboratory. OLS provides a web service interface to query multiple ontologies from a single location with a unified output format. These three community cultures differ from each other in terms of recruitment selectivity, growth rate, turnover and decision making style.

- **Recruitment selectivity** indicates the threshold that determines whether a scientist begins to contribute or leaves a community after the process of enculturation. Exploratory communities are highly selective, because contributions need to converge to expectations of central leadership that guides the direction of the project. When a community of core members, instead of a central single project leader, shares governance a scientist can have more flexibility in making contributions as long as majority of the core group finds the submission acceptable. Such groups are

Table 1. GPS Community Cultures

Types of Community Cultures		
Decision-making style	**Coordination Style**	
	Centralized	**Distributed**
Centralized	Exploration-oriented	
Distributed	Service-oriented	Utility-Oriented

less selective in comparison to a central governance scheme.

- **Growth rate** for each community indicates the number of new individuals entering the community at regular intervals of time.

- **Turnover** specifies the threshold that determines whether or not a scientist leaves the community during the innovation process. If the reputation is less than the threshold, the agent will leave the community. Those communities with high recruitment selectivity results in community members that are highly enculturated and motivated. Such members are less likely to leave their communities; hence, exploratory communities are more cohesive compared to service and utility communities.

- **Decision making style** involves the process that determines whether to accept or decline a contribution. A single evaluator that represents the leader of the project performs centralized decision making, which is often observed in exploratory communities. In service-oriented communities, core members of the group are allowed to vote. Majority of votes is considered to make a final decision. Emergent selection delays evaluation for a specific time interval, at the end of which the number of individuals who adopt the contribution is taken into account to make a decision.

Paradox of Creativity and its Relation to Conflict

Our position is based on the observation that conflict theory provides a sound framework by which collective creativity can be examined. The observation is predicated on the premise that group dynamics and conflict are strongly interrelated in that high levels of diversity among team members can potentially cause conflicts as a result of communication (Kraut and Streeter, 1995) and coordination difficulties (Kirton, 1976,

1989). For example, Carnevale and Probst (1998) demonstrated that when individuals anticipate conflict, their thought processes become more narrow and rigid than when they anticipate cooperation; even the suggestion of conflict, without the actual experience, can be enough to trigger this limitation in thinking. Because creative ideas thrive on openness of thought, it would seem that conflict should affect creativity. Even though it is theoretically possible to suppress all conflict in group work (Thomas, 1992), this may not be in the team's best interest because it can hinder both the team's productivity and its creativity (Elliott and Scacchi, 2005; Nemeth, 1992). Others have proposed that total agreement throughout a group's process can leave the team susceptible to the dangerous occurrence of "groupthink" (Janis, 1972), in which the psychological drive for consensus at any cost suppresses dispute and consideration of alternatives. Based on a similar logic, Kolb and Gidden (1986) argued that project leaders can legitimatize conflict in groups to use conflict as a creative force.

The conflict resolution approaches available to communities vary depending on the members' desire to be assertive and cooperative. That is, the types of conflict resolution that the leadership (e.g., project leader and core members) utilizes can be analyzed in two dimensions: assertiveness - concern about one's outcomes and cooperativeness - concern about the outcome of others). As shown in Table 2, these dimensions can be used to identify approaches that can be used by the core leadership for conflict resolution.

Simulation-Based Study of GPS Communities

Although significant research has been conducted on social aspects of scientific com munities, simulation modeling of such communities is rare. One notable example is (Gilbert, 1997), where the citation patterns and growth of knowledge are simulated to exhibit empirical regularities

Table 2. Conflict Management

Conflict Handling Styles		
Concern for Others	Concern for Self	
	High	Low
High	Integrating	Obliging
Low	Dominating	Avoiding

observed in scientific communities. Yet, this study does not aim to consider social processes pertaining to enculturation and innovation. On the other hand, the simulation study presented in (Edmonds, 2007) views scientific discovery as a social process. However, unlike the model presented in this article, its underlying generative process does not take interactions between agents (i.e., scientists) into account. In the context of innovation, the use of simulation of collective invention and innovation diffusion (Cowan and Jonard, 2004) revealed the significance of social network and communication structure in knowledge creation and diffusion. Building on these earlier studies, the model introduced herein (1) explicitly specifies the underlying generative mechanisms related social dynamics of knowledge creation and (2) examines the implications of these mechanisms within the context of emergent virtual forms of scientific communities.

Similar studies have been conducted to better understand the dynamics of Open Source Software communities. These studies involved the use of formal simulation models to study project growth patterns (Antoniades et al. 2003a) and decision-making processes of individuals participating in such projects (Dalle and David 2003). In (Antoniades et al. 2003b), authors present a formal model that reveal growth processes in various phases in the lifecycle of GPS communities and demonstrate how the findings align with empirical observations observed in the APACHE project.

One of the early agent-based models of GPS communities developed by Madey et al. (2002) specifies a GPS community as a self-organizing ad-

hoc social network of heterogeneous agents. The model is used to investigate social psychological aspects of communication and team effectiveness and generate power-law distributions observed in SourceForge data. Agent-based modeling (ABM) paradigm provides a framework to examine the impact of the behavior of decentralized and autonomous individuals (agents) and their interactions over time in terms of emergent properties that are based on self-organizing processes. As such, ABM provides a useful methodology to explore the consequences of possibly hypothetical assumptions pertaining to open innovation communities such as GPS. Taking advantage of the spatial and temporal features, Smith et al. (2006) present a model of the evolution of GPS communities over time and examine the distribution of activities over the project space defined in terms of a projection grid similar to the approach presented in our model.

A CONCEPTUAL MODEL FOR OPEN SOURCE INNOVATION

A model of collectivity creativity and innovation requires explicit representation of a generator and evaluator to examine the impact of alternative community cultures and critic styles on the creative output of the community. The frequency of oscillation between individual contributions and the evaluation component, as well as the degree of harshness in the critics, and hence the receptivity of community leadership in new novel and useful ideas play a critical role in the emergent creative outcome. As discussed earlier, certain level of critical analysis and constraints are needed to avoid chaotic pseudo-random exploration of the space of contributions. On the other hand, low levels of receptivity and strict constraints may also be unproductive, because it penalizes experimentation too severely. Therefore, a balance between exploration and exploitation is critical.

Complex Systems Perspective: The Basis for Modeling Collective Creativity

Collective creativity occurs as a result of the interaction between individual contributions, the field (the core leadership), and the domain of knowledge, practices, norms, and values as suggested by the systems model of creativity. The process of collective creativity may be viewed as the creation and exploration of autopoietic attractors through an evolutionary system where contributions of individuals are based on combination and mutation of ideas in the spirit of genetic algorithms, as well as analogical spreading of ideas. (Goertzel, 1997) The search for such autopoietic attractors and phase transitions is similar to exploring where

this dynamic process leads to a convergence - in the sense of what type product and community climate the collective is going to have.

Hence, a complex system model is useful to gain insight about the interactions between the three major components of the systems model of creativity. In such a model, the *individual* serves the role of generator, whereas the *field* is the evaluator. Both components operate under the constraints imposed by the *domain*. With these observations, the conceptual structure for the strategy is presented in Figure 3.

The purpose of the evaluator is to judge the novelty and value of the contribution. The generator is skilled at producing rather than evaluating. The evaluator plays the role of external world and of the critic. Too much critic is not productive, as it inhibits the generator, which, in order to be innovative, must have spontaneity. Yet, too little critic can also be unproductive, as the output of the creator can be random at times. Therefore, novel and useful outputs involve some degree of oscillation between generator and evaluator, and the frequency of the oscillation should correspond roughly to the amount of constraint involved in the problem domain. Using the complex systems

Figure 3. Components of the Model

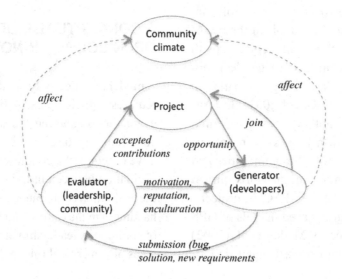

perspective we model an innovation community in terms of autonomous agents that interact to generate a global self-organizing behavior yielding emergent patterns that are amenable to analysis to make inference about the conditions under which innovation emerges.

Project Space

A *project* is defined in terms of a two-dimensional space over the function areas and associated problems. The cells in the project space denote components and artifacts of the project. Figure 4 depicts the two-dimensional representation of the project as a problem space. Cells with blue colors indicate new artifacts or modules with low complexity. As the complexity of an artifact increases due to accepted contributions of community members, the color of the cell changes toward pink.

Those regions with high artifact complexity also indicate where most development activity is taking place. Community members, including the project leader and core members, move within

Figure 4. Open Source Project Space

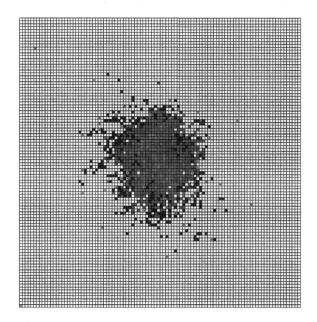

the project space and behave in accordance with specific rules defined in the following sections. To establish conceptual validity of simulations, these behavioral rules are selected to mimic the way contributors behave according to their roles (e.g., reader, peripheral contributor, active contributor). The cells with the color brown represent new artifact requirements (e.g., problems) proposed by the community members. These problems, when accepted by the project leadership, are replaced by artifacts with a randomly selected complexity. The color of the cell depicting the new artifact is based on its initial complexity.

Community Members: The Generator Component

Agents modeled in this study represent community members. Agents (i.e., community members) join a project, orient themselves to be familiar with the culture of the community, contribute by submitting solutions or revisions to existing artifacts, get promoted to become a member of the core group, exit the community to join new subprojects, or leave the GPS community. This high-level behavior is depicted in terms of the agent life-cycle shown in Figure 5.

GPS communities are specific forms of Collective Production Communities (von Hippel 2005). The organizational structure of GPS communities is frequently compared to the layers of an onion. This is also known as core/periphery network topology, and as shown in Figure 6, a snapshot of the social network of the Gene Ontology group within the OBO community exhibits this regularity. According to Von Hippel (2005), the project leader(s) is often the person, who initiates the project. Core contributors are responsible for collective guidance and coordination of the project. Active developers regularly contribute new features and fix bugs. Peripheral contributors occasionally contribute new functionality or revisions. Their contribution is irregular and the period of involvement is sporadic and short. GPS

Figure 5. Agent Lifecycle

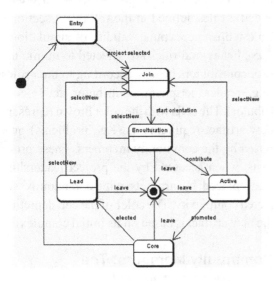

systems and communities co-evolve through the contributions of large number of participants.

The statechart presents the phases (i.e., states) that a new agent goes through after entering into the simulation. When the simulation is initialized, agents are selected to start from a specific state depending on their type (e.g., active contributor, leader, member of the core group). However, as the simulation unfolds, new agents start from the

Figure 6. The Core/Periphery Network of the Gene Ontology group within OBO

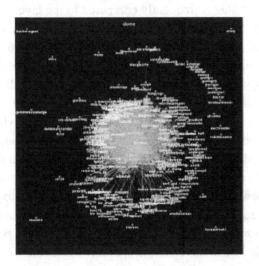

initial state so that they can autonomously start enculturation, and then continue with potential contributions, as well as get promoted into the governing group within the community.

Enculturation

An agent that joins the project starts familiarizing itself with the project. Following the conceptual framework proposed by Harrison and Carrol (2006), we abstract the enculturation process by means of a single variable indicating the propensity of an individual to embrace the values, norms, and practice of the community. A new member joining to the project may already be familiar with the technology and the scientific artifact (e.g., model, ontology, software) under development. That is, enculturation begins before the agent joins the community. This is captured in the model by assigning a randomly selected enculturation value in the range *[0,1]*. At every unit time interval, the enculturation of an agent *i* at time *t+1* is defined as follows:

$$C_{i,t+1} = f(C_{i,t}, I_{i,t}) \tag{1}$$

where $f(C_{i,t}, I_{i,t})$ is a function of the current enculturation level and the influence that the agent receives from the community members that it interacts with. At each time interval the agent interacts with a random number of other agents selected from the pool of contributors that are actively engaged in the artifact that the agent is visiting in the project space. The total influence the agent receives is defined as

$$I_{i,t} = \frac{1}{N} \sum_{j \neq i} M_{ji,t}(C_j - C_i) \tag{2}$$

where N is the number of agents active in the same artifact during the same time interval. The variable $M_{ji,t}$ denotes the intensity of influence that is exerted by agent *j* on agent *i*. The intensity is a function of the reputation of the agent exerting the influence:

$$M_{ji,t} = vR(j,t)$$

v used as a weighting parameter in the range between 0 and 1, and v is proportional to the frequency of communication and increases with successive interactions among pairs of agents. The initial values for v are chosen randomly. Given the current enculturation level of the agent along with the overall influence received from its peers, the new enculturation level of the agent is defined as

$$C_{i,t+1} = C_{i,t} + \beta I_{i,t} \tag{3}$$

where β, which is in the range of (0,1], refers to susceptibility of the agents to influence. Enculturation occurs more slowly for smaller values of β indicating inertia as a result of tenure of the agent. That is, the longer the agent is involved with the community, the less susceptible it is to influence and enculturation. Agents that do not have enculturation levels larger than activation threshold leave the community after a pre-specified interval of time. Depending on the type of the community a specific arrival rate is use to create a random number of agents to join the community and initiate their enculturation process.

Active Community Member

An agent decides to become an active member, if it is sufficiently enculturated and is fit to make proposals to contribute to the project. The rate of shifting from a passive state to active state depends on community threshold. The style of the community culture directly affects an agent's decision to become an active member. For instance, in exploration-oriented communities, the threshold to move to center of the community is high, whereas

utility-oriented communities such as Linux have low thresholds for entry. There are two types of active agents: peripheral contributors and active contributors. Active participants (see Figure 7) regularly contribute new features.

Peripheral contributors occasionally contribute new functionality or update existing artifacts. Their contribution is irregular and the period of involvement is sporadic and short. The degree of motivation triggers the agent's transition to a new role or exit from the community. If the motivation of the active contributor falls below a medium threshold, it reverts back to a role as peripheral participant. If the active contributor is a member of leadership or the project leader, then the agent can increase the complexity of an artifact or add new artifacts without peer evaluation. It is assured that the members of this group, based on their experience and reputation, are given privileges to make changes in the project space. The motivation and reputation of an agent is updated by the evaluator component, which is the agent that represents the project leader, core membership, or the community at large depending on the type of mechanism used to select contributions submitted by the agent. The rules for updating motivation and reputation will be discussed later.

Figure 7. Active Contributor

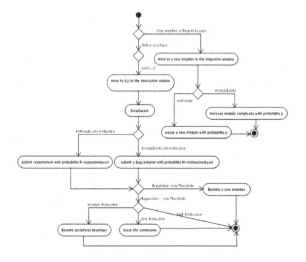

The Field: Evaluator Component

To examine the impact of alternative evaluation strategies on the creative output of a GPS community, we considered three community cultures that differ from each other in terms of entry thresholds, decision-making style, and growth and turnover rates. Along with community cultures, four different conflict resolution strategies are used to specify evaluation and critical analysis process to influence the growth of the project. Table 3 depicts the specification of community cultures in terms of their recruitment selectivity, growth rate, turnover, and decision-making style. The evolution of a project is heavily influenced by the growth/turnover in membership defined in terms of inter arrival rates of agents. We use a Poisson process to represent the growth rates of exploratory, service-oriented, and utility communities. The turnover for agents is defined in such a way to reflect the type of community they are affiliated with. In exploratory and service-oriented communities, decisions are influenced by the conflict management style of the project leadership.

Project leadership tends to focus on specific functional areas at any given point in time. Those contributions that relate to current hot zones and extend them in a meaningful way consistent with the objectives of the core group. Therefore, the probability of acceptance of a contribution is defined as a function of the distance between the project leader and the member who submits the contribution. As the distance increases, the probability first sharply decreases. The rate of decrease slows down for larger distances and reaches an asymptotic level. Specifically, we specify R_i, the probability of accepting a contribution submitted by an agent that is d units away in the project space from the decision maker (e.g., project leader) agent i with the following equation. Euclidean distance in the project space between the contributor and the leader is used to compute d. To compute the Euclidean distance, the (x,y) cell dimensions of agents' present location are used.

$$P_{acc}(i) = \beta_0 + \exp(-\beta_1 - \beta_2 d), \qquad (4)$$

where β_0 is associated with the asymptotic level for likelihood of acceptance, β_1 inversely related with the level of receptivity to others' contributions, and β_2 with the degree of concern for self. Large values of β_2 in the range [0,1] results in sharper decline as distance d increases, whereas small values of β_1 in the range [0,1] leads to higher receptivity for a given level β_2, resulting in higher level of concern for others. Figure 8 depicts the behavior of the function with different ($\beta_0, \beta_1, \beta_2$) combinations. To mimic alternative

Table 3. Specification of Community Types

Community Type	Community Characteristics
Exploration-oriented	Recruitment selectivity: HIGH Growth rate: LOW Turnover: LOW Decision-making style: Centralized
Utility-oriented	Recruitment selectivity: MODERATE Growth rate: HIGH Turnover: MODERATE Decision-making style: Emergent Selection
Service-oriented	Recruitment selectivity: LOW Growth rate: MODERATE Turnover: High Decision-making style: Council Style

conflict management styles, we sample ($\beta_0, \beta_1, \beta_2$) as follows:

Integrating: $<\beta_0 = [0.1, 0.3], \beta_1 = [0.1, 0.5], \beta_2 = [0.5, 1]>$

Obliging: $<\beta_0 = [0.1, 0.3], \beta_1 = [0.1, 0.5], \beta_2 = [0.1, 0.5]>$

Dominating: $<\beta_0 = (0, 0.1], \beta_1 = [0.5, 1.0], \beta_2 = [0.5, 1]>$

Avoiding: $<\beta_0 = [0.1, 0.3], \beta_1 = [0.5, 1.0], \beta_2 = [0.1, 0.5]>$

Besides the quality of the contribution, the reputation of a community member plays a critical role in having contributions accepted. To reflect the impact of reputation in the evaluation process, we extend the earlier acceptance probability formula by factoring in the reputation of the agent by means of the following equation:

$$P'_{acc}(i) = \min(1, (0.5 + R(i))[\beta_0 + \exp(-\beta_1 - \beta_2 d)]), \tag{5}$$

where R_i denotes the reputation of agent i and lies in the range $[0,1]$. In exploratory projects, the decision to accept a contribution submitted by agent i is based on the value of $P'_{acc}(i)$ as computed by the project leader. On the other hand, in service-oriented communities, each core group member, including the project leader, votes to accept or decline, and the results are aggregated to derive the collective decision. In the current model, each vote has the same weight; yet, this may easily be changed by giving higher weights to the votes of the project leader as well as the core group members that are closer to the contribution in the project space. For utility-oriented projects, we use the emergent selection style, where the decision to accept or decline is based on how much interest a contribution attracts. The degree of adoption of a contribution by others in the community is used as a measure to include or remove the artifact in the project space at a future scheduled time. As such, all proposed contributions are allowed with the stipulation that those contributions that do not add value and acceptance by the broader community would be dropped. The project complexity is used as a proxy metric to determine the extent to which community members contribute and adopt an artifact. If the complexity exceeds a predefined threshold, the artifact is accepted for inclusion in the project space; otherwise, it is removed.

Decisions feed back stimulation or frustration on the community members through updating their

Figure 8. Probability of Accepting a Contribution as a Function of Leader-Contributor Distance

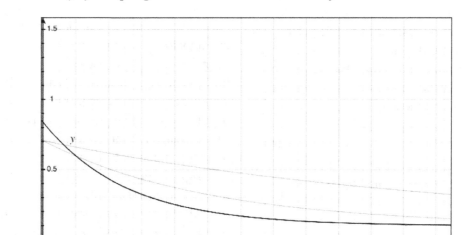

reputation, as well as motivation. Motivation, reputation, and enculturation levels of individuals define the climate of the community, because they influence the perceptions of members with respect to community type and leadership. Based on the expectancy theory of motivation (Vroom, 1964), the motivation and reputation levels of agents change depending on whether their incremental suggestions to improve artifacts or new problems are accepted for inclusion in the project. For incremental improvements to existing artifacts, inclusion of a contribution to an artifact, *MOD*, submitted by a community member, *i*, effect its motivation *M(i)* and reputation *R(i)* as follows:

$$R'(i) = R(i) + (1 - R(i))\min(\alpha d, 1)) \qquad (6)$$

$$M'(i) = M(i) + (1 - M(i))(1 - m(MOD) + \varepsilon)\gamma, \qquad (7)$$

where α and γ define parameters that control the step size for the increase in reputation and motivation respectively, *d* specifies the degree to which the accepted contribution involves an artifact that is differentiated from the current focus of the project leader. In the case of motivation, the level of increase depends on the degree of maturity of the artifact, defined as *m(MOD)*. That is, contributions to features that have lower complexity bring more satisfaction. The increments in motivation and reputation pull the new values toward 1, which is the largest possible value for motivation and reputation.

Declines of submitted contributions by the project leadership influence motivation and reputation in the other direction.

$$R'(i) = R(i) - R(i))\delta \qquad (8)$$

$$M'(i) = M(i) - M(i)(1 - m(MOD) + \varepsilon)\theta, \qquad (9)$$

The drop in reputation is higher for large values of reputation and the degree of drop is controlled by the parameter $0 < \delta < 1$. Similarly, decrease in motivation is proportional to current level of motivation and degree of complexity of the artifact. The change in reputation and motivation in the case of decisions involving proposed new features and requirements are defined similarly, with the exception that artifact maturity does not play a role, because the proposals are for new artifacts as opposed to existing components.

MEASURING COLLECTIVE CREATIVITY

Two measures are used in this study to develop proxy indicators for collective creativity. Next, we examine each metric and its derivation.

Collectivity Creativity and Community Climate

The first metric is predicated on the theory of organizational climate to determine the degree of boldness (divergent thinking tendency) of individuals and the receptivity of a community. The receptivity measure refers to the frequency and harshness of critical intervention of the environment facing the creative members of the community. In evolutionary biology terms, one may establish the analogy that maximum evolutionary innovation occurs in a moderately but not excessively constrained environment. On the other hand, high receptivity and criticism-free environment, places no constraints on the creative output and is unlikely to lead to useful novelty. These arguments can be formulated in the form of a proposition as follows:

Proposition: Those projects with strong normative climates (i.e., individuals usually *act in a certain way (norm) and often are punished (e.g., rejected contributions) when seen not to be acting according to the norm)* have fewer innovations.

Developing a metric to measure the degree of normativeness of a community and extent of punishment, we need to develop operational definitions of normative behavior and punishment. One way is to define the boldness or divergent thinking potential of a community member along with the receptivity of the community based on the decisions made by the project leadership. In our formulation, we consider *boldness* or divergent thinking as a function of motivation, reputation, and enculturation. The basic premise for the use of these parameters is that a divergent thinker and a bold member of a community needs to be motivated to continue to support the community and should have sufficient reputation to attract community members as well as project leaders and persuade them to accept contributions that are not necessarily aligned with the current direction and scope of the project. However, such divergent thinkers should rather be loosely coupled with the leadership to avoid group thinking or bias. Hence, those individuals with lower enculturation levels, while experiencing high motivation and reputation levels are likely to exhibit the characteristics of a divergent thinker. So far as *receptivity* is concerned, the ratio of accepted contributions to all submitted requests serves as a proxy metric to measure overall receptivity of the community. Specifically, the boldness, *B(i,t)*, of a community member, *i* at time *t* is defined as:

$$B\left(i,t\right) = \frac{MoT\left(i,t\right) \times R\left(i,t\right)}{C\left(i,t\right)} \quad (10)$$

where $MoT(i,t)$ and $R(i,t)$ denote motivation and reputation of the community member, while $C(i,t)$ depicts its enculturation level. Aggregating and then averaging the level of boldness of individuals within the community, we compute the overall boldness level of the community at time t:

$$\overline{B_t} = \frac{1}{N} \sum_{i \in 0} B\left(i,t\right) \quad (11)$$

where N denotes the number of members in community O. The receptivity, $RP(O)$, of the same community is computed as follows:

$$RP\left(O,t\right) = \frac{A\left(t\right)}{A\left(t\right) + D\left(t\right)} \quad (12)$$

where $A(t)$ and $D(t)$ represents the number of contributions accepted and declined.

Propositions on Complexity and Creativity

The second metric that we use in this study is grounded in complexity theory and influenced by the foundational hypotheses of the systems model of creativity. In (Csikszentmihalyi, 1999), the complexity of the society that constitutes the field and members of the community, as well as the domain are defined as fundamental hypotheses concerning and explaining how culture and domain affects the incidence of creativity. Specifically, Csikszentmihalyi (1999) proposes the following questions and explanations:

- How differentiated is the domain? The more differentiated the domain (e.g., the project contributions in the case of GPS ecologies), the more specialized the information, hence, advances occur rapidly.
- How integrated is the domain? The more integrated a domain, the advances in one subdomain will be relevant to the overall domain. While this may decrease the chance of acceptation and incorporation of new contribution, but once it is approved for inclusion in the domain, its diffusion will be rapid.

- How complex is the community? Both differentiation and integration within society affect the rate of generation and adoption of novelty.

Based on these critical hypotheses, we suggest a principled mechanism to measure the community as well as the produced artifact to determine the likelihood of incidence of creativity. Specifically, based on the theory of complexity, one can conjecture that there are two major and opposite tendencies in evolutionary systems. Changes in the community structure and climate, as well as the project growth may either lead to harmony or entropy (conflict and disorder). Harmony is achieved by evolutionary changes involving an increase in a system's complexity, that is, an increase in both differentiation and integration between complete order and disorder. Differentiation refers to the degree to which a system is composed of components that are different in structure or function from other parts. Integration refers to the extent to which different parts of a system are related, unified, and interact to enhance each other's goals. A system that is more differentiated and integrated is considered as complex. Therefore, our second measure utilized this synergy between complexity and creativity by measuring the entropy in the project state space.

The degree of complexity of a community, as well as a balanced degree of differentiation and integration of domain are critical for the incidence of creativity (Csikszentmihalyi, 1999). Creativity occurs at the edge of disorder and where the index of creativity and innovation self-organizes itself at a critical point beyond and below which chaotic disorder and orderliness lies, respectively. Both disorder and orderliness impede creativity. Disorder results in disintegration, as opposed to differentiation. On the other hand, mere orderliness leads to increasing impoverishment and finally to the lowest possible level of structure, no longer distinguishable from chaos, which is the absence of order. What distinguishes disorder and stagna-

tion through order (tightly coupled homogeneous set of ideas and contributions to the project) from novel and useful creativity is the degree of entropy that exists in the system. Hence, we use entropy as a proxy metric to measure the complexity of the community and the domain to analyze the degree of their differentiation and integration.

The *entropy* of a system can be defined by means of a probabilistic description of its states. If we consider the GPS community as a socio-technical system, the energy (e.g., motivation, boldness) of its members can take a discrete number of states. We have thus as set of possible degrees of motivation (or boldness), and we can define the set of probabilities associated with the possible motivation states. For instance, let P_j be the probability of observing an agent with motivation level M_j (with j =1,2,...S). The entropy of the community climate in relation to motivation is defined as follows:

$$H = -\sum_{j=1}^{s} P_j \log P_j \qquad (13)$$

In this study, we apply the entropy metric to project complexity to measure the degree of differentiation and determine if specific community styles and conflict management policies lead to disintegration, which inhibits useful and integrated novelty. Application of the same metric to motivation and enculturation levels across members of the community would measure the degree of differentiation and integration of the community, and hence its complexity, which relates to incidence of creativity.

IMPLEMENTATION, EXPERIMENTATION, AND DISCUSSION

GPSSim simulation framework is built over the RePast Simphony environment as a reusable package to facilitate extensions toward a library of components for simulating innovation communities.

Implementation and Face Validity of the Simulation

Figure 9 demonstrates the initial state of the simulation as well as parameter specification template. In the left pane, five parameters are used to initialize the simulation. The *community style* parameter is used to select alternative community cultures. Currently, three community cultures are supported: exploratory, utility, and service-oriented. Two parameters are used to select one of the four conflict management styles discussed earlier. The parameter values and their interpretation is as follows: Avoiding: [Concern for Others = 0, Concern for Self =0], Dominating: [Concern for Others = 0, Concern for Self =1], Obliging: [Concern for Others = 1, Concern for Self =0], Integrating: [Concern for Others = 1, Concern for Self =1]. Finally, the last parameter is used to specify if reputation plays a role in decision-making or not. The value *of Selection Criterion* parameter takes the value random or reputation. The simulation starts with 10 agents, one being the leader, while the remaining are the core, active, and peripheral members that are randomly selected at the time of

initialization. At each time tick new agent enter or leave the community in accordance with the model specification presented in section 3.

GPSim is conceptually grounded and based on empirical observations pertaining to mode of production and community types reported literature (Ye et al. 2005). Since the model is used to examine the performance of normative community designs/cultures and which behavioral assumptions confer incidence of innovation, as opposed to empirical insight, the operational behavior of the model is not compared to existing communities. However, for face validity, we plot the size of the communities generated by the simulation in Figure 10. We observe that most community members in all community types are peripheral contributors, while core project leadership and active contributors are significantly low compared to both readers and peripheral members. Also, as expected the size of utility communities is significantly larger compared to service and utility communities.

Experimentation, Preliminary Results, and Evaluation

As shown in Figure 11, we simulated a hypothetical GPS community using three factors; culture, conflict management style, and contribution

Figure 9. Initial State and Parameter Set-up

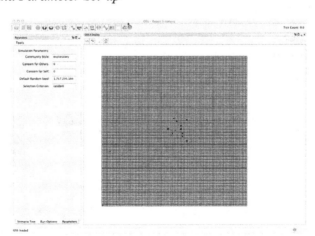

Figure 10. Member Distributions

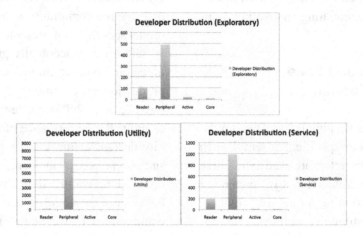

selection criterion. The number of replications performed for each scenario is 30. The outcomes of interest in the study are the effects of the identified independent variables on the degree of differentiation and integration of the domain and the community, as well as the characteristics of the emergent organizational climate as it pertains to collective creativity.

First, the GPS community model is simulated under different scenarios to examine emergent patterns in the project space. These emergent patterns not only provide qualitative insight, but also help achieve face validity to instill confidence

in the operational validity of the model. To this end, we look at the evolution over time of the project space of an exploratory community with avoiding style for conflict management. Figure 12 presents the snapshots of the projects at time t=100, 500, and 1000. The blue colored squares indicate artifacts that have low complexity and maturity. Those artifacts that attract community members and become complex over time due to acceptance of contributions are represented by the pink squares. The red squares denote new feature requests or requirements that have not yet

Figure 11. Experiment Scenarios

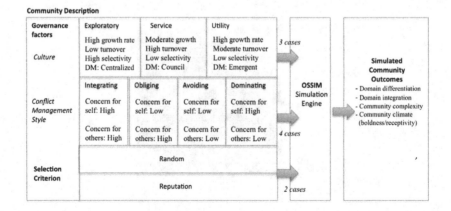

Figure 12. Project Growth

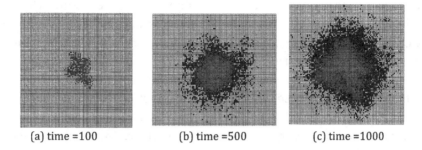

(a) time =100   (b) time =500   (c) time =1000

been confirmed or accepted by the project leadership.

As the simulation unfolds, a clear pattern in the project space emerges to depict those areas that receive more attention and attraction. The coherent and unified pattern that starts emerging at time t=500 becomes dissolving and exploration of new paths starts at time t=1000. The structural theme starts disintegrating over time. The patterns shown in Figure 13 present the emergent patterns pertaining to accepted contributions across alternative conflict management styles within a hypothetical exploratory community. Under the avoiding style, the community is willing to consider paths that are closely linked to the structural and functional theme. However, the project has a scope and boundary, which the project leadership is not willing to extend. The dominating style leads to a similar pattern, with the exception that the size of the project is smaller compared to alternative conflict management styles.

An interesting observation is that under the obliging style, despite the fact that project leadership is willing to accommodate, the community members tend to flock toward center of the project. The integrating style tends to create a uniform and coherent scope for the project. The project

Figure 13. Exploratory Project

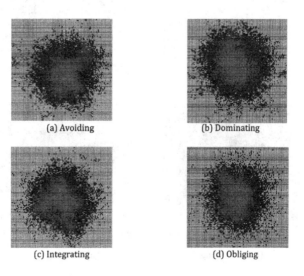

(a) Avoiding   (b) Dominating

(c) Integrating   (d) Obliging

leadership is willing to accommodate contributions in new directions, and the scope of the project is more prone to extension.

Yet, the core of the project continues to have a uniform and coherent structure, as most members do not have incentive to contribute in emergent artifacts, unless they are well integrated into the exploratory project, the direction of which is maintained by a central decision maker.

The patterns shown in Figure 14 present emergent patterns for the service-oriented style. Similar to the observations in exploratory community, the avoiding style under the service-oriented management leads to disintegrated project structure, which lacks a coherent and unified core, which is a critical requirement in service-oriented projects. One major distinction between the exploratory and service-oriented projects is that the level of receptivity in service communities is smaller.

This is evident based on the significant increase in submissions, which are declined and excluded from the project. An interesting observation is

that similar to the case of obliging style in exploratory project, the obliging (low degree of assertiveness and high level of cooperativeness) style under a service-oriented community generates a unified and coherent project structure, while explorations across new directions are enabled. The level of receptivity under accommodation style is also higher compared to integrating style.

In Figure 15, we observe the emergent project space, when contributions are considered for inclusion based on emergent selection principle, where those contributions that receive sufficient level of attraction from others are kept within the project to grow. As seen in both figures, regardless of whether attraction to new artifacts is by reputation or random selection, the emergent patterns are more differentiated from previous community styles. Yet, the patterns are neither as ordered as other types of communities, nor are completely disordered. There is a core project in the middle, while artifacts with low complexity and maturity are pursued to expand the features. In the case of

Figure 14. Service-oriented Project

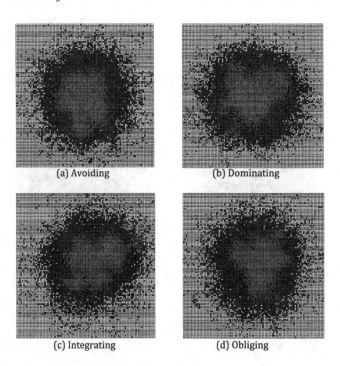

(a) Avoiding

(b) Dominating

(c) Integrating

(d) Obliging

Figure 15. Utility-oriented Project

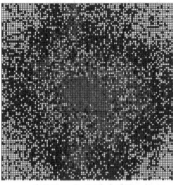

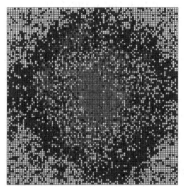

(a) Random Selection   (b) Reputation-based Selection

random selection, the pattern suggests a potential for the existence of percolation threshold, a point where the contributions propagate from top to bottom in the project space.

To reinforce our qualitative insight regarding the comparative analysis of the degree of differentiation in project growth across community types and conflict management styles, we compute the entropy in artifact complexity. Figure 16 depicts the existence of expected differences and lends support to qualitative observations. The x-axis of the chart denotes the community type, where the letters E and S represent exploratory

and service-oriented communities respectively. The letters appended to community type indicate the type of the conflict management style (i.e., A-Avoiding, I: Integrating, D-Dominating, and O-Obliging). The y-axis represents the computed entropy.

The results shown in Figure 16 indicate that as expected utility-oriented communities exhibit the highest degree of entropy. This is because either the project is disintegrated and lies within the boundary of complete disorder or it lies at the edge of chaos and order, where incidence of collective creativity is expected to be highest. Given

Figure 16. Entropy Distribution

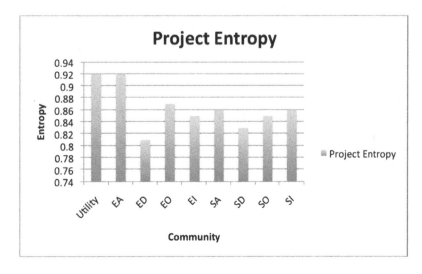

the qualitative insight gleaned from Figure 15, however, we observe that the project growth is not completely disordered and that there exists a pattern that enables the system to self-organize at this critical threshold. Another observation is that despite the orderliness of exploratory communities under avoiding style of conflict management, there is significant entropy, hence differentiation within the project space. Also, given the fact that exploratory communities generate projects that are well integrated compared to utility-oriented communities, this result may be indicative of the fact that exploratory communities can be conducive to innovation if proper conflict management style is utilized.

Finally, we measure the distribution of boldness and receptivity scores to see whether the qualitative insights above can be reinforced. In Figure 17 the distribution of boldness/receptivity values for alternative communities is presented. An interesting observation is that for both the service and exploratory communities, the average boldness of the community converges to a fixed small value, while exploratory communities exhibit slightly higher score in terms of receptivity. We also observe that the boldness and receptivity scores for the exploratory and service communities across alternative conflict management styles

are clustered and converge to a similar neighborhood in the scatter plot. On the other hand, for utility-oriented communities both the boldness and receptivity levels are significantly higher, suggesting increased potential for incidence of creativity and innovation.

In utility-oriented projects, collective decision making results in significantly better performance compared to exploratory and service communities. Therefore, overall, the results tend to support the expectation that emergent selection, by which the community decides which contributions are novel and useful, lead to higher incidence of creativity. This is similar to the notion of collective wisdom in decision making within prediction markets where the prediction accuracy tends to be higher when a community uses a market mechanism to make forecasts about the likelihood of outcomes for future events. When a group of community members as part of the project leadership submit votes on the acceptability of a contribution with equal weights reflecting the degree of their interest, the boldness and receptivity values tend to be minimized. This suggests rigid control over the project growth is likely to lead stagnation in divergent thinking.

Figure 17. Boldness-Receptivity Distribution

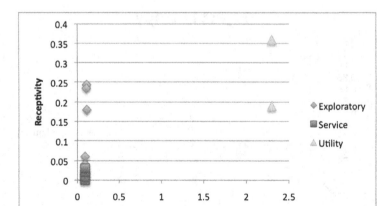

CONCLUSION

We examined the impact of community cultures and conflict management styles of project leadership on collective creativity in innovation communities such as open source ecologies. The view advocated in the study is that innovation communities exhibit the characteristics of self-organizing complex adaptive systems and the tools in complexity science can bring useful insight into the study of creativity and innovation. Such studies can help understand the nature of creativity and help determine minimal structural and behavioral conditions, that is, the simplest set of assumptions, for the emergence and sustainment of collective creativity in open innovation. To this end, we presented a model of the dynamics of GPS development communities based the existing empirical observations published in the literature so that the model is conceptually grounded and credible in terms of its congruence to conceptual elements of such communities. The dynamics of the model is patterned after the systems model of creativity.

A strong analogy between the mode of production in GPS ecologies and systems model of creativity is substantiated, and the processes underlying the systems model of creativity is realized within the context of GPS development. Metrics are proposed and formalized to measure the potential for incidence of creativity in such collectives. The measures are specified in terms of the boldness and receptivity observed in the community, as well as the degree of differentiation and integration of the project and the community, both of which are related to complexity of the domain and the field. Findings suggest that decentralized coordination schemes such as emergent selection such as found in utility communities and moderate degrees of assertiveness and cooperation for conflict management result in higher incidence of innovation.

The findings and experiences gained in using the complexity perspective to study creativity open new directions and interesting avenues for future research. One future challenge is to identify parameters of interest and explore self-organized criticality (SOC) as a property and attractor for innovation communities, toward which innovative open source ecologies may tend to converge.

ACKNOWLEDGMENT

This work is partially based upon work supported by the National Science Foundation under CreativeIT program funding NSF- IIS-0718648 with Grant No: G00003258. The views and conclusions contained in this document are those of the author and should not be interpreted as representing the official policies, either expressed or implied, of the U.S. government.

REFERENCES

Amabile, T. M. (1988). A model of creativity and innovation in organizations. *Research in Organizational Behavior, 10,* 123–167.

Anderson, N., De Dreu, C., & Nijstad, B. A. (2004). The routinization of innovation research: A constructively critical review of the state-of-the-science. *Journal of Organizational Behavior, 25,* 147–173. doi:10.1002/job.236

Antoniades, I. P., Samoladas, I., Stamelos, I., Angelis, L., & G. L. Bleris G. L. (2003b). Dynamical simulation models of the Open Source Development process, in Free/Open Source Software Development, Idea Group Inc., PA, USA (2003), 174-202.

Antoniades, I. P., Stamelos, I., Aggelis, L., & Bleris G.L. (2003a). A Novel Simulation Model for the Development Process of Open Source Software Projects. *International Journal of Software Process: Improvement and Practise (SPIP),* special issue on Software Process simulation and modeling, 7, 3-4, (2003), 173-188.

Carnavale, P. J., & Probst, T. M. (1998). Social values and social conflict in creative problem solving and categorization. *Journal of Personality and Social Psychology*, *74*, 1300–1309. doi:10.1037/0022-3514.74.5.1300

Cowan, R., & Jonard, N. (2004). Network Structure and the Diffusion of Knowledge. *Journal of Economic Dynamics and the Diffusion of Knowledge*, *28*, 1557–1575.

Csikszenthmihalyi, M. (1999). Implications of a systems perspective for the study of creativity. In *Handbook of Creativity*, (313-338).

Dalle, J. M., & David, P. M. (2003). The allocation of software development resources in "open source" production mode, SIEPR Discussion Paper No. 02-27, Stanford Institute For Economic Policy Research, Stanford, CA.

David A. P & Spence, M. (2003). . Toward institutional infrastructures for e-science: The scope of challenges. Technical Report: Oxford Technical Institute, May.

Dennis, A. R., & Valacich, J. S. (1993). Computer brainstorms: More heads are better than one. *The Journal of Applied Psychology*, *78*, 531–537. doi:10.1037/0021-9010.78.4.531

DeRosa, D. M., Smith, C. L., & Hantula, D. A. (2007). The medium matters: Mining the long-promised merit of group interaction in creative idea generation tasks in a meta-analysis of the electronic group brainstorming literature. *Computers in Human Behavior*, *23*, 1549–1581. doi:10.1016/j.chb.2005.07.003

Diehl, M., & Stroebe, W. (1991). Productivity loss in idea-generating groups: Tracking down the blocking effect. *Journal of Personality and Social Psychology*, *61*, 392–403. doi:10.1037/0022-3514.61.3.392

Edquist, C. (1997). *Systems of Innovation: Technologies, Institutions, and Organizations.* London, UK: Pinter.

Elliott, S. M., & Scacchi, W. (2005). Free Software Development: Cooperation and Conflict in a Virtual Organization Culture. In Koch, S. (Ed.), *Free/Open Software Development*, (152-172). Idea Group Inc.

Foster, I. (2005, May). Service-oriented science. *Science*, *308*, 814–817. doi:10.1126/science.1110411

Furst, S., Blackburn, R., & Rosen, B. (1999). Virtual teams: A proposed agenda for research. *Information Systems Journal*, *9*, 249–269. doi:10.1046/j.1365-2575.1999.00064.x

Gallupe, R. B., Bastianutti, L. M., & Cooper, H. W. (1991). Unlocking brainstorming. *The Journal of Applied Psychology*, *76*, 137–142. doi:10.1037/0021-9010.76.1.137

Gilbert, N. (1997). A Simulation of the Structure of Academic Science. *Sociological Research Online*, *2*(2). http://www.socresonline.org.uk/socresonline/2/2/3.html. doi:10.5153/sro.85

Goertzel, B. (1997). *From Complexity to Creativity: Explorations in Evolutionary, Autopoietic, and Cognitive Dynamics*. Plenum.

Harrison, R. J., & Carroll, R. G. (2006). *Culture and Demography in Organizations*. New Jersey, NJ: Princeton University Press.

Hars, A., & Shaosong, O. Working for free motivations of participating in open source software projects. In *Proceedings of the 34th Hawaii International Conference on System Sciences*, 25-31.

Hertel, B., Niedner, S., & Herrmann, S. (2003). Motivation of software developers in open source software projects: An internet-based survey of contributors to the linux kernel. *Research Policy*, *32*(7), 1159–1172. doi:10.1016/S0048-7333(03)00047-7

Janis, I. L. (1972). *Victims of Groupthink: A Psychological Study of Foreign Policy Decisions and Fiascoes*. Boston, MA: Houghton Mifflin.

Kirton, M. (1976). Adaptors and innovators: A description and measure. *The Journal of Applied Psychology*, *61*, 622–629. doi:10.1037/0021-9010.61.5.622

Kirton, M. (1989). *Adaptors and Innovators: Styles of creativity and problem-solving*. New York, NY: Routledge.

Koch, S., & Schneider, G. (2002). Effort, cooperation, and coordination in an open source software project: GNOME. *Information Systems Journal*, *12*(1), 27–42. doi:10.1046/j.1365-2575.2002.00110.x

Kolb, D. M., & Gidden, P. A. (1986). Getting to know your conflict options: Using conflict as a creative force. *The Personnel Administrator*, *31*, 77–90.

Kraut, R. E., & Streeter, A. L. (1995). Coordination in software development. *Communications of the ACM*, *28*(3), 69–81. doi:10.1145/203330.203345

Lakhani, K., & Wolf, B. (2005). Why hackers do what they do: Understanding motivation and effort in free/open source software projects . In *Perspectives on Free and Open Source software*. Cambridge, Massachusetts: MIT Press.

Lawler, E. E. (1992). *The ultimate advantage: Creating the high involvement organization*. San Francisco, CA: Jossey-Bass.

Madey, G., Freeh, V., & Tynan, R. (2005). Modeling the Free/Open Source Software Community: A Quantitative Investigation. In Koch, S. (Ed.), *Free/Open Software Development*, (203-220). Idea Group Inc.

McKelvey, M. (1996). *Evolutionary Innovation: The Business of Genetic Engineering*. Oxford, UK: Clarendon.

Miller, H. J., & Page, E. S. (2007). *Complex Adaptive Systems: An Introduction to Computational Models of Social Life*. Princeton, New Jersey: Princeton University Press.

Mockus, A., Fielding, R. T., & Herbsleb, J. D. (2002). Two case studies of open source software development: Apache and mozilla. *ACM Transactions on Software Engineering and Methodology*, *11*, 309–346. doi:10.1145/567793.567795

Nelson, R. (1995). Recent Evolutionary Theorizing about Economic Change. *Journal of Economic Literature*, *33*, 48–90.

Nemeth, C. J. (1992). Dissent as Driving Cognition, Attitudes, and Judgments. *Social Cognition*, *13*, 273–291. doi:10.1521/soco.1995.13.3.273

Nijstad, B. A., Stroebe, W., & Lodewijkx, H. F. M. (2006). The illusion of group productivity: A reduction of failures explanation. *The Journal of Social Psychology*, *36*, 31–48.

Smith, B., Ashburner, M., Rosse, C., Bard, J., Bug, W., & Ceusters, W. (2007). The Obo Foundry: Coordinated Evolution of Ontologies to Support Biomedical Data Integration. *Nature Biotechnology*, *25*(11), 1251–1255. doi:10.1038/nbt1346

Smith, N., Andrea, C., & Juan, F. R. (2006). Users and Developers: an Agent-Based Simulation of Open Source Software Evolution. In Proceedings of the SPW/ProSim2006 Workshop, LNCS, Springer-Verlag, Vol. 3966, pp. 234-241, Shanghai, China.

Stewart, D. (2005). Social status in an open source software community. *American Sociological Review*, *70*(5), 823–842. doi:10.1177/000312240507000505

Thomas, K. W. (1992). Conflict and negotiation processes in organizations. In M. Dunette & L. Hough (Eds.), *Handbook of Industrial and Organizational Psychology*, (651-718).

Von Hippel, E. (2005). *Democratizing Innovation.* Cambridge, Massachusetts: MIT Press.

Von Hippel, E., & Von Krogh, G. (2003). Open source software and the private-collective innovation model: Issues for organization science. *Organization Science, 14,* 209–223. doi:10.1287/orsc.14.2.209.14992

Vroom, V. (1964). *Work and Motivation.* New York, NY: Wiley and Sons.

West, M. A., & Farr, J. L. (1990). Innovation at work. In West and Far (Eds.) *Innovation and creativity at work: Psychological and organizational strategies,* (145-172).

Ye, Y., Nakakoji, K., Yamamoto, Y., & Kishida, K. (2005). The co-evolution of systems and communities in free and open source software development. In Koch, S. (Ed.), *Free/Open Software Development,* (59-82). Idea Group Inc.

Chapter 12
Communication Network Characteristics of Open Source Communities

David Hinds
Nova Southeastern University, USA

Ronald M. Lee
Florida International University, USA

ABSTRACT

Empirical research has shown that social network structure is a critical success factor for various kinds of work groups. The authors extended this research to a new type of work group—the open source software project community—with the objective of exploring the role of communication networks within these intriguing projects. Using archival data from 143 open source project groups, the authors compiled six measures of social network structure and analyzed these in relation to four measures of group success. This study found that the social network structures of these project communities did not appear to be critical success factors at all, but rather they had no significant impact on success or their effect was opposite of that seen in prior studies of work groups. Various conjectures were suggested that might explain these results, offering opportunities for further research.

INTRODUCTION

In the Art History (Kunsthistorische) Museum in Vienna hangs a famous painting by Pieter Breughel (1563), his vision of the Tower of Babel, supposedly built around 2000 B.C. According to

the Biblical account, construction on the tower failed when God scrambled up the languages of the workers. They could no longer coordinate. Work groups, then as now, depend on effective communication for their success. This seems to be especially true of software projects (Figure 1).

Back in the 1970's, Fred Brooks, project manager for what was then the largest software proj-

DOI: 10.4018/978-1-60960-513-1.ch012

Figure 1. A failure to communicate

ect ever, the operating system for the IBM 360, wrote a classic book, *The Mythical Man Month* (1975/ 1995). In it, he formulated Brook's Law: "adding manpower to a late software project makes it later". This has two aspects. One is the learning curve of new staff: it takes time to learn the complexities of the project. The other is the combinatorics of communication. The number of different communication channels increases exponentially with the number of people involved.

A key factor for project management of any kind is the complexity of the artifact being produced. Brooks (1986) claims that large software systems are among the most complex: "Software entities are more complex for their size than perhaps any other human construct because no two parts are alike (at least above the statement level). If they are, we make the two similar parts into a subroutine--open or closed. … The complexity of software is an essential property, not an accidental one" (Brooks, 1986). As one would expect, composite systems are correspondingly more complex: "A programming systems product takes about nine times as much effort as the component programs written separately for private use" (1995, Ch1).

Brooks, and many others after him, have argued that the only way around the software productivity bottleneck is improved design: "My rule of thumb is 1/3 of the schedule for design, 1/6 for coding,

1/4 for component testing, and 1/4 for system testing" (Brooks, 1995).

Recent research, for example Pendharkar and Rodger (2009), indicates that current software work still encounters many of the same communication difficulties as in the 1970's. However, they note that these may be mitigated by improved methods such as the use of CASE tools. Paulley (2009) notes that these gains may nonetheless be offset by the added communication difficulties of geographically dispersed software development teams.

Against the backdrop of conventional software project management, the notion that software might be developed based on an ad-hoc, evolutionary style framework seems implausible. Eric Raymond (1999b) comments:

In The Mythical Man-Month, Fred Brooks … argued that the complexity and communication costs of a project rise with the square of the number of developers, while work done only rises linearly. Brooks's Law has been widely regarded as a truism. But … the process of open-source development falsifies the assumptions behind it—and, empirically, if Brooks's Law were the whole picture Linux would be impossible.

This is a remarkable observation. Is it really the case that open source projects do not suffer the same communication challenges as traditional software projects? Or is it perhaps that some communication structures work better than others?

In this paper we present a study that examines the communication structures of open source project communities. In particular, we explore the relationship, if any, between the communication network structure of an open source software project community and the success of the project.

Our approach employs techniques of social network analysis. We focused on social network structural factors that past research has shown to most strongly affect work group success and effectiveness, namely that closure, bridging and leader centrality all have a positive influence.

The results of this empirical study were surprising, and indeed in support of Raymond's claim that open source constitutes a different kind of project management strategy. Contrary to the prior research on social network structure and work group effectiveness, the results of our study did not provide evidence that social network constructs such as closure, bridging or leader centrality were success factors for these projects. Rather, we found that these constructs either had no significant impact or that their effect on project success was opposite of that seen in other kinds of work groups. This led us to reflect on the implications of these results with respect to the unique nature of the open source process and the extent to which further research along this track may contribute to an expanded understanding of this process.

In the remainder of this paper, we begin with a brief discussion of social network analysis and theory. We review the empirical literature on social network structure and work group performance across various types of work groups. We then describe open source software project communities as work groups and we review the limited literature which connects social network structure with open source software community success. This is followed by a presentation of our research model which suggests the expected relationship between social network structure and open source project group success. The details of our empirical study are then presented including the definition of the study population and the research variables, the sample selection and filtering methods, and the statistical analysis methods. This is followed by a discussion of results, along with conjectures which may help to explain the anomalous findings. Concluding remarks include study limitations, implications for practice, and future research directions.

SOCIAL NETWORK ANALYSIS AND THEORY

Social networks are mathematical representations of the relationships between social entities. People or organizations are represented as a set of nodes and the relationships, such as advice-giving or trade, are represented as a set of links connecting the nodes (Wasserman & Faust, 1994). Social network analysis is based on formal graph theory, and the related analytical methods draw heavily upon matrix algebra for coding and manipulating network data. Social network variables can reveal patterns not discernable with other methods, and these patterns may be reflected in quantitative social network measurements or they may be observed qualitatively in two- or three-dimensional graphical network representations. These variables are most commonly defined at the group level or the individual level, although they are also sometimes applied at a subgroup level.

In contrast to social network analysis, the domain of social network theory involves the application of network concepts and perspectives to various aspects of social psychology, sociology, and organizational science. More broadly, social network theory is considered a subset of computational and mathematical organization theory (Carley, 1995). One of the most prominent of the social network theoretical domains is the structural dimension of social capital theory. Social capital theory is very broad and has been applied in many areas of management and organizational research (Bordeau, 1986; Burt, 1992; Granovetter, 1985; Putnam, 2000). This theory is based on the premise that certain kinds of social attributes have value to the group and/or to individuals within the group. These attributes can be viewed as a kind of "capital", similar to how one might think of financial capital or human capital. These attributes are referred to as "social capital".

Nahapiet and Ghoshal (1998) identify three dimensions of social capital including cognitive, relational, and structural. The cognitive dimension includes the shared vocabulary and narratives of the social group. The relational dimension considers the constructs of trust, norms, and identification. The structural dimension considers constructs of network ties, network configuration, and appropriable resources. In a structural context, social capital theory uses an information processing paradigm to explain how social network structure affects social outcomes at the individual level and at the group level. Social ties are viewed as conduits for the flow of information, knowledge, and other resources.

The structural dimension of social capital theory refers to the constructs of closure and bridging, where closure is the extent to which members of a group are inter-connected with each other and bridging is the extent to which members of a group are connected to individuals outside of the group. Social capital theory suggests that a structure with high closure within a group will support activities which require the utilization of the knowledge of the group, while a structure with many bridging ties between group actors and non-group actors will support activities which require access to knowledge which is beyond the boundaries of the group (and which is non-redundant with respect to knowledge shared within the group).

WORK GROUPS AND SOCIAL NETWORK STRUCTURE

One application area of social capital theory is work groups. Work groups consist of collections of individuals whose joint efforts lead to a work output, such as the creation of a product or the provision of a service. Work groups might include teams, departments, or other collective forms such as communities. In the case of software development, the most common form used for commercial development is the team, while open source development typically involves a community-like structure.

Empirical social network studies of work groups have shown that, consistent with social capital theory, the group network attributes of closure and bridging are positively associated with group effectiveness and success. In these groups, social networks are seen as playing a critical role as channels of communication, where such communication may be needed to support activities such as coordination, problem-solving, task completion, and learning, all of which are necessary for successful work group outcomes. In addition to closure and bridging, the centrality of the leader has also been found to be a success factor, where leader centrality is most commonly defined as the extent to which the group leader is directly connected with the other group members.

The bulk of this work group research is summarized in a meta-analysis of 37 studies over 50 years regarding the effect of social network structure on work group effectiveness (Balkundi & Harrison, 2006). The authors of this meta-analysis conclude that work groups with a high density of ties (closure) within the group are more effective, and that groups that are more central within a network of other groups (bridging) are also more effective. In addition, group performance is positively associated with the centrality of the group leader within the group network (leader centrality). These results were applicable for both instrumental ties (associated with task-oriented activities) and for expressive ties (associated with socially-oriented activities). The Balkundi and Harrison (2006) meta-analysis included studies involving various kinds of work groups including military teams, top management teams, project teams, and work groups involving both production and service. However, no studies of software development teams were included in that meta-analysis.

One study which did examine the social network structures of software development groups was reported by Yang and Tang (2004). The authors concluded that group cohesion was positively related with performance and that the group structures were critical to the overall team effectiveness. In this study, cohesion was defined to be a density measure in which only "positive" relationships are counted. However, measures which directly reflect closure, bridging, and/or leader centrality were not considered.

OPEN SOURCE SOFTWARE PROJECT COMMUNITIES

The individuals participating in open source software projects are often seen as comprising a community which performs software development work activities. These communities have been described as having an onion-like structure, with a central core of highly active individuals, surrounded by other layers of progressively less active individuals. One example of this is presented by Ye et al. (2005) in which the central core is composed of the project leaders and core members, with five outer layers containing active developers, peripheral developers, bug reporters, passive users, and stakeholders, respectively.

Open source software project communities are typically initiated by a single founding individual (or small group of individuals) who provides the initial source code and sets the general direction for the project. The host platform is usually provided by a third-party hosting organization (e.g., SourceForge), although larger and more mature projects may form organizations to host their own communities. The key technological components of this platform include a source code repository (version control system), public forum facilities, and project web pages. The initial source code provided by the community founder is entered into the project source code repository and this initial code represents the seed work product for further community development activity. Policies and rules for the project are sometimes provided in part by the hosting organization (e.g., requirement of transparency and use of an open source license) and partly by each project community

manager/administrator (e.g., commit privileges, norms of behavior).

In contrast with most other types of work groups, the members of non-corporate sponsored open source project groups are mostly volunteers who are motivated by instrumental factors associated with fulfilling a need, expertise development (learning), or enhanced reputation, as well as by psychological needs involving self-fulfillment, basic fun and enjoyment (Lakhani & Wolf, 2005; Raymond, 1999a). Many open source developers are seen as "hackers" who are highly proficient but whose "fun" comes not from social activities but from the solitary exercise of their programming skills.

With regard to social network research of open source software projects and communities, most of the prior work has employed social network analytical methods to describe and characterize the projects, the project developers, and the connections among developers across many different projects. Very few studies have attempted to relate social network structural variables to community success at the individual project level.

Some studies have focused on the individual developer as the unit of analysis (Dahlander & Wallin, 2006; Sowe et al., 2006). Some works take the most active or successful projects and then describe their social networks (Concas et al., 2008). However, such studies do not distinguish between successful and unsuccessful projects and therefore cannot be used to identify the structural correlates of project success. Some studies are focused on the overall open source community (across many projects), and do not address the networks associated with particular projects (Gao et al., 2003; Madey et al., 2002; Wagstrom et al., 2005; Xu et al., 2005). Lopez-Fernandez et al. (2004) apply this overall community approach to the analysis of code commit data obtained from project CVS repositories. Spaeth (2005) also uses CVS repository data to create descriptive measures of 29 open source projects. Crowston and Howison (2004, 2006) describe the social networks of individual projects but do not relate these variables to measures of success.

Regarding social network studies of success in open source software project groups, the literature is quite sparse. One study which was identified in this regard was reported in a recent paper by Grewel et al. (2006). In this study, the authors collected data from 108 open source software project communities on SourceForge and related various measures of bridging (which they refer to as "network embeddedness") with the number of code commits and the number of downloads (used as measures of project success). Overall, the authors obtained a mixed set of positive, negative, and "no-effect" relationships between bridging and success. Another study by Kidane and Gloor (2007) defined creativity and performance measures for open source projects and then related these measures to static and dynamic measures of social network structure (density and centralization). The authors found that density was positively correlated with performance but that centralization was not. They also found that certain temporal changes in social network structure were correlated with creativity and performance.

Similar to the works of Grewel et al. (2006) and Kidane and Gloor (2007), our work attempts to relate social network structural variables to measures of community success across a relatively large-scale sample of projects. However, to the best of our knowledge, our study is unique in its use of a social network theoretical foundation and in our comparison of open source software project communities with other types of work groups.

RESEARCH MODEL

In order to address the aims of this research, a conceptual research model was formulated and is presented on Figure 2. The model incorporates the three fundamental social network structural constructs of closure, bridging, and leader centrality. The closure and bridging constructs are

suggested based on the assertions of social capital theory as previously discussed. The leader centrality construct refers to prior social network studies regarding team leaders and the effect of their network position on the effectiveness of the work group.

In the model, group success is conceptualized as consisting of two dimensions: output and activity. The output dimension consists of the quantity of software that is produced by the project group while the activity dimension reflects the quantity of participation by group members as well as other software users who are not members of the group as defined in this study. These two dimensions are modeled as having a reciprocal relationship. This is based on the suggestion that the production of more software will generally lead to greater community participation and software usage, and that increased software usage will tend to attract and motivate even more developers to produce more software. To the extent that higher quality software will tend to generate a greater level of activity than lower quality software, it is suggested that activity can also be viewed as a proxy for software product quality.

It is recognized that various factors may mediate the relationship between social network structure and success. These factors include group size, project type, project maturity, process/task structure, community norms, and organizational

Figure 2. Conceptual research model

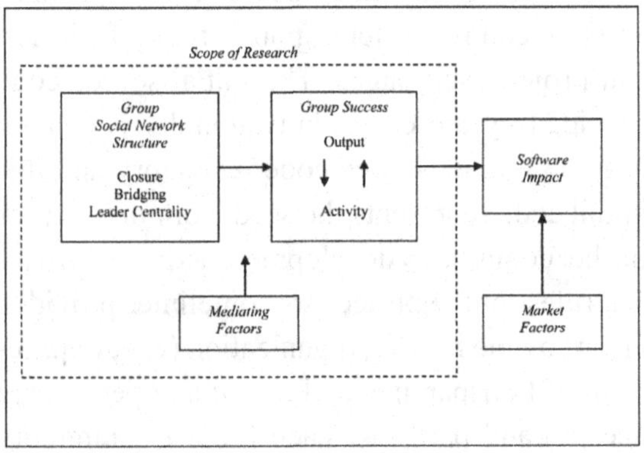

environment. As discussed in later sections of this paper, the group size factor is controlled as a regression variable while the other factors are controlled through limitations to the definition of the study population.

The model suggests that group success in terms of output and activity will be related to the impact of the group-produced software beyond the group boundaries, and that such software impact will be affected by market factors such as user population size or competition. Examples of software impact might include the incorporation of the produced software into the broader internet infrastructure (e.g., Linux) or the widespread acceptance of the software by the public (e.g., Mozilla).

EMPIRICAL STUDY

We conducted an empirical study using an unobtrusive method (Babbie, 2005) and a cross-sectional study design in which archival data from the public records[1] of SourceForge were extracted, compiled and analyzed. SourceForge is the most prominent hosting organization for open source software project communities, and over 100,000 projects have been registered with this organization. We selected the individual project community as our unit of analysis. While it is possible to think of all SourceForge participants as a single community, we chose to focus on individual projects to define our communities because each project is associated with its own particular platform, including specific interaction protocols defined and implemented by the project administrator. In effect, the "project community" is a kind of work group that emerges to participate in the project.

Study Population

A study population was defined in consideration of the need to control for various factors which may mediate the relationship between social network structure and open source community success. Specifically, the study population was defined to include early-stage projects which are developer-targeted and community-sponsored.

An early-stage project is one which has completed two years of activity following the first release of executable software. The study population was limited to early-stage projects in order to control for the effects of project maturity. In their meta-analysis, Balkundi and Harrison (2006) found that the structural effects on group effectiveness are weakened as a group matures and members become more familiar with each other. This implies that structural effects, if they exist, are more likely to be found in these early-stage projects. In order to address the concern that early-stage projects might not have sufficient communication activity to generate measurable social network patterns, we also limited the population to projects with at least 50 message postings to the public forums. It is recognized that project age could have been reflected as a control variable. However, this option was not chosen because we wished to exclude the more mature and larger projects on the basis that they may have substantially different organizational structures and communication patterns.

Some projects involve software which is targeted to developers (e.g., operating systems) while other software is targeted to users (e.g., web browsers). We limited the population to developer-targeted projects in order to control for the project type and the process/task structure, considering that the involvement of non-developer users may change the task structure because of the need to incorporate user input. In addition, corporate-sponsored projects often involve paid developers and direct corporate participation. Therefore, only community-sponsored projects were selected in order to control for community norms and organizational environment.

Research Variables

In order to operationalize the research model, six variables were selected for social network structure and four variables were selected for group success. Additionally, three variables were defined to be used as control variables in the multivariate analysis. All of these variables were captured over the two-year period following the date of first software release (regardless of the actual start date of the project).

In defining these research variables, we considered that open source project communities have features that differ from other types of work groups. Work groups typically have only one leader and they usually do not have core and peripheral subgroups. In contrast, open source project groups often have more than one leader (administrator) and they usually exhibit a core-peripheral structure typical of communities (Wenger, 1998). In order to reflect these unique features, we defined three member subgroups to include core developers, peripheral developers, and administrators.

A group member is defined as an individual that has either formally registered with the project or has posted a message to a project public forum. An individual is considered to be a core developer if that individual was formally registered with the focal project during the two-year observation window. An individual is recognized to be a peripheral developer if that individual posted a message to a project public forum during the two-year window (but was not formally registered with the project). Thus, the core developer subgroup and the peripheral developer subgroup are mutually exclusive and exhaustive subsets of the total set of group members. An individual is further considered to be an administrator if that individual is formally registered as an administrator with the focal project on the SourceForge records. Because registered administrators are also registered members, the administrators are also core developers. The three defined subgroups were used in devising the six *social network variables,* as discussed below.

Closure. The closure construct is represented by the density of the ingroup conversational network, where density is calculated as the observed number of conversational links in the network divided by the total possible number of links. The ingroup conversational network consists of project community members and their conversational links, where a link is defined if two members participated in at least one threaded discussion on the project public forums during the two-year observation window. Crowston and Howison (2004) used a similar type of social network definition to study the social structural patterns of open source software projects by extracting textual data from bug report trackers.

Three closure variables were defined including Group Density, Core Density, and Peripheral Two-Mode Density. Group Density is the density measured across the entire ingroup network, Core Density considers only connections within the core subgroup, and Peripheral Two-Mode Density considers only links between the peripheral subgroup and the core subgroup. Group Density and Core Density represent two different perspectives with regard to the perceived boundaries of the work group. The Peripheral Two-Mode Density was defined because the open source literature suggests that peripheral-core connections might relate to the instrumental and psychological needs of the peripheral subgroup members such as perceiving a sense of identification with the project, as well as feelings of satisfaction and challenge.

Bridging. The bridging construct is represented by the average nodal degree of community members, calculated as the average number of links in the affiliation network which are attached to a community member node. The affiliation network is a two-mode network in which community members are one mode (node type) and SourceForge projects are the other mode.[2] A bridging link is defined as being present if a member of the focal project is a member of a SourceForge project. Gao et al. (2003) defined a similar type of project membership network in studying the connections between various open source software projects hosted by SourceForge.

In effect, these measures consider the members of a focal project community and they represent the average number of projects in which these individuals are a member. Two bridging variables were defined for the core subgroup and the administrator subgroup. Core Membership Degree is based upon connections between the core subgroup and other projects while Administrator Membership Degree is based upon connections between the administrator subgroup and other projects.

Leader Centrality. The leader centrality construct is represented by the degree class centrality of the administrator subgroup within the same ingroup conversational network that was defined for the closure variables. We utilized the class centrality concept defined by Everett and Borgatti (1999) in which the centrality measures normally applied to individual nodes are extended to subgroups. The class centrality measure is useful because it provides a meaningful equivalent of the team leader centrality measure commonly applied to individual leaders within work groups to administrator subgroups which are often seen in open source communities. If the administrator subgroup includes only one leader, then the class centrality measure collapses mathematically to the common individual centrality measure. We define our leader centrality variable to be Administrator Class Centrality, which is the class centrality of the administrator subgroup.

With regard to *group success variables* for commercial product development groups, success is typically defined in terms of sales and profitability. For open source projects, those measurements are not meaningful. We therefore need to identify some kind of proxy measurements. In this choice, we were also influenced by the availability of data in the archives of the SourceForge platform. We eventually decided on two kinds of variables – those measuring coding output, and those measuring the activity of users of the resulting software. We defined two variables for coding

output, Code Commits and Software Releases, and two variables for usage activity, Software Downloads, Page Views, all of which were measured over the two-year observation window.[3] These variables were selected based on success criteria associated with open source software project communities, as compiled by Crowston et al. (2004), together with a consideration of the availability of data within the SourceForge project archives.

Code Commits. As any software developer knows, software is an iterative process, proceeding with various versions. In open source projects, a versioning system is used to manage the process. Each new installment of code is entered with a 'commit' command. Thus, the variable Code Commits is a count of the number of these "commits" that were made over the two-year observation window (Healy & Schussman, 2003).

Software Releases. At various points in time, based on the discretion of the administrators, the current production source code repository is "compiled" and a new release of executable software is made. This is essentially a working version of the software which can be used by developers or by non-technical users. Each release of this software is recorded in the project archives, and the variable Software Releases (Crowston, Annabi, Howison, & Masango, 2004; Stewart & Ammeter, 2002) is a count of the number of such releases during the two-year window.

Page Views. The Page Views (Healy & Schussman, 2003) variable is measured by the number of times that any one of the project web pages is viewed. The project web pages include a home page, developer's page, and various other pages of interest to project developers and software users. The number of views which are made to these pages are recorded in the project archives, and the variable Page Views is a count of the number of such viewing actions which occur during the two-year window.

Software Downloads. As software releases are made by the project administrators, new software versions are made available to the public. An individual who wishes to acquire and use this software is required to download the executable version from the project web site. Each user download of the software is recorded in the project archives, and so the variable Software Downloads (Healy & Schussman, 2003) is a count of the number of such download actions which occur during the two-year window.

The above group success variables can be compared with the performance dimension of the group effectiveness construct commonly used in the work group literature. Work group performance is often aligned with the extent to which a group achieves its objectives and produces suitable output. An open source software project community which produces software that is widely downloaded and viewed can be said to have achieved its objectives. Therefore, the group success variables as defined above are generally equivalent to performance in work groups with regard to the accomplishment of task and group objectives.

With regard to the *control variables*, previous studies have identified group size as having an effect on team effectiveness and this effect might also be expected in open source project communities. In addition, some social network variables, such as those involving density measurements, are sensitive to the total size of the group. Therefore, both Group Size and Core Size are identified as controls, defined respectively as the number of project community members and the number of core subgroup members as of the midpoint in the two-year observation window. In addition, it is plausible that the success of the project community could be related to the total volume of conversation, rather than the structure of the conversational network itself. Therefore, an additional control variable is defined to be Conversation Volume, which is measured as the sum of the number of forum posts over the two-year observation window.

Sample Selection and Filtering

A randomized probability sample (Babbie, 2005) of projects was selected from the archives of SourceForge based on a filtering procedure which applied the previously-described study population definitions (early-stage, developer-targeted, community-sponsored), along with other criteria which required a sufficient level of data availability and data integrity. A search for projects on SourceForge as of January 2006 which survived the filtering process produced a total of 160 project communities. Of these, 17 projects were rejected based on an outlier analysis[4], resulting in a final sample of 143 project communities. Descriptive statistics for the sampled project groups are shown on Table 1. Of the 143 sampled projects, 49% involved a single administrator while 51% involved more than one administrator.

Statistical Analysis Methods

We first created a research dataset by calculating measures for each research variable and for each project, using data which was extracted from the project communities contained in the selected sample. A series of preliminary statistical and analytical procedures were applied to this dataset. The distributions of the variables were first checked for normality and based on the findings, the dependent variables were log transformed.

We then analyzed the research variables by applying a multiple linear regression technique with ordinary least squares (Tabachnick & Fidell, 2007). A total of 24 regression analyses were performed - one for each of the 24 combinations of the 6 social network variables (independent variable) and the 4 group success variables (dependent variable). Each regression analysis consisted of a two-step hierarchical procedure which involved a regression of the selected dependent variable on the three control variables of Group Size, Core Size, and Conversation Volume ("model 1"), followed by a regression of the dependent variable

Table 1. Descriptive statistics of subgroups and research variables

	Unit	Min.	Max.	Mean	Median	S.D.
Subgroups:						
Peripheral Developers	# members	2	313	61.8	37.0	62.6
Core Developers	# members	2	21	5.4	4.0	3.9
Administrators	# members	1	8	2.0	2.0	1.4
Controls:						
Group Size	# members	7	326	67.3	44.0	63.0
Core Size	# members	2	21	5.4	4.0	3.9
Conversation Volume	# 2yr posts	50	3,258	326	159	451
Group Success:						
Code Commits	# 2yr commits	50	43,594	2,336	1,058	4,511
Software Releases	# 2yr releases	0	79	11.3	8.0	11.1
Software Downloads	# 2yr downloads	758	222,510	23,893	12,808	35,910
Page Views	# 2yr views	4,825	1,243,073	165,180	88,219	227,992
Social Network Structure:						
Group Density	0-to-1 index	.006	.429	.078	.054	.074
Core Density	0-to-1 index	.000	1.000	.288	.100	.357
Periph. Two-Mode Density	0-to-1 index	.000	.642	.210	.184	.155
Core Member. Degree	# projects	1.00	7.20	2.03	1.75	0.99
Admin. Member. Degree	# projects	1.00	11.50	2.49	2.00	1.82
Admin. Class Centrality	0-to-1 index	.000	1.000	.554	.596	.282

on the three control variables and the selected independent variable ("model 2"). For each test, we calculated statistics to check for compliance with appropriate assumptions including normality, homoscedasticity, linearity, and multicollinearity. The results of all of these tests were within acceptable thresholds.

DISCUSSION OF RESULTS

Results of the multivariate regression analysis are shown in Table 2. As seen on Table 2, a generally negative relationship was found for the 12 tests on the closure variables. The strongest negative relationship was found between Group Density and the two community activity variables, Software Downloads and Page Views (at p-values <.001). There is also evidence of a negative relationship between Group Density and the community output variables, although the relationship is not as strong (with p-values of .066 and .063). For Core Density, a mostly negative relationship with community success was observed, with three of four regressions showing a negative result. The negative relationship was stronger and more consistent for the output variables than for the activity variables. The strongest result was between Core Density and Software Releases (p <.05). For Peripheral Two-Mode Density, the results of

Table 2. Summary of regression test results

Independent Variable	Dependent Variable	Success Dimension	Observed Relationship
Closure:			
Group Density	Code Commits	Output	Negative (p=.066)
Group Density	Software Releases	Output	Negative (p=.063)
Group Density	Software Downloads	Activity	Negative ***
Group Density	Page Views	Activity	Negative ***
Core Density	Code Commits	Output	Negative (p=.057)
Core Density	Software Releases	Output	Negative *
Core Density	Software Downloads	Activity	Negative (p=.067)
Core Density	Page Views	Activity	None
Peripheral Two-Mode Density	Code Commits	Output	None
Peripheral Two-Mode Density	Software Releases	Output	None
Peripheral Two-Mode Density	Software Downloads	Activity	Negative (p=.092)
Peripheral Two-Mode Density	Page Views	Activity	None
Bridging:			
Core Membership Degree	Code Commits	Output	None
Core Membership Degree	Software Releases	Output	None
Core Membership Degree	Software Downloads	Activity	None
Core Membership Degree	Page Views	Activity	None
Admin. Membership Degree	Code Commits	Output	None
Admin. Membership Degree	Software Releases	Output	None
Admin. Membership Degree	Software Downloads	Activity	None
Admin. Membership Degree	Page Views	Activity	None
Leader Centrality:			
Administrator Class Centrality	Code Commits	Output	None
Administrator Class Centrality	Software Releases	Output	Positive **
Administrator Class Centrality	Software Downloads	Activity	None
Administrator Class Centrality	Page Views	Activity	None
Notes: *p<.05, **p<.01, ***p<.001, n=143 groups			

these regressions contained only one weak negative relationship (p =.092) on just one of the four success variables - Software Downloads - with no effect seen on the other three variables. A total of 8 tests were performed for the bridging variables of Core Membership Degree and Administrator Membership Degree. The results of all 8 tests showed no significant or near-significant linear relationships. A total of 4 tests were performed for the leader centrality variable of Administrator Class Centrality. For these tests, only the one test involving Software Releases showed a significant positive relationship (p <.01), while the remaining three showed no significant linear result.

In summary, we found a generally negative relationship between closure and success, no relationship between bridging and success, and no relationship between leader centrality and success with one exception involving software releases. This is in marked contrast with the results of prior work group research which indicate that closure, bridging, and leader centrality all have positive relationships with group success.

In the Appendix, we further discuss these findings and compare them with the literature regarding social network structure and success in open source projects. In the following section, we offer conjectures which may help to explain these anomalous results.

CONJECTURES

Our results show that closure, bridging, and leader centrality have no significant positive effect on the success of open source software project communities, with one exception (Administrator Class Centrality and Software Releases) which, as discussed in the Appendix, may well be a spurious result. Some negative relationships were found between closure and success, supporting the conjecture that closure may be an indicator of insufficiencies with respect to software architecture, software documentation, and/or project rules; however, they do not support a causal relationship between closure and success. In summary, we found no cogent evidence that any of these fundamental social network structural variables are critical success factors for open source project groups.

We would like to understand the reasons for these anomalous results. In particular, we seek to understand why social network structural variables of closure, bridging and leader centrality are critical success factors for many other types of work groups, but are not critical success factors for this type of work group – the open source software

project community. In this section, we offer various possible explanations for this surprising result. In presenting these explanations, we are assuming that the relevant project communications were actually captured from the public forum messages. The possibility that some relevant communications were not actually captured is considered in the Study Limitations section of the paper. The conjectures are presented below.

Modular Software Architecture

Modular software architecture permits changes to source code within one module without significant effects on code contained in other modules. This reduces the need for coordinating communication between developers who are working on different modules, compared with software development projects which do not utilize a modular architecture.

Accepted Standards and Tools

The use of well-known coding standards, design approaches, and programming languages may act to reduce the need for coordinating communication because developers will already be familiar with these tools and will not require additional knowledge in order to use them.

Highly Skilled Developers

Project community members may be so highly skilled and experienced that coordinating communication is not very important for learning and problem solving. Open source is known to attract such highly skilled "hacker" developers (Raymond, 1999a). These experienced individuals may not need direction from a central leader but rather are self-directed such that their choice of task and work method productively contributes to the overall software development task. They may also not need or want help from other members of the project community or from individuals outside of the project community.

Developer as User

In developer-targeted software projects (part of our target population), the developer is also the user and therefore the communication that would normally occur between user and developer is not necessary. This would result in a reduction in the need for coordinating communication compared with other software development processes in which external users are consulted in developing software requirements and in evaluating the project output.

Open Source Culture

The culture of the broader open source software community is characterized as a kind of meritocracy in which a rational approach is favored over other approaches which resort to hierarchical position or relationships of power and influence (Raymond, 1999a). Such a culture may result in limited exchanges of knowledge compared with hierarchical cultures which require more protracted and extensive coordinating communications as may be seen within a bureaucratic structure (Yamauchi, 2000).

Shared Mental Models

To the extent that participants have shared mental models, it is possible that these shared models may reduce the need for knowledge flows associated with coordination and other development activities (Scozzi et al., 2008). In some respects, this may be related to the notion of familiarity, in which familiarity among the members of a work group can act to weaken the relationship between social network structure and group performance, implying a reduced need for coordinating communications (Balkundi & Harrison, 2006). Perhaps open source developers are very experienced and

therefore familiar with the task. However, we note that the study population involved the two-year period following the first release of software, and therefore the familiarity effect may not be so important in this study as compared with the familiarity that develops in other work groups over the span of many years.

Technical Artifact Mediation

Open source software developers operate within a socio-technical environment involving many types of tools and other technical artifacts such as source code repositories, programming languages, project web pages, and others (Scacchi, 2002). In general, the mediating effect of software artifacts on computer supported cooperative work has been broadly recognized (Ngwenyama & Lyytinen, 1997). The scenario in which artifacts can successfully mediate information transfer (thus reducing the need for communication) is feasible to the extent that the artifacts can be inscribed with information and that the task can be structured to allow for workflows from person to artifact to person, rather than from person to person. In this case, the artifacts become the mediators of information transfer and they act as a substitute for the social network in this regard. This is somewhat similar to the "knowledge ecology" view offered by Lanzara and Morner (2003). For example, the statement sequence, algorithmic logic, and general organization of the code can be viewed as a kind of inscription of information. When a developer checks out a batch of code from the source code repository, the information that was inscribed by all of the previous contributors to that code becomes available to that developer. In a sense, these prior developers are "speaking" to the new developer through the code. As this developer makes changes to the code, he or she is inscribing their own information into the code, and this new information becomes available to other developers as soon as the new code is committed into the repository. This process may allow for key information transfers to occur without the need for dense social networks.

CONCLUDING REMARKS

Our original motivation was to investigate the success factors for open source software project communities. Taking the perspective of open source communities as a form of work group, we studied various fundamental social network structural variables to determine their relationship with group success. Considering that these structural variables were critical success factors for various other types of work groups, we were surprised to find no evidence that they positively influenced success in open source groups. In this final section, we consider the study's limitations, some of the implications for practice and potential future research directions.

Study Limitations

The choice of SourceForge as the sole research setting is a limitation in that it is possible that the projects hosted by SourceForge are not representative of the broader population of projects which may be found on other hosting sites and/or which may have their own hosting platform. Also, the extensive transparency associated with SourceForge may not be representative of other hosting sites. However, SourceForge is, by far, the largest of the available hosting platforms and SourceForge projects include a wide variety of software types, application domains, and open source licenses.

With regard to the choice of research method, it is recognized that the use of historical statistics may result in reliability issues (Babbie, 2005). Existing statistical records are usually kept for purposes other than research, and various changes can occur in record-keeping methods, information processing systems, definition of fields, and so forth. These matters are addressed by taking proactive steps to identify changes in recording method and other changes which might affect data reliability. Fortunately, the SourceForge organization is well aware that they are the source of considerable research efforts and, along with their open policy; they appear to be conscientious about publishing their record-keeping methods and announcing any changes. These announcements were carefully reviewed to determine the impact on data reliability and other steps were taken to check the integrity of the data.

In the case of the conversational networks used to compile the ingroup variables of closure and leader centrality, the networks were built from online public forum records. It is possible that there were other conversations among project members which involved other modes such as mailing lists, direct email or IRC communications, and therefore were not captured in our data. While we recognize this to be a possibility, we note that the norms of open source software promote a high level of openness and transparency which will tend to limit the extent to which non-public conversations actually take place. We further note that the dominant public communication method used in our sampled projects was the public forum and that other methods such as mailing lists were not frequently used.

Regarding the outgroup bridging variables, we note that the network definition was limited by the availability of data, and that we used membership data rather than conversational data. It is possible that conversational links existed between a member of the focal group and members of other groups in which the focal group member was not registered with the other groups. However, we suggest that such outgroup conversations would often occur between developers who are co-members of the other project group, and therefore the membership link is a reasonable proxy for a conversational link. In effect, membership ties with another group are expected to be associated with conversational ties with members of that other group.

Finally, a cross-sectional study design normally results in ambiguity with respect to the direction of the causal arrow between independent and dependent variables, since time precedence cannot be established. Various conjectures were offered and their implications regarding causal direction were discussed. However, these conjectures are not tested in this study and would require longitudinal studies to more strongly support an argument of causality.

Implications for Practice

With regard to practice, the results for closure may be useful to individuals and firms who sponsor, manage, and/or participate in open source software projects. Even though social network structures were not established as likely causes of success, the closure structure was noted as having a negative relationship with success. Therefore, the results of this work with respect to closure may provide practical measurement tools which can be efficiently applied to pre-existing digital archives such as email, instant messaging and online forums (Hinds & Lee, 2009). Open source software project administrators might use such measures to assess their own communities and to determine if they have the right kinds of structures or if changes might be necessary. Further, the possible role of software architecture, software documentation, and project rules is noted with regard to success and administrators and host platform designers should be aware of the potential importance of these artifacts and should take actions to ensure that they are properly designed. If problems arise, these artifacts should be carefully evaluated to see if there are any deficiencies that can be corrected.

In more general terms, perhaps the most important implication for practice is the recognition that open source may represent a fundamentally new form of collaborative development with different knowledge flow characteristics compared with other work groups. Practitioners should expand their perspectives and reconsider their assumptions that, for example, a team is the only organizational work group form which can be used for collaboratively developing a knowledge product. Open source methods have been shown to be a useful and interesting alternative to team-based software development methods. Practitioners should be aware that other possible applications of open source methods may be feasible in areas such as the development of innovative product designs, knowledge repositories, and other kinds of knowledge-based products.

Future Research Directions

A number of future research directions can be envisioned. In the short-term, attempts to generalize the results of this work to other types of open source software projects would be worthwhile. This would involve relaxing some of the restrictions imposed by the study population definition and applying these tests to projects of different maturity levels, projects involving user-targeted software, and projects which are corporate-sponsored rather than community-based. Projects from host organizations other than SourceForge should also be considered.

Because of the anomalous nature of the results, it is important that alternative research methods be used to either confirm or refute the observed deviation from theories of work groups and social capital theories. This might involve more intensive field studies in which a small number of project communities are investigated in order to evaluate some of the conjectures that have been offered but have not been empirically tested. These studies can search for the presence of alternative forms of communication among project developers.

With regard to the explanation of these surprising results, various propositions should be developed based on the previously suggested conjectures and related testable hypotheses should be elaborated. Alternative research methods might be applied depending upon the nature of the hypotheses that are suggested. In the short-term, these efforts would be focused on explaining the anomalous results that were seen in open source software project communities. In the longer term, it is possible that these efforts could be expanded to consider other types of virtual development communities that may utilize open source methods and principles in building a more general theory of collaborative development (Benkler, 2006).

In addition, it may be appropriate in testing these propositions to define a two-mode "socio-technical network", in which one type of node is a person and the other type of node is a technical artifact. In this way, such a socio-technical network could be investigated as a mediator of knowledge flows and perhaps various structural measures of this kind of network would be found to be critical success factors for open source project groups.

Finally, there appears to be significant potential in considering the role and impact of technical artifacts with regard to the open source development process. Initially, this work might involve comparative studies of artifacts and their roles in the development process, for example as in comparing a prominent open source software project with the development of a non-software product such as the Wikipedia. More generally, there is the potential to conduct design research studies which use laboratory and field experimental methods to test the impact of different design strategies on the nature and success of the work group that emerges.

REFERENCES

Babbie, E. (2005). *The basics of social research.* Stamford, CT: Thomson Wadsworth.

Balkundi, P., & Harrison, D. (2006). Ties, leaders, and time in teams: Strong inference about network structure's effects on team viability and performance. *Academy of Management Journal, 49*(1), 49–68.

Benkler, Y. (2006). *The wealth of networks: How social production transforms markets and freedom.* New Haven, CT: Yale University Press.

Bordieu, R. (1986). The forms of capital. In Richardson, J. G. (Ed.), *Handbook of Theory and Research for the Sociology of Education* (pp. 241–258). New York: Greenwood Press.

Breughel, Pieter the Elder (1563). *Tower of Babel.* Retrieved from http://en.wikipedia.org/wiki/File:Brueghel-tower-of-babel.jpg

Brooks, F. Jr. (1986). No silver bullet—essence and accidents of software engineering. In Kugler, H. J. (Ed.), *Information Processing* (*Vol. 86*, pp. 1069–1076). Amsterdam, The Netherlands: Elsevier Science Publishers.

Brooks, F., Jr. (1975, 1995). *The mythical man month.* Reading, MA: Addison-Wesley.

Burt, R. (1992). *Structural holes: The social structure of competition.* Cambridge, MA: Harvard University Press.

Carley, K. (1995). *Computational and mathematical organization theory: perspective and directions.* Paper presented at the Informs meetings, Los Angeles, CA.

Concas, G., Lisci, M., et al. (2008). Open source communities as social networks: An analysis of some peculiar characteristics. In *Proceedings of the 19th Australian Conference on Software Engineering* (pp. 387-391).

Crowston, K., Annabi, H., Howison, J., & Masango, C. (2004). *Towards a portfolio of FLOSS project success measures.* Paper presented at the 4th Workshop on Open Source Software Engineering, Edinburgh, Scotland.

Crowston, K., & Howison, J. (2004). *The social structure of free and open source software development* (Syracuse FLOSS Working Paper).

Crowston, K., & Howison, J. (2006). Hierarchy and centralization in free and open source software team communications. *Knowledge, Technology, &. Policy, 18*(4), 65–85.

Dahlander, L., & Wallin, M. W. (2006). A man on the inside: Unlocking communities as complementary assets. *Research Policy, 35*, 1243–1259. doi:10.1016/j.respol.2006.09.011

Everett, M. G., & Borgatti, S. P. (1999). The centrality of groups and classes. *The Journal of Mathematical Sociology, 23*(3), 181–201.

Free Software Foundation (FSF). (n.d.). Retrieved from http://www.fsf.org/

Fukuyama, F. (1995). *The social virtues and the creation of prosperity*. London: Hamish Hamilton.

Gao, Y., Freeh, V., & Madey, G. (2003). *Analysis and modeling of open source software community*. Paper presented at the North American Association for Computational Social and Organizational Science Conference.

Gorla, N., & Lam, Y. W. (2004). Who should work with whom? Building effective software project teams. *Communications of the ACM, 47*(6), 79–82. doi:10.1145/990680.990684

Granovetter, M. (1985). Economic action and social structure: the problem of embeddedness. *American Journal of Sociology, 91*(3), 481–510. doi:10.1086/228311

Grewal, R., Lilien, G. L., & Mallapragada, G. (2006). Location, location, location: How network embeddedness affects project success in open source systems. *Management Science, 52*(7), 1043–1056. doi:10.1287/mnsc.1060.0550

Healy, K., & Schussman, A. (2003). *The ecology of open-source software development (Tech. Rep.)*. Arizona, USA: University of Arizona, Department of Sociology.

Hinds, D. (2008). *Social network structure as a critical success condition for open source software project communities*. Unpublished doctoral dissertation, Florida International University, Florida, USA. Retrieved March 2008 from http://etd.fiu.edu/ETD-db/available/etd-0501108-124416/

Hinds, D., & Lee, R. M. (2009). Assessing the social network health of virtual communities. In Whitworth, B., & deMoor, A. (Eds.), *Handbook of research on socio-technical design and social networking systems*. Hershey, PA: IGI Global.

Kidane, Y. H., & Gloor, P. A. (2007). Correlating temporal communication patterns of the Eclipse open source community with performance and creativity. *Computational & Mathematical Organization Theory, 13*, 17–27. doi:10.1007/s10588-006-9006-3

Lakhani, K. R., & Wolf, R. G. (2005). Why hackers do what they do: understanding motivation and effort in free/open source software projects. In Feller, J., Fitzgerald, B., Hissam, S., & Lakhani, K. R. (Eds.), *Perspectives on free and open source software*. Cambridge, MA: MIT Press.

Lanzara, G. F., & Morner, M. (2003). *The knowledge ecology of open-source software projects*. Paper presented at the 19th European Group of Organizational Studies Colloquium, Copenhagen, Denmark.

Lee, G. K., & Cole, R. E. (2003). From a firm-based to a community-based model of knowledge creation: The case of the Linux kernel development. *Organization Science, 14*(6), 633–649. doi:10.1287/orsc.14.6.633.24866

Libresoft. (2006). Libre *software research*. Retrieved October 2008 from http://libresoft.es/

Lopez-Fernandez, L., Robles, G., & Gonzalez-Barahona, J. M. (2004). *Applying social network analysis to the information in CVS repositories*. Retrieved from http://opensource.mit.edu/papers/llopez-sna-short.pdf

MacCormack, A., Rusnak, J., & Baldwin, C. Y. (2006). Exploring the structure of complex software designs: An empirical study of open source and proprietary code. *Management Science, 52*(7), 1015–1030. doi:10.1287/mnsc.1060.0552

Madey, G., Freeh, V., & Tynan, R. (2002). The open source software development phenomenon: An analysis based on social network theory. In *Proceedings of the Americas Conference on Information Systems (AMCIS 2002)* (pp. 1806-1813).

Moreno, J. (1934). *Who shall survive?* New York: Beacon Press.

Nahapiet, J., & Ghoshal, S. (1998). Social capital, intellectual capital, and organizational advantage. *Academy of Management Review, 23*(2), 242–266. doi:10.2307/259373

Nakakoji, K., & Yamamoto, Y. (2005). The co-evolution of systems and communities in free and open source software development. In Koch, S. (Ed.), *Free/open source software development* (pp. 59–82). Hershey, PA: IGI Global.

Ngwenyama, O. K., & Lyytinen, K. J. (1997). Groupware environments as action constitutive resources: a social action framework for analyzing groupware technologies. *Computer Supported Cooperative Work, 6*, 71–93. doi:10.1023/A:1008600220584

Paulley, G. (2009, January 26). Fred Brooks is still right. *Sybase, iAnywhere.* Retrieved February 21, 2009 from http://iablog.sybase.com/paulley/2009/01/fred-brooks-is-still-right/

Pendharkar, P. C., & Rodger, J. A. (2009). The relationship between software development team size and software development cost. *Communications of the ACM, 52*(1), 141–144. doi:10.1145/1435417.1435449

Putnam, R. D. (2000). *Bowling alone: The collapse and revival of American community.* New York: Simon and Schuster.

Raymond, E. S. (1999a). *The cathedral and the bazaar: Musings on Linux and open source by an accidental revolutionary.* Sebastopol, CA: O'Reilly & Associates, Inc.

Raymond, E. S. (1999b). The social context of open source. [http://www.catb.org/~esr/writings/cathedral-bazaar/cathedral-bazaar/ar01s11.html] (Retrieved 21 February 2009)

Scacchi, W. (2002). Understanding the requirements for developing open source software systems. *IEE Software Proc, 149*(1), 24–39. doi:10.1049/ip-sen:20020202

Scozzi, B., Crowston, K., Eseryel, U. Y., & Li, Q. (2008). Shared mental models among open source software developers. In *Proceedings of the 41st Hawaii International Conference on System Sciences,* Hawaii.

Sowe, S., Stamelos, I., & Angelis, L. (2006). Identifying knowledge brokers that yield software engineering knowledge in OSS projects. *Information and Software Technology, 48*(11), 1025–1033. doi:10.1016/j.infsof.2005.12.019

Spaeth, S. (2005, June). *Coordination in open source projects: A social network analysis using CVS data.* Unpublished doctoral dissertation, University of St. Gallen, St. Gallen, Switzerland. Retrieved from http://www.unisg.ch/www/edis.nsf/7acbc805e9219074c1256d28004777d9/cf2cd20cdc0551a6c12570540023f6bf!OpenDocument

Stewart, K. J., & Ammeter, T. (2002). *An Exploratory Study of Factors Influencing the Level of Vitality and Popularity of Open Source Projects.* Paper presented at the Twenty-Third International Conference on Information Systems.

Tabachnick, B. G., & Fidell, L. S. (2007). *Using Multivariate Statistics.* Boston, MA: Pearson.

Teigland, R., & Wasko, M. M. (2003). Integrating knowledge through information trading: examining the relationship between boundary spanning communication and individual performance. *Decision Sciences, 34*(3), 261–286. doi:10.1111/1540-5915.02341

University of Notre Dame. (2006). Research project on the free/open source software development phenomenon. Retrieved October 2008 from http://www.nd.edu/~oss/

Von Krogh, G., Spaeth, S., & Haefliger, S. (2005). Knowledge reuse in open source software: An exploratory study of 15 open source projects. In *Proceedings of the 38th Hawaii International Conference on System Sciences,* Hawaii.

Von Krogh, G., & Von Hippel, E. (2006). The promise of research on open source software. *Management Science, 52*(7), 975–983. doi:10.1287/mnsc.1060.0560

Wagstrom, P. A., Herbsleb, J. D., et al. (2005). *A social network approach to free/open source software simulation.* Paper presented at the First International Conference on Open Source Systems, Genova.

Wasserman, S., & Faust, K. (1994). *Social network analysis: methods and applications.* Cambridge, UK: Cambridge University Press.

Wenger, E. (1998). *Communities of practice: learning, meaning, and identity.* Cambridge, UK: Cambridge University Press.

Xu, J., Gao, Y., et al. (2005). *A topological analysis of the open source software development community.* Paper presented at the 38th Hawaii International Conference on System Sciences, Hawaii.

Yamauchi, Y., Yokozawa, M., Shinohara, T., & Ishida, T. (2000). *Collaboration with lead media: How open source software succeeds.* Paper presented at the ACM Conf. Comput. Supported Cooperative Work, Philadelphia, PA.

Yang, H., & Tang, J. (2004). Team structure and team performance in IS development: A social network perspective. *Information & Management, 41,* 335–349. doi:10.1016/S0378-7206(03)00078-8

ENDNOTES

[1]   We utilized data obtained directly from SourceForge.net, as well as data contained in SourceForge-based research databases which are compiled by the University of Notre Dame (2006) and by the Libre Project of Universidad Rey Juan Carlos (Libresoft, 2006).

[2]   Conversational data between project group members and members of other groups were not available and therefore membership affiliation links were used as a proxy for conversational links.

[3]   Two other variables – Trackers Opened and Trackers Closed – were considered but were eliminated based on the results of principal component analysis.

[4]   The 17 projects were excluded as outliers based on a univariate criterion of at least three standard deviations from the mean and a multivariate criterion involving the chi-square statistic (p <.001) for the Mahalanobis distance.

APPENDIX

EXTENDED DISCUSSION OF RESULTS

Closure

With regard to closure, there are no positive relationships between any of the 3 closure variables and the 4 success variables. Rather, we find that 8 of the 12 possible combinations exhibit a significant or near-significant negative relationship, while the remaining 4 combinations show no significant result.

For *Group Density*, the negative result was more pronounced for the activity variables (Software Downloads and Page Views) as compared with the output variables. The Group Density variable applies to the conversations within the entire group including both core developers and peripheral developers. On average, peripheral developers outnumber core developers by a 10-to-1 ratio, and the peripheral developers are mostly involved with beta testing, bug reporting, and/or general usage. Therefore, it is likely that more software downloads and page views (activity variables) are generated by peripheral developers than by core developers which may result in the strong relationship between Group Density and these two variables.

For *Core Density*, the negative result was more pronounced for the output variables (Code Commits and Software Releases) than for the activity variables. The Core Density variable only applies to conversations within the core subgroup. These are the core developers who produce most of the source code, and therefore these individuals generate most of the activity associated with the output variables of code commits and software releases. As a result, this may lead to the strong relationship between Core Density and the two output variables.

For *Peripheral Two-Mode Density*, the negative result was minor with just one near-significant result obtained. This structural variable is a measure of the density of conversation between the core subgroup and the peripheral subgroup. A greater level of two-mode density implies a higher level of involvement between the peripheral developers and the core developers, which may lead to a greater sense of identification with the project, as well as feelings of satisfaction and challenge. As Raymond (1999a) notes, it is important to "listen to the beta testers". Greater two-mode closure may translate into increased feelings of obligation and commitment, which may produce beneficial effects which offset the negative effects seen in the other density variables.

Crowston and Howison (2006) reported the results of an empirical study of bug report forums. The authors calculated and reported density of the conversation networks and found a negative relationship between conversational density and group size. This result corresponds with the findings of our work that group density and group size are negatively correlated (Pearson correlation value of -.52). However, the Crowston and Howison (2006) study did not consider a success variable in their regression. They regressed density on group size, while our study regressed success on density while controlling for group size. Thus, our study controlled for the relationship between density and group size, and we still found a negative relationship between density and success. Crowston and Howison did not perform such an analysis, and therefore the results cannot be directly compared.

In another study, Kidane and Gloor (2007) found a positive correlation between group density and open source software project performance. Their measure of performance was calculated as the portion of reported software bugs that were fixed within a given period of time. We note that this measure of "success" is specific to one aspect of open source project functioning and that it is not comparable to the output and activity measures of success which we employed in our study in an attempt to relate our results to the results obtained for other work groups.

The closure of a network is essentially the proportion of the total possible links in a network that are actually connected. Therefore, a higher closure value indicates more connected links while a lower closure value indicates fewer connected links. If the causal arrow is assumed to point from structure to outcome, then the observed negative relationship between closure and success would imply that a lack of network links can somehow cause or logically lead to success. No plausible conjectures were identified which could explain such a relationship. Therefore, it must be concluded that closure is not a critical success factor in our study.

With regard to the observed negative relationship between closure and success, we argue that a third factor may exist which affects both closure and success. In particular, we suggest that insufficiencies in software architecture, software documentation, and project rules are leading to higher levels of closure and lower levels of success. Thus, the observed negative relationship may be evidence that closure is an indicator of problems, but it does not support the conclusion that closure is a critical success factor.

With regard to the effects of insufficient software architecture, we note that the modularity of the software architecture is recognized as an important success factor for open source software projects (MacCormack et. al., 2006). Modular software architecture permits changes to source code within one module without significant effects on code contained in other modules. Ineffective software modularity will tend to increase closure as a result of the increase in coding interdependencies, and at the same time, it will tend to decrease output due to losses in productivity and effort, and will decrease activity due to negative impacts on software quality. The suggested positive relationship between modularity ineffectiveness and closure and the suggested negative relationship between modularity ineffectiveness and success will result in a negative correlation between closure and success. However, because this negative correlation arises from the effects of a third variable (software modularity ineffectiveness), the closure-success relationship would be viewed as spurious and no causal relationship would be suggested between closure and success. Similar arguments can be made for the impact of insufficiencies in software documentation and project rules.

Bridging

No significant relationship was found for any of the 8 combinations of the 2 bridging variables and the 4 success variables. Considering that a positive relationship is typically seen in work groups, it was surprising to find that the extensiveness of bridging ties did not seem to have an effect on success, implying that such bridging ties are not an important factor in open source software project communities.

In a recent study by Grewal et. al. (2006), the authors collected data from 108 open source software project communities on SourceForge and related various measures of bridging (which they refer to as "network embeddedness") with the number of code commits and the number of downloads (used as measures of project success). Overall, the authors obtained a mixed set of positive, negative, and "no-effect" relationships between bridging and success. Their suggestion that bridging has "powerful but subtle effects on project success" is generally inconsistent with our finding that bridging had no relationships with success. However, due to methodological differences, the comparability of the two studies is questionable. For example, Grewal et. al. (2006) used many different bridging measures which were not comparable to the measures used in our work. In addition, their study utilized a nominalist sampling approach in which 10 projects were selected based on their common platform technology and then other projects were selected based on known bridging ties with these original 10 projects. This is in contrast with our study in which a randomized sampling strategy was used. It is possible that the bridging results for a sample of projects with known bridging connections may be different than the results for a randomly selected sample of projects.

Leader Centrality

Of the 4 combinations of leader centrality with success, a positive relationship was observed between Administrator Class Centrality and Software Releases. Otherwise, leader centrality had no significant relationship with the success variables. The one positive result is consistent with the results of prior work group studies, while the other three results are not. Does this provide some evidence that leader centrality is a critical success factor for open source project communities?

No studies of open source software project communities were identified in which leader centrality variables were measured and related to success. However, the literature does suggest that open source administrators tend to operate in low key roles, avoiding power relationships and delegating as much as possible. These observations are consistent with the finding that leader centrality had no significant relationship with 3 of the 4 success variables, but they are inconsistent with the finding of the one positive relationship with Software Releases.

Regarding the positive finding for Software Releases, we first reflect on the observation that this was a strong relationship ($p < .01$) in comparison with the other three variables in which no significant or even near-significant relationship was seen. This leads us to consider whether there may be other reasons for this result. Is it possible that a third variable is involved and that this positive relationship is spurious? We believe that the answer is "yes" as further argued below.

The decision to make a software release is typically made by the administrator. While a high level of coding activity (Code Commits) is logically associated with frequent releases (Software Releases), it is possible for an administrator to make frequent releases even if there is a relatively low volume of code commits. In effect, the decision to release is somewhat arbitrary and it is possible that certain administrators are biased towards frequent releases and therefore they have a higher "propensity to release" than others. If this were the case, then those administrators with high propensity to release would make frequent releases resulting in a high level of Software Releases. In this situation, the frequent releases would tend to generate questions and comments from developers who download the releases and these conversations would tend to dominate the forums and would be directed to the releasing administrator, resulting in high levels of Administrator Class Centrality. In effect, these administrators would be generating their own centrality. If this conjecture were true, then the implication would be that the causal arrow points in a reverse direction from the assumption of the research model – that is, it would point from outcome (Software Releases) to social network structure (Administrator Class Centrality).

This work was previously published in International Journal of Open Source Software and Processes (IJOSSP), edited by Stefan Koch, pp. 26-48, copyright 2009 by IGI Publishing (an imprint of IGI Global).

Chapter 13

Strategies for Improving Open Source Software Usability:
An Exploratory Learning Framework and a Web-based Inspection Tool

Luyin Zhao
Rutgers University, USA

Fadi P. Deek
New Jersey Institute of Technology, USA

James A. McHugh
New Jersey Institute of Technology, USA

ABSTRACT

The Open Source Software (OSS) movement has had enormous impact on how software is created and continues to attract interest from researchers, software developers and users. A factor that may be inhibiting OSS from achieving greater success is usability, a fundamental characteristic to user acceptance of software. Motivated by the uniquely user-driven nature of the open source model and the extensive user base that participates in OSS projects, the authors propose an exploratory learning method and an associated web-based inspection environment that enables non-experts to contribute to open source usability inspection. This tool uses pattern-based usability guidelines to help identify usability knowledge during inspection. The method emphasizes outlining and exploration features which the authors have formally evaluated and the results of which are described. Data collected from a qualitative study indicates positive impact of the proposed method in helping end-users inspect software and achieve better results in discovering usability problems.

DOI: 10.4018/978-1-60960-513-1.ch013

INTRODUCTION

The Open Source Software development model is distinguished from traditional software development models by its distributed, collaborative developer participation, its use of highly public distributed peer review, the common use of frequent development releases, and the use of open licensing arrangements (principally via the General Public License). Open invitation to developers is a cornerstone of the open source paradigm, and the distinction between the developers and users of software may be fluid. While numerous studies have examined the OSS model from a development point of view, there has been much less concern with open source usability and how users can effectively improve software usability.

It is questionable as to whether OSS projects devote adequate resources to usability improvement, and whether there is a positive correlation between the OSS development model and better software usability (Nichols & Twidale, 2003) (Twidale & Nichols, 2004). Widely recognized motivations for participating in OSS development include personal satisfaction or technical needs, increasing one's technical skills, as well as a desire to enhance one's technical reputation in the broad open source community. These motivations and the culture of the community have potential implication for usability. For example, it is often said that "when programmers produce open source software, since they are largely "scratching their own itch", they tend to produce software for themselves and to be content with a (programmer-oriented) user interface" (Pemberton, 2004). Furthermore, since algorithmic or functional problems have greater value in the developer 'reputation market' than contributions to usability (Nichols et al., 2002), it is more difficult for usability proponents to establish and promote the legitimacy of their focus vis-à-vis the functionality perspective of expert-users (Twidale & Nichols, 2004).

User involvement at the level of identifying software bugs or suggesting new features has been a major factor in OSS success. However, this kind of participation has been less effective in recognizing "soft" interests like usability in applications programs, and even less so at accommodating the kind of user diversity which is the objective of fine usability engineering as described by (Shneiderman, 1998). On the other hand there is a kind of inherited deep usability knowledge that is captured by the OSS model precisely because the software is often designed based on a "following the tail-lights" approach. The idea of this OSS strategy is to imitate successful existing systems' functionality and their external shells. Assuming these systems have sound usability characteristics, then the imitative system should acquire many of these characteristics by default. Despite this, Messerschmitt (2004) cogently argues that software (usability) defects expose a fundamental weakness in the open source paradigm itself: an inability to adequately grasp the needs of application users. He argues that for most application users, critical usability information comes from marketers, salespeople, customer service, testers, and program managers who play a crucial role in surfacing, clarifying, and understanding the real needs of end users. These users are typically unable to participate in OSS development. Consequently their perspectives may be marginalized with the result that most OSS projects lack crucial direct usability information from these users.

The empirical study by Zhao and Deek (2005) contrasted the usability problems identified using a formal usability test method (protocol analysis) versus those submitted through voluntarily user participation. The study indicated that:

- Only a small portion of the usability problems found by formal usability testing were reported by users contributing through the regular OSS project bug reporting channel and subsequently addressed by the project developers. In other words, the existing

OSS bug reporting paradigm is apparently not considered an appropriate channel for reporting usability problems.

- Feature requests do form a large proportion of usability enhancement proposals. However, these requests are mainly submitted by advanced users who frequently look for features that facilitate "flexibility and efficiency of use" and "visibility of system status." These represent only limited aspects of usability and do not cover the range of possible needs of the entire user group.

In the absence of formal usability evaluations, open source projects lack key mechanisms for discovering usability problems. This is based on the OSS status quo, so there clearly remains great potential for open source development to address usability. Indeed there are significant reasons for optimism: OSS projects have begun to attract usability engineers; the OSS paradigm has the flexibility to allow usability professionals to contribute; and most importantly, the community provides a large user base for usability testing. Furthermore, it is possible to build remote reporting features into OSS software that allow users to report not only bugs, but also usability problems identified after deployment. For example, establishing explicit channels for "usability bug reporting" might guide and encourage potential contributing users to report more usability problems.

This paper is intended to provide deeper insight into these issues and offer empirical data to support the viewpoints presented. We argue that getting the large contributing user base involved in the usability improvement process is the most feasible way to address these limitations and key to improving the usability outcomes of open source development. To provide effective support for such user involvement, we propose a new learning-by-doing method supported by a web-based tool that enables ordinary users to learn and adapt established usability knowledge during usability inspection.

It is notable that our approach coheres well with the classic GQM (Goal-Question-Metric) method for continuous improvement using goal-driven metrics, originally elaborated by Victor Basili (see Basili & Weiss, 1984; Solingen & Berghout, 1999 for a detailed exposition.) The GQM method underscores the necessity of maintaining a clear connection between the goals of a project or organization and metrics for their improvement. It is worth making the correspondence explicit to put our work in proper context. In our instance, the project is a software engineering product and its development process, specifically one developed in an open source environment. The goals are to improve the quality of the software development process and the product produced. The aspect of quality focused on is the usability of the product. A key challenge is the difficulty of doing usability engineering in an open source context. The software tool and method we present is intended to facilitate improving the product by using usability patterns to guide the user/developers in identifying usability issues. The usability patterns utilized are well-established and their use is tantamount to posing specific questions about the product interface: is the interface effective or defective with respect to such and such characteristics which are widely recognized as requisite to proper interface design. The GQM method is implicit in this framework. Though questions are not explicitly formulated as such in the tool we design, the underlying patterns are equivalent to usability questions which the user/developer is led to address when seeking to identify defects in the product interface. The corresponding metrics are the user critiques that identify product features that fail to adhere to usability principles, and user recommendations for their correction or improvement. Unlike the traditional GQM method, the role of questions and metrics is implicit in our process. The user pool that applies this improvement analysis is in fact not even assumed to be expert in the usability rules underlying the tool. This flexibility is precisely a key benefit of the tool. The improvement is accomplished and the GQM-like process implemented without requiring that the user/developers be expert in the quality improvement criteria applied. The result is not only product improvement but two kinds of software process improvements. First, the usability process is structured to be friendly and adapted to the abilities, attitudes and characteristics of the user/developer pool in order to promote its actual use and application. Secondly, the knowledge base of the users about usability principles is enhanced so their acquired expertise can be brought to bear not only on the present product/project but also in subsequent projects.

RELATED WORK ON OSS USABILITY IMPROVEMENT

Current research has focused on potential deficiencies in the open source development model as it relates to usability, especially when potential contributors are not usability experts. In light of this problem, researchers and software engineers have proposed a number of refinements to the standard OSS paradigm including:

- Establishing formal processes for promoting usability guidelines within the OSS communities. This is obviously challenging in the OSS environment since it is difficult for project leaders to exercise control and channel/allocate the resources needed to support such efforts. For instance, while the well-known GNOME and KDE projects have published Human Interface Guidelines to help developers design applications that are consistent with the GNOME and KDE environment, it is unclear as to how and to what degree the guidelines are actually followed. Even though establishing such guidelines seems

to be a priori feasible, it in fact represents a cultural problem in OSS since it attempts to bring a more formalized usability process and style into OSS development that has not been characteristic of the OSS ethos. Moreover, there are obvious drawbacks to guidelines that are too vague to be effective. For example, guidelines can range from general recommendations to specific style guide (Jeffries *et al.*, 1991) and tend to be maintained as prescriptive checklists without context or examples.

- Automated usability testing is intended to reduce cost, increase consistency and reduce the level of human involvement, all of which are significant advantages given the limitations of OSS projects with their significantly volunteer-driven membership. (Nichols et al., 2003). However, despite the fact that automated testing would require less resources, it is questionable whether usability testing would even then get enough attention from development teams. The teams already invest insufficient time in functionality testing since they assume peer review and user contributions are adequate for finding and reporting bugs (Zhao & Elbaum, 2003).

- Researchers like Nichols et al. (2003) have emphasized that improving the design of the bug reporting capabilities of OSS projects would capitalize on the large, geographically distributed OSS user base. This provides a promising opportunity for improving OSS usability because it opens up new venues for additional users to contribute. Not only can automated methods for extracting usability information be used (Hilbert & Redmiles, 2000), but a well-designed bug reporting process can assist in capturing cognitive information from users. Such methods depend critically on establishing accessible communication channels that allow non-expert us-

Figure 1. Bug reporting embedded in the software

ers to contribute. This is essential because such users may be put off by complicated procedures for recording bugs in repositories. One example of this approach, called critical incident reporting, is to embed a bug-reporting mechanism in the software so that both system state information and subjective, user comments can be reported during system usage (Castillo & Hartson, 1998). The screenshot in Figure 1, taken from the open source software "more. groupware", illustrates this method.

Despite the fact that methods like critical incident reporting open new ways to engage currently non-active users to contribute, there remains a limitation on the effectiveness of such approaches: without preparation akin to that received by trained usability experts, typical users lack adequate knowledge about usability. This significantly hinders their ability to identify usability problems. Unfortunately, these end-users tend to blame themselves for the difficulties they encounter with awkward user interfaces (McCoy, 2002).

We believe that significant benefits can accrue from studying how to train end-users to inspect software and discover usability problems by providing them with appropriate strategies. Learning how to do this need not require extensive training but can simply focus on readily acquired, context-based knowledge of usability, such as usability patterns (van Welie & van der Veer, 2003). In the

following, we introduce a method for acquiring such knowledge on-the-fly in the context of OSS usability inspection. The method is inspired by the theory of exploratory learning. Exploratory learning aims to achieve rapid learning outcomes for novice users through a learning-by-doing approach (Piaget, 1972) (Carroll et al., 1985).

THE EXPLORATORY INSPECTION METHOD

The proposed method is based on a theory called exploratory learning. One of its key characteristics is that it encourages acquiring skills and knowledge by exploring and experimenting, with less attention to the more didactic mode of instruction called learning-by-doing. The theoretical basis for exploratory learning is found in Piaget's constructivist theory (Piaget, 1972). The idea is that people learn best by actively constructing their own understanding of a subject area. Following this line of thought, a number of exploratory learning models have been developed with the goal of investigating how to develop and deploy information systems that require little or no upfront training. Promising results have been reported by Carroll et al. (1985) and Polson and Lewis (1990) who applied the method to learning how to use a software system.

The Exploratory Inspection Model

John and Kieras (1996) define exploratory learning as a "task-oriented, time-constrained process, whose primary goal is performance of the current task, with learning as a second aspect." This definition coheres well with usability inspection where identifying usability problems is the primary goal, but with usability knowledge also acquired during the inspection process. Early research indicates that exploratory learning can be an effective way for novice software users to acquire important knowledge about software systems (Carroll et al., 1985).

Thus, our research goal is to extend the scope of exploratory learning to usability knowledge learning (hereafter referred to as *Exploratory Inspection*) and investigate whether it can be applied to acquiring usability knowledge. Theories and empirical studies of exploratory learning are usually based on the principle of minimal instruction (Carroll et al., 1985) and task-oriented learning. Some basic observations follow.

First, didactic or rote learning is unsuitable for acquiring usability knowledge. This is especially so for the case of volunteer open source contributors who are unlikely to spend a significant amount of time studying extensive and lengthy usability guidelines in advance of conducting an inspection. This is the fundamental barrier that exploratory learning seeks to overcome for task-oriented disciplines. Our hypothesis is that exploratory learning is a better method to impart usability knowledge to non-expert inspectors.

Second, exploratory learning is a type of problem solving methodology (van Oostendorp & Walbeehm, 1995) where the learner has little or no specific domain knowledge. Usability inspection relies strongly on critical thinking, one of the pillars of problem solving. Since non-expert inspectors can be assumed to have little prior usability knowledge before conducting such inspections, exploratory learning is a logical choice for this type of problem solving.

Figure 2. Conceptual comparison of exploratory inspection vs. exploratory learning

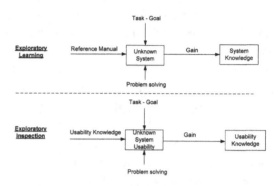

Finally, exploratory learning is based on using task-oriented learning to help maintain exploration goals. It is especially appropriate in situations where sticking to a goal is needed to learn effectively, like when learning about usability.

Figure 2 illustrates how exploratory learning is suited to the needs of usability inspection. The unknown domain to be explored is the unknown system usability. This is also the target of usability inspection or inquiry. The objective for learners of exploratory inspection is not only to gain usability knowledge, but also to identify usability problems and gain a better understanding of the unknown system usability. Here "learning" refers to "learning usability knowledge" while "task" refers to "usability inspection." A distinguishing characteristic of inspection-based learning is that, unlike for the case of using a software system, the inspection task itself may not provide learners with sufficient usability knowledge. This is because inspection is essentially a critiquing task rather than an applications task directed at a concrete goal like composing a document. That is, the target of the exploration is the system's unknown usability characteristics. The creative application of exploratory learning on usability inspection makes it a new paradigm with unique elements as already discussed.

Below, we discuss two key components that support the exploratory inspection model.

Exploration Guidance

When exploring an unknown software system, completely open-ended unguided exploration is inefficient and rarely used (Rieman, 1996). On the other hand, if excessive guidance or instruction is provided, exploration can degenerate into a mere exercise, thwarting the entire purpose of exploratory learning. Hitherto, the conventional strategy has been to provide the learner/inspector with the minimal amount of instruction needed to initiate exploration without undermining freedom of exploration (Carroll et al., 1987).

Exploratory inspection requires the guidance to be suitable for inspectors with little prior experience in usability inspection. Expert-based guidelines like Nielsen's usability heuristics do not appear to be good candidates for this purpose (Molich & Nielsen, 1990) because they are free-style guidelines intended for usability experts. We decided instead to choose usability patterns (van Welie & van der Veer, 2003) for inspection guidance. Unlike abstract, expert-oriented usability guidance, usability patterns represent a valuable form of usability knowledge that allows for easy adoption by ordinary developers and users without prior formal usability training. Such patterns have been successfully used to provide usability knowledge to software developers who were typically not usability experts. So it is plausible that usability patterns can also provide expert knowledge to open source users to contribute to OSS usability improvement. Many of these OSS users are themselves software developers.

The description of a usability pattern can range from a few sentences to many pages. To effectively use these patterns as inspection guidelines we need to keep in mind that if a large volume of information is presented in a pattern, especially at the beginning of the learning process, the novice usability inspector may either lose interest in or become distracted from the actual task. As Rieman (1996) indicates, using references, online help, documents (like quick sketches or outlines of content), or simply trying things out on a system are typical strategies used in exploratory learning. To support this kind of learning, "training-wheel" methods have been proposed and tested that reduces the strain on a learners' cognitive capacity and try to minimize errors at the initial learning stage, the phase where learners have little knowledge of the system. It turns out that not only do users learn faster using this approach, they also perform system functions better compared to users who begin their exploration on a full-blown system (Catrambone & Carroll, 1987).

Given this background, we designed a two-phase *outlining* method for our research model. In the first phase, a core usability pattern is extracted and presented to an inspector. Pattern details are made available as the inspector needs more information when doing the actual inspection task (the second phase). This is consistent with the training-wheel principle wherein one reduces cognitive load at the initial stage (especially for learning complicated patterns) and maintains motivation by focusing on real inspection tasks.

Freedom of Exploration

The principle underlying exploratory learning is to keep learners motivated by letting them focus on real tasks and activities that are intrinsically meaningful to them. In studies that compare two types of learning, exercise and exploration, a fundamental difference is that exploration allows more freedom in goal setting, which is identified by Carroll (Carroll et al., 1987) as a key to maintaining high levels of learning motivation (Wiedenbeck & Zila, 1997).

Although freedom of exploration seems to be a key factor in the success of exploratory learning, critics argue that novices are unprepared to set goals at the start of the learning process because they lack familiarity with the system. Another concern about using exploratory learning in usability inspection is cognitive load, specifically the burden imposed when novices must learn

Figure 3. Exploratory learning based usability inspection

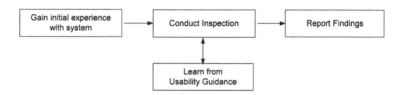

multiple aspects of usability knowledge at the same time. This arises, for instance, when a usability evaluator has to retain a possibly daunting set of newly acquired heuristics in their working memory, overburdening the natural limitations of memory and attention (Kurosu et al., 1997). This is why Nielsen's heuristic evaluation limits to just ten the number of heuristics used. In another study that investigated the effectiveness of inspection by novice inspectors, the so-called "perspective based usability inspection" method was used to compel every inspector to focus attention on one of three perspectives (novice use, expert use, and error handling) (Zhang et al., 1999). The experimental results were promising. Motivated by the same principle, Kurosu et al. (1997) proposed dividing the entire set of usability heuristics into subcategories, asking each evaluator to focus on one subcategory at a time, but no experimental results were reported.

We need to understand how these factors can affect the exploratory inspection outcome. In our research model, we favor giving a greater degree of exploratory freedom to inspectors for the following reasons:

Firstly, in the open source community, the majority of user contributions (e.g., bugs reports and improvement suggestions) are submitted based on actual software use by users. The exploratory inspection model should be understood as a learning process that begins with gaining real experience with the software, with a learning goal as only a secondary objective.

Secondly, compared with the traditional use of exploratory learning in software education, the inspector ends up with a clearer understanding of what they need to learn to find relevant usability knowledge and support/strengthen their recognition of possible usability problems. It is important to clarify this point since the traditional application of exploratory learning in software education assumes a learning goal must be set before the entire learning process begins. Making such an implicit assumption for the exploratory learning model may be misleading. Figure 3 depicts the exploratory learning based inspection process.

The preceding discussion shows how the cognitive load may be reduced since, although an inspector may be given a large number of guidelines to choose from, there is no need to keep a large amount of information in mind if a clear learning goal has already been established.

In summary, we believe that in exploratory inspection in an open source environment, greater freedom with regard to how to do an inspection encourages inspectors to work on usability aspects they are already aware of or on which they have encountered problems and are interested in exploring, while conversely limiting the scope (or freedom) of the process reduces the effectiveness of the exploration.

A Web-Based Inspection Tool

The preliminary step in validating the proposed model is to develop a web-based inspection tool based on which subsequent validation can proceed. It is appropriate for the tool to be web-based since that modality coheres well with the distributed collaborative framework of the OSS

Figure 4. Web-based exploration inspection system

model. The design and development of the tool will follow the theoretical model outlined above with an emphasis on making it easy for open source participants to use.

Tool Design and Development

A system screenshot is shown in Figure 4. The design and layout of the window elements and its rationale are described below. The overall design is intentionally simple so inspectors can focus their attention on the actual task of inspection, rather than expending a significant effort in learning how to use the tool. The programming language used is Perl.

As shown in Figure 4, the upper portion of the window includes simple instructions and text fields for recording usability problems and suggestions for improvement. The main purpose of this part of the interface is to clearly explain the need for usability inspection and provide guidance on how to complete an inspection task so the results are useful. The following points are specifically addressed:

1) What is usability.

Clearly explaining what usability means helps prevent inspectors avoid reporting large numbers of functionality bugs, like system crashes, broken

hyperlinks, database errors, and deadlocks. One objective has been to avoid jargon or fuzzy words when describing what usability is. For example, we replace the term "usability" by the more self-explanatory and familiar phrase "user interface problem". Examples provide a quick way for intuitively understanding ideas. So a link to typical examples of usability problems is provided as illustrated in Figure 5. Both examples represent problems found in an open source project named *dotproject*, primarily because it fits well into our

Figure 5. Usability problem examples

research context but also for a number of other reasons. First, we were still in the midst of the development process (i.e., the project was in Beta version). The number of usability problems that remained to be found and the level of user contribution were both expected to reach a high level at that point, making it the best time to apply any user contribution based methods. Second, through a pre-screening, we found it convenient to observe many usability problems on this single software application, avoiding the use of multiple OSS projects and the between-subject effect. Third, the theme of the application – project management – is one that is easily understood by a majority of users without much investment in upfront training. And, finally, the web-based application allows users to participate without local installation and configuration.

2) How to report a usability problem.

Usability experts not only need to find usability problems, but also need to be able to effectively report them. Again, we use an example to guide inspectors to report problems by filling out a form with three key fields: a description of the usability problem, its severity level, and suggestions for its improvement.

3) How to use the guidelines or patterns.

These are provided at the lower part of the window. It is important to explicitly encourage inspectors to take advantage of usability patterns (called "guidelines" in the tool). Different sets of patterns can be used for different types of applications. For instance, Welie.com presents a set of web site design patterns that we used in designing the tool. As shown, the left frame organizes the patterns according to a tree-like structure based on categories for easy navigation. The right frame provides details about a pattern when an inspector clicks a specific pattern on the left. The two model components, Outlining and Freedom of Exploration, are supported in the following ways:

• **Outlining:** Instead of presenting the complete pattern information in the right frame, a pattern extraction that includes Problem, Context, Solution and Reason, is displayed when the inspector clicks a pattern. The option to view the complete pattern is given if the inspector needs extra information about the pattern. Figure 6 shows an example of pattern extraction.

• **Freedom of exploration:** As discussed in the previous section, inspectors should be given enough freedom to get helpful information. Therefore, instead of providing a limited amount of usability knowledge like usability heuristics and "focused" inspec-

Figure 6. Pattern extractions (left: the complete rendered pattern, right: the outlining pattern)

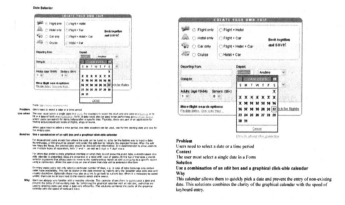

227

tion methods like "perspective-based us-ability inspection" (Zhang et al., 1999), the complete set of patterns are identified but organized in a tree-like view with top level categories shown for easy navigation.

An Evaluation

To test the adequacy of the proposed research model, collect preliminary data, and assess the feasibility of a more comprehensive study, a qualitative observation experiment was conducted. Results of this evaluation would inform the next phase of our research and lays out ground for a more comprehensive quantitative, hypotheses-based experiment.

An invitation was sent to the user community of sourceforge.net, the world's largest open source web site, asking for voluntarily participation in the study. Fifty-five participants elected to log onto the web-based tool to inspect a web-based OSS application called *dotproject*. To examine the impact of two model components - "Outlining" and "Freedom or exploration," we distributed participants across four categories as shown in Table 1. The web-based tool was adapted based on the requirements of each category:

Outlining vs. Complete rendering

Complete rendering: *Full pattern details were presented to the inspector without pattern extraction.*

Outlining: *Pattern extraction was presented first, with full pattern details available when needed.*

Table 1. Number of usability problems found in different categories

	High freedom	Low freedom
Complete Rendering	22	25
Outlining	35	21

High freedom vs. Low freedom

High freedom: *All web-based patterns were organized in a tree structure and presented to the inspectors.*

Low freedom: *Only one category of patterns (e.g. Searching) was presented to an inspector at a time. To obtain another set of random patterns, the inspector had to click a button.*

Unlike the case in formal usability testing where participants may spend hours inspecting software, contributions from OSS users are often voluntary and "light-weight". We attempted to preserve this characteristic by asking each participant to report a minimum of one usability problem. More specifically, each participant was instructed to initially spend 10-20 minutes getting familiar with *dotproject* by carrying out a task of their choosing. Next, the participants were asked to log onto the exploratory inspection system and record at least one usability problem and suggestions for improvement. The users were also encouraged to make use of the guidance provided (i.e., patterns or heuristics) and if any of the problems they located were in fact due to knowledge learned from this guidance, they were required to indicate so. A total of 103 usability problems were found. Of these, 32 were discovered with the help of patterns explicitly indicated by the inspectors. Comparing problems found with versus without help from patterns, we observed that problems identified without the use of patterns tended to be preliminary in nature like "too many choices at any stage," "highlighting colors hard on eyes," and "creation button are far from list they refer to, for example [new company] is far from [company list]." In contrast, participants who used patterns found more in-depth and diverse usability problems. Two examples follow:

Example 1: Based on a pattern called "Paging", one problem discovered was that "tabbed contents have the potential to grow into a large list of items." It was proposed that the system "present the results grouped in pages with a fixed number of items when the user needs to browse through a large tabbed contents".

Example 2: Based on a pattern called "Alternating Row Colors", a problem discovered was that "Tasks per user Page is very hard to read at a glance because the information shows no clear separation between entries." The proposed remedy was to "Alternate task per section in different colors to make the table more readable".

Comparing the conditions "Outlining" versus "Complete rendering", 56 vs. 47 problems were found. For "High Freedom" versus "Low Freedom" the number of problems found was 67 versus 47. The low freedom participants also tended to complain about the number of times they had to click a button to find the help they needed. These observations provide an early indication of the positive impact of usability guidelines for helping non-expert inspectors.

Additionally, patterns used for assisting inspection were distributed according to the usability profile of *dotproject* (i.e., the aspects of software that do have usability problems), rather than based on how often each pattern has been browsed. This also confirms that the users were able to control their exploration process by using only the relevant patterns, not the most viewed patterns.

CONCLUSION AND NEXT STEP

This paper addresses usability in open source software development from both theoretical and practical perspectives. We began by highlighting the lack of usability expertise and the subsequent limited contributions to usability bug reporting from active and other potential OSS users. We then argued that current functional bug reporting channels offered by OSS hosting web sites like sourceforge.net are inadequate for reporting usability problems and providing supporting knowledge for contributing users. Thus developing an effective method for usability analysis and a corresponding software tool is critical for helping non-expert users learn about usability and contribute to OSS usability improvement. We then proposed an exploratory inspection model supported by a web-based inspection tool that facilitates usability analysis and reporting. The tool features pattern-based usability guidelines. These provide practical inspection assistance and represent a form of usability knowledge that can easily be adopted by ordinary users without prior formal usability training.

Even though this model is designed to specifically address usability in open source software, we do not limit the scope of application only to the open source community. This method is indeed useful for any type of software engineering, including commercial software development, as long as user participation is taken as a measure to improvement usability. However, we believe that this method has a much higher value for OSS than for commercial software, not only because OSS cannot afford the costly usability lab evaluation methods and usability still remains a deficiency in the OSS environment, but also because this method is established on the unique characteristic of OSS development model – mass user participation, which is what differentiates OSS from commercial development models. The overall objective of our model is to help non-expert inspectors develop usability knowledge while they are actively performing inspection tasks. This kind of learning-by-doing model especially suits the open source development process because ad-hoc user contributions form such an important cornerstone of the OSS environment. We preliminarily validated the method using an evaluation. Given the limited scope of the study, we refrain from making firm statistical conclusions, nonetheless the results are highly suggestive that there is a positive relationship between the proposed exploratory inspection model and the effectiveness of the inspection.

Figure 7. The refined research model

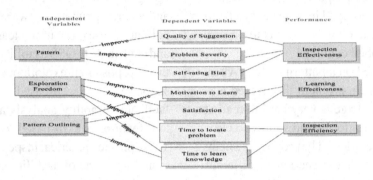

Based on the evaluation, we expanded our research model as shown in Figure 7. Specifically, we plan to investigate the impact of three independent variables: type of guidance (usability pattern vs. traditional heuristics), exploration freedom (high vs. low), and outlining (yes vs. no), on inspection and learning. Inspection and learning are both important. Effective inspection can bring immediate usability improvements to OSS projects. Effective learning increases the knowledge base about usability in the OSS community. Specific measurements (dependent variables) for the effectiveness/efficiency of learning and inspection include: Problem Severity, Quality of Improvement Suggestions, Self-rating Bias (how severity ratings by OSS users deviates from usability experts), Motivation to Learn Usability Knowledge, Learning/Inspection Satisfaction, Time to locate usability problems and Time to Learn Usability Knowledge. The general hypotheses made by the research model are:

- For exploratory inspection, Usability Pattern-based guidance provides more effective inspection than traditional Heuristics-based guidance.
- Both Pattern Outlining and Freedom of Exploration lead to better learning effectiveness

The next phase of our research – a quantitative oriented validation – constitutes a more comprehensive experiment involving over 300 OSS users from the largest OSS host site www. sourceforge.net. Results obtained from this study have provided motivation and evidence to further validate the proposed model. In the meanwhile, we have set up a project website on Sourceforge for our inspection tool and named it "exploratory Inspection". The objective is to make the source code and tool available to the OSS community, to solicit contributions in support of the tool's further development as an OSS project, and to create a long-term open research and data collection environment. Results of this work will be disseminated to the research and user community periodically.

REFERENCES

Basili, V., & Weiss, D. (1984). A Methodology for collecting valid software engineering data. *IEEE Transactions on Software Engineering*, *10*(6), 728–738. doi:10.1109/TSE.1984.5010301

Carroll, J. M., Mack, R. L., Lewis, C. H., Grischkowsky, N. L., & Robertson, S. P. (1985). Exploring a word processor. *Human-Computer Interaction*, *1*(3), 283–307. doi:10.1207/s15327051hci0103_3

Carroll, J. M., Smith-Kerker, P. L., Ford, J. R., & Mazur-Rimetz, S. A. (1987). The minimal manual. *Human-Computer Interaction*, *3*(2), 123–153. doi:10.1207/s15327051hci0302_2

Castillo, J. C., Hartson, H. R., & HIX, D. (1998). *Remote usability evaluation: can users report their own critical incidents?* Paper presented at the Catrambone, R., & Carroll, J. M. (1987). *Learning a word processing system with training wheels and guided exploration.* Paper presented at the SIGCHI/GI conference on Human factors in computing systems and graphics interface (pp. 169-174).

CHI 98 conference summary on Human factors in computing systems.

Deek, F. P., & McHugh, J. A. (2007). *Open Source - Technology and Policy.* Cambridge, UK: Cambridge University Press.

Hilbert, D. M., & Redmiles, D. F. (2000). Extracting usability information from user interface events. [CSUR]. *ACM Computing Surveys, 32*(4), 384–421. doi:10.1145/371578.371593

Jeffries, R., Miller, J. R., Wharton, C., & Uyeda, K. (1991). *User interface evaluation in the real world: A comparison of four techniques.* Paper presented at the SIGCHI conference on Human factors in computing systems: Reaching through technology (pp. 119-124).

John, B. E., & Kieras, D. E. (1996). The GOMS family of user interface analysis techniques: Comparison and contrast. *ACM Transactions on Computer-Human Interaction, 3*(4), 320–351. doi:10.1145/235833.236054

Kurosu, M., Matsuura, S., & Sugizaki, M. (1997). *Categorical inspection method-structured heuristic evaluation (shem).* Paper presented at the IEEE International Conference on Systems, Man, and Cybernetics (pp. 2613-2618).

McCoy, T. (2002). The politics of usability. *The Usability SIG Newsletter, 8*(4).

Messerschmitt, D. G. (2004). Back to the user (open source). *IEEE Software, 21*(1), 89–91. doi:10.1109/MS.2004.1259234

Molich, R., & Nielsen, J. (1990). Improving a human-computer dialogue. *Communications of the ACM, 33*(3), 338–348. doi:10.1145/77481.77486

Nichols, D. M., McKay, D., & Twidale, M. B. (2003). Participatory usability: Supporting proactive users. In *Proceedings of the 4th ACM SIGCHI NZ Symposium on Computer-Human Interaction (CHINZ'03)*, Dunedin, New Zealand (pp. 63-68). New York: ACM.

Nichols, D. M., Thomson, K., & Yeates, S. A. (2001). *Usability and open-source software development.* Retrieved from http://opensource.mit.edu/papers/nichols.pdf

Nichols, D. M., & Twidale, M. B. (2003). The usability of open source software. *First Monday, 8*(1).

Pemberton, S. (2004). Scratching someone else's itch (why open source can't do usability). *Interaction, 11*(1), 72. doi:10.1145/962342.962366

Piaget, J. (1972). *To understand is to invent.* New York: The Viking Press, Inc.

Polson, P. G., & Lewis, C. H. (1990). Theory-based design for easily learned interfaces. *Human-Computer Interaction, 5*(2/3), 191–220. doi:10.1207/s15327051hci0502&3_3

Rieman, J. (1996). A field study of exploratory learning strategies. *ACM Transactions on Computer-Human Interaction, 3*(3), 189–218. doi:10.1145/234526.234527

Shneiderman, B. (1998). *Designing the user interface: Strategies for effective human-computer-interaction* (3rd ed.). New York: Addison Wesley Longman.

Solingen, van. R., & Berghout, E. (1999). *The Goal/Question/Metric Method: A practical guide for quality improvement of software development.* London: McGraw-Hill.

Twidale, M. B., & Nichols, D. M. (2004). *Usability discussions in open source development (Tech. Rep.)*. Hamilton, New Zealand: University of Waikato.

van Oostendorp, H., & Walbeehm, B. J. (1995). Towards modeling exploratory learning in the context of direct manipulation interfaces. *Interacting with Computers*, 7(1), 3–24. doi:10.1016/0953-5438(95)90817-5

van Welie, M., & van der Veer, G. C. (2003). *Pattern languages in interaction design: Structure and organization*. Paper presented at the Ninth IFIP TC13 International Conference on Human-Computer Interaction.

Wiedenbeck, S., & Zila, P. L. (1997). Hands-on practice in learning to use software: A comparison of exercise, exploration, and combined formats. *ACM Transactions on Computer-Human Interaction*, 4(2), 169–196. doi:10.1145/254945.254967

Zhang, Z., Basili, V., & Shneiderman, B. (1999). Perspective-based usability inspection: An empirical validation of efficacy. *Empirical Software Engineering*, 4(1), 43–69. doi:10.1023/A:1009803214692

Zhao, L., & Deek, F. P. (2005). *Improving open source software usability*. Paper presented at the 2005 Americas Conference on Information Systems.

Zhao, L., & Elbaum, S. (2003). Software quality under the open source model. *Journal of Systems and Software*, 66(1), 65–75.

Chapter 14

Motivation of Open Source Developers:
Do License Type and Status Hierarchy Matter?

Mark R. Allyn
Montclair State University, USA

Ram B. Misra
Montclair State University, USA

ABSTRACT

The motivational drivers of open source software developers have been researched by various investigators since about 2000. This work shows that developers are motivated by different extrinsic and intrinsic drivers, among them community aspirations, reciprocity and fairness, creative impulses, and monetary and career ambitions. There has been some work done in studying whether the profile of developer motivations is constant across open source projects or is sensitive to project organizational design. Among the many factors that could influence the mix of motives of OS developers is the license under which the work is performed. Licenses range in openness between those such as the GNU GPL that severely restrict the freedom of developers to mingle their OS code with proprietary code to those such as BSD licenses which allow programmers much greater latitude in integrating open source code with proprietary code. In addition to formal rules, meritocracies emerge to reward effort and performance, and also to direct, coordinate, and control other participants. The authors discuss these variables and how they may be related to motivations.

DOI: 10.4018/978-1-60960-513-1.ch014

INTRODUCTION

Open source software projects have become ubiquitous. Sourceforge.net open currently hosts more than 200,000 projects, from small to large. In the open source environment, many programmers work without direct monetary compensation and yet they create high quality products that result from their willingness to share their knowledge (code and algorithms) with other programmers. Setting aside the problem of how their efforts are directed and coordinated, these open source projects present a fascinating instance of knowledge sharing without compensation and with only limited safeguards on exploitation by renegades who can hijack the code for their own ends. Sharing knowledge and code is costly for the contributor, both in terms of current effort and foregone opportunities. What is the reward?

INCENTIVE SYSTEMS

Beginning with Hars and Ou (2002), many investigators have asked this question and proposed various answers supported by differing amounts of empirical evidence. The answers have fallen into two broad categories, and it appears from the evidence that no single driver is the impetus for contributing, but a mix of motives is present in all projects that have been studied. In an important survey, Krishnamurthy (2006) summarizes the major threads of the panoply of motivators, and makes the important observation that the empirical evidence indicates that both extrinsic and intrinsic motives can coexist in an OS context.

A. Extrinsic Motivation

Lerner and Tirole (2000) group extrinsic motivations into two clusters, immediate payoff and delayed payoff. The *immediate* payoffs may come simply because the code must be written to solve an existing problem. The *delayed* reward payoffs derive from ego gratification, applause from an appreciative and sophisticated audience, or career incentives. Career concerns stem from future anticipated job opportunities.

As distinct from penalties arising from infringing licenses, there are norms that punish those who defect from (for example, "forking") the community and rules that determine status and benefits for making substantial contributions to the product. One norm that is mentioned often is "generalized reciprocity", the willingness to share with no expectation of immediate benefits. Sharing widely and freely what one knows can be a powerful signaling device that shows others, in particular employers, one's level of competence in a domain in which it may be difficult and costly for the employer to discern skill levels.

Hann, Roberts, Slaughter, and Fielding (2002) show that employer compensation is linked with rank in an OS project, but contributions to the project are not correlated with pay. As noted by these authors, leaders provide valuable services to the project in terms of "vision", architecture decisions, and enforcing the rules of project. Thus, a hierarchy rather naturally develops in these projects if they are to sustain themselves and higher employer pay is a compensation for the leadership behaviors of the leaders.

It is a common illusion (see, for instance, Benkler, 2002) that open communities are flat, decentralized "full mesh" peer-to-peer networks ("bazaars", as Raymond tells it). In fact, there is strong evidence that a substantial and powerful hierarchy emerges, typically starting with a founder such as Linus Torvalds (1999), who controls the final release of each point version of the Linux program. In addition to the founder, additional bureaucratic levels ("user", or "bug fixer", "programmers", administrators, (Lattemann & Stieglitz, 2005) appear in mature open source environments. In one of the few social sciences investigations, Stewart (2005) examined an open source community of about 5000 programmers and found a very distinct four-level status hierarchy.

Leadership is vital to the survival of an open software environment (Lerner & Tirole, 2000). The leader is responsible for providing what Lerner & Tirole call "vision", do the job of dicing the project into modules, attract other programmers, prevent fragmentation ("forking") of the project into renegade camps. Hierarchy in an OS project provides this leadership.

Open systems projects employ self-selection as the method of assigning tasks to workers. On the basis of the information about a particular module a worker makes voluntary contributions to the module. However, although individual programmers make decisions about which tasks to undertake, the hierarchy determines which "patches" will be included in the working version of the code.

There are many ways programmers can profit directly (Koenig, 2004; Watson et al., 2008) from creating an open source project or contributing to one. Some firms and individuals collect revenue through complementary services such as consulting, selling subscriptions for maintenance and upgrades, hosting applications, and so forth. Firms that have commercialized open source projects tend to hire those developers who have worked on the code and know the software (Watson et al., 2005). Besides compensation for ancillary services there are at least two other mechanisms, dual licensing and Dynamic Link Library techniques that have been used extensively for packaging OS licensed software with proprietary code. OS projects are widely commercialized even though the OS code per se cannot be modified without making modifications public goods.

B. Intrinsic Motivation

In addition to extrinsic motives, intrinsic motives are also at work in open source contributors. In a very thorough study of open source motivators, Ghosh et al. (2002) found evidence that the most frequently mentioned motivation for joining open source communities was learn and develop new skills without much mentioning of monetary and career aspirations. Lakhani and Wolf (2005) found that the level of effort on an open source project was related more strongly to the perceived level of creativity in the project than to financial payoffs or the feeling of obligation to help others. In another study, Lakhani and von Hippel (2003) report that 28 percent of their respondents indicated that posting answers to questions from Apache users was fun. Most importantly, and supporting the view that generalized reciprocity is an active norm in these communities, Lakhani and von Hippel (2002) report that about half of their respondents say they help other users because they have been previously helped. There is, in other words, evidence of a social conscience that doles out internal praise for doing good deeds to one's fellows. These findings are bolstered by Constant et al. (1996) who, using a different taxonomy from Lakhani and von Hippel, find that in their sample 16% reported that they helped users because they "enjoy helping others" and 12% say that they "expect others to help me, so it's only fair to help them". We treat the reciprocity motive as an intrinsic motivation since the rewards are self-administered.

Some programmers appear to be driven by moral antipathy towards proprietary software. The moral conviction that code should be readily exchanged and modifiable appears to be an important motivator at least for some. This ideology is the core of the GNU GPU and the Free Software Foundation. Presumably, when one creates code and liberally exchanges it with others one seeks to promote a moral code. We consider that the reward for supporting a moral code by one's actions is self-administered. Therefore, we consider this ideology as an intrinsic motivation.

PROPERTY RIGHTS

Property rights rules and their enforcement and incentives for contributing patches complement the purely technical features and reward contributors for their effort. Siobhan O'Mahony (2003) has discussed the social and legal mechanisms that protect the community property created by open source developers.

Licenses are the fundamental legal safeguard that protects the code as a public good and limits, but does not prevent completely, the use of open source code for commercial purposes. Developers are free to choose whatever kind of license, including none at all, under which to protect the code. Intellectual property rights are typically defined by some version of the Open Software Development license. This appears to be a variant of the original "copyleft" agreement associated with the GNU project at MIT. In general, an OSD license defends the identity of the originator of the particular code contained in the overall product and guarantees widespread distribution of the source code.

There are many different licenses that fall within the OSD definition. Lerner and Tirole (2000, 2002) identified the openness of the licenses as an important dimension on which the licenses differ. At one extreme is the GNU GPL and LGPL that are most open while at the other pole are licenses like BSD that are much more permissive. Two determinants of permissiveness are:

1. All derivatives of the source code are subject to the same license, and
2. Open and closed (proprietary) source software is not mixed in a new distribution of the code.

Because of item 1, any changes to the code (modifications) must be made publicly available. For this reason it would appear as though commercial opportunities would be drastically curtailed. This has not, however, been the case. Besides offering consulting services, developers also sell applications built around OS licensed code. These applications take advantage of porosity in the interpretation of item 2. What exactly constitutes mixing code, and what counts as a modification? If the developer uses a DLL available in an OS licensed library and invokes the executable at runtime via a call from a proprietary application, has the DLL been modified? Besides this approach, the method of dual licensing (see Valmaki (2003), for a discussion of several real cases) has been used. In this case, two versions, one OS licensed and the other proprietary, that allows protection from any lawsuits arising out of any potential infringement of OS licenses, are offered to users. This is legally permissible provided the developer retains the copyright.

MySQL and other projects that have been commercialized have shown that it is feasible to exploit OS code and extract considerable financial gain. Thus, it is by no means the case that open licenses like the various versions of the GPL appeal only to hobbyists, amateurs, and lovers of beautiful code. As Marc Fleury, a JBOSS founder, has stated (January 30, 2008):

As a general rule of thumb, reciprocal licenses (GPL) help the developer make a living, academic licenses (BSD) help the competing vendor.

RESEARCH PROBLEM

Investigators have identified a variety of extrinsic and intrinsic motivations exhibited by open source programmers. Not studied by any other researcher until now is how these motivations are modulated by the nature of the license governing the project. More specifically, does the types and mix of motivations (both extrinsic and intrinsic) correlate with the degree of openness of the license selected for OS development?

Licenses that are most open make it more difficult (ex. GPL) for individual programmers to convert the community's product into private financial gain. However, at the other extreme, less open licenses (BSD) make it much easier for others to convert the code to their own private gains. Open licenses become safe havens for entrepreneurs who desire protection from competitors. In addition, this feature (openness) could enhance some other extrinsic rewards. Since there is less potential for cheating to occur (and higher confidence that that one's code will not be misused for private gains by others), higher quality code is more likely to be shared. Because the code is higher quality the usefulness of the code for signaling reputation to employers is likely to go up and those motivated by this desire would more frequently become seriously involved. Furthermore, since the level of trust is higher, those seeking the joys of reciprocity are more likely to have more opportunities to enjoy helping others rather than being disappointed by bad behavior. With respect to intrinsic rewards, higher quality code might be more aesthetically pleasing and those developers inspired by beauty might be more interested in participating.

As license openness diminishes, it becomes easier for code to be hijacked for commercial gain (Fleury, 2008). This will reduce the quality of the contributed code because developers will not want others to "cash in" on their efforts. Because the code base quality is lower, it will not attract the best programmers and will at the same time be a less reliable indicator of their competence level. Because the signaling of competence becomes noisier, employers will not pay attention to rank in the community and (rank linked) compensation will decline. On the other hand, it is also much easier to commercialize the code. This should enhance the strength of extrinsic rewards.

Status hierarchies emerge in successful open source projects. These appear to be based primarily on technical competence. Hierarchies serve several functions. First, they are a reward system. To rise in the hierarchy is to gain recognition as a superior developer and enjoy the benefits of social approval. Increased rank enables the second reward to emerge. With higher status comes the authority to determine courses of action. Others will pay more attention to your opinions and suggestions. Your plans are more likely to be accepted as the correct choice. More authority gives access to the means of disciplining other developers.

Access to enforcement rules is important because rules direct the behavior of other contributors and therefore coordinate the work of the community. We suppose that motives are highly modulated by the position in the hierarchy of developers. It seems reasonable, for example, to hypothesize that at the lowest level of the hierarchy intrinsic motives relating to the joy of creating code are more salient than at higher levels. Over time, as one achieves greater rank, increases in signaling value are likely to diminish. At higher levels of the hierarchy, career and reputation motives may be more prominent than pecuniary gain. All of these motives are extrinsic.

Finally, we will investigate the interaction of license type and hierarchical position on the level of motivation types. What this means is that the salience of a particular type of motive depends upon both the openness of the license and also on the programmer's level in the hierarchy.

HYPOTHESES

We hypothesize that:

H1: *(License openness and Motivations) As licenses become more open, the strengths of both extrinsic and intrinsic motivations increase.*

Rationale: Open licenses make it easier to reap pecuniary gains for programmers, but less open licenses make it much easier for commercial companies to co-opt the economic benefits programmers might otherwise capture. Therefore, we expect to observe greater levels of extrinsic motivation in projects with open licenses. Since extrinsic rewards increase under a more open license, the overall quality of the code should increase too. The increased code quality should increase the pleasure of writing code for its own sake. Higher quality code in open projects is likely to provide more intrinsic motivation. We expect therefore that both types of motivation will increase when projects are governed by more open licenses.

H2: *(Developer status and motivations) As developer status increases, the strength of both extrinsic and intrinsic motivations will increase.*

Rationale: The people who are driven by intrinsic motivations will tend to continue making beautiful and useful contribution to the project. The evidence shows that there is no tradeoff between extrinsic and intrinsic motives and so talented programmers who enjoy coding do not have to sacrifice this motive. Moreover, as programmers' skills become more widely known and more refined they will receive gratifying social approval from other members of the project team and code users.

Higher status developers are more likely to have the opportunity to convert their knowledge of the project into economic gains. Their reputation becomes an instrument by which employment opportunities outside the immediate scope of the project become available. This leads inexorably to higher compensation. The extrinsic benefits arising from working on high-quality code increase as well because higher quality code provides better signals to employers. In addition, because they have more influence on project decisions they can direct the project into more commercially rewarding activities. They also become bridges between the project and other projects with commercial potential.

H3: *License openness x status interaction and motivations - There might be a tradeoff between these two governance mechanisms in determining the frequency (or strength) of developer motivation.*

Rationale: Open licenses will require less hierarchy to protect property rights; conversely, open source projects with strong hierarchies and less open licenses can also protect property rights. This means that it becomes more difficult to extract

private gains when either the hierarchy is strong or the license is open.

PREVIOUS RESEARCH

Although all the variables we have identified have received at least some attention in the literature, to the best of our knowledge, no published work has studied the combined effect of status and license openness on motivations. The study which comes closest to ours is by Shah (2006). This study investigated developer motivations and development activity in two different communities: one governed by an open license (unidentified type) and the other having a corporate sponsor ("gated community") that owned all rights to the code. This study developed a number of interesting hypotheses, but did not involve measuring status or measuring motivations. Moreover, it confounds license types with corporate sponsorship inasmuch as the open source developers sampled were working under some form of open source license while the sponsored owned all the rights to the code in the gated community. Among the more interesting findings of the Stewart et al. (2006) study were that developers contributing to the gated community reported being driven primarily by the need of the developed software while the open source developers more frequently reported "fun" as their motivator.

VARIABLES AND MEASURES

We developed a survey questionnaire that contains measures of motivations and status that are based on previous studies of open source developers, for example, Lakhani and Wolf (2005). We used nearly verbatim the items used by predecessors in an effort to bolster validity and also to ensure the comprehensiveness of our motivation inventory. Appendix 1 presents a listing of the specific wording of these items.

From our survey data we were able to derive a respondent's own self-assessed status and also whether or not they were able to commit patches to the codebase.

In addition to the respondent motivation variables and status assessments, we also extracted from Sourceforge the following information:

1. License type. Licenses vary in openness. We used the 8-point ordinal scale proposed by Lin et al. (2005), but unlike these writers we assigned lower scale values to more open (GNU GPL) licenses and higher values to less open licenses (BSD).
2. Hierarchy. We extracted the ratio of developers to administrators and used this as an objective measure of hierarchy. This supplemented our knowledge of hierarchy based on self-reports described above.

We posted the survey on the internet and invited developers from a number of Sourceforge projects to participate. Our invitation was emailed to individual users and promised a summary of results to those who participated. More than 1400 invitations were emailed to the sample firms. Respondents were asked to name their OS project in the survey and through this item we were able to link the survey results to the project in the Sourceforge database, except for 5 cases. We received 137 responses from 87 projects. A total of 166 projects were included in the sample so the project response rate was about 52%. However, on an individual respondent basis the rate was slightly less than 10%.

DATA AND ANALYSIS

Aside from demographic data, most of the items in the survey were 7 point Likert-scale type statements for which the respondent indicated the extent to which they agreed or disagreed with the item or the degree of importance they gave to the item.

In several items, for example, the demographic items, the respondent merely picked the appropriate category. A few items, such as their estimates of the number of patches they had contributed, were simply handled as magnitude estimates and coded as such.

Our statistical treatment of these subjective data follows a conventional approach. First we conducted a factor analysis of the items. This was done using conventional principle components analysis followed by Varimax rotation to assist in identifying the factors. For those items with loadings of more than 0.5 we constructed simple additive scales. We then checked the internal validity of the resulting scales and if coefficient alpha was acceptable (generally 0.7 or above), the scale was deemed sufficiently reliable for analytic purposes.

a. Demographic Characteristics of the Sample

The sample profile is what one might expect based on previous findings. Full-time employees are two-thirds of the sample, but students are the next most frequently reported group. The educational achievements of the sample are impressive. About thirty percent respondents have a master's degree; sixty percent have a college or master's degree. An additional eight percent have Ph. D.'s. Close to 60 percent received their degree in computer science and another 20 percent received an engineering degree. Interestingly, one category, social science, was not mentioned even once as the degree field. The sample also tends to be young, more than forty percent reporting that they are in the age range of twenty-five to thirty-five years old. A quarter of the sample is in the fifteen to twenty-five year group, so altogether about 60 percent were between 15 and 35 years old.

Probably the most striking observation is the total lack of female OS participation. This reflects the fact that women are significantly under-represented in the engineering field, especially

Table 1. Participant social status

	Component	
Survey Item		
	1	2
LISTEN2 [1]	0.857	0.316
IMPLEAD	0.875	0.182
KNOWME	0.235	0.874
PRGMSKIL	0.633	-0.538
TEKCONTR	0.879	-8.69E-02
ORGCONTR	0.732	7.90E-02
Extraction Method: Principal Component Analysis.		
Rotation Method: Varimax with Kaiser Normalization.		

computer science. The absence of women is a matter of conjecture. One possibility is the "after dinner effect". Previous research has indicated that developers do their OS programming during out-of-work hours. Women's family roles in our society call for women when at home to take care of many family duties that husbands are able to avoid. Even women in technical fields are likely to feel that their time at home should be directed towards domestic work, not extensions of their working life. Hence, getting on the Internet to do open source programming during off hours seems likely to attract more men simply because more men are free to participate,

b. Developer Social Status

The research problem called for measuring the developer's status within the project team. Ideally, we would have preferred to gather complete team sociometric data that would have allowed us to identify the team hierarchy with greater certainty. Recognizing that sociometric data would be very hard to obtain for each project, our survey did not ask respondents to rate the status of other developers. As a matter of fact, we averaged only about 1.6 respondents per project. We had to fall back on each developer's own evaluation of his status

within the project plus ratings from other several items as shown in Table 1.

We subjected the items to a factor analysis and found that they loaded on two factors. These two factors account for about 74.1 percent of the variance, of which the first accounts for about 54 percent. Based on the items, it is just the first factor that seems most clearly to contain the status. The item with the highest loading (tekcontr) is "compared to other developers my contributions to technical issues on this project are;") and the second highest loading is on "implead" ("other developers on this project consider you to be one of the most important leaders of the development effort"). The second dimension loads most heavily on just a single item (knowme) which refers to the relative number of other programmers who know the respondent. We decided to capture programmer status using just the first factor. We converted the item scores to a single scale by averaging the individual item scores. A check on internal reliability showed that coefficient alpha for the derived scale was 0.85.

c. Motivations for Contributing

To get to the heart of the research goals required measuring developer motivations. Our tactic to identify these motivations was to factor analyze the items we had collected from previous developer surveys to verify that the factors others had observed were also present in our sample. This proved to be the case as a glance at Table 2 will show.

If one simply selects a solution based on all eigenvalues greater than one, and a principal components analysis, a seven-factor solution accounting for about 67 percent of the variance emerges. But, the last three factors are difficult to interpret and scales constructed from them have very low reliability. Instead, we chose a 5 factor solution that accounted for 57 percent of the variance. It had the advantage, however, of more interpretable dimensions, especially for the third, fourth, and fifth components. Table 2 shows the loadings of each item on the rotated components.

In either the seven or the five factor solutions the first two components were identical. These are clearly associated with instrumental usefulness in gainful employment (Factor 1) and professional status enhancement (Factor 2). We named the first factor "jobmot" and the second factor "repmot". There is evidence for non-instrumental motivators too. These show up in Factor 3. This factor has to do with the joy of problem solving, and especially, intellectual stimulation. Factor 4 included three items that did not appear to be clearly related,

"myspecreq", "goodidea", and "slovlprob". We did not attempt to name this factor and a scale constructed from it had extremely poor reliability (alpha = 0.373). We thus dropped it from further consideration. Factor 5 had loadings on just two items, "empsuprt", and "ansquest". These seemed to have to do mostly with extending help to people, and so we called this motive "helpmot".

As we did for other items, we collapsed the individual items onto a single scale for each factor. We checked the internal reliability of the resulting scales and found coefficient alphas of 0.82, 0.867,

Table 2. Participant motivations

Survey Item	Component				
	1	2	3	4	5
PAYPROJ	0.728	0.115	-0.006	-0.078	0.153
EMPSUPRT	0.409	0.124	-0.069	0.034	0.565
MARKCOMP	0.623	0.001	0.091	-0.019	-0.213
ADVNSKIL	-0.157	0.403	0.238	0.232	0.405
IMPJOBOP	0.237	0.567	0.174	0.130	0.371
GETREP	0.182	0.907	0.089	0.102	-0.017
ENHNCREP	0.152	0.913	0.060	0.076	-0.046
GNPFSTAT	0.291	0.753	0.092	0.029	0.110
OKPAID	0.297	-0.071	0.135	0.307	0.188
IMPRTCOM	0.843	0.171	0.168	0.012	0.150
MYSPCREQ	0.200	0.022	0.169	0.493	0.318
USEONJOB	0.745	0.290	-0.011	0.216	0.008
IMPRTJOB	0.838	0.276	0.067	0.071	0.078
ANSQUEST	0.086	-0.024	0.342	0.282	-0.713
ENJTEKPR	0.016	-0.169	0.543	0.363	-0.076
ENJYREC	0.085	0.353	0.616	0.067	-0.092
SLOLVPRB	0.021	0.105	-0.083	0.631	-0.078
GOODIDEA	-0.057	0.169	0.094	0.596	-0.156
BEAUTFUL	-0.019	0.076	0.502	0.469	0.060
CREATCMP	0.286	0.040	0.651	-0.098	0.069
LOSETIME	-0.042	0.056	0.585	0.105	-0.339
INTLSTIM	0.040	0.180	0.808	-0.006	0.061
Extraction Method: Principal Component Analysis.					
Rotation Method: Varimax with Kaiser Normalization.					

0.696, and -0.712 for scales based on "jobmot", "repmot", "joymot", and "helpmot".

d. Reciprocity Norm

Reciprocity has been mentioned in the literature as a motive for contributing to OS projects. We measured the influence of this norm with four items and it turns out that they loaded on just a single factor that accounts for 51 percent of the variance. Results of the factor analysis are shown in Table 3. The items refer to feeling obliged to answer questions from others ("feeloblg"), helping others who have helped you ("fairhelp"), trusting that others will exert high effort ("hieffrt"), and a belief that every member will do her/his share of the work ("hrshr"). As with other factor analysis results, we converted these four items into just a single scale. Its coefficient alpha is 0.661. As with the previous four scales, we considered this to be a motive for contributing to open source projects.

e. Ideology

Richard Stallman and other leaders in the OS community seem committed to the view that computer code should be freely available to all who wish to use it. In addition, any recipient of code who makes changes is bound by a higher morality (and GPL) to share those changes freely with others. Code should never be proprietary. Our findings indicate that there exists a strong belief that software should be "free" (meaning

"open", not monetarily costless). For instance, 50% of the sample agreed or strongly agreed that the power of large software companies should be limited, and 47 percent agreed or strongly agreed with the statement that software should not be a proprietary asset.

Table 4 shows the results for our three items intended to measure the strength of the belief that software should be open. The three items load on just one factor that accounts for 69 percent of the variance. We therefore added up individual item scores to get an overall ideology score for the free software ethic. The alpha of this scale is 0.77. As have others, we considered motive for contributing to open source projects, and we named this factor "ideolmot".

We asked respondents for the number of hours per week spent on their OS project. It was a point of some interest to determine which of these developers' views on their status, motivations, feelings of social obligation, and ideology were significantly related to the intensity of their work on the projects To make this check we simply regressed the rated hours of work per week for each developer on socstat, the four motivation scales, recipmot, and ideolmot.

The results of this regression showed that the scales for socstat, jobmot, and joymot were all significant predictors of programming hours, and the signs of the regression coefficients were all the same. People who rated their social status higher, their job motivation higher, and the joy they took in open source programming indicated they spent more time in open source programming (r-square

Table 3. Reciprocity norm

Survey Item	Component 1
FEELOBLG	0.761
FAIRHELP	0.75
HIEFFRT	0.705
HERSHR	0.624
Extraction Method: Principal Component Analysis.	

Table 4. Ideology

Survey Item	Component 1
CODEOPEN	0.837
NOTPROP	0.875
LIMPOWR	0.768
Extraction Method: Principal Component Analysis.	

= 0.381; F= 12.027, p<0.01). This finding is consistent with the results from Stewart et al. (2006) and Krishnamurthy's (observation) that intrinsic and extrinsic motives do not compete with each other in determining level of contributions.

Tests of Hypotheses

We undertook this research to determine how license openness and social hierarchy affected programmer motivations. As a byproduct of our Sourceforge data we also have been able to examine whether these two independent factors might also affect open source project outputs and productivity.

We divided our motivation variables into two groups, extrinsic and intrinsic. The extrinsic group contained job motive, reputation motive, and reciprocity motives. We put help motive, ideology motive, and joy motive into the intrinsic set. Initially, we simply did bivariate correlations of the contribution motives with socstat, our measure of the individual's perceived status and licopen, the measure of license openness. We also created an interaction variable, licstat by computing the product of the two component scales.

The bivariate correlations showed that just three of the six motivation variables were correlated at better than a 5-percent alpha level with licopen and socstat. These were job motive, ideology motive, and joy motive. The remainder of the analysis concentrated on the relationship of these three motivation variables to license openness and social status.

For this purpose we used individual multiple regressions of the three independent variables on licopen, socstat, and licstat

H1: *License openness and motivations - As licenses become more open, the strengths of both extrinsic and intrinsic motivations increase. Furthermore, on a relative scale, the increase in extrinsic motivations is higher than the gains in intrinsic motivation. Our data partially support*

this hypothesis. Ideology motives turned out to be positively correlated with the openness of the license, as one would expect. To reiterate, by a open license we mean generally that it is more difficult to modify and use the open source code for one's own purposes without making public the additional code. The most open of the open source licenses is the GNU GPL. Our data showed that those most strongly motivated by a belief that code should not be proprietary turned out to be more associated with projects where more open licenses were in place (p <.001). Ideology motive was the only intrinsic motive to be related to the license openness.

We examined the relationship of license openness and the joy motive ("joymot") and found no significant increase in this variable as license openness declined. Job motives such as the importance of the code to one's employer were significantly (p<.039) related to the openness of the license. Job motives were mentioned more often as the license became more open. However, the other important extrinsic motivator, reputation, was not significantly related to license openness. We found a significant (p<.001) positive correlation between job motives and reputation, but reputation itself proved not to be related to license openness.

H2: *Developer status and motivations - As developer status increases, the strength of intrinsic and extrinsic motivations will increase.*

We found only partial support for the hypothesis. The multiple regressions showed that socstat – the extent to which the respondent rated himself as a high status person – was positively related to joy motivation (an intrinsic variable). The coefficient is significant at p<.003 and positive, meaning that as the self-perceived status of the programmer went up, so too did the joy of programming. However, we did not find any relation between either job motivation or reputation and self-reported social status. In short, the data show that if a developer perceives he or she is higher in status in the project hierarchy he or she will report greater pleasure in doing the work, but no increase in extrinsic motivation.

H3: *License openness x status interaction and motivations -There might be a tradeoff between these two governance mechanisms in determining the frequency (or strength) of developer intrinsic motivation. However, our results show that there was no interaction between social status and license openness in determining the motivation levels.*

SUMMARY AND CONCLUSION

Our investigation began by cataloging previously studied motives and from a list of these we selected items for our questionnaire that covered the gamut of variables implicated by previous researchers. The results of our investigation regarding motives are in complete accord with many others, for example, Lakhani and Wolf (2005), who identified a similar set of intrinsic and extrinsic drivers for participation.

While the literature on developer motives is extensive what has not previously been investigated is whether the motives expressed by developers are shaped by the type of license restrictions governing their projects. We were interested to see if the motives expressed by developers were influenced by the license openness. It was, we supposed, possible that more open licenses would be associated with much stronger extrinsic motivators such as the reputation of the developer or the potential to use the code on the job or in the commercial market. Developers with strong extrinsic motivation would be more concerned to keep their work efforts within the community and not to be exploited by others. In contrast, those programmers who simply enjoy coding for pleasure might well be more indifferent as to the ways it might be exploited by others.

This research was a snapshot study of a cross-section of current OS projects. Because it is a snapshot it cannot reveal the dynamics of the evolving social structure of the projects. There is little question that the social structure and norms of these project teams change in interesting ways over time. It is possible that the license effects have an initial impact on developer motivations but that this impact changes as the group evolves, perhaps diminishing over time. One might also conjecture the converse: that the license effects become more salient as the project matures and becomes more susceptible to "hijacking". Unfortunately, we do not have the ability in our snapshot to isolate these changes.

Our data partially support this hypothesis. Of the motives we measured, the ideology motive was found to be clearly related to license openness. The more open the license, the more the programmers indicated that they believed code should not be proprietary. Most respondents in our study indicated they were aware of the nature of the license before participating in their projects. Hence, it is hardly surprising that those with strong feelings about keeping code open would select projects with most open license. There was no indication that other intrinsic or extrinsic motives were differentially related to the openness of the license. In addition, we found that the motive to improve one's employment circumstances also was positively related to the openness of the license. Reputation, our other major extrinsic motive, was not found to be significantly related to the license nor was the joy of coding. All in all, we found partial support for H1.

A second novel feature of our work was its attempt to see whether social status might affect developer motivations. We must admit that our measure of social status is rather unsatisfactory. It is based on a self-assessment of the worker's own status. The limitation is clear: aside from the questions of whether the self-assessment is accurate, the person reporting the status is also the person reporting on motivation. The measure is likely to be inflated compared to how others on the team might evaluate the developer's status. A much better measure of status would be derived from a social network analysis of the extent to which a project's developers had evolved a status hierarchy. Unfortunately, we had no such measure. Notwithstanding the limitation of our status measure, our data contradict any notion that higher status suppresses the joy of coding.

We were left with no choice but to use the developers' self-assessments instead as proxies for a status hierarchy. We hypothesized those intrinsic motives such as the joy of programming would increase as would extrinsic motives. As expected, we found that higher self-perceived status was positively related to the pleasure of programming. However, we found no relationship between extrinsic motives and self-perceived social status. We may not have observed the effects of status on job motivation and reputation because of the flawed nature of the measure and this possibility should be explored in a careful study of communication patterns in open source projects.

The data did allow us to check on the social status measurement with an independent, objective measure of status. We derived a variable based on the ratio of administrators to developers. Presumably, this is a crude measure of social hierarchy in a project. When we did correlations of this measure with the motivation variables, however, there were no significant relationships.

What about the dynamics of the social hierarchy as a mechanism of governing the OS community acting as a substitute for a formal open license? In other words, is there an interaction between license openness and social hierarchy? We supposed that open source license rules are enforced to varying degrees by a social hierarchy within a given open source project. The hierarchy controls a system of sanctions which determine who may contribute and how participants are to be dealt with in the event they transgress the license or informal protocols that the community has developed. In our view, it was possible that there might be a tradeoff between social authority and license openness.

We did not, however, find evidence of a tradeoff. Notwithstanding the faulty measure of hierarchy, as discussed above, we conclude tentatively that no interactions between perceived hierarchy and license openness exist.

The major dependent variable we consider here is the mix of motives, intrinsic and extrinsic, that are reported by developers as a function of the degree of the openness of the formal license and the position of the developer in the status hierarchy. We implemented a study of these variables using data available from the Sourceforge hosting site. Sourceforge is especially attractive because they capture activity data and user interest data in accurate measures.

REFERENCES

Benkler, Y. (2002). Coase's Penguin, or, Linux and the Nature of the Firm. *The Yale Law Journal, 3*, 112.

Bitzer, J., Schrettl, W., & Schroder, P. (2004.) *Intrinsic Motivation in Open Source Software Development*. Diskussionsbeitrage des Fachbereichs Wirtschaftswissenschafrt der freien Universitat Berlin (ISBN 3-935058-89-6).

Constant, D., Sproull, L., & Kiesler, S. (1996). The Kindness of Strangers: The Usefulness of Electronic Weak Ties for Technical Advice. *Organization Science, 7*, 119–135. doi:10.1287/orsc.7.2.119

Fitzgerald, B. (2006). The Transformation of Open Source Software. *Management Information Systems Quarterly, 30*(3), 587–598.

Ghosh, R. A., Glott, R., Krieger, B., & Robles, G. (2002). *Survey of Developers, Free/Libre and Open Source Software: Survey and* Study (FLOSS Final Report). Maastricht, The Netherlands: University of Maastricht, International Institute of Infonomics. Retrieved from http://www.infonomics.nl/FLOSS/report/Final4.pdf

Hars, A., & Ou, S. (2002). Working for Free? Motivations of Participating in open source projects. *International Journal of E-Commerce, 42*(3), 25–39.

Koenig, J. (2004, March 14). Seven Open Source Business Strategies for Competitive Advantage. *IT Manager's Journal*. Retrieved from http://management.itmanagersjournal.com/article.pl?sid=04/05/10/2052216&tid=85

Krishnamurthy, S. (2006). On the Intrinsic and Extrinsic Motivation of Free/Libre/Open Source (FLOSS) Developers. *Knowledge, Technology, &. Policy, 18*(4), 17–39.

Lakhani, K. R., & von Hippel, E. (2001). How Open Source Software Works: Free user-to-user assistance. *Research Policy, 32*, 923–943. doi:10.1016/S0048-7333(02)00095-1

Lakhani, K. R., & Wolf, R. G. (2005). Why Hackers Do What They Do: Understanding Motivation and Effort in Free/Open Source Software Projects. In Feller, J., Fitzgerald, B., Hissam, S., & Lakhani, K. R. (Eds.), *Perspectives on Free and Open Source Software*. Cambridge, MA: MIT Press.

Lattemann, C., & Stieglitz, S. (2005). Framework for Governance in Open Source Communities. In *Proceedings of the 38ᵗʰ Hawaii International Conference on Systems Sciences* (pp. 1-11). Washington, DC: IEEE.

Lerner, J., & Tirole, J. (2000). *The Simple Economics of Open Source* (Working Paper 7600). The National Bureau of Economic Research, Inc.

Lerner, J., & Tirole, J. (2002). *The Scope of Open Source Licensing* (Working Paper). Boston, MA: Harvard Business School.

Lin, Y.-H., Ko, T.-M., Tyung-Ruey, C., & Lin, K.-J. (2005). Open Source Licenses and the Creative Commons Framework: License Selection and Comparison. *Journal of Information Science and Engineering, 22*, 1–17.

Moon, J. Y., & Sproull, L. (2000). The Essence of Distributed Work: The Case of the Linux Kernel. *First Monday, 5*, 11.

O'Mahony, S. (2003). Guarding the commons: how community managed software projects protect their work. *Research Policy, 32*, 1179–1198. doi:10.1016/S0048-7333(03)00048-9

Raymond, E. S. (1998). The Cathedral and The Bazaar. *First Monday, 3*(3).

Roberts, J. A., Hann Il-H., & Slaughter, S. A. (2006). Understanding the Motivations, Participation, and Performance of Open Source Software Developers: A Longitudinal Study of the Apache Projects. *Management Science, 52*(7), 984–999. doi:10.1287/mnsc.1060.0554

Schweik, C. M., & Semenov, A. (2003). The Institutional Design of Open Source Programming: Implications for Addressing Complex Public Policy and Management Problems. *First Monday, 8*, 1.

Shah, S. K. (2006). Motivation, Governance, and the Viability of Hybrid Forms in Open Source Software Development. *Management Science, 52*(7), 100–1014. doi:10.1287/mnsc.1060.0553

Stewart, D. (2005). Social Status in an Open-Source Community. *American Sociological Review, 70*(5), 823–842. doi:10.1177/000312240507000505

Stewart, K., Ammeter, A. P., & Maruping, L. (2006). Impacts of License Choice and Organizational Sponsorship on User Interest and Development Activity in Open Source Software Projects. *Information Systems Research, 17*(2), 126–144. doi:10.1287/isre.1060.0082

Stewart, K., & Gosain, S. (2006). The Impact of Ideology on Effectiveness in Open Source Software Development Teams. *Management Information Systems Quarterly, 30*(2), 291–314.

Torvalds, L. (1999). *Interview with Linus Torvalds: What Motivates Free Software Developers*? Retrieved from http://www.firstmonday.dk/issues3_3/torvalds/index.html

Valimaki, M. (2003, January). Dual Licensing in Open Source Software Industry. *Systemes d'Information et Management*.

Watson, R. T., Boudreau, M.-C., York, P. T., Greiner, M. E., & Wynn, D. (2008). The Business of Open Source. *Communications of the ACM*, *51*(4), 41–46. doi:10.1145/1330311.1330321

Watson, R. T., Wynn, D., & Boudreau, M.-C. (2005). JBOSS: The Evolution of Professional Open Source Software. *MIS Quarterly Executive*, *4*(3), 329–341.

Wenger, E. C., & Snyder, W. M. (2000, January-February). Communities of Practice: The Organizational Frontier. *Harvard Business Review*, 139–14.

ENDNOTE

[1] For a complete listing of all items, please see Appendix 1.

APPENDIX 1

Social status:

Know Me Among the persons who are involved in this project how well known you?

Listen2 When there are technical issues that need resolving in this project, how much weight does your opinion carry with other developers?

Implead Other developers in this project consider you to be one of the most important leaders of the development effort.

Prgmskil Compared to other developers in this project I consider my programming skills as...

Tekcontr Compared to other developers my contributions to technical issues on this project (future development, quality of code) are:

Orgcontr Compared to other developers on this project my contributions to organizational issues (e.e. coordination, mailing lists) are:

Individual motivations:

Payproj If you are full- or part-tune employed, is part of yur pay from this job compensation for working on this project?

Empsupport Some companies support open source projects financially or with other contributions in addition to allowing employees to contribute their time. Other companies encourage employees to work on open source projects but do not contribute any other resources. How does your employer support this project, if at all?

Markcomp Have you received any market compensation by commercializing some portion (including all) of this project's code?

Advnskil Advancing my skills at software development is ___ to me.

Impjobop Improving my job opportunities due to experience gained in open source projects is ____ to me.

Getrep I am working on this open source project to get a reputation in OS/FS community.

Enhncrep I am working on this open source project to ENHANCE my reputation in the F/OSS community.

Gnpfstat I am working on this open source project to enhance my professional status in general.

Okpaid I think it is OK if people get paid for working on this open source project.

Imprtcom The problem we are working on in this OS project is important to my company.

Myspcreq Being able to modify this open source product to meet my specific requirements is ____ to me.

Useonjob I will use (or am using) this open source product I helped develop in my regular job.

Imprtjob Participating in this open source project has been an important part of my job.

Ansquest I answer questions about this project in user forums and mailing lists for fun.

Enjtekpr I enjoy solving technical problems that come up in this project.

Enjyrec I enjoy earning recognition as a developer in this project.

Solvprob I got involved in this open source project to solve a problem that could not be solved by proprietary software.

Goodidea I got involved in this project to get help in realizing a good idea for a software program.

Beautiful I got involved in this project to write beautiful and aesthetically pleasing programs.

Createmp Compared to your most creative endeavor, how creative is this project?

Losetime How likely are you to lose track of time when programming on this project?

Intlstim Code for this project is intellectually stimulating to write.

Reciprocity:

Feeloblg Others have helped me in the past and I feel an obligation to reciprocate by answering mailing list and forum questions.

Fairhelp I expect others to help me on this project so it's only fair to help them.

Hieffrt I trust that the other developers put high effort in the development of this project.

Hershr Every member of our project team does her/his share of the work.

Ideology:

Notprop I think that software should not be a proprietary asset.

Limpowr I believe in limiting the power of large software companies.

Codeopen I believe that source code should generally be open.

Compilation of References

Adams, P., Capiluppi, A., & de Groot, A. Detecting agility of Free Software projects through developer engagement. In Proceedings of the 4th International Conference on Open Source Systems, 2008.

Agerfalk, P., & Fitzgerald, B. (2008). Outsourcing to an Unknown Workforce: Exploring Opensourcing as a Global Sourcing Strategy. *Management Information Systems Quarterly, 32*(3), 385–410.

Ajzen, I. (1985). From Intentions to Actions: A Theory of Planned Behavior. In Kuhl, J., & Beckmann, J. (Eds.), *Action Control: From Cognition to Behavior* (pp. 11–39). New York, NY: Springer.

Algorithms and Theory of Computation Handbook. CRC Press LLC, 1999, "Levenshtein distance", in Dictionary of Algorithms and Data Structures [online], Paul E. Black, ed., U.S. National Institute of Standards and Technology. 11 June 2007. (Accessed 15 June 2007) Available from: http://www.nist.gov/dads/HTML/Levenshtein.html

Amabile, T. M. (1988). A model of creativity and innovation in organizations. *Research in Organizational Behavior, 10*, 123–167.

Amor, J. J., Robles, G., & González-Barahona, J. M. (2006). Discriminating development activities in versioning systems: A case study. In *Proceedings PROMISE 2006: 2nd. International Workshop on Predictor Models*.

Analysis of the linux kernel. (2004). Research report. (Coverity Incorporated)

Anderson, N., De Dreu, C., & Nijstad, B. A. (2004). The routinization of innovation research: A constructively critical review of the state-of-the-science. *Journal of Organizational Behavior, 25*, 147–173. doi:10.1002/job.236

Antoniades, I., Samoladas, I., Stamelos, I., Angelis, L., & Bleris, G. L. (2005). Dynamical simulation models of the open source development process. In Koch, S. (Ed.), *Free/open source software development* (pp. 174–202). Hershey, PA: Idea Group, Incorporated.

Antoniades, I. P., Samoladas, I., Stamelos, I., Angelis, L., & G. L. Bleris G. L. (2003b). Dynamical simulation models of the Open Source Development process», in Free/Open Source Software Development, Idea Group Inc., PA, USA (2003), 174-202.

Antoniades, I. P., Stamelos, I., Aggelis, L., & Bleris G.L. (2003a). A Novel Simulation Model for the Development Process of Open Source Software Projects. *International Journal of Software Process: Improvement and Practise (SPIP)*, special issue on Software Process simulation and modeling, 7, 3-4, (2003), 173-188.

Antwerp, M. V., & Madey, G. (2008). Advances in the sourceforge research data archive. In *WoPDaSD*.

Arundel, A. (2001). Patents in the Knowledge-Based Economy. *Beleidstudies Technology Economie, 37*, 67–88.

Atkins, D. L., Ball, T., Graves, T. L., & Mockus, A. (2002). Using version control data to evaluate the impact of software tools: A case study of the version editor. *IEEE Transactions on Software Engineering, 28*(7), 625–637. doi:10.1109/TSE.2002.1019478

Axelrod, R. (1984). *The evolution of cooperation.* New York: Basic Books.

Azoulay, P. (2004). Capturing Knowledge within and across firm boundaries: Evidence from clinical development. *The American Economic Review, 94*(5), 1591–1612. doi:10.1257/0002828043052259

Babbie, E. (2005). *The basics of social research.* Stamford, CT: Thomson Wadsworth.

Baldwin, C., & Clark, K. (2006). The architecture of participation: Does code architecture mitigate free riding in the open source development model? *Management Science, 52*(7), 1116–1127. doi:10.1287/mnsc.1060.0546

Balkundi, P., & Harrison, D. (2006). Ties, leaders, and time in teams: Strong inference about network structure's effects on team viability and performance. *Academy of Management Journal, 49*(1), 49–68.

Basili, V., & Weiss, D. (1984). A Methodology for collecting valid software engineering data. *IEEE Transactions on Software Engineering, 10*(6), 728–738. doi:10.1109/TSE.1984.5010301

Batini, C., Lenzerini, M., & Navathe, S. (1986). A comparative analysis of methodologies for database schema integration. *ACM Computing Surveys, 18*(4), 323–364. doi:10.1145/27633.27634

Bauer, A., & Pizka, M. (2003). The contribution of free software to software evolution. In *Proceedings of the International Workshop on Principles of Software Evolution (IWPSE)*, Helsinki, Finland. IEEE Computer Society.

Beck, K. Extreme Programming Explained: Embrace Change. Addison-Wesley Professional, October 1999. A. Capiluppi and M. Michlmayr. From the cathedral to the bazaar: An empirical study of the lifecycle of volunteer community projects. In J. Feller, B. Fitzger- ald, W. Scacchi, and A. Silitti, editors, Open Source Development, Adoption and Innovation, pages 31–44. International Federation for Information Processing, Springer, 2007.

Benkler, Y. (2006). *The wealth of networks: How social production transforms markets and freedom.* New Haven, CT: Yale University Press.

Benkler, Y. (2002). Coase's Penguin, or, Linux and the Nature of the Firm. *The Yale Law Journal, 3*, 112.

Bessen, J. (2006). Open Source Software: Free Provision of Complex Public Goods. In Bitzer, J., & Schraeder, P. J. H. (Eds.), *The Economics of Open Source Software Development.* Elsevier B. V. doi:10.1016/B978-044452769-1/50003-2

Bessen, J. (2002). What good is free software? In Hahn, R. W. (Ed.), *Government policy toward open source software* (pp. 12–33). Washington, DC: Brookings Institution Press.

Bettenburg, N., Premraj, R., Zimmermann, T., & Kim, S. (2008). Extracting structural information from bug reports. In *MSR '08: Proceedings of the 2005 Working Conference on Mining software repositories.*

Bitton, D., & David, J. (1983, June). DeWitt, Duplicate record elimination in large data files [TODS]. *ACM Transactions on Database Systems, 8*(2), 255–265. doi:10.1145/319983.319987

Bitzer, J., & Schröder, P. J. (2005, July). Bug-fixing and code-writing: The private provision of open source software. *Information Economics and Policy, 17*(3), 389–406. doi:10.1016/j.infoecopol.2005.01.001

Bitzer, J., & Schröder, P. J. H. (Eds.). (2006). *The Economics of Open Source Software Development.* Elsevier Science Publishers.

Bitzer, J., Schrettl, W., & Schroder, P. (2004.) *Intrinsic Motivation in Open Source Software Development.* Diskussionsbeitrage des Fachbereichs Wirtschaftswissenschafrt der freien Universitat Berlin (ISBN 3-935058-89-6).

Bonaccorsi, A., Giannangeli, S., & Rossi, C. (2006). Entry strategies under competing standards: Hybrid business models in the open source software industry. *Management Science, 52*(7), 1085–1098. doi:10.1287/mnsc.1060.0547

Bonaccorsi, A., & Rossi, C. (2003). Why Open Source software can succeed. *Research Policy, 32*(7), 1243–1258.

Bonaccorsi, A., Lorenzi, D., Merito, M., & Rossi, C. (2007). Business Firms' Engagement in Community Projects. Empirical Evidence and Further Developments of the Research. In the Proceedings of First International Workshop on Emerging Trends in FLOSS Research and Development, 2007

Bordieu, R. (1986). The forms of capital. In Richardson, J. G. (Ed.), *Handbook of Theory and Research for the Sociology of Education* (pp. 241–258). New York: Greenwood Press.

Breughel, Pieter the Elder (1563). *Tower of Babel.* Retrieved from http://en.wikipedia.org/wiki/File:Brueghel-tower-of-babel.jpg

Brooks, F. P. (1975). *The mythical man-month: Essays on software engineering.* Reading, MA: Addison-Wesley.

Brooks, F. Jr. (1986). No silver bullet—essence and accidents of software engineering. In Kugler, H. J. (Ed.), *Information Processing* (*Vol. 86*, pp. 1069–1076). Amsterdam, The Netherlands: Elsevier Science Publishers.

Brooks, F., Jr. (1975, 1995). *The mythical man month.* Reading, MA: Addison-Wesley.

Bulchand, J., Osorio, J., & Rodríguez, J. (2007). Information Technology for Education Management and Open Source Software: Improving Education Management through Open Source. In *Knowledge Management for Educational Innovation* (pp. 115–122). Boston: Springer. doi:10.1007/978-0-387-69312-5_15

Burt, R. (1992). *Structural holes: The social structure of competition.* Cambridge, MA: Harvard University Press.

Cameron, L. (2003). Challenges for ELT from the expansion in teaching children. *ELT Journal, 57,* 105–112. doi:10.1093/elt/57.2.105

Capiluppi, A. (2004). Improving comprehension and cooperation through code structure. In *Proceedings of the 4th Workshop on Open Source Software Engineering, 26th International Conference on Software Engineering,* Edinburg, Scotland, UK.

Capiluppi, A., Lago, P., & Morisio, M. (2003). Evidences in the evolution of OS projects through changelog analyses. In *Proceedings of the 3rd International Workshop on Open Source Software Engineering,* Orlando, Florida, USA.

Capiluppi, A., Lago, P., & Morisio, M. (2002). Characterizing the OSS Process. In Proceedings of the 2nd Workshop on Open Source Software Engineering, Orlando, FL, May 2002.

Capiluppi, A., Morisio, M., & Ramil, J. F. (2004). Structural evolution of an Open Source system: a case study. In *Proceedings of the 12th International Workshop on Program Comprehension,* pages 172–183, Bari, Italy.

Carley, K. (1995). *Computational and mathematical organization theory: perspective and directions.* Paper presented at the Informs meetings, Los Angeles, CA.

Carnavale, P. J., & Probst, T. M. (1998). Social values and social conflict in creative problem solving and categorization. *Journal of Personality and Social Psychology, 74,* 1300–1309. doi:10.1037/0022-3514.74.5.1300

Carroll, J. M., Mack, R. L., Lewis, C. H., Grischkowsky, N. L., & Robertson, S. P. (1985). Exploring a word processor. *Human-Computer Interaction, 1*(3), 283–307. doi:10.1207/s15327051hci0103_3

Carroll, J. M., Smith-Kerker, P. L., Ford, J. R., & Mazur-Rimetz, S. A. (1987). The minimal manual. *Human-Computer Interaction, 3*(2), 123–153. doi:10.1207/s15327051hci0302_2

Carter, L., & Belanger, F. (2006). The Influence of Perceived Characteristics of Innovating on e-Government Adoption, *Electronic. Journal of E-Government, 1*(2).

Casadesus-Masanell, R., & Ghemawat, P. (2006). Dynamic Mixed Duopoly: A Model Motivated by Linux vs. Windows. *Management Science, 52,* 1072–1084.

Castillo, J. C., Hartson, H. R., & HIX, D. (1998). *Remote usability evaluation: can users report their own critical incidents?* Paper presented at the Catrambone, R., & Carroll, J. M. (1987). *Learning a word processing system with training wheels and guided exploration.* Paper presented at the SIGCHI/GI conference on Human factors in computing systems and graphics interface (pp. 169–174).

Chang, H.-F., & Mockus, A. (2008). Evaluation of source code copy detection methods on FreeBSD. In *MSR '08: Proceedings of the 5th Working Conference on Mining software repositories.*

Chelf, B. (2006). *Measuring software quality: a study of open source software. Research report.* Coverity Incorporated.

CHI 98 conference summary on Human factors in computing systems.

Chua, W. (1986). Radical Developments in Accounting Thought. *Accounting Review, 61,* 601.

Cohen, W. M., & Levinthal, D. A. (1990). Absorptive Capacity: A New Perspective on Learning and Innovation. *ASQ, 35,* 128–152. doi:10.2307/2393553

Cohen, W., Nelson, R., & Walsh, P. (2000). Protecting Their Intellectual Assets: Appropriability Conditions and Why U.S. Manufacturing Firms Patent (or Not). NBER Working Paper No. W7552.

Comino, S., & Manenti, F. M. (2008). *Dual licensing in open source software markets*. Communication to the 2nd International Workshop on FLOSS Rennes, June.

Command and Control Research Program (The). CCRP, www.dodccrp.org.

Concas, G., Lisci, M., et al. (2008). Open source communities as social networks: An analysis of some peculiar characteristics. In *Proceedings of the 19th Australian Conference on Software Engineering* (pp. 387-391).

Conklin, M. Beyond low-hanging fruit: seeking the next generation of FLOSS data mining. In Proc. 2nd Intl. Conf. on Open Source Systems. (Como, Italy, June 2006). Springer, New York, NY, 2006. 47-56.

Constant, D., Sproull, L., & Kiesler, S. (1996). The Kindness of Strangers: The Usefulness of Electronic Weak Ties for Technical Advice. *Organization Science*, *7*, 119–135. doi:10.1287/orsc.7.2.119

Cowan, R., & Jonard, N. (2004). Network Structure and the Diffusion of Knowledge. *Journal of Economic Dynamics and the Diffusion of Knowledge*, *28*, 1557–1575.

Cremer, J., & Gaudeul, A. (2004). Some economics of the open-source software. *Reseaux*, *22*(124), 111–139.

Crowston, K., Howison, J., & Annabi, H. (2006, March/April). Information systems success in free and open source software development: Theory and measures. *Software Process Improvement and Practice*, *11*(2), 123–148. doi:10.1002/spip.259

Crowston, K., & Scozzi, B. (2002). Open source software projects as virtual organizations: competency rallying for software development. *IEE Proceedings. Software*, *49*, 3–17. doi:10.1049/ip-sen:20020197

Crowston, K., & Howison, J. (2006). Hierarchy and centralization in free and open source software team communications. *Knowledge, Technology, &. Policy*, *18*(4), 65–85.

Crowston, K., & Howison, J. (2004). *The social structure of free and open source software development* (Syracuse FLOSS Working Paper).

Crowston, K., Annabi, H., Howison, J., & Massango, C. Effective work practices for software engineering: Free/libre open source development. In ACM Workshop on Interdisciplinary Software Engineering Research, 2004. B. During. Sprint driven development: Agile methodologies in a distributed open source project (pypy). In P. Abrahamsson, M. Marchesi, and G. Succi, editors, XP, volume 4044 of Lecture Notes in Computer Science, pages 191–195. Springer, 2006.

Crowston, K., Annabi, H., Howison, J., & Masango, C. (2004). *Towards a portfolio of FLOSS project success measures*. Paper presented at the 4th Workshop on Open Source Software Engineering, Edinburgh, Scotland.

Csikszenthmihalyi, M. (1999). Implications of a systems perspective for the study of creativity. In *Handbook of Creativity*, (313-338).

Dahlander, L., & Magnusson, M. G. (2005). Relationships between open source software companies and communities: Observations from nordic firms. *Research Policy*, *34*(4), 481–493.

Dahlander, L., & Wallin, M. W. (2006). A man on the inside: Unlocking communities as complementary assets. *Research Policy*, *35*(8), 1243–1259. doi:10.1016/j.respol.2006.09.011

Dalle, J. M., & David, P. M. (2003). The allocation of software development resources in "open source" production mode, SIEPR Discussion Paper No. 02-27, Stanford Institute ForEconomic Policy Research, Stanford, CA.

Dalle, J.-M., & David, P. A. (2004, November 1). *SimCode: Agent-based simulation modelling of open-source software development* (Industrial Organization). EconWPA.

Daniel, S., Agarwal, R., & Stewart, K. (2006) An absorptive capacity perspective on OSS development group performance, *27th International Conference on Information Systems,* Milwaukee Dec 2006.

Darmon, E., Le Texier, T., & Torre, D. (2007). *Commercial or Open Source Software? Winner-Takes-All Competition, Partial Adoption and Efficiency*. GREDEG Working paper.

David A. P & Spence, M. (2003).. Toward institutional infrastructures for e-science: The scope of challenges. Technical Report: Oxford Technical Institute, May.

Davis, F. (1989). Perceived Usefulness, Perceived Ease of Use, and User Acceptance of Information Technology. *Management Information Systems Quarterly*, *13*, 319–340. doi:10.2307/249008

Deek, F. P., & McHugh, J. A. (2007). *Open Source - Technology and Policy*. Cambridge, UK: Cambridge University Press.

Defense industry daily, DID, online information service at www.defenseindustrydaily.com.

Defense information systems agency (the), DISA, www. disa.mil, and more specifically the information letter *The Grid*, volume 7 number 1, June 2008.

Dennis, A. R., & Valacich, J. S. (1993). Computer brainstorms: More heads are better than one. *The Journal of Applied Psychology*, *78*, 531–537. doi:10.1037/0021-9010.78.4.531

DeRosa, D. M., Smith, C. L., & Hantula, D. A. (2007). The medium matters: Mining the long-promised merit of group interaction in creative idea generation tasks in a meta-analysis of the electronic group brainstorming literature. *Computers in Human Behavior*, *23*, 1549–1581. doi:10.1016/j.chb.2005.07.003

Diehl, M., & Stroebe, W. (1991). Productivity loss in idea-generating groups: Tracking down the blocking effect. *Journal of Personality and Social Psychology*, *61*, 392–403. doi:10.1037/0022-3514.61.3.392

Doan, A., Domingos, O., & Halevy, A. Reconciling schemas of disparate data sources: A machine learning approach. In Proc. of the SIGMOD conference. (Santa Barbara, CA, USA, 2001). ACM Press, New York, NY, 2001, 509-520.

Doan, A., Lu, Y., Lee, Y., & Han, J. Object matching for information integration: A profiler-based approach. In Proc. of the IJCAI Workshop on Information Integration and the Web. (Acapulco, Mexico, 2003). 53-58.

Dombrowski, P., Gholz, E., & Ross, A. L. (2002). *Military transformation and the Defense industry after next, The Defense industrial implications of Network Centric Warfare*. Naval war college Newport papers #18, New Port (RI): Naval war college.

Economides, N., & Katsamakas, E. (2006). Two-sided Competition of Proprietary vs. Open Source Technology Platforms and the Implications for the Software Industry. *Management Science*, *52*(7), 1057–1071.

Edquist, C. (1997). *Systems of Innovation: Technologies, Institutions, and Organizations*. London, UK: Pinter.

Eisenhardt, K. (1989). Building theory from case study research. *Academy of Management Review*, *14*(4), 532–550. doi:10.2307/258557

Elliott, S. M., & Scacchi, W. (2005). Free Software Development: Cooperation and Conflict in a Virtual Organization Culture. In Koch, S. (Ed.), *Free/Open Software Development*, (152-172). Idea Group Inc.

English, R., & Schweik, C. M. (2007). Identifying success and tragedy of FLOSS commons: A preliminary classification of Sourceforge.net projects. In *FLOSS '07: Proceedings of the first international workshop on emerging trends in FLOSS research and development* (p. 11). Washington, DC, USA: IEEE Computer Society.

Everett, M. G., & Borgatti, S. P. (1999). The centrality of groups and classes. *The Journal of Mathematical Sociology*, *23*(3), 181–201.

Federal computer week, FCW, www.fcw.com, section dedicated to "Stories".

Feller, J., Finnegan, P., Fitzgerald, B., & Hayes, J. (2008). From peer production to productization: a study of socially-enabled business exchanges in open source service networks. *Information Systems Research*, *19*(4). doi:10.1287/isre.1080.0207

Fichman, R. G. (2004). Going Beyond the Dominant Paradigm for IT Innovation Research: Emerging Concepts and Methods. *Journal of the Association for Information Systems*, *5*(8).

Fichman, R. G., & Kemerer, C. F. (1999). The Illusory Diffusion of Innovation: An Examination of Assimilation Gaps. *Information Systems Research*, *10*(3), 255–275. doi:10.1287/isre.10.3.255

Fichman, R. G. (1992). Information Technology Diffusion: A Review of Empirical Research," in J.l. DeGross, J.D. Becker, and J.J. Elam (Eds.), *13th International Conference on Information Systems*, Dallas, TX, pp. 195-206.

Fichman, R. G., and Kemerer, C. F. The Assimilation of Software Process Innovations: An Organizational Learning Perspective, *Management Science* (43:10), 1997, pp. 1345-1363.

Fitzgerald, B. (2006). The Transformation of Open Source Software. *Management Information Systems Quarterly*, *30*(3), 587–598.

Foster, I. (2005, May). Service-oriented science. *Science*, *308*, 814–817. doi:10.1126/science.1110411

Fox, J., & Guyer, M. (1977, June). Group size and others' strategy in an n-person game. *The Journal of Conflict Resolution*, *21*(2), 323–338.

Free Software Foundation (FSF). (n.d.). Retrieved from http://www.fsf.org/

Fukuyama, F. (1995). *The social virtues and the creation of prosperity*. London: Hamish Hamilton.

Furst, S., Blackburn, R., & Rosen, B. (1999). Virtual teams: A proposed agenda for research. *Information Systems Journal*, *9*, 249–269. doi:10.1046/j.1365-2575.1999.00064.x

Gallivan, M. (2001). Organizational adoption and assimilation of complex technological innovations: development and application of a new framework. *Database*, *32*(3), 51–85.

Gallupe, R. B., Bastianutti, L. M., & Cooper, H. W. (1991). Unlocking brainstorming. *The Journal of Applied Psychology*, *76*, 137–142. doi:10.1037/0021-9010.76.1.137

Galoppini, R. (2008). *Open Source at Microsoft: an analysis of Microsoft Open Source Strategy*, http://robertogaloppini.net/2008/03/20/open-source-at-microsoft-an-analysis-of-microsoft-open-source-strategy/

Gao, Y., Freeh, V., & Madey, G. (2003). *Analysis and modeling of open source software community*. Paper presented at the North American Association for Computational Social and Organizational Science Conference.

Gao, Y., Madey, G., & Freeh, V. (2005, April). Modeling and simulation of the open source software community. In Agent-Directed Simulation Conference (pp. 113–122). San Diego, CA.

Garcia-Molina, H. 2006. Pair-Wise entity resolution: overview and challenges. In Proceedings of the 15th ACM international Conference on information and Knowledge Management (Arlington, Virginia, USA, November 06 - 11, 2006).CIKM '06. ACM, New York, NY, 1-1.

Gaudeul, A. (2003). The (La)TeX project: a case study of open source software. *TUGboat*, 24(1), Proceeding of the 2003 Annual Meeting, (pp. 132-145).

Germán, D. M. (2004). Mining CVS repositories, the softChange experience. In *Proceedings of the International Workshop on Mining Software Repositories*, Edinburgh, UK.

Gholz, E. (2003). In Prencipe, A., Davies, A., & Hobday, M. (Eds.), *Systems integration in the US Defence industry: who does it and why is it important?* (pp. 279–306).

Ghosh, R and Glott, R (2005) Results and policy paper from survey of Government authorities, Technical report, MERIT, University of Maastricht, Free/Libre and Open Source Software: Policy Support.

Ghosh, R. A., Glott, R., Krieger, B., & Robles, G. (2002). *Survey of Developers, Free/Libre and Open Source Software: Survey and Study (FLOSS Final Report)*. Maastricht, The Netherlands: University of Maastricht, International Institute of Infonomics. Retrieved from http://www.infonomics.nl/FLOSS/report/Final4.pdf

Ghosh, R., & Glott, R. (2005). FLOSSPOLS Skill Survey Report, available from: http://flossproject.org/papers/20050415/RishabGHOSH-padua-skills.pdf

Gilbert, N. (1997). A Simulation of the Structure of Academic Science. *Sociological Research Online*, *2*(2). http://www.socresonline.org.uk/socresonline/2/2/3.html. doi:10.5153/sro.85

Glaser, B., & Strauss, A. (1967). *The Discovery of Grounded Theory*. Chicago: Aldine.

Gobeille, R. (2008). The fossology project. In *MSR '08: Proceedings of the 5th Working Conference on Mining software repositories*.

Goertzel, B. (1997). *From Complexity to Creativity: Explorations in Evolutionary, Autopoietic, and Cognitive Dynamics*. Plenum.

González-Barahona, J. M., Izquierdo-Cortazar, D., & Squire, M. (2010). Repositories with public data about software development. *International Journal of Open Source Software and Processes*, 2(2), 1–13.

Gonzalez-Barahona, J. M., Robles, G., & Dueñas, S. (2010). Collecting data about floss development: the flossmetrics experience. In *FLOSS '10: Proceedings of the 3rd International Workshop on Emerging Trends in Free/Libre/Open Source Software Research and Development*, pages 29–34, New York, NY, USA. ACM.

Gorla, N., & Lam, Y. W. (2004). Who should work with whom? Building effective software project teams. *Communications of the ACM*, 47(6), 79–82. doi:10.1145/990680.990684

Goth, G. (2007). Sprinting toward open source development. *IEEE Software*, 24(1), 88–91. doi:10.1109/MS.2007.28

Government accountability office, GAO, (2004). *Defense acquisition, Stronger management practices are needed to improve DoD's software intensive weapon acquisitions*, Report to the committee on armed services, US Senate, reference GAO-04-393. Available from www.gao.gov.

Government accountability office, GAO, (2008). *Defense acquisitions, Assessment of selected weapon programs*, Report to congressional committees, reference GAO-08-467SP. Available from www.gao.gov.

Government computer news, GCN, www.gcn.com, sections dedicated to "Hot topics" and "White papers".

Granovetter, M. (1985). Economic action and social structure: the problem of embeddedness. *American Journal of Sociology*, 91(3), 481–510. doi:10.1086/228311

Graves, T. L., & Mockus, A. (1998). Inferring change effort from configuration management databases. In *5th IEEE International Software Metrics Symposium*, pages 267–, Bethesda, Maryland, USA.

Grewal, R., Lilien, G. L., & Mallapragada, G. (2006). Location, location, location: How network embeddedness affects project success in open source systems. *Management Science*, 52(7), 1043–1056. doi:10.1287/mnsc.1060.0550

Hahsler, M., & Koch, S. (2005). Discussion of a large-scale open source data collection methodology. In *Proceedings of the Hawaii International Conference on System Sciences (HICSS-38)*, Big Island, Hawaii, USA.

Halstead, M. H. (1977). *Elements of Software Science*. New York, USA: Elsevier.

Hamel, G., & Prahalad, C. K. (1990). The core competence of the corporation. *Harvard Business Review*, 68(may-june), 79–91.

Harrison, R. J., & Carroll, R. G. (2006). *Culture and Demography in Organizations*. New Jersey, NJ: Princeton University Press.

Hars, A., & Ou, S. (2002). Working for Free? Motivations of Participating in open source projects. *International Journal of E-Commerce*, 42(3), 25–39.

Hars, A., & Shaosong, O. Working for free motivations of participating in open source software projects. In *Proceedings of the 34th Hawaii International Conference on System Sciences*, 25-31.

Healy, K., & Schussman, A. (2003). *The ecology of open-source software development (Tech. Rep.)*. Arizona, USA: University of Arizona, Department of Sociology.

Henderson, R. M., & Clark, K. B. (1990). Architectural innovation: The reconfiguration of existing product technologies and the failure of established firms. *Administrative Science Quarterly*, 35(1), 9–30. doi:10.2307/2393549

Henkel, J. (2006a). Selective revealing in open innovation processes: the case of embedded *Linux. Research Policy*, 35(7), 953–969.

Henkel, J., & Gruber, M. (2006b). New ventures based on open innovation - an empirical analysis of start-up firms in embedded Linux. *International Journal of Technology Management*, 33(4), 256–372.

Hernandez, M. A. and Stolfo, S. J. 1995. The merge/purge problem for large databases. SIGMOD Rec. 24, 2 (May. 1995), 127-138.

Herraiz, I., Izquierdo-Cortazar, D., Rivas-Hernandez, F., Gonzalez-Barahona, J. M., & Robles, G. nas Dominguez, S. D., Garcia-Campos, C., Gato, J. F., & Tovar, L. (2009). FLOSSMetrics: Free / libre / open source software metrics. In *Proceedings of the 13th European Conference on Software Maintenance and Reengineering (CSMR)*. IEEE Computer Society.

Hertel, B., Niedner, S., & Herrmann, S. (2003). Motivation of software developers in open source software projects: An internet-based survey of contributors to the linux kernel. *Research Policy*, *32*(7), 1159–1172. doi:10.1016/S0048-7333(03)00047-7

Herz, J. C., Lucas, M., & Scott, J. (2006). Open technology development – Roadmap plan. http://www.acq.osd.mil/actd/OTDRoadmapFinal.pdf

Hilbert, D. M., & Redmiles, D. F. (2000). Extracting usability information from user interface events. [CSUR]. *ACM Computing Surveys*, *32*(4), 384–421. doi:10.1145/371578.371593

Hindle, A., Herraiz, I., Shihab, E., & Jiang, Z. M. (2010). Mining Challenge 2010: FreeBSD, GNOME Desktop and Debian/Ubuntu. In *Proceedings of the 7th IEEE International Working Conference on Mining Software Repositories*, pages 82–85. IEEE Computer Society.

Hinds, D., & Lee, R. M. (2009). Assessing the social network health of virtual communities. In Whitworth, B., & deMoor, A. (Eds.), *Handbook of research on socio-technical design and social networking systems*. Hershey, PA: IGI Global.

Hinds, D. (2008). *Social network structure as a critical success condition for open source software project communities*. Unpublished doctoral dissertation, Florida International University, Florida, USA. Retrieved March 2008 from http://etd.fiu.edu/ETD-db/available/etd-0501108-124416/

Hissam, S., Weinstock, C. B., Plakosh, D., & Asundi, J. (2001). *Perspectives on open source software*, Carnegie Mellon Software Ingineering Institute, Technical report CMU/SEI-2001-TR019, november 2001.

Hopenhayn, H. A., & Mitchell, M. F. (2001). Innovation Variety and Patent Breadth. *The Rand Journal of Economics*, *32*(1), 152–166. doi:10.2307/2696402

Howells, J. (1996). Tacit knowledge, innovation and technology transfer. *Technology Analysis and Strategic Management*, *8*(2), 91–106. doi:10.1080/09537329608524237

Howells, J., James, A., & Malik, K. (2003). The sourcing of technological knowledge: distributed innovation and dynamic change. *R & D Management*, *33*(4), 395–409. doi:10.1111/1467-9310.00306

Howison, J., Conklin, M., & Crowston, K. (2006). Flossmole: A collaborative repository for floss research data and analyses. *International Journal of Information Technology and Web Engineering*, *1*, 17–26.

Howison, J., & Crowston, K. (2004). The perils and pitfalls of mining SourceForge. In *Proceedings of the International Workshop on Mining Software Repositories*, pages 7–11, Edinburg, Scotland, UK.

Howison, J., Conklin, M., & Crowston, K. OSSmole: A collaborative repository for FLOSS research data and analyses. In Proc. 1st Intl. Conf. on Open Source Systems. (Genova, Italy, June 2005). 54-59.

Janis, I. L. (1972). *Victims of Groupthink: A Psychological Study of Foreign Policy Decisions and Fiascoes*. Boston, MA: Houghton Mifflin.

Jeffries, R., Miller, J. R., Wharton, C., & Uyeda, K. (1991). *User interface evaluation in the real world: A comparison of four techniques*. Paper presented at the SIGCHI conference on Human factors in computing systems: Reaching through technology (pp. 119-124).

Jerdee, T. H., & Rosen, B. (1974). Effects of opportunity to communicate and visibility of individual decisions on behavior in the common interest. *The Journal of Applied Psychology*, *59*(6), 712–716. doi:10.1037/h0037450

John, B. E., & Kieras, D. E. (1996). The GOMS family of user interface analysis techniques: Comparison and contrast. *ACM Transactions on Computer-Human Interaction*, *3*(4), 320–351. doi:10.1145/235833.236054

Johnson, J. P. (2002). Open source software: Private provision of a public good. *Journal of Economics & Management Strategy*, *11*(4), 637–662. doi:10.1162/105864002320757280

Kan, S. H. (2003). *Metrics and Models in Software Quality Engineering* (2nd ed.). Addison-Wesley Professional.

Kaplan, B., & Duchon, D. (1988). Combining qualitative and quantitative methods in IS research: a case study. *Management Information Systems Quarterly, 12*(4), 571–587. doi:10.2307/249133

Katsamakas, E., & Georgantzas, N. (2007). Why most open source development projects do not succeed? In *FLOSS '07: Proceedings of the first international workshop on emerging trends in FLOSS research and development* (p. 3). Washington, DC, USA: IEEE Computer Society.

Katz, M.L., and Shapiro, C. "Technology Adoption in the Presence of Network Externalities," *Journal of Political Economy* (94:4) 1986, pp 822-841.

Keirsey, D. (1998). *Please Understand Me II*. Del Mar, CA: Prometheus Nemesis Book Company.

Kicinger, R., Arciszewski, T., & De Jong, K. A. (2005). Evolutionary computation and structural design: A survey of the state of the art. *Computers & Structures, 83*(23-24), 1943–1978. doi:10.1016/j.compstruc.2005.03.002

Kidane, Y. H., & Gloor, P. A. (2007). Correlating temporal communication patterns of the Eclipse open source community with performance and creativity. *Computational & Mathematical Organization Theory, 13*, 17–27. doi:10.1007/s10588-006-9006-3

Kirsch, L. (2004). Deploying common systems globally: the dynamics of control. *Information Systems Research, 15*(4), 374–395. doi:10.1287/isre.1040.0036

Kirton, M. (1976). Adaptors and innovators: A description and measure. *The Journal of Applied Psychology, 61*, 622–629. doi:10.1037/0021-9010.61.5.622

Kirton, M. (1989). *Adaptors and Innovators: Styles of creativity and problem-solving*. New York, NY: Routledge.

Klein, H. K., & Myers, M. D. (1999). A Set of Principles for Conducting and Evaluating Interpretive Field Studies in Information Systems. *Management Information Systems Quarterly, 23*(1), 67–93. doi:10.2307/249410

Klemperer, P. (1990). How Broad Should the Scope of Patent Protection Be? *The Rand Journal of Economics, 21*(1), 113–130. doi:10.2307/2555498

Koch, S., & Schneider, G. (2002). Effort, cooperation, and coordination in an open source software project: GNOME. *Information Systems Journal, 12*(1), 27–42. doi:10.1046/j.1365-2575.2002.00110.x

Koch, S. (2008). Exploring the effects of SourceForge.net coordination and communication tools on the efficiency of open source projects using data envelopment analysis. In Morasca, S. (Ed.), *Empirical Software Engineering*. Springer.

Koch, S. (2008). Effort Modeling and Programmer Participation in Open Source Software Projects. *Information Economics and Policy*.

Koch, S. Agile principles and open source software development: A theoretical and empirical discussion. In Extreme Programming and Agile Processes in Software Engineering: Proceedings of the 5th International Conference XP 2004, number 3092 in Lecture Notes in Computer Science (LNCS), pages 85–93. Springer Verlag, 2004. E. Raymond. The Cathedral and the Bazaar, chapter The Cathedral and the Bazaar. O'Reilly & Associates, Inc., 1999.

Koenig, J. (2004, March 14). Seven Open Source Business Strategies for Competitive Advantage. *IT Manager's Journal*. Retrieved from http://management.itmanagersjournal.com/article.pl?sid=04/05/10/2052216&tid=85

Kogut, B., & Metiu, A. (2001, Summer). Open-source software development and distributed innovation. *Oxford Review of Economic Policy, 17*(2), 248–264. doi:10.1093/oxrep/17.2.248

Kolb, D. M., & Gidden, P. A. (1986). Getting to know your conflict options: Using conflict as a creative force. *The Personnel Administrator, 31*, 77–90.

Kowalczykiewicz, K. (2005). Libre projects lifetime profiles analysis. In *Free and open source software developers' European meeting 2005*. Brussels, Belgium.

Kraut, R. E., & Streeter, A. L. (1995). Coordination in software development. *Communications of the ACM, 28*(3), 69–81. doi:10.1145/203330.203345

Krishnamurthy, S. (2002, June). Cave or community?: An empirical examination of 100 mature open source projects. *First Monday, 7*(6).

Krishnamurthy, S. (2003). A managerial overview of open source software. *Business Horizons, 9-10*, 47–56. doi:10.1016/S0007-6813(03)00071-5

Krishnamurthy, S. (2006). On the Intrinsic and Extrinsic Motivation of Free/Libre/Open Source (FLOSS) Developers. *Knowledge, Technology, &. Policy, 18*(4), 17–39.

Kuk, G. (2006) Strategic Interaction and Knowledge Sharing in the KDE Developer Mailing List," *Management Science,* (52:7), pp 1031-1042

Kurosu, M., Matsuura, S., & Sugizaki, M. (1997). *Categorical inspection method-structured heuristic evaluation (shem)*. Paper presented at the IEEE International Conference on Systems, Man, and Cybernetics (pp. 2613-2618).

Lakhani, K., & Wolf, B. (2005). Why hackers do what they do: Understanding motivation and effort in free/open source software projects. In *Perspectives on Free and Open Source software*. Cambridge, Massachusetts: MIT Press.

Lakhani, K. R., & von Hippel, E. (2001). How Open Source Software Works: Free user-to-user assistance. *Research Policy, 32*, 923–943. doi:10.1016/S0048-7333(02)00095-1

Lakhani, K. R., & Wolf, R. G. (2005). Why Hackers Do What They Do: Understanding Motivation and Effort in Free/Open Source Software Projects. In Feller, J., Fitzgerald, B., Hissam, S., & Lakhani, K. R. (Eds.), *Perspectives on Free and Open Source Software*. Cambridge, MA: MIT Press.

Lakhani, K., & Wolf, B. (2005) Motivation and Effort in Free/Open Source Software Projects: The Interplay of Intrinsic and Extrinsic Motivations, in Feller, J, Fitzgerald, B, Hissam, S, and Lakhani, K. (2005) (Eds) *Perspectives on Free and Open Source Software*, MIT Press, Cambridge.

Lanzara, G. F., & Morner, M. (2003). *The knowledge ecology of open-source software projects*. Paper presented at the 19th European Group of Organizational Studies Colloquium, Copenhagen, Denmark.

Lattemann, C., & Stieglitz, S. (2005). Framework for Governance in Open Source Communities. In *Proceedings of the 38th Hawaii International Conference on Systems Sciences* (pp. 1-11). Washington, DC: IEEE.

Lawler, E. E. (1992). *The ultimate advantage: Creating the high involvement organization*. San Francisco, CA: Jossey-Bass.

Lechner, D., & Kaiser, H. (2005). The fortress and the bazaar: Open-source and DoD software. *Defense Acquisition Review Journal*, december, (pp. 374-391).

Lee, A. S., & Baskerville, R. L. (2003). Generalizing Generalizability in Information Systems Research. *Information Systems Research, 14*(3), 221–243. doi:10.1287/isre.14.3.221.16560

Lee, G. K., & Cole, R. E. (2003). From a firm-based to a community-based model of knowledge creation: The case of the Linux kernel development. *Organization Science, 14*(6), 633–649. doi:10.1287/orsc.14.6.633.24866

Lerner, J., & Tirole, J. (2005, April). The scope of open source licensing. *Journal of Law Economics and Organization, 21*(1), 20–56. doi:10.1093/jleo/ewi002

Lerner, J., & Tirole, J. (2002). Some simple economics of open source. *The Journal of Industrial Economics, 50*(2), 197–234. doi:10.1111/1467-6451.00174

Lerner, J., & Tirole, J. (2002). Some Simple Economics of Open Source. *The Journal of Industrial Economics, 50*(2), 197–234.

Lerner, J., & Tirole, J. (2000). *The Simple Economics of Open Source* (Working Paper 7600). The National Bureau of Economic Research, Inc.

Lerner, J., & Tirole, J. (2002). *The Scope of Open Source Licensing* (Working Paper). Boston, MA: Harvard Business School.

Levenshtein, V. I. (1966). Binary codes capable of correcting deletions, insertions, and reversals. *Soviet Physics, Doklady, 10*, 707–710.

Levin, R., Klevorick, A., Nelson, R., Winter, S., Gilbert, R., & Griliches, Z. (1987). Appropriating the Returns from Industrial Research and Development. *Brookings Papers on Economic Activity, 3*, 783–831. doi:10.2307/2534454

Libresoft. (2006). Libre *software research*. Retrieved October 2008 from http://libresoft.es/

Lin, Y.-H., Ko, T.-M., Tyung-Ruey, C., & Lin, K.-J. (2005). Open Source Licenses and the Creative Commons Framework: License Selection and Comparison. *Journal of Information Science and Engineering, 22*, 1–17.

Linux kernel software quality and security better than most proprietary enterprise software, 4-year Coverity analysis finds. (2004). Press release. (Coverity Incorporated)

Lopez-Fernandez, L., Robles, G., & Gonzalez-Barahona, J. M. (2004). *Applying social network analysis to the information in CVS repositories.* Retrieved from http://opensource.mit.edu/papers/llopez-sna-short.pdf

Lundell, B., Lings, B., & Lindqvist, E. (2006). Perceptions and uptake of open source in Swedish organizations. In *Damiani, E, Fitzgerald, B, Scacchi, W and Succi, G (2006) Open Source Systems* (pp. 155–164). New York: Springer-Verlag.

Lundell, B., Persson, A., & Lings, B. (2007). Learning Through Practical Involvement in the OSS Ecosystem: Experiences from a Masters Assignment. In Proceedings of the Third International Conference on Open Source Systems 2007, 289-294

MacCormack, A., Rusnak, J., & Baldwin, C. Y. (2006). Exploring the structure of complex software designs: An empirical study of open source and proprietary code. *Management Science, 52*(7), 1015–1030. doi:10.1287/mnsc.1060.0552

Macleod, C. (1988). *Inventing the Industrial Revolution: The English Patent System, 1660-1800.* Cambridge.

Madey, G., Freeh, V., & Tynan, R. (2005). Modeling the Free/Open Source Software Community: A Quantitative Investigation. In Koch, S. (Ed.), *Free/Open Software Development,* (203-220). Idea Group Inc.

Madey, G., Freeh, V., & Tynan, R. (2002). The open source software development phenomenon: An analysis based on social network theory. In *Proceedings of the Americas Conference on Information Systems (AMCIS 2002)* (pp. 1806-1813).

Mansfield, E. (1985). How Rapidly Does New Industrial Technology Leak Out? *The Journal of Industrial Economics, 34*(2), 217–223. doi:10.2307/2098683

Markus, M. L. (1987). Toward a 'Critical Mass' Theory of Interactive Media: Universal Access, Interdependence and Diffusion. *Communication Research, 14*, 491–511. doi:10.1177/009365087014005003

Markus, M. L., & Robey, D. (1988). Information Technology and Organizational Change: Causal Structure in Theory and Research. *Management Science, 34*(5), 583–598. doi:10.1287/mnsc.34.5.583

McCabe, T. J. (1976). A complexity measure. *IEEE Transactions on Software Engineering, 2*(4), 308–320. doi:10.1109/TSE.1976.233837

McCoy, T. (2002). The politics of usability. *The Usability SIG Newsletter, 8*(4).

McCue. (2004) London council ditches Linux plans, http://news.zdnet.co.uk/software/0,1000000121,39118909,00.htm, last accessed on 8 Jan 2007.

McKelvey, M. (1996). *Evolutionary Innovation: The Business of Genetic Engineering.* Oxford, UK: Clarendon.

Meiszner, A., Sowe, S., & Glott, R. (2008). Preparing the Ne(x)t Generation: Lessons learned from Free/Libre Open Source Software. Fourth International Barcelona Conference on Higher Education: new challenges and emerging roles for human and social development, 2008. Jaccheri, L., Osterlie, T. (2007). Open Source Software: A Source of Possibilities for Software Engineering Education and Empirical Software Engineering. First International Workshop on Emerging Trends in FLOSS Research and Development, 2007.

Mérindol, V., & Versailles, D. W. (2007). Towards a re-interpretation of ICT impact on command and control. *Defence Studies, 7*(2), 232–237.

Messerschmitt, D. G. (2004). Back to the user (open source). *IEEE Software, 21*(1), 89–91. doi:10.1109/MS.2004.1259234

Michlmayr, M. (2005). Software process maturity and the success of free software projects. In Zielinski, K., & Szmuc, T. (Eds.), *Software engineering: Evolution and emerging technologies* (pp. 3–14). Krakow, Poland: IOS Press.

Miles, M., & Huberman, A. (1994). *Qualitative Data Analysis: A Sourcebook of New Methods.* Sage, Beverley Hills.

Military information technology online edition, available at www.military-information-technology.com online archives volumes 7 (2003) to 12 (2008).

Miller, H. J., & Page, E. S. (2007). *Complex Adaptive Systems: An Introduction to Computational Models of Social Life*. Princeton, New Jersey: Princeton University Press.

Mitre corporation (The). (2003). *Use of Free and Open source software (FOSS) in the US Department of Defence*, version 1.2.04, January 2nd, 2003, prepared for the DISA, report number MP W 02 0000101; approved for public release yet unpublished; downloaded in pdf format on October 16th, 2008, from http://terrybollinger.com/.

Mockus, A., Fielding, R. T., & Herbsleb, J. D. (2002). Two case studies of open source software development: Apache and mozilla. *ACM Transactions on Software Engineering and Methodology*, *11*, 309–346. doi:10.1145/567793.567795

Mockus, A., & Votta, L. G. (2000). Identifying reasons for software changes using historic databases. In *Proc Intl Conf Softw Maintenance*, pages 120–130.

Mohr, L. B. (1982). *Explaining Organizational Behavior*. San Francisco, CA: Jossey-Bass.

Molich, R., & Nielsen, J. (1990). Improving a human-computer dialogue. *Communications of the ACM*, *33*(3), 338–348. doi:10.1145/77481.77486

Moon, J. Y., & Sproull, L. (2000). The Essence of Distributed Work: The Case of the Linux Kernel. *First Monday*, *5*, 11.

Moore, G. C., & Benbasat, I. (1991). Development of an Instrument to Measure Perceptions of Adapting an Information Technology Innovation. *Information Systems Research*, *2*(3), 192–222. doi:10.1287/isre.2.3.192

Moreno, J. (1934). *Who shall survive?* New York: Beacon Press.

Mustonen, M. (2003). Copyleft - The economics of Linux and other open source software. *Information Economics and Policy*, *15*(1), 99–121. doi:10.1016/S0167-6245(02)00090-2

Nahapiet, J., & Ghoshal, S. (1998). Social capital, intellectual capital, and organizational advantage. *Academy of Management Review*, *23*(2), 242–266. doi:10.2307/259373

Nakakoji, K., & Yamamoto, Y. (2005). The co-evolution of systems and communities in free and open source software development. In Koch, S. (Ed.), *Free/open source software development* (pp. 59–82). Hershey, PA: IGI Global.

Narduzzo, A., & Rossi, A. (2003). Modularity in action: GNU/Linux and Free/Open source software development model unleashed. Working paper.

Nelson, R. (1995). Recent Evolutionary Theorizing about Economic Change. *Journal of Economic Literature*, *33*, 48–90.

Nemeth, C. J. (1992). Dissent as Driving Cognition, Attitudes, and Judgments. *Social Cognition*, *13*, 273–291. doi:10.1521/soco.1995.13.3.273

Newman, M., & Robey, D. (1992). A Social-Process Model of User-Analyst Relationships. *Management Information Systems Quarterly*, *16*(2), 249–265. doi:10.2307/249578

Ngwenyama, O. K., & Lyytinen, K. J. (1997). Groupware environments as action constitutive resources: a social action framework for analyzing groupware technologies. *Computer Supported Cooperative Work*, *6*, 71–93. doi:10.1023/A:1008600220584

Niccolai, J. (2005) Scottish police pick Windows in software line-up, *InfoWorld*, http://www.infoworld.com/article/05/08/11/HNscottishpolice_1.html, last accessed 20 Dec 2006

Nichols, D. M., & Twidale, M. B. (2003). The usability of open source software. *First Monday*, *8*(1).

Nichols, D. M., McKay, D., & Twidale, M. B. (2003). Participatory usability: Supporting proactive users. In *Proceedings of the 4th ACM SIGCHI NZ Symposium on Computer-Human Interaction (CHINZ'03)*, Dunedin, New Zealand (pp. 63-68). New York: ACM.

Nichols, D. M., Thomson, K., & Yeates, S. A. (2001). *Usability and open-source software development*. Retrieved from http://opensource.mit.edu/papers/nichols.pdf

Nijstad, B. A., Stroebe, W., & Lodewijkx, H. F. M. (2006). The illusion of group productivity: A reduction of failures explanation. *The Journal of Social Psychology, 36*, 31–48.

Nonneke, B., & Preece, J. (2000). Lurker demographics: Counting the silent. *Proceedings of the SIGCHI conference on Human factors in computing systems*, New York: ACM Press, (pp. 73-80).

Nordhaus, W. (1969). *Invention, Growth and Welfare: A Theoretical Treatment of Technological Change*. M.I.T. Press.

Nussbaum, L., & Zacchiroli, S. (2010). The Ultimate Debian Database: Consolidating Bazaar Metadata for Quality Assurance and Data Mining. In *7th IEEE Working Conference on Mining Software Repositories (MSR)*. IEEE Computer Society.

Nuvolari, A. (2002). Collective invention ancient and modern: A reappraisal. ECIS working paper.

O'Mahony, S. (2003). Guarding the commons: how community managed software projects protect their work. *Research Policy, 32*, 1179–1198. doi:10.1016/S0048-7333(03)00048-9

On, B.-W., Lee, D., Kang, J., & Mitra, P. Comparative study of name disambiguation problem using a scalable blocking-based framework. In Proc. of 5th ACM/IEEE-CS Joint Conf. on Digital Libraries. (Denver, CO, USA, 2005). 344-353.

Onetti, A., & Capobianco, F. (2005) Open source and business model innovation. the Funambol case, in Scotto, M and Succi, G (Eds) *Proceedings of First International Conference on Open Source (OSS2005)*, Genoa, 11-15 July 205, pp. 224-227.

Osterloh, M., & Rota, S. (2007). Open source software development – Just another case of collective invention? *Research Policy, 36*(2), 157–171. doi:10.1016/j.respol.2006.10.004

Ostrom, E., Gardner, R., & Walker, J. (1994). *Rules, games and common pool resources*. Ann Arbor, MI: University of Michigan Press.

Papadopoulos, P., Demetriadis, S., & Stamelos, I. (2006). Online Case-Based Learning: Design and Preliminary Evaluation of the eCASE Environment. Sixth IEEE International Conference on Advanced Learning Technologies, ICALT, 2006.

Parker, G., & Van Alstyn, M. (2008). *Innovation through Optimal Licensing in Free Markets and Free Software*. Available at SSRN: http://ssrn.com/abstract=639165.

Paulley, G. (2009, January 26). Fred Brooks is still right. *Sybase, iAnywhere*. Retrieved February 21, 2009 from http://iablog.sybase.com/paulley/2009/01/fred-brooks-is-still-right/

Pemberton, S. (2004). Scratching someone else's itch (why open source can't do usability). *Interaction, 11*(1), 72. doi:10.1145/962342.962366

Pendharkar, P. C., & Rodger, J. A. (2009). The relationship between software development team size and software development cost. *Communications of the ACM, 52*(1), 141–144. doi:10.1145/1435417.1435449

Petrenko, M., Poshyvanyk, D., Rajlich, V., & Buchta, J. (2007). Teaching Software Evolution in Open Source. *IEEE Computer, 40*(11), 25–31.

Piaget, J. (1972). *To understand is to invent*. New York: The Viking Press, Inc.

Pollock, R. (2006). *The Value of the Public Domain*. Published by the Institute for Public Policy Research as part of a series on IP and the Public Sphere.

Polson, P. G., & Lewis, C. H. (1990). Theory-based design for easily learned interfaces. *Human-Computer Interaction, 5*(2/3), 191–220. doi:10.1207/s15327051hci0502&3_3

Postema, M., Miller, J., & Dick, M. (2001). Including Practical Software Evolution in Software Engineering Education. In Proceedings of the 14th Conference on Software Engineering Education and Training, CSEET 2001, 127-135.

Prencipe, A., Davies, A., & Hobday, M. (Eds.). (2003). *The business of systems integration*. Oxford: Oxford university press. doi:10.1093/0199263221.001.0001

Putnam, R. D. (2000). *Bowling alone: The collapse and revival of American community*. New York: Simon and Schuster.

Rahm, E., & Bernstein, P. (2001). A survey of approaches to automatic schema matching. *The VLDB Journal, 10,* 334–350. doi:10.1007/s007780100057

Raymond, E. (1998). The Cathedral and the Bazaar. *First Monday, 3*(3). http://www.firstmonday.org/issues/issue3_3/raymond/index.html.

Raymond, E. S. (1999a). *The cathedral and the bazaar: Musings on Linux and open source by an accidental revolutionary*. Sebastopol, CA: O'Reilly & Associates, Inc.

Raymond, E. S. (1999b). The social context of open source. [http://www.catb.org/~esr/writings/cathedral-bazaar/cathedral-bazaar/ar01s11.html] (Retrieved 21 February 2009)

Raymond, E. S. (2000, September 11). *The cathedral and the bazaar* (Tech. Rep. No. 3.0). Thyrsus Enterprises.

Rieman, J. (1996). A field study of exploratory learning strategies. *ACM Transactions on Computer-Human Interaction, 3*(3), 189–218. doi:10.1145/234526.234527

Roberts, J. A., Hann Il-H., & Slaughter, S. A. (2006). Understanding the Motivations, Participation, and Performance of Open Source Software Developers: A Longitudinal Study of the Apache Projects. *Management Science, 52*(7), 984–999. doi:10.1287/mnsc.1060.0554

Robles, G., González-Barahona, J. M., & Guervós, J. J. M. (2006a). Beyond source code: The importance of other artifacts in software development (a case study). *Journal of Systems and Software, 79*(9), 1233–1248. doi:10.1016/j.jss.2006.02.048

Robles, G., González-Barahona, J. M., Izquierdo-Cortazar, D., & Herraiz, I. (2009). Tools for the study of the usual data sources found in libre software projects. *International Journal of Open Source Software and Processes, 1*(1), 24–45.

Robles, G. (2010). Replicating msr: A study of the potential replicability of papers published in the mining software repositories proceedings. pages 171 –180.

Robles, G., & Gonzalez-Barahona, J. Developer identification methods for integrated data from various sources. In Proc. of Mining Software Repositories Workshop (MSR 2005) (St. Louis, MO, USA, 2005). 1-5.

Robles, G., Gonzalez-Barahona, J. M., Michlmayr, M., & Amor, J. J. (2006b). Mining large software compilations over time: Another perspective of software evolution. In *Third International Workshop on Mining Software Repositories*, pages 3–9, Shanghai, China.

Robles, G., González-Barahona, J. M., & Michlmayr, M. (2005). Evolution of volunteer participation in libre software projects: evidence from Debian. In *1st International Conference on Open Source Systems*, pages 100–107, Genoa, Italy.

Robles, G., Koch, S., & González-Barahona, J. M. (2004). Remote analysis and measurement of libre software systems by means of the CVSAnalY tool. In *Proc 2nd Workshop on Remote Analysis and Measurement of Software Systems*, pages 51–56, Edinburg, UK.

Robles, G., Prieto-Martínez, J. L., & González-Barahona, J. M. (2006c). Assessing and evaluating documentation in libre software projects. In *Proceedings of the Workshop on Evaluation Frameworks for Open Source Software (EFOSS 2006)*.

Rogers, E. (1962). *Diffusion of Innovations*. NY: The Free Press.

Rogers, E. (2003). *Diffusion of Innovations* (5th ed.). NY: The Free Press.

Rosenberg, D., & Stephens, M. (2007). *Use Case Driven Object Modeling with UML: Theory and Practice*. New York: Springer-Verlag.

Rossi, B., Russo, B., & Succi, G. (2006). A study of the introduction of OSS in public administration. In *Damiani, E, Fitzgerald, B, Scacchi, W and Succi, G (2006) Open Source Systems* (pp. 165–172). New York: Springer-Verlag.

Rossi, M. A. (2004). *Decoding the "Free/Open Source (F/OSS) Software Puzzle" a survey of theoretical and empirical contributions. Department of Economics University of Siena 424*. Department of Economics, University of Siena.

Rossi, M. A. (2004, April). *Decoding the "Free/Open Source(F/OSS) Software puzzle" a survey of theoretical and empirical contributions* (Quaderni No. 424). Dipartimento di Economia Politica, Università degli Studi di Siena.

Sambamurthy, V., & Poole, M. S. (1992). The Effects of Variations in Capabilities of GDSS Designs on Management of Cognitive Conflict in Groups. *Information Systems Research, 3*(3), 225–251. doi:10.1287/isre.3.3.224

Sanders, J. (1998). Linux, open source, and software's future. *IEEE Software, 15*(5), 88–91. doi:10.1109/52.714831

Sayyad Shirabad, J., & Menzies, T. (2005). *The PROMISE Repository of Software Engineering Databases*. Canada: School of Information Technology and Engineering, University of Ottawa.

Scacchi, W. (2001). Understanding the Requirements for Developing Open Source Software Systems. *IEE Proceedings. Software, 149*(1), 24–39. doi:10.1049/ip-sen:20020202

Scherer, F. (1972). Nordhaus' Theory of Optimal Patent Life: A Geometric Reinterpretation. *The American Economic Review, 62*(3), 422–427.

Schmidt, K., & Schnitzer, M. (2003). Public subsidies for open source? Some economic policy issues of the software market. *Harvard Journal of Law & Technology, 16*(2), 473–505.

Schwaber, K., & Beedle, M. Agile Software Development with Scrum. Prentice Hall, October 2001. A. Sigfridsson, G. Avram, A. Sheehan, and D. K. Sullivan. Sprint-driven development: working, learning and the process of enculturation in the pypy community. In J. Feller, B. Fitzgerald, W. Scacchi, and A. Sillitti, editors, OSS, volume 234 of IFIP, pages 133–146. Springer, 2007.

Schweik, C. M., & Semenov, A. (2003). The Institutional Design of Open Source Programming: Implications for Addressing Complex Public Policy and Management Problems. *First Monday, 8*, 1.

Scotchmer, S., & Green, J. (1990). Novelty and Disclosure in Patent Law. *The Rand Journal of Economics, 21*(1), 131–146. doi:10.2307/2555499

Scott, J., Lucas, M., & Herz, J.-C. (2006). *Open technology development Roadmap plan*. version 3.1 (final), prepared for the Deputy Under Secretary of Defense, Advanced Systems and Concepts, cleared for open publication on June 7th, 2006, available from www.acq.osd.mil/asc/.

Scozzi, B., Crowston, K., Eseryel, U. Y., & Li, Q. (2008). Shared mental models among open source software developers. In *Proceedings of the 41st Hawaii International Conference on System Sciences,* Hawaii.

Sfetsos, P., Stamelos, I., Angelis, L., & Deligiannis, I. (2006). Investigating the Impact of Personality Types on Communication and Collaboration-Viability in Pair Programming - An Empirical Study. In *Proceedings of eXtreme Programming (XP) 2006* (pp. 43–52). Springer-Verlag. doi:10.1007/11774129_5

Shah, S. (2006). Motivation, governance and the viability of hybrid forms in open source software development. *Management Science, 52*(7), 1000–1014. doi:10.1287/mnsc.1060.0553

Shah, S. K. (2006). Motivation, Governance, and the Viability of Hybrid Forms in Open Source Software Development. *Management Science, 52*(7), 100–1014. doi:10.1287/mnsc.1060.0553

Shaikh, M. (2006) Version Control Software in the Open Source Process: A Performative View of learning and Organizing in the Linux Collectif, Unpublished Thesis, London School of Economics.

Shaw, T., & Jarvenpaa, S. L. (1997). Process Models in Information Systems, *IFIP WG8.2 Working Conference on Information Systems and Qualitative Research,* May 31-June 3, Philadelphia, PA.

Shneiderman, B. (1998). *Designing the user interface: Strategies for effective human-computer-interaction* (3rd ed.). New York: Addison Wesley Longman.

SIPRI. (2006). *SIPRI Yearbook 2006, Armaments, disarmaments and international security*. Stockholm: SIPRI.

Smith, B., Ashburner, M., Rosse, C., Bard, J., Bug, W., & Ceusters, W. (2007). The Obo Foundry: Coordinated Evolution of Ontologies to Support Biomedical Data Integration. *Nature Biotechnology, 25*(11), 1251–1255. doi:10.1038/nbt1346

Smith, N., Andrea, C., & Juan, F. R. (2006). Users and Developers: an Agent-Based Simulation of Open Source Software Evolution. In Proceedings of the SPW/ProSim2006 Workshop, LNCS, Springer-Verlag, Vol. 3966, pp. 234-241, Shanghai, China.

Smith, S. C., & Sidorova, A. (2003). Survival of open-source projects: A population ecology perspective. In *ICIS 2003. Proceedings of international conference on information systems 2003.* Seattle, WA.

Smith, T. (2002, October 1). *Open source: Enterprise ready – with qualifiers.* theOpenEnterprise. (http://www.theopenenterprise.com/story/TOE20020926S0002)

Solingen, van. R., & Berghout, E. (1999). *The Goal/Question/Metric Method: A practical guide for quality improvement of software development.* London: McGraw-Hill.

Sowe, S., Angelis, L., & Stamelos, I. (2006c). Identifying Knowledge Brokers that Yield Software Engineering Knowledge in OSS Projects. *Information and Software Technology, Elsevier, 48*(11), 1025–1033. doi:10.1016/j.infsof.2005.12.019

Sowe, S., & Stamelos, I. (2006a). A Framework for Teaching Software Testing using F/OSS Methodology. In Proceedings of the 2nd International Conference on Open Source Systems 2006, Springer Verlag, 261-266.

Sowe, S., Angelis, S., & Stamelos, I. (2006b). An Empirical Approach To Evaluate Students Participation In Open Source Software Projects. In the Proceedings of IADIS Cognitive and Exploratory Learning in the Digital Age (CELDA) 2006, 304-308.

Spaeth, S. (2005, June). *Coordination in open source projects: A social network analysis using CVS data.* Unpublished doctoral dissertation, University of St. Gallen, St. Gallen, Switzerland. Retrieved from http://www.unisg.ch/www/edis.nsf/7acbc805e9219074c1256d28004777d9/cf2cd20cdc0551a6c12570540023f6bf!OpenDocument

Spinellis, D. (2006). Prof. Diomidis Spinellis, Personal communication, Athens, 2006.

Staring, K., & Titlestad, O. H. (2006). Networks of Open Source Health Care Action. In the Proceedings of the 2nd International Conference on Open Source Systems, Springer-Verlag, 135-141.

Staring. K., Titlestad, O. H., Gailis, J. (2005). Educational transformation through open source approaches, IRIS'28 Meeting. http://wwwold.hia.no/iris28/Docs/IRIS2028-1106.pdf

Stewart, K., & Gosain, S. (2006). The impact of ideology on effectiveness in open source software development teams. *Management Information Systems Quarterly, 30*(2), 291–314.

Stewart, K. J., Ammeter, A. P., & Maruping, L. M. (2006, June). Impacts of license choice and organizational sponsorship on user interest and development activity in open source software projects. *Information Systems Research, 17*(2), 126–144. doi:10.1287/isre.1060.0082

Stewart, D. (2005). Social Status in an Open-Source Community. *American Sociological Review, 70*(5), 823–842. doi:10.1177/000312240507000505

Stewart, K., Ammeter, A. P., & Maruping, L. (2006). Impacts of License Choice and Organizational Sponsorship on User Interest and Development Activity in Open Source Software Projects. *Information Systems Research, 17*(2), 126–144. doi:10.1287/isre.1060.0082

Stewart, K., & Gosain, S. (2006). The Impact of Ideology on Effectiveness in Open Source Software Development Teams. *Management Information Systems Quarterly, 30*(2), 291–314.

Stewart, K. J., & Ammeter, T. (2002). *An Exploratory Study of Factors Influencing the Level of Vitality and Popularity of Open Source Projects.* Paper presented at the Twenty-Third International Conference on Information Systems.

Tabachnick, B. G., & Fidell, L. S. (2007). *Using Multivariate Statistics.* Boston, MA: Pearson.

Tajfel, H. (1981). *Human groups and social categories: Studies in social psychology.* Cambridge, UK: Cambridge University Press.

Teece, D. J. (1986). Profiting from technological innovation: Implications for integration, collaboration, licensing and public policy. *Research Policy, 15*(6), 285–305. doi:10.1016/0048-7333(86)90027-2

Teigland, R., & Wasko, M. M. (2003). Integrating knowledge through information trading: examining the relationship between boundary spanning communication and individual performance. *Decision Sciences, 34*(3), 261–286. doi:10.1111/1540-5915.02341

The, S. QO-OSS Project Consortium. D7 – Novel Quality Assessment Techniques, February 2008. J. Warsta and P. Abrahamsson. Is open source software development essentialy an agile method? In 3rd Workshop on Open Source Software Engineering, 2003.

Thomas, K. W. (1992). Conflict and negotiation processes in organizations. In M. Dunette & L. Hough (Eds.), *Handbook of Industrial and Organizational Psychology,* (651-718).

Thurston, R. (2006), Criticism mounts over Birmingham's Linux project, last accessed on 15 Jan 2007 at: http://www.zdnet.com.au/news/software/soa/Criticism_mounts_over_Birmingham_s_Linux_project/0,130061733,339272293,00.htm

Tornatzky, L., & Klein, K. (1982). Innovation Characteristics & Innovation Adoption Implementation: A Meta-Analysis of Findings. *IEEE Transactions on Engineering Management, EM-29,* 28–45.

Torvalds, L. (1999). *Interview with Linus Torvalds: What Motivates Free Software Developers?* Retrieved from http://www.firstmonday.dk/issues3_3/torvalds/index.html

Tsoukas, H. (1996). The firm as a distributed knowledge system: a constructionist approach. *Strategic Management Journal, 17*(winter), 11-25.

Tuomi, I. (2004). Evolution of the Linux Credits file: Methodological challenges and reference data for Open Source research. *First Monday, 9*(6). http://www.firstmonday.dk/issues/issue9_6/ghosh/.

Turner, A. (2005), Linux misses Windows of opportunity, last accessed on 15 Jan 2007 at http://www.theage.com.au/articles/2005/09/26/1127586780339.html?from=top5

Twidale, M. B., & Nichols, D. M. (2004). *Usability discussions in open source development (Tech. Rep.).* Hamilton, New Zealand: University of Waikato.

University of Notre Dame. (2006). Research project on the free/open source software development phenomenon. Retrieved October 2008 from http://www.nd.edu/~oss/

Valimaki, M. (2003, January). Dual Licensing in Open Source Software Industry. *Systemes d'Information et Management.*

van Oostendorp, H., & Walbeehm, B. J. (1995). Towards modeling exploratory learning in the context of direct manipulation interfaces. *Interacting with Computers, 7*(1), 3–24. doi:10.1016/0953-5438(95)90817-5

Van Reijswoud, V. (2005) OSS for development: myth or reality? last accessed 17 Jan 2007 at http://www.calibre.ie/events/limerick/docs/calibre_Reijswoud_presentation.pdf

van Welie, M., & van der Veer, G. C. (2003). *Pattern languages in interaction design: Structure and organization.* Paper presented at the Ninth IFIP TC13 International Conference on Human-Computer Interaction.

van Wendel de Joode, R., & Egyedi, T. M. (2005). Handling variety: the tension between adaptability and operability of open source software. *Computer Standards & Interfaces, 28*(1), 109–121. doi:10.1016/j.csi.2004.12.004

Varian, H. R., & Shapiro, C. (2003). Linux adoption in the public sector: An economic analysis. Working paper.

Ven, K., Van Nuffel, D., & Verelst, J. (2006). The introduction of OpenOffice.org on the Brussels Public Administration. In *Damiani, E, Fitzgerald, B, Scacchi, W and Succi, G (2006) Open Source Systems* (pp. 123–134). New York: Springer-Verlag.

Versailles, D.W. (2005). La nouvelle gouvernance des programmes de Défense: les relations entre l'Etat et l'industrie. *Revue d'économie industrielle, 112*(4), 83-105.

Villa, L. (2003). How gnome learned to stop worrying and love the bug. In *Otawa Linux Symposium*, Otawa.

Villa, L. (2005). Why everyone needs a bugmaster. In linux.conf.au, Canberra.

von Hippel, E. (1987). Cooperation between rivals: informal know-how trading. *Research Policy, 16*(6), 291–302. doi:10.1016/0048-7333(87)90015-1

Von Hippel, E. (2005). *Open Source Software Projects as User Innovation Networks* (pp. 267–278). Cambridge, London: Perspectives on Free and Open Source Software.

Von Hippel, E. (2005). *Democratizing Innovation.* Cambridge, Massachusetts: MIT Press.

Von Hippel, E., & Von Krogh, G. (2003). Open source software and the private-collective innovation model: Issues for organization science. *Organization Science, 14*, 209–223. doi:10.1287/orsc.14.2.209.14992

von Krogh, G., & von Hippel, E. (2003). Special Issue on Open Source Software Development [Editorial]. *Research Policy, 32*(7), 1149–1157. doi:10.1016/S0048-7333(03)00054-4

Von Krogh, G., & Von Hippel, E. (2006). The promise of research on open source software. *Management Science, 52*(7), 975–983. doi:10.1287/mnsc.1060.0560

Von Krogh, G., Spaeth, S., & Haefliger, S. (2005). Knowledge reuse in open source software: An exploratory study of 15 open source projects. In *Proceedings of the 38th Hawaii International Conference on System Sciences,* Hawaii.

Vroom, V. (1964). *Work and Motivation.* New York, NY: Wiley and Sons.

Wagstrom, P. A., Herbsleb, J. D., et al. (2005). *A social network approach to free/open source software simulation.* Paper presented at the First International Conference on Open Source Systems, Genova.

Wagstrom, P., Herbsleb, J., & Carley, K. (2005). A social network approach to free/open source software simulation. In *First international conference on open source systems* (pp. 16–23).

Walli, S., Gynn, D., & von Rotz, B. (2005) The Growth of Open Source Software in Organizations, available at http://www.optaros.com/en/publications/white_papers_reports (last accessed 31 Jul 2006)

Walsham, G. (1993). *Interpreting Information Systems in Organizations.* UK: Wiley.

Wang, Y. (2007). *Prediction of success in open source software development.* Master of science dissertation, University of California, Davis, Davis, CA.

Wasserman, S., & Faust, K. (1994). *Social network analysis: methods and applications.* Cambridge, UK: Cambridge University Press.

Watson, R. T., Boudreau, M.-C., York, P. T., Greiner, M. E., & Wynn, D. (2008). The Business of Open Source. *Communications of the ACM, 51*(4), 41–46. doi:10.1145/1330311.1330321

Watson, R. T., Wynn, D., & Boudreau, M.-C. (2005). JBOSS: The Evolution of Professional Open Source Software. *MIS Quarterly Executive, 4*(3), 329–341.

Weinstock, C. B., & Hissam, S. A. (2005). Making lightning strike twice. In Feller, J., Fitzgerald, B., Hissam, S. A., & Lakhani, K. R. (Eds.), *Perspectives on Free and Open Source Software* (pp. 143–159). Cambridge: The MIT Press.

Weiss, D. (2005). Quantitative analysis of open source projects on SourceForge. In M. Scotto & G. Succi (Eds.), *Proceedings of the first international conference on open source systems (OSS 2005)* (pp. 140–147). Genova, Italy.

Weißgerber, P., Neu, D., & Diehl, S. (2008). Small patches get in! In *MSR '08: Proceedings of the 2005 Working Conference on Mining software repositories.*

Wenger, E. (1998). *Communities of practice: learning, meaning, and identity.* Cambridge, UK: Cambridge University Press.

Wenger, E. C., & Snyder, W. M. (2000, January-February). Communities of Practice: The Organizational Frontier. *Harvard Business Review*, 139–14.

West, J. (2003). How open is open enough? Melding proprietary and open source platform strategies. *Research Policy, 32*(7), 1259–1285. doi:10.1016/S0048-7333(03)00052-0

West, M. A., & Farr, J. L. (1990). Innovation at work. In West and Far (Eds.) *Innovation and creativity at work: Psychological and organizational strategies*, (145-172).

Wheeler, D. A. (2001). More than a gigabuck: Estimating GNU/Linux's size. http://www.dwheeler.com/sloc/redhat71-v1/redhat71sloc.html.

Wiedenbeck, S., & Zila, P. L. (1997). Hands-on practice in learning to use software: A comparison of exercise, exploration, and combined formats. *ACM Transactions on Computer-Human Interaction, 4*(2), 169–196. doi:10.1145/254945.254967

Wilcoxon, F. (1945). Individual comparisons by ranking methods. *Biometrics Bulletin, 1*(6), 80–83. doi:10.2307/3001968

Winkler, W. (1999). *The State of Record Linkage and Current Research Problems. Technical Report, Statistical Research Division.* US Bureau of the Census.

Xu, J., Gao, Y., et al. (2005). *A topological analysis of the open source software development community.* Paper presented at the 38th Hawaii International Conference on System Sciences, Hawaii.

Yamauchi, Y., Yokozawa, M., Shinohara, T., & Ishida, T. (2000). *Collaboration with lead media: How open source software succeeds.* Paper presented at the ACM Conf. Comput. Supported Cooperative Work, Philadelphia, PA.

Yang, H., & Tang, J. (2004). Team structure and team performance in IS development: A social network perspective. *Information & Management, 41*, 335–349. doi:10.1016/S0378-7206(03)00078-8

Ye, Y., Nakakoji, K., Yamamoto, Y., & Kishida, K. (2005). The co-evolution of systems and communities in free and open source software development. In Koch, S. (Ed.), *Free/Open Software Development*, (59-82). Idea Group Inc.

Yin, R. (1994). *Case Study Research: Design and Methods* (2nd ed.). California: Sage Publications.

Zachary, G. (2003) Ghana, Information Technology and Development in Africa, http://www.cspo.org/products/articles/BlackStar.PDF (Current 11 Aug 2006)

Zaltman, G., Duncan, R., & Holbeck, J. (1973). *Innovations & Organizations.* New York: Wiley & Sons.

Zhang, Z., Basili, V., & Shneiderman, B. (1999). Perspective-based usability inspection: An empirical validation of efficacy. *Empirical Software Engineering, 4*(1), 43–69. doi:10.1023/A:1009803214692

Zhao, L., & Elbaum, S. (2003). Software quality under the open source model. *Journal of Systems and Software, 66*(1), 65–75.

Zhao, L., & Deek, F. P. (2005). *Improving open source software usability.* Paper presented at the 2005 Americas Conference on Information Systems.

Zimmermann, T., Weißgerber, P., Diehl, S., & Zeller, A. (2005). Mining version histories to guide software changes. *IEEE Transactions on Software Engineering, 31*(6), 429–445. doi:10.1109/TSE.2005.72

Zuliani, P., & Succi, G. (2004) Migrating public administrations to open source software, *Proceedings of e-Society IADIS International Conference,* Avila, Spain, 2004.

About the Contributors

Stefan Koch is Associate Professor and Vice Chair at Bogazici University, Department of Management. His research interests include user innovation, cost estimation for software projects, the open source development model, the evaluation of benefits from information systems and ERP systems. He has published over 15 papers in peer-reviewed journals, including *Information Systems Journal, Information Economics and Policy, Decision Support Systems, Empirical Software Engineering, Electronic Markets, Journal of Database Management, Journal of Software Maintenance and Evolution, Enterprise Information Systems* and *Wirtschaftsinformatik,* and over 30 in international conference proceedings and book collections. He has also edited a book titled 'Free/Open Source Software Development' for an international publisher in 2004, and serves as Editor-in-Chief of the International Journal on Open Source Software & Processes.

* * *

Paul Adams joined Sirius from academia where he was a researcher within the Centre for Research on Open Source Software at the University of Lincoln. Paul's particular research specialisms are in Open Source software engineering, agile development and quality assessment, where he has more than a dozen publications in major international conferences, workshops and journals. In addition to his research, Paul brings a wealth of software development experience having been involved with many Free Software projects. Paul is a Chartered member of the British Computer Society (for which he is Chairman and founder of the BCS Open Source Specialist Group) and a full member of the IEEE (including the Computer Society).

Mark Allyn is currently Associate Professor, Department of Management & Information Systems at Montclair State. Dr. Allyn teaches courses in human resources management, entrepreneurship, and strategic management in the undergraduate and MBA programs at Montclair State. His research interests include worker productivity and computers, and human resource determinants of knowledge sharing among workers. Dr. Allyn obtained his Ph.D. in experimental psychology from Stanford University in 1971. Following this he spent nearly 30 years in the telecommunications industry in a variety of research and planning roles. Recently he has focused primarily on Open Source computer projects as social systems. He has written and co-authored a number of papers, proceedings and presentations in organizational behavior and strategic human resource management.

Andrea Capiluppi has obtained his PhD from the Politecnico di Torino, Italy. He has been a visiting Researcher in the In the Grupo de Sistemas y Comunicaciones of Universidad Rey Juan Carlos, Madrid, Spain, during October 2003. From January 2004 to present, he has been a Visiting Researcher in the Department of Maths and Computing, at the Open University, UK, working in collaboration with Drs. Juan Ramil, Neil Smith, Helen Sharp, Alvaro Faria and Sarah Beecham. The appointment has been renewed till December 2008. In January 2006, he joined the University of Lincoln as a Senior Lecturer.

James Collofello is currently Computer Science and Engineering Professor and Associate Dean for the Engineering School at Arizona State University. He received his Ph.D. in Computer Science from Northwestern University. His teaching and research interests lie in the software engineering area with an emphasis on software quality assurance, software project management and software process modeling and simulation.

Eric Darmon is Associate Professor at the University of Rennes 1 and CREM (Centre de Recherche en Economie et Management, UMR 6211 of CNRS and University or Rennes 1) since 2006. His PhD thesis was on the impact of ICT on Market organization and performance. He is now a member of M@RSOUIN (consortium of research centers dedicated to ICT-related issues) and is carrying research into two interconnected directions: economics of ICT (economics of software with an emphasis on competition/cooperation between Open Source/commercial approaches and piracy, economics of online markets and communities) and behavioral economics (learning on markets). He also organized a series of workshops on Open Source.

Fadi Deek received his B.S. Computer Science, 1985; M.S. Computer Science, 1986; and Ph.D. Computer and Information Science, 1997 all from New Jersey Institute of Technology (NJIT). He is Dean of the College of Science and Liberal Arts, Professor of Information Systems, Information Technology, and Mathematical Sciences at NJIT where he began his academic career as Teaching Assistant in 1985. He is also a member of the Graduate Faculty - Rutgers University Business School.

Brian Fitzgerald holds the Frederick A Krehbiel II Chair in Innovation in Global Business and Technology at the University of Limerick, where he is also Director of the Lero Graduate School in Software Engineering (www.lgsse.ie). He holds a PhD from the University of London and his research interests include open source software, agile methods, and distributed software development. He has published 10 books and more than 130 book chapters and papers in the leading journals and conferences in the Information Systems and Software Engineering fields. He has served as a guest editor for several prominent journals, including Information Systems Research, Communications of the ACM, European Journal of Information Systems, Software Process: Improvement and Practice and the Information Systems Journal.

Alexia Gaudeul is an industrial economist with an interest in the Internet, open source software and new media. Her current work deals with the role of intermediaries in the exchange of information goods, and with the dynamics of knowledge production on the Internet. Alexia completed a case study of the LATEX open-source typesetting software and is now working on an empirical study of bloggers and their activities. She holds a PhD from the University of Toulouse, France and works as a lecturer in Economics at the University of East Anglia. Alexia is also a member of the ESRC Centre for Competition Policy.

Jesus Gonzalez-Barahona teaches and researches in Universidad Rey Juan Carlos, Móstoles (Spain). He started to be involved in the promotion of libre software in 1991. Since then, he has carried on several activities in this area, including the organization of seminars and courses, and the participation in working groups on libre software, both at the Spanish and European levels. Currently he collaborates with several libre software projects (including Debian) and associations, writes in several media about topics related to libre software, and consults for companies and public administrations on issues related to their strategy on these topics. His research interests include understanding libre software development, where he has published several papers, and is participating in some international research projects. He is also one of the promoters of the idea of an European master program on libre software, and has specific interest in the education in that area.

Israel Herraiz teaches and researches in Universidad Alfonso X el Sabio in Madrid, Spain. He obtained a PhD from Universidad Rey Juan Carlos, while working at the GSyC/Libresoft research group. His research interests lie in the intersection between software evolution, mining software repositories and empirical software engineering, with an emphasis in large scale studies and statistical analysis of software proijects. He he as contributed to several FLOSS projects, and collaborates in the Master on Free Software as a FLOSS expert. He is a member of the editorial review board of the International Journal of Open Source Software and Processes.

David Hinds is Assistant Professor of Decision Sciences in the Huizenga School of Business at Nova Southeastern University. He presently teaches business decision modeling and enterprise information systems within the MBA program. His research and consulting interests involve new forms of social and work-oriented groups which have emerged around Web 2.0 technologies and their impact on strategy, operations, management and entrepreneurship. He previously held senior management positions with Deloitte Consulting, Cordis Corporation (now Johnson & Johnson), and the Wurth Group. He was also President and owner of Trend Distributors, a building supply distribution company. David is a licensed Professional Engineer in Florida. He received a BS in Engineering Science and an MS in Operations Research from the University of Miami, and an MBA and a PhD in Business Administration / Information Systems from Florida International University.

Daniel Izquierdo-Cortazar is a PhD student at the Universidad Rey Juan Carlos in Móstoles, Spain. He earned a degree in computer science from the same university and obtained his master degree in computer networks and computer science systems in 2006. His research work is centered in the assessment of libre software communities from an engineering point of view and especially with regard to quantitative and empirical issues. Right now he holds a grant from the Universidad Rey Juan Carlos to dedicate part of his time to his PhD's thesis. He is also involved in European-funded projects such as QualOSS or FLOSSWorld. He also teaches in Universidad Rey Juan Carlos, Móstoles (Spain) in the Master on Free Software.

Marco Janssen is Assistant Professor on formal modeling of social and social-ecological systems within the School of Human Evolution and Social Change at Arizona State University. He is also the Associate Director of the Center for the Study of Institutional Diversity. His formal training is within the area of Operations Research and Applied Mathematics. His current research focuses on the fit between behavioral, institutional and ecological processes. In his research he combines agent-based models with laboratory experiments and case study analysis. Janssen also performs research on diffusion processes of knowledge and information, with applications in marketing and digital media.

Thomas Le Texier holds a PhD degree in Economics from the University of Nice - Sophia Antipolis and a doctoral position at the GREDEG – UMR CNRS 6227 (Valbonne, France). He also holds a research associate position in Economics at the Research Center of the French Air Force (CReA), in the Defense and Knowledge Management laboratory (Salon de Provence, France). His current research topics are closely related to open innovation and digital economics, dealing with both managerial and market-based aspects. Thomas Le Texier is particularly interested in analyzing the economic scope of open source software development, file-sharing networks and digital piracy. He teaches information economics, microeconomics and statistics at the University of Nice – Sophia Antipolis, and knowledge management at the French Air Force Academy.

Ronald Lee has more than 30 years of research experience in electronic commerce, web-based initiatives, and formal modeling. Since 2002, he has conducted research at Florida International University on open sourced e-learning, e-tourism, e-culture, and virtual world environments, including intelligent 'bots'. For the previous ten years, he was Director of the Erasmus University Research Institute for Decision Information Systems (Euridis), in the Netherlands. He previously held positions at the University of Pennsylvania, the University of Texas, Universidad Nova de Lisboa, Portugal, and the International Institute for Applied Systems Analysis (IIASA), in Vienna, Austria. Lee holds a BA in Mathematics, an MBA, and a PhD in Decision Sciences from the University of Pennsylvania (Wharton).

James McHugh received his A.B. Mathematics from Fordham College and Ph.D. in Applied Mathematics from the Courant Institute of Mathematical Sciences. He is Professor of Computer and Information Science with a joint appointment in the Information Technology program at NJIT. He has also served as Director of the Information Technology Program, Director of Ph.D. Program in Computer and Information Science, and Acting Chair of the Department of Computer and Information Science.

Ram Misra is currently Professor of Management and Information Systems at Montclair State University, Montclair, NJ, USA. Prior to joining Montclair State University, Ram was an executive director at Bell Communications Research (now Telcordia Technologies). He worked in telecom industry (Bell Labs and Bell Communications Research) in various technical and management positions for 24 years. Ram received his Ph.D. in Industrial engineering (Operations Research) from Texas A&M University, College Station, Texas. He has published in IEEE Transactions, the International Journal of Management Research, the International Journal of Production Research, the Naval Logistics Review and the Decision Sciences Journal of Innovative Education, the Journal of IT Cases and Applications, the Journal of Information Technology and Applications, the International Journal of Pharmaceutical and Healthcare Marketing, and the i-Manger's Journal of Management.

Rufus Pollock obtained his PhD in Economics from the University of Cambridge in 2008 and is currently the Mead Research Fellow in Economics at Emmanuel College, University of Cambridge. As an economist, the present focus of his research is on innovation and IP, with particular attention to open models of innovation. Other areas of interest include two-sided/platform industries (e.g. Operating Systems, Search Engines), and research on happiness and well-being.

Nicholas Radtke is a Ph.D. candidate in Computer Science at Arizona State University. His research focuses on understanding and modeling Free/Libre Open Source Software engineering processes.

Gregorio Robles is Associate Professor at the Universidad Rey Juan Carlos in Móstoles, Spain. He earned a degree on electrical engineering from the Universidad Politécnica de Madrid (studying his last year and submitting his master thesis at the Technical University of Berlin) and obtained his PhD in 2006. His research work is centered in the study of libre software development from an engineering point of view and especially with regard to quantitative and empirical issues. Other, not-technical related, matters have also been of his interest like volunteer-driven software development and social network analysis in the libre software phenomenon. He has developed or collaborated in the design of programmes to analyse libre software and the tools used to produce them. He was also involved in the FLOSS study on libre software financed by the European Commission IST programme and in other European-funded projects such as FLOSSMetrics or QualOSS.

Megan Squire is an associate professor in the Department of Computing Sciences at Elon University. Her primary research focus is on data mining and large database systems, particularly as they apply to the collection of open source software engineering data. She is one of the leaders of the FLOSSmole project, which is a collection of tools designed to gather and analyze data about open source software development. Megan has a BA in Art History and Public Policy from the College of William and Mary in Virginia, and a PhD in computer science from Nova Southeastern University.

Ioannis Stamelos; an Associate Professor with the Department of Informatics, received his PhD in Computer Science from the Aristotle University of Thessaloniki in 1988. His research activity focuses on Software Engineering, with emphasis on software management, empirical software engineering, Free/Libre Open source software. He has over 90 publications including papers in international journals and conference proceedings, and book chapters. He is a member of IEEE, a reviewer for 10 scientific Journals and has participated in several conference committees. He has also participated in 20 funded educational and research & development projects. Recently, he was ranked 12th top scholar worldwide in the field of Systems and Software Engineering for the period 2000-2004 by the Journal of Systems and Software, Elsevier.

Dominique Torre is Professor at University Nice-Sophia Antipolis (UNS) and GREDEG (UMR 6227 of CNRS and UNS) where he heads DEMOS research department. His research topics are currently (i) Economics of ICT (economics of Open Source Software, software piracy, e-recruitment, e-tourism, electronic platforms, online communities), (ii) Economics of Financial Intermediaries (venture capital, banking networks, economics of Central Banking) and (iii) History of Economic Thought (the monetary debates between 1870 and 1939). He organized a series of workshops and Conferences and / or coordinated special issues of scientific reviews on Open Source, Financial Intermediation, Monetary Economics and History of Monetary Economics.

David Versailles is an economist who created in 2002 the multidisciplinary research center of the French Air Force (CreA) and served as its Director until 2008. At CReA, he was the head of the research laboratory dedicated to Knowledge management and supervised the Master and PhD programs in management, economics, and leadership. He also managed as principal investigator the research program commissioned to CReA by the MoD. David has been previously in charge of the office for statistics and economic research at the French MoD (Directorate for financial affairs and Observatoire économique de la Défense), where he was running the (in-house and outsourced) research program commissioned by the Conseil économique de la Défense. David has been lecturing on a regular basis at the Master and PhD level for several universities in Europe. He is regularly invited as an expert on Defense-, Security- and aeronautics-related industrial policies in Europe (eg for the European Defense agency, the Security and Defense Agenda…). David holds a PhD degree in economics from the University Paul Cezanne (Aix Marseille 3) and an habilitation in economics from the University of Nice. He devotes his research to industrial economics, to knowledge theory, and to business intelligence.

Levent Yilmaz is Associate Professor of Computer Science and Software Engineering and holds a joint appointment with the department of Industrial and Systems Engineering at Auburn University. He received his M.S. and Ph.D. degrees from Virginia Tech. His research focuses on Modeling and Simulation, Agent-directed Simulation, and Complex Adaptive Systems with a focus in advancing the theory and methodology via novel formalisms and their use in creative intelligent systems, computational modeling of scientific discovery, robust decision-making, and exploratory analysis of complex adaptive socio-technical, cognitive, and cultural systems. Dr. Yilmaz is a member of ACM, IEEE Computer Society, Society for Modeling & Simulation International (SCS), and Upsilon Pi Epsilon. He is a member of the board of directors of SCS and serves as the Editor-in-Chief of the Simulation journal. His email and web addresses are yilmaz@auburn.edu and www.eng.auburn.edu/~yilmaz.

Luyin Zhao received his B.S. computer science from Beijing University of Aeronautics and Astronautics, M.S. in computer science from Beijing University, M.E. Software Engineering from the J. D. Edwards Honors Program at the University of Nebraska-Lincoln, and Ph.D. Management from Rutgers University. His research interests include open source software, software engineering, medical decision support systems, computer-aided diagnosis, and management information systems.

Index

T

U

V

version control systems 96
virtual communities 67

W

Wayne State University 69
weapon systems 99, 104, 106, 109
web-based application 227
web-based inspection 218, 225, 229
web-based programs 30
web browsers 30

welfare 128, 129, 130, 131, 132, 133, 134,
135, 136, 137, 138, 139, 141, 151
Wikipedia 114
Windows NT 102, 104, 107
work flows 57, 58
work groups 195, 197, 198, 199, 200, 202,
203, 204, 207, 208, 209, 210, 216
WTA-equilibria (for Winner-Takes-All equilibria) 157, 158, 160, 161, 163